PLATO

Plato, with Socrates and Aristotle, is the founder of the Western intellectual tradition. Like his mentor Socrates, he was essentially a practical philosopher who found the abstract theory and visionary schemes of many contemporary thinkers misguided and sterile. He was born about 429 B.C. in Athens, the son of a prominent family that had long been involved in the city's politics. Extremely little survives of the history of Plato's youth, but he was raised in the shadow of the great Peloponnesian War, and its influence must have caused him to reject the political career open to him and to become a follower of the brilliantly unorthodox Socrates, the self-proclaimed "gadfly" of Athens.

Socrates' death in 399 B.C. turned Plato forever from politics, and in the next decade he wrote his first dialogues, among them *Apology* and *Euthyphro*. At age forty, Plato visited Italy and Syracuse, and upon his return he founded the Academy—Europe's first university—in a sacred park on the outskirts of Athens. The Academy survived for a millennium, finally closed by the emperor Justinian in A.D. 529. Plato hoped his school would train its pupils to carry out a life of service for their communities and to investigate questions of science and mathematics. In time, the Academy attracted young men from across Greece and became a major seat of learning. Plato's old age was probably devoted to teaching and writing, and he died in Athens in 348 B.C.

Bantam Classics
Ask your bookseller for these other World Classics

THE BHAGAVAD-GITA (translated by Barbara Stoler Miller)

CHEKHOV: FIVE MAJOR PLAYS, Anton Chekhov
A DOCTOR'S VISIT: SHORT STORIES, Anton Chekhov

THE INFERNO, Dante (translated by Allen Mandelbaum)
PURGATORIO, Dante (translated by Allen Mandelbaum)
PARADISO, Dante (translated by Allen Mandelbaum)

THE BROTHERS KARAMAZOV, Fyodor Dostoevsky
CRIME AND PUNISHMENT, Fyodor Dostoevsky
THE IDIOT, Fyodor Dostoevsky
NOTES FROM UNDERGROUND, Fyodor Dostoevsky

THE COUNT OF MONTE CRISTO, Alexandre Dumas
THE THREE MUSKETEERS, Alexandre Dumas

MADAME BOVARY, Gustave Flaubert

FAUST, Johann Wolfgang von Goethe

THE COMPLETE FAIRY TALES OF THE BROTHERS GRIMM (translated by
Jack Zipes)

THE HUNCHBACK OF NOTRE DAME, Victor Hugo

FOUR GREAT PLAYS, Henrik Ibsen

THE METAMORPHOSIS, Franz Kafka

LES LIAISONS DANGEREUSES, Pierre Choderlos de Laclos

THE PHANTOM OF THE OPERA, Gaston Leroux (translated by Lowell
Bair)

THE PRINCE, Niccolo Machiavelli

DEATH IN VENICE, Thomas Mann (translated by David Luke)

CYRANO DE BERGERAC, Edmond Rostand

THE CHARTERHOUSE OF PARMA, Marie-Henri Beyle de Stendhal
(translated by Lowell Bair)

THE RED AND THE BLACK, Marie-Henri Beyle de Stendhal (translated
by Lowell Bair)

ANNA KARENINA, Leo Tolstoy
THE DEATH OF IVAN ILYICH, Leo Tolstoy

FATHERS AND SONS, Ivan Turgenev

AROUND THE WORLD IN EIGHTY DAYS, Jules Verne
20,000 LEAGUES UNDER THE SEA, Jules Verne

CANDIDE, Voltaire

The Dialogues
of Plato

With an Introduction by
Erich Segal

BANTAM BOOKS

NEW YORK · TORONTO · LONDON · SYDNEY · AUCKLAND

THE DIALOGUES OF PLATO

A Bantam Book / June 1986

Crito *is reprinted with the permission of the publisher, Bobbs-Merrill Educational Publishing, from* Plato, Euthyphro, Apology, and Crito, *translated by F. J. Church, revised by Robert D. Cumming, LLA 4 © 1956, The Bobbs-Merrill Company, Inc.*

Euthyphro *is reprinted with the permission of the publisher, Yale University Press, from* The Dialogues of Plato, Volume I, *translated by R. E. Allen. © 1984 by Yale University.*

Phoedo *is reprinted with the permission of the publisher. Routledge & Kegan Paul PLC, from Plato's* Phaedo, *translated by R. S. Bluck. © 1955 by Routledge & Kegan Paul PLC.*

Protagoras *is reprinted with the permission of the publishers. Gerald Duckworth and Company Ltd. and The University of Chicago Press, from* Protagoras, *translated by B. A. F. Hubbard and E. S. Karnofsky. © 1982 by B. A. F. Hubbard and E. S. Karnofsky.*

Gorgias, Part III *is reprinted with the permission of the publisher. Bobbs-Merrill Educational Publishing (The Liberal Arts Press), from Plato's* Gorgias, *translated by W. C. Hembold, copyright 1952. The Bobbs-Merrill Company, Inc.*

Cover painting, "The School of Athens" by Raphael, a fresco located in the Stanze, Vatican City. Used by kind permission of Scala/Art Resource, New York City.

ISBN 0-553-21371-7

Published simultaneously in the United States and Canada

Bantam Books are published by Bantam Books, a division of Bantam Doubleday Dell Publishing Group, Inc. Its trademark, consisting of the words "Bantam Books" and the portrayal of a rooster, is Registered in U.S. Patent and Trademark Office and in other countries. Marca Registrada. Bantam Books, 1540 Broadway, New York, New York 10036.

PRINTED IN THE UNITED STATES OF AMERICA

O   18   17   16

CONTENTS

INTRODUCTION
by Erich Segal

> It is impossible to tell what deep levels of the Western mind Platonic notions have penetrated. The simplest sort of person regularly employs expressions and portrays views which are derived from Plato.
>
> JOSÉ ORTEGA Y GASSET

For Eric Havelock, *magistro Socratico*

It is one of the great paradoxes of history that the birth of "modern" philosophy should coincide with the death of its first practitioner. For one may seriously question whether Plato would ever have begun to set down thoughts for posterity had he not been so moved by the execution of his great teacher, Socrates, in 399 B.C. This tragic event marked the end of what is perhaps the most intense period of intellectual creativity the world has ever known.

Fifth-century Athens had seen the development of comedy and tragedy to the point of sublimity and significant advances in science and the art of medicine, as well as in historiography and oratory. It also saw a radical change in the methods of educational theory (establishing the paradigm of the modern university).

Philosophy Before Plato

Though Plato is the first Western philosopher in the modern sense of the word (indeed the first to employ the term *philosophos*),[1]

---

[1] Writing in the 1st century B.C., Cicero (*Tusculan Disputations* 5.3.9) claims that Pythagoras, who lived more than a hundred years before Plato, was the first to coin the term *philosophos*. But the question of nomenclature is of secondary importance.

he was preceded by a series of what one might call proto-philosophical thinkers, which may be divided into two groups:

1. The so-called *pre-Socratics*, beginning with the sage Thales of Miletus (early sixth century B.C.). They were a diverse collection of natural scientists generally centered in Asia Minor (e.g., Anaximander, Heraclitus) or in the Greek cities of southern Italy (e.g., Pythagoras and Empedocles). But their work exists merely in fragments and, with rare exceptions—such as Parmenides' denial of the possibility of motion or Zeno's paradoxes—did not generate a long productive tradition of inquiry.[2]

2. The *Sophists*, who flourished in the fifth century B.C. The original connotation of *sophistēs* was merely "wise man" or "master of a craft," and totally lacked the pejorative connotation of the modern word. These "experts" came to Athens from all parts of the Greek world and claimed to be able to teach all types of *technai*—"skills," "techniques," "tricks"—to the young men of the city.

While some of the Sophists were mere hucksters, others were what we might call free-lance professors, whose specialty was teaching the art of rhetorical persuasion. The latter was a potentially pernicious technique inasmuch as it twisted morality merely for the sake of winning an argument. Socrates' unyielding determination to achieve *absolute* truth is in one sense a reaction to the Sophists' "moral relativism."

The principal Sophists, Protagoras, Gorgias, Hippias, and Prodicus, appear in many of Plato's dialogues as Socrates' antagonists, and more often than not Socrates demolishes their theories. Indeed, the Platonic dialogues have been viewed as giving the coup de grace to their pseudoscience.

Plato constantly disputes the Sophists' claim that they are philosophers in the true sense and often satirizes them for their long, ornamented speeches, their penchant for nitpicking debate, and their confusion of opinion with knowledge.

Though their work also survives only in fragmentary form, we should note that it was not totally devoid of later influence.

---

[2]This point is not undisputed. In "Back to the Presocratics," *Proceedings of the Aristotelian Society* 59 (1958–59): 1–24, Karl Popper argues that these thinkers were the first practitioners of the experimental method in science. Popper's essay is reprinted in his anthology *Conjectures and Refutations* (London: 1963), 136–153.

For Plato seems to have some respect for Protagoras, the most eminent of them, and Socrates, even though he opposes them, is quite often obliged to employ their terminology and adopt some of the methods to his dialectic.[3]

Plato himself was born around 429 B.C. (the third year of the Peloponnesian War, and the year Pericles died). He was of noble lineage, the sort of youth who might well have studied with the Sophists. There is also some evidence that as a young man he was a champion wrestler (a sign of excellence in the "old-style" education) and that at some point he aspired to enter politics. There is also a tradition that he composed dramas, which he went home and burned after he heard his first lecture by the man destined to change his life—and the world's thought—Socrates.

Plato ultimately founded a school, the eponymous Academy, and devoted himself to setting down the ideas of his master, complemented by his own. Scholars commonly distinguish three phases in Plato's work, dividing the dialogues as follows:

Early: *Euthyphro, Apology, Crito* (the last days of Socrates);

      Laches, Lysis, Charmides ("aporetic" dialogues)
      Hippias Minor, Ion;

      Protagoras, Meno, Gorgias (longer dialogues with Sophists culminating in the major doctrines that virtue is knowledge and that no man willingly acts unjustly);

      Phaedo (on the immortality of the soul, this work is sometimes ascribed to the next phase);

Middle: *Menexenus, Euthydemus, Cratylus;*

      Republic (the centerpiece of Platonic thought, containing a full exposition of his theory of forms; the concept of the philosopher-king; the philosopher's method of dialectic; the analogies of the sun, the line, and the cave; the pessimistic discussion of democracy; the banning of most poetry from the ideal state on the ground that it has a bad moral influence);

      Symposium (the famous discussion of *erōs*. Perhaps Plato's most artistic, dramatic, and vivid dialogue);

---

[3] Cf. G.B. Kerferd, *The Sophistic Movement* (Cambridge: Cambridge University Press, 1981), the best general introduction to the Sophists in the English language.

Late: *Phaedrus, Parmenides, Sophist, Statesman, Theaetetus,*
           Critias, Philebus, Timaeus, Laws.

The evidence for these divisions is mainly subjective. The periods are distinguished mainly by stylistic criteria and the way the philosopher seems to be developing his thought, beginning with the figure of Socrates and branching out into his own more complex direction. The continuing debate about what is Socratic, what purely Platonic, and what an admixture will rage eternally. This is further complicated by the possible influence of Pythagorean ideas.[4]

Moreover as R. M. Hare has expressed it, "the extremely deep and difficult investigations of metaphysical and logical questions which occupy many of the later dialogues are fairly obviously the result of Plato's own perplexities . . . their solution did not become clear before the work of Aristotle, if then."[5]

Plato's Main Theories

Plato's main theories will of course be referred to at the appropriate points in the commentary on individual dialogues, but for the sake of convenience the following is an overview of basic Platonic concepts:

1. *Dialectic* as a means to truth. Socrates believed that the authentic method of the philosopher is the analysis and intellectual progression through question-and-answer dialogue. (Cf. *Apology, Protagoras.*)

2. Virtue is knowledge and therefore teachable. (Cf. *Protagoras.*)

3. All knowledge is recollection (*anamnēsis*) based on previous experience of "what the soul has learned." (Cf. *Meno, Phaedo.*)

4. No man does harm willingly. (Cf. *Protagoras.*)

5. To cause injury to another is worse than suffering it, since one is harming one's own soul. (Cf. *Gorgias.*)

6. The theory of *Forms* or "Ideas": What we see in this

---

[4]The Pythagoreans anticipated such Platonic concepts as the transmigration of souls, the notion of the philosopher-king, organizing a separate community according to their philosophical principles, etc.

[5]R.M. Hare, *Plato* (Oxford: Oxford University Press, 1982), 15.

world is a pale reflection of true reality. (Cf. *Phaedo*, *Republic*.)

7. Justice is the harmony of the three parts of the soul in the individual and the harmony of the three classes of citizens in the state (*Republic*).

8. The leader of the ideal state would be a philosopher-king, whose business would be to cling to the "form of the good" (*Republic*).[6]

Plato's Style

The oft-quoted dictum that "the medium is the message" was never more appropriate than when applied to Plato's mode of expression. For by choosing to present his ideas in dialogue form, Plato is probably coming as close as possible to imitating the so-called Socratic method, the pedagogical technique of his mentor.

Despite arguments by scholars that the form has roots in Homeric speeches, Euripidean dramatic debates, and the general Greek fascination for verbal jousting and agonal argument, Plato's use of dialogue as a vehicle for conveying philosophy may be justifiably regarded as one of his most significant achievements. After all, none of his predecessors used this style. Sophists wrote handbooks, and the pre-Socratics for the most part composed in hexameter verse or pithy maxims (e.g., Heraclitus' "everything flows, nothing stays"). Thus, the philosophical dialogue would seem to be a genuinely Platonic invention.

Plato also writes an exquisite and versatile prose, making eloquent use of simile, metaphor, parody, irony, and personification. At significant points he creates memorable allegories to illustrate his arguments. One thinks of the resurrection of the hero Er in *Republic* X or the soul as two steeds and a charioteer in the *Phaedrus*. He also employs striking images—such as democracy as a wild beast (*Republic*), the philosopher as a midwife of ideas (*Theaetetus*), and the shadows in the cave to illustrate his Theory of Forms (*Republic*).

Though Plato was notorious for banishing poetry from the ideal state, his entire work is a tapestry woven of strands from the "classical poets" such as Homer and Pindar and echoes of

---

[6]Numbers 7 and 8 are beyond the scope of this anthology but are too essential to Plato's thought to have been omitted. I have not, however, listed the rather esoteric doctrines of the later dialogues.

the more recent masterpieces of Greek tragedy. Perhaps, like the Roman philosopher Lucretius, he realized that, although poetry was dangerous, it could also be the most powerful mode of captivating a wide public.[7]

There is another significant characteristic of Plato's art that is less frequently remarked upon. Viewed as a whole, the dialogues present a kind of rich tableau of intellectual life in Athens of the late fifth century B.C. Significant historical personages appear and reappear in major and minor roles. We encounter the controversial politician Alcibiades, leading Sophists such as Protagoras and Gorgias, the dean of comic poets Aristophanes, the avant-garde tragic playwright Agathon, the pretentious scholar-poet Ion, and various scientists and physicians. Stretching a point only slightly, one might say that Plato's oeuvre depicts the entire Athenian intelligentsia as Balzac's did the nineteenth-century French bourgeoisie. Thus Plato is conveying not only ideas but a portrait of the society in which they were formed.

Of course, the most important and compelling figure in the dialogue is Socrates himself. The great philosopher was born in 469 B.C. and, after being indicted for "subversive" teaching, was tried and executed in 399. His personal crisis, which was also symptomatic of Athens' own paranoid state of mind, is the subject of the earliest four dialogues.

In his own words, Socrates was a "gadfly" for the Athenian conscience, relentlessly asking such essential philosophical questions as "what is virtue," "how should life be lived," and the like.

The fact that he was an eccentric, odd-looking character is attested to not only by Plato but by Xenophon and, perhaps most famously, by the caricature in Aristophanes' *Clouds*.

Despite his comical appearance he was a man of extraordinary strength both physical and moral (the latter is demonstrated throughout the dialogues, the former by his conspicuous bravery at Potidaea and other battles during the Peloponnesian War). Moreover, quite unlike the Sophists, with whom Aristophanes playfully associates him merely for dramatic purposes, Socrates never demanded payment for his teaching. He was an extraordinary altruist and one of the noblest figures who ever lived.

---

[7] Cf. Lucretius, *On the Nature of Things* IV.8ff., in which he offers the charming explanation that his philosophy is like a harsh medicine that sick children must take to make them better. Hence just as physicians rub honey around the rim of a child's cup to entice him to swallow the bitter liquid, the poet similarly coats his philosophy with sweet verse to make it more palatable to the general reader.

How then could he have met such an unjust fate? We may never know for certain, but there are a number of plausible hypotheses.

To begin with, his new-style education, emphasizing independence of thought, unsettled conservative "aristocrats" (*kaloikagathoi*). It is also possible that he became suspect because many of his friends, such as Critias and Alcibiades, had either been involved in the subversion of the democracy or (equally important) were viewed as fundamentally antidemocratic.

There is another simple, if bitter, explanation. Athens fell in 404 B.C., and frightened people were looking for scapegoats. Even before its actual defeat, the city had been rife with anti-intellectual persecution, and as Sir Kenneth Dover has cogently argued, the trial of Socrates was "the last episode in a chapter of persecution."[8]

Whatever the reason, it is clear that Socrates could have survived had he been willing to compromise. But he was not. Indeed, the *Apology* shows him as gently defiant. Even if he is acquitted, he says, he will not change his life-style. Further, he argues that far from punishment, he deserves the kind of rewards and honor due an Olympic champion.

In the *Crito* he is given a chance to escape but refuses. This is not, as some have suggested, a display of self-willed martyrdom, but of genuine heroism. For like a Sophoclean hero, he will not yield his principles and would rather die to preserve them. Indeed, the manner of his death is perhaps his greatest object lesson.

Before briefly discussing the individual dialogues, one transcendent irony must be noted. Not only did Socrates, the first great systematic thinker, never publish anything, he was deeply ambivalent about the value of the written word.[9] The true philosopher, he seems to say, lives in the realm of ideas not of books, which merely offer pale reflections of the truth. As he remarks in

[9]E.A. Havelock has made many thought-provoking observations about how contemporary ambivalence toward the written word affected the thought of Plato. For, according to Havelock, Plato composed at a very crucial period of Greek intellectual history, namely the moment when what had previously been an oral culture was becoming an age of (literate) analytical rationalism. Cf. *Preface to Plato* (Oxford: Basil Blackwell, 1963), and more recently, *The Literate Revolution in Greece* (Princeton: Princeton University Press, 1982).

a discussion about uncontested authority near the conclusion of *Phaedrus*:

> Anyone who leaves behind him anything in writing and likewise anyone who takes it over from him supposing that such writing will provide something reliable and permanent would be a fool.

Paradoxically he speaks this just when his contemporary Thucydides is composing a work that the historian intends to be *ktēma es aiei*—"a possession for all time." While Thucydides was not wrong, he lacked the sublime humility of the philosopher who was wise enough to recognize the limits of the human mind.

Notes on the Individual Dialogues

The *Apology* purports to be the actual words spoken at Socrates' trial in 399 B.C. Most critics agree that it is very close to what he actually said (indeed some hold to the extreme view that this is the only truly "Socratic" dialogue). Socrates was being tried for corrupting youth and introducing new gods into the city, but in his speech he purposely notes "My opponents are of two kinds; one recent, the other ancient." By the latter he seems to mean the general anti-intellectual prejudices of the times and alludes to the fact that Aristophanes' (originally affectionate) parody seems to have subsequently gained ominous credence.[10]

Socrates' speech is in two parts, the first before the conviction, the second after, when the jury is deliberating the penalty.

Professor J. J. Keaney has recently put forth the provocative theory that Plato is here presenting Socrates as a kind of "Achilles-figure."[11] For at the dialogue's end Socrates mentions his war record, his adamant refusal to act illegally on two occasions when he was under great public pressure to do so, and his readiness to die so that he can meet the great Trojan heroes in the underworld (p. 25). Indeed, Socrates makes a direct reference to Achilles' willingness to risk death (p. 14).

On an equally heroic level there seems to be a similarity between Socrates and Antigone, for example, in Socrates' re-

---

[10]For a detailed discussion see K.J. Dover's introduction to his edition of Aristophanes' *Clouds* (Oxford: Oxford University Press, 1968).

[11]J.J. Keaney, "Plato," in *Ancient Writers: Greece and Rome*, ed. T. James Luce (New York: Charles Scribner's Sons, 1982), 359ff.

fusal even under threat of execution to mend his ways, and, still more specifically, in his statement (p. 14) that he prefers to obey the divine, rather than civic, law.

Socrates' intention to continue in his manner of philosophizing is exemplified within the *Apology* itself, for near the dialogue's beginning he briefly cross-examines Meletus his accuser. Thus, even when his life is in the balance, he persists with the "Socratic method."

There are many well-known aspects of this famous dialogue. It touches on, for example, the fact that the Delphic oracle had called Socrates the wisest man in the world because Socrates had insisted that he knew nothing and had made his entire life a quest for truth. There is also a reference to the "inner voice" that divinely guided him at crucial moments (p. 17). In a touch that is both poignant and ironic, Socrates says at one point that he could perhaps afford a modest fine, one of his guarantors being none other than Plato.

This dialogue also contains the oft-quoted utterance of Socrates, "the unexamined life is not worth living" (p. 22). Heroic to the last, he has composed his own—most appropriate—epitaph.

Scholars commonly refer to the *Apology, Crito, Euthyphro,* and *Phaedo* as a tetralogy, since they all deal with the trial and suicide of Socrates. Set in Socrates' prison during the last days before his death, *Crito* describes the visit of the title character, an elderly friend, who has come to urge the philosopher to flee into exile. Ignoring even the pleas that he consider his family's welfare, Socrates refuses, arguing that escape would be a conscious injury to the laws, who are like our parents. And however greatly he has been wronged, Socrates cannot justify "requiting evil with evil."

Just after the midpoint of *Crito* (p. 36), Socrates begins an imaginary dialogue with personifications of the laws and the state. There is even a touch of humor in this ingenious discourse as the philosopher depicts them employing his own "Socratic method" on *him*. The essential concept is that the laws are parents who have given birth to and nurtured mankind and therefore deserve filial respect whatever the circumstances.

The subject of the *Euthyphro* is *hosiotēs*, "piety." Its dramatic chronology places it prior to the trial of Socrates when the philosopher is preparing himself for his ordeal. He encounters Euthyphro, a soothsayer, who is engaged in prosecuting his own father for accidental homicide—according to the narrow interpretation of the "old religion" and traditional morality. The dialogue is poignantly framed in references to Socrates' own forthcoming trial, whose outcome is already known to the reader.

With cutting irony Socrates keeps pressing Euthyphro to define piety, but he never receives a satisfactory answer. Indeed, the dialogue ends almost on a comic note as the much-discomfited soothsayer ultimately beats a hasty retreat, claiming, like the White Rabbit, that he is late for a very important date.

This type of dialogue, in which crucial questions are posed but left unanswered, is called "aporetic" (from *aporia,* "impasse"). We have similar examples in the *Lysis* on friendship, in *Charmides* on temperance, and in *Laches* on courage.

Phaedo, the longest, richest, and philosophically the most important dialogue of the Socratic tetralogy, takes place on the morning of Socrates' death.[12] During the discussion, most of the major tenets of Platonic philosophy are referred to: the doctrine of recollection, the immortality of the soul, the theory of Ideas. And we also have one of the great Platonic myths—the progress of the soul after death and the nature of the world and the underworld—that appears near the dialogue's conclusion (pp. 122–129).

Phaedo, the narrator, is retelling events that have occurred sometime earlier. This artistic distancing, that is, having one character tell another what has happened on an earlier occasion, is a typically Platonic narrative device—that per se has philosophical significance. For it implicitly undermines the validity of the written word to reproduce "truth" accurately. Socrates' principal interlocutors are Simmias and Cebes, with minor appearances by Crito, Apollodorus (who will again be present in the *Symposium*), as well as the sympathetic jailor. Plato is explicitly said to have been absent with illness (p. 67). The long and complex argument centers about the immortality of the soul, which is related to Plato's theory of Ideas (most fully exposed in the *Republic*).

The notion of the soul's eternal life is not new in Greek thought. It was expressed to some extent by Anaxagoras, the Pythagoreans, and even such poets as Homer and Pindar. But the novelty in Plato is that the doctrine is here not merely described but demonstrated by cogent argument.

The removing of Socrates' chains is a symbolic prefiguration of the argument he will shortly put forth, namely that the true philosopher should rejoice when he is about to die, for it

---

[12]Despite its chronologically earlier subject matter, the *Phaedo* is frequently ascribed to Plato's "middle" period.

releases him from the prison house of the body. As Socrates expresses it (p. 92), philosophy is "the practice of death" (*meletē thanatou*).

The proof itself concentrates first on showing that man's soul existed prior to birth (cf. the doctrine of recollection: we "learn" during life by "remembering" encounters from a prior existence). The second part, which argues that the soul must exist after death, elicits more objections from Simmias and Cebes. But they are finally satisfied (p. 122), when Socrates shows them that the *psychē* ("soul"), as part of its essence, is imperishable and can never have anything to do with its opposite, that is, mortality.

The dialogue concludes with the famous death scene. The touching vignette of Socrates stroking Phaedo's hair (p. 101) is a subtle link to the *Symposium*. Socrates' final words, "Crito, we owe a cock to Asclepius," show us a human being who died as piously as he lived. Crito closes Socrates' eyelids, marking the earthly end of the man who, in Plato's words, was the "best, wisest, and most righteous" who ever lived.

Protagoras, Meno, Cratylus, and *Symposium* constitute what might be called the "Sophistic tetralogy." For the dramatis personae of these dialogues constitute a veritable legion of avant-garde intellectuals. In addition to the title character, the *Protagoras* includes Prodicus, Hippias, and the rich amateur Callias. Meno himself, in the dialogue that bears his name, professes to be a student of Gorgias the Sophist, and the discussion begins with a very sophistic question, "Can virtue be taught?" The entire *Cratylus* discusses whether words have their meanings by convention (*nomos*) or nature (*physis*). The opposition of *nomos* and *physis* was extremely popular among the new thinkers, who were generally preoccupied with pinning down the precise definition of words (e.g., Prodicus, who is parodied in *Protagoras*). Although the subject of *Symposium* is *erōs* ("love"), we have a parody of the newfangled rhetoric in the "Gorgianic" (i.e., elaborately balanced, tintinnabulating, antithetical) speech of the tragedian Agathon.

In *Protagoras,* Socrates starts the discussion by asking the title character what will happen if Hippocrates becomes a student in Protagoras' classes. The Sophist replies that the young man will become better. Socrates demands to know in what way. The professor answers that he will instruct him in the art of politics (*politikē technē*) and how to become a good citizen.

The structure of the dialogue resembles an hourglass. At the outset, Protagoras affirms that *politikē technē* and *aretē* ("virtue") are teachable, while Socrates doubts it. By the conclusion, the positions are completely reversed.

The *Protagoras* conveys some of the real excitement caused by the Sophists' arrival in Athens. Though Socrates is playfully ironic, it does not diminish his genuine regard for his antagonist. At the same time, the Socratic-Platonic mistrust for the new rhetoric is clearly expressed (e.g., in the debate about long speeches versus short question-and-answer on pp. 162–64).

Protagoras' myth about man's primitive state (which he calls a *mythos*, "story") and his subsequent explanation (pp. 149–151) are among the great "set-pieces" in Plato.[13]

The most important philosophical aspect of *Meno* is the demonstration of the doctrine of recollection (*anamnēsis*). Socrates postulates that the soul is immortal (p. 207), and then leads Meno's young slave through a mathematical exercise. Since the boy did not already "know" this through teaching or learning, he must have "known" it in a previous existence and recollected it.

The dialogue opens with Meno's question (reminiscent of the *Protagoras*), "Is virtue teachable?" But the discussion quickly turns to another, more basic set of problems: a) What is virtue? and b) Is it singular (unitary) or plural?

At one point the young man tells Socrates that a man's virtue is being able to engage in politics in such a way as to do good to his friends and harm his enemies (p. 196). This is the old-fashioned ethical code of heroic society as presented, for example, in the *Ajax* of Sophocles.[14] Plato's *Gorgias* devotes a great deal of attention to demolishing this barbaric morality.

If we were to translate the title of Plato's *Symposium* as "the cocktail party," we might run the risk of being anachronistic, but we would not be inaccurate. For the entire dialogue may be seen as presenting intellectual chitchat of the kind one usually encounters at a social gathering. This famous dialogue is very much like a theater piece—in fact, it has many of the qualities of an Aristophanic comedy.

---

[13]For the importance of these myths in Greek cultural history see Thomas Cole, *Democritus and the Sources of Greek Anthropology* (American Philological Association Monograph no. XXV, 1967), 50ff. Also E.A. Havelock, *The Liberal Temper in Greek Politics* (New Haven: Yale University Press, 1957), 407–9.

[14]See B.M.W. Knox, "The *Ajax* of Sophocles," *Harvard Studies in Classical Philology* 67 (1961), reprinted in *Word and Action: Essays on the Ancient Theatre* (Baltimore: Johns Hopkins University Press, 1979), 125ff.

There are seven principal speakers, each of whom does a kind of solo turn in a style appropriate to his character.[15] In all cases, the subject is eros, in theory and practice.

Another stylistic aspect must at once be noted. The narrative structure emphasizes our great distance both from the words and from the events reported (cf. the remarks on the *Phaedo*, p. xvi). At the very outset we find Apollodorus repeating to an anonymous companion a report of the "cocktail party," which *he* has heard from someone else who was present. In addition, it is emphasized that the occasion was to celebrate the first dramatic victory of the playwright Agathon—which occurred "many a year ago." As noted earlier, this distancing must inevitably blur the accuracy of what is reported, making the narrative a kind of verbal equivalent of the shadows on the cave in *Republic* VII.

Phaedrus, the first "soloist," gives a superficial performance consisting mostly of ragtag quotations from other authors. Pausanias, who follows, posits the existence of two kinds of eros, the "vulgar" (*pandēmos*) and the "heavenly." The first sort is inferior to the second, involving love for women as well as boys and the body rather than the soul. "Heavenly" love is, of course, of the male alone. Indeed, it is impossible to understand Platonic society without realizing that by hallowed tradition it involved bonds of affection between men. This aspect is far too complex a matter to deal with in the confines of this essay, but all students of Greek culture should make themselves familiar with the definitive study of this phenomenon, K. J. Dover's *Greek Homosexuality* (Cambridge, MA: Harvard University Press, 1978).

The physician Eryximachus, who speaks next, picks up the distinction between the two kinds of eros and expresses it in physiological terms.

The fourth soloist is the comic poet Aristophanes who recounts the famous and amusing myth of the three sexes—male, female, and androgynous—all of whom were once curious chimerical creatures with double the "normal" number of limbs and members. The gods, in anger, split them in half. And "love," according to the playwright, is the passionate search of two natural halves to find each other again.

Agathon follows with a speech more notable for its form (sophistic) than its actual content. His ornate effusion sets the

---

[15]R.G. Bury analyzes the artistry of Plato's "rhetorical characterization" in his edition of the *Symposium* (Cambridge: Cambridge University Press, 1909), xxiv–xxxvi.

stage for the plain (and profound) speech of the man all have been waiting to hear. Socrates, with his typical irony, claims to know nothing about the subject himself, having acquired what knowledge of eros he possesses, from the priestess Diotima (note how this further increases the stylistic distancing).

In a lively dialectic Socrates had learned from the priestess that love is neither human nor divine but rather an intermediary (*metaxu*) between the two completing the bond between god and man. Eros yearns for wisdom (*philosophei*), especially the absolute form of the Beautiful. Socrates' image of the "ladder of love" has subsequently been a source of inspiration to poets in every age (one thinks immediately of the entire concept of Dante's *Divine Comedy*).

There is another arresting image in Socrates' speech, namely that all men are "pregnant" and desire to give birth. On the simplest level it is like parents who seek immortality through their children; on the loftiest it is a "pregnancy" of the soul, which achieves its immortality by begetting the Beautiful.

The finale of the *Symposium* is almost identical to the typical conclusion of an Aristophanic comedy: Alcibiades breaks drunkenly into the proceedings, a flute girl on his arm, a troupe (one might even say a chorus) of revelers in his train.

He will be the seventh and last speaker on love, and his address differs significantly from all the others. For whereas the first six symposiasts spoke—each according to his métier—in theoretical terms, Alcibiades relates actual events, specifically the details of his many attempts to seduce Socrates. While his account is piquantly entertaining, it also tells us something significant about Socrates, namely that he has practiced what he has just preached. He has, in the literal sense, "sublimated" his fleshly desires to a lofty spiritual plane.

The dialogue concludes with the memorable "morning-after" anecdote in which the only partyers left awake, Agathon the tragedian and Aristophanes the comedian, are listening to Socrates theorizing that a real genius could compose both types of drama. One may argue that his claim was only later to be substantiated by the work of Shakespeare, but there is cogent evidence that such a genius was nearer at hand—namely Plato himself.

The *Gorgias,* a product of Plato's mature years, is divided into three parts: the first section presents Socrates in an encounter with the title character, a Sophist, who had come to Athens in

427 B.C. and created a sensation with his theory (and practice) of rhetoric. Socrates demolishes Gorgias' elevated claims for the value of his art, arguing that he is merely a purveyor of opinion rather than the truth.

The second section pits Socrates against Polus, a follower of Gorgias, who claims that the greatest good is power and that the happiest man is the tyrant. But Socrates confutes him too and argues that it is better to suffer injustice than to commit it—a notion that runs counter to the Greek heroic tradition.

The final portion is a confrontation between Socrates and Callicles—a figure who may be a fictional creation of Plato's. In any case, we here find the philosopher dropping his playful ironic mask and speaking in deadly earnest. It is almost as if his antagonist's doctrines are so dangerous that Plato thinks special measures are required. Callicles claims that might makes right and that the happiest man is he who can allow free rein to his passions. Justice and virtue are merely the artificial constructs of weak and hypocritical men, who praise such myths as "self-control" because they are impotent to take what they want.

Callicles is without doubt the most cynical and brutal of Socrates' interlocutors in all the dialogues. Plato underscores this on page 334, where he has Callicles refer to the possibility of Socrates being haled into court by a worthless man. To this the philosopher responds that "no honest man could ever deal so with the innocent." This is wounding, tragic irony.[16]

Some commentators have compared Callicles' doctrines to those of Nietzsche. Perhaps their closest analogue is the contention of the Sophist Thrasymachus, in *Republic* I, that justice is the interest of the stronger.

The *Gorgias* is especially notable for its articulation of the then radical doctrine that it is better to suffer evil than commit it. This is the exact opposite of the traditional Greek heroic code (classically formulated in, among other places, Euripides' *Medea*. Cf. our discussion of the *Meno* above, p. xviii). This notion

---

[16]There is a deeply moving irony that seems to inform all of the dialogues to a greater or lesser extent. Though Socrates is already dead by the end of Plato's earliest works, Plato's subtle artistry creates a kind of "retroactive anticipation" by alluding to the ultimate judgment of Socrates (playfully, theoretically) in the dialogues, which are chronologically set at a time when the philosopher was in no mortal danger. The Callicles reference is one such ominous example; then there are instances such as *Symposium* p. 282 where Alcibiades jocularly calls upon the other party guests (*dikastai*, "judges") to put Socrates on trial—for resisting Alcibiades' charms. Clearly, the traumatic event of Socrates' unjust condemnation haunted Plato throughout his life.

marks a significant turning point in the history of Western ethics, anticipating as it does the teachings of the New Testament.

The dialogue concludes with a myth in which Socrates discusses the judgment of souls after death. He again warns men to be on guard against committing wrong (rather than suffering it). The peroration is among his noblest speeches—and his bluntest. For in the concluding words of the dialogue, he dismisses Callicles' philosophy as "completely worthless."

Plato may have created the brutal interlocutor merely to provide a dramatic pretext to display the fury of Socrates' righteous indignation. To meet his adversary's repugnant theories, Socrates utters his famous dictum on p. 311 that the most serious question a man must ask is "in what way should one live one's life?"

He was one of the few men in history who truly knew the answer.

The Dialogues
of Plato

APOLOGY

Translated by Benjamin Jowett

How you, O Athenians, have been affected by my accusers, I cannot tell; but I know that they almost made me forget who I was—so persuasively did they speak; and yet they have hardly uttered a word of truth. But of the many falsehoods told by them, there was one which quite amazed me;—I mean when they said that you should be upon your guard and not allow yourselves to be deceived by the force of my eloquence. To say this, when they were certain to be detected as soon as I opened my lips and proved myself to be anything but a great speaker, did indeed appear to me most shameless—unless by the force of eloquence they mean the force of truth; for if such is their meaning, I admit that I am eloquent. But in how different a way from theirs! Well, as I was saying, they have scarcely spoken the truth at all; but from me you shall hear the whole truth: not, however, delivered after their manner in a set oration duly ornamented with words and phrases. No, by heaven! but I shall use the words and arguments which occur to me at the moment; for I am confident in the justice of my cause:[1] at my time of life I ought not to be appearing before you, O men of Athens, in the character of a juvenile orator—let no one expect it of me. And I must beg of you to grant me a favor:—If I defend myself in my accustomed manner, and you hear me using the words which I have been in the habit of using in the agora, at the tables of the money-changers, or anywhere else, I would ask you not to be surprised, and not to interrupt me on this account. For I am more than seventy years of age, and appearing now for the first time in a court of law, I am quite a stranger to the language of the place; and therefore I would have you regard me as if I were really a stranger, whom you would excuse if he spoke in his native

[1]Or, I am certain that I am right in taking this course.

tongue, and after the fashion of his country:—Am I making an unfair request of you? Never mind the manner, which may or may not be good; but think only of the truth of my words, and give heed to that: let the speaker speak truly and the judge decide justly.

And first, I have to reply to the older charges and to my first accusers, and then I will go on to the later ones. For of old I have had many accusers, who have accused me falsely to you during many years; and I am more afraid of them than of Anytus and his associates, who are dangerous, too, in their own way. But far more dangerous are the others, who began when you were children, and took possession of your minds with their false-hoods, telling of one Socrates, a wise man, who speculated about the heaven above, and searched into the earth beneath, and made the worse appear the better cause. The disseminators of this tale are the accusers whom I dread; for their hearers are apt to fancy that such enquirers do not believe in the existence of the gods. And they are many, and their charges against me are of ancient date, and they were made by them in the days when you were more impressible than you are now—in childhood, or it may have been in youth—and the cause when heard went by default, for there was none to answer. And hardest of all, I do not know and cannot tell the names of my accusers; unless in the chance case of a comic poet. All who from envy and malice have persuaded you—some of them hav-ing first convinced themselves—all this class of men are most difficult to deal with; for I cannot have them up here, and cross-examine them, and therefore I must simply fight with shadows in my own defense, and argue when there is no one who answers. I will ask you then to assume with me, as I was saying, that my opponents are of two kinds; one recent, the other ancient: and I hope that you will see the propriety of my answer-ing the latter first, for these accusations you heard long before the others, and much oftener.

Well, then, I must make my defense, and endeavor to clear away in a short time, a slander which has lasted a long time. May I succeed, if to succeed be for my good and yours, or likely to avail me in my cause. The task is not an easy one; I quite understand the nature of it. And so leaving the event with God, in obedience to the law I will now make my defense.

I will begin at the beginning, and ask what is the accusation which has given rise to the slander of me, and in fact has encouraged Meletus to prefer this charge against me. Well, what do the slanderers say? They shall be my prosecutors, and I will sum up their words in an affidavit: "Socrates is an evildoer, and a curious person, who searches into things under the earth and in heaven, and he makes the worse appear the better cause; and he teaches the aforesaid doctrines to others." Such is the nature of the accusation: it is just what you have yourselves seen in the comedy of Aristophanes,[2] who has introduced a man whom he calls Socrates, going about and saying that he walks in air, and talking a deal of nonsense concerning matters of which I do not pretend to know either much or little—not that I mean to speak disparagingly of any one who is a student of natural philosophy. I should be very sorry if Meletus could bring so grave a charge against me. But the simple truth is, O Athenians, that I have nothing to do with physical speculations. Very many of those here present are witnesses to the truth of this, and to them I appeal. Speak then, you who have heard me, and tell your neighbors whether any of you have ever known me hold forth in few words or in many upon such matters. . . . You hear their answer. And from what they say of this part of the charge you will be able to judge of the truth of the rest.

As little foundation is there for the report that I am a teacher, and take money; this accusation has no more truth in it than the other. Although, if a man were really able to instruct mankind, to receive money for giving instruction would, in my opinion, be an honor to him. There is Gorgias of Leontium, and Prodicus of Ceos, and Hippias of Elis, who go the round of the cities, and are able to persuade the young men to leave their own citizens by whom they might be taught for nothing, and come to them whom they not only pay, but are thankful if they may be allowed to pay them. There is at this time a Parian philosopher residing in Athens, of whom I have heard; and I came to hear of him in this way:—I came across a man who has spent a world of money on the Sophists, Callias, the son of Hipponicus, and knowing that he had sons, I asked him: "Callias," I said, "if your two sons were foals or calves, there would be no difficulty in finding some one to put over them; we should hire a trainer of horses, or a farmer, probably, who would improve and perfect them in their own proper virtue and excellence; but as they are human beings, whom are you thinking of placing over them? Is there any one who understands human and political virtue? You must have thought about the matter, for you have sons; is there

---

[2]Aristophanes, *Clouds*, 225 ff.

any one?" "There is," he said. "Who is he?" said I; "and of what country? and what does he charge?" "Evenus the Parian," he replied; "he is the man, and his charge is five minae." Happy is Evenus, I said to myself, if he really has this wisdom, and teaches at such a moderate charge. Had I the same, I should have been very proud and conceited; but the truth is that I have no knowledge of the kind.

I dare say, Athenians, that some one among you will reply, "Yes, Socrates, but what is the origin of these accusations which are brought against you; there must have been something strange which you have been doing? All these rumors and this talk about you would never have arisen if you had been like other men: tell us, then, what is the cause of them, for we should be sorry to judge hastily of you." Now, I regard this as a fair challenge, and I will endeavor to explain to you the reason why I am called wise and have such an evil fame. Please to attend then. And although some of you may think that I am joking, I declare that I will tell you the entire truth. Men of Athens, this reputation of mine has come of a certain sort of wisdom which I possess. If you ask me what kind of wisdom, I reply, wisdom such as may perhaps be attained by man, for to that extent I am inclined to believe that I am wise; whereas the persons of whom I was speaking have a superhuman wisdom, which I may fail to describe, because I have it not myself; and he who says that I have, speaks falsely, and is taking away my character. And here, O men of Athens, I must beg you not to interrupt me, even if I seem to say something extravagant. For the word which I will speak is not mine. I will refer you to a witness who is worthy of credit; that witness shall be the god of Delphi—he will tell you about my wisdom, if I have any, and of what sort it is. You must have known Chaerephon; he was early a friend of mine, and also a friend of yours, for he shared in the recent exile of the people, and returned with you. Well, Chaerephon, as you know, was very impetuous in all his doings, and he went to Delphi and boldly asked the oracle to tell him whether—as I was saying, I must beg you not to interrupt—he asked the oracle to tell him whether any one was wiser than I was, and the Pythian prophetess answered, that there was no man wiser. Chaerephon is dead himself; but his brother, who is in court, will confirm the truth of what I am saying.

Why do I mention this? Because I am going to explain to you why I have such an evil name. When I heard the answer, I said to myself, What can the god mean? and what is the interpretation of his riddle? for I know that I have no wisdom, small or great. What then can he mean when he says that I am the wisest of men? And yet he is a god, and cannot lie; that would be against his nature. After long consideration, I thought of a method of trying the question. I reflected that if I could only find a man wiser than myself, then I might go to the god with a refutation in my hand. I should say to him, "Here is a man who is wiser than I am; but you said that I was the wisest." Accordingly I went to one who had the reputation of wisdom, and observed him—his name I need not mention; he was a politician whom I selected for examination—and the result was as follows: When I began to talk with him, I could not help thinking that he was not really wise, although he was thought wise by many, and still wiser by himself; and thereupon I tried to explain to him that he thought himself wise, but was not really wise; and the consequence was that he hated me, and his enmity was shared by several who were present and heard me. So I left him, saying to myself, as I went away: Well, although I do not suppose that either of us knows anything really beautiful and good, I am better off than he is,—for he knows nothing, and thinks that he knows; I neither know nor think that I know. In this latter particular, then, I seem to have slightly the advantage of him. Then I went to another who had still higher pretensions to wisdom, and my conclusion was exactly the same. Whereupon I made another enemy of him, and of many others besides him.

Then I went to one man after another, being not unconscious of the enmity which I provoked, and I lamented and feared this: but necessity was laid upon me,—the word of God, I thought, ought to be considered first. And I said to myself, Go I must to all who appear to know, and find out the meaning of the oracle. And I swear to you, Athenians, by the dog I swear!—for I must tell you the truth—the result of my mission was just this: I found that the men most in repute were all but the most foolish; and that others less esteemed were really wiser and better. I will tell you the tale of my wanderings and of the "Herculean" labors, as I may call them, which I endured only to find at last the oracle irrefutable. After the politicians, I went to the poets; tragic, dithyrambic, and all sorts. And there, I said to myself, you will be instantly detected; now you will find out that you are more ignorant than they are. Accordingly I took them some of the most elaborate passages in their own writings, and asked what was the meaning of them—thinking that they would teach me something. Will you believe me? I am almost ashamed to confess the truth, but I must say that there is hardly a person present who would not have talked better about their poetry than they did themselves. Then I knew that not by wisdom do poets write poetry, but by a sort of genius and inspiration; they are like diviners or soothsayers who also say many fine things, but do not understand the meaning of them. The poets appeared to me to be much in the same case; and I further observed that upon the strength of their poetry they believed themselves to be the wisest of men in other things in which they were not wise. So I departed, conceiving myself to be superior to them for the same reason that I was superior to the politicians.

At last I went to the artisans. I was conscious that I knew nothing at all, as I may say, and I was sure that they knew many fine things; and here I was not mistaken, for they did know many things of which I was ignorant, and in this they certainly were wiser than I was. But I observed that even the good artisans fell into the same error as the poets;—because they were good workmen they thought that they also knew all sorts of high matters, and this defect in them overshadowed their wisdom; and therefore I asked myself on behalf of the oracle, whether I would like to be as I was, neither having their knowledge nor their ignorance, or like them in both; and I made answer to myself and to the oracle that I was better off as I was.

This inquisition has led to my having many enemies of the worst and most dangerous kind, and has given occasion also to many calumnies. And I am called wise, for my hearers always imagine that I myself possess the wisdom which I find wanting in others: but the truth is, O men of Athens, that God only is wise; and by his answer he intends to show that the wisdom of men is worth little or nothing; he is not speaking of Socrates, he is only using my name by way of illustration, as if he said, He, O men, is the wisest, who, like Socrates, knows that his wisdom is in truth worth nothing. And so I go about the world obedient to the god, and search and make enquiry into the wisdom of any one, whether citizen or stranger, who appears to be wise; and if he is not wise, then in vindication of the oracle I show him that he is not wise; and my occupation quite absorbs me, and I have no time to give either to any public matter of interest or to any concern of my own, but I am in utter poverty by reason of my devotion to the god.

There is another thing:—young men of the richer classes, who have not much to do, come about me of their own accord; they like to hear the pretenders examined, and they often imitate me, and proceed to examine others; there are plenty of persons, as they quickly discover, who think that they know something, but really know little or nothing; and then those who are examined by them instead of being angry with themselves are angry with me: This confounded Socrates, they say; this villainous misleader of youth!—and then if somebody asks them, Why, what evil does he practice or teach? they do not know, and cannot tell; but in order that they may not appear to be at a loss, they repeat the ready-made charges which are used against all philosophers about teaching things up in the clouds and under the earth, and having no gods, and making the worse appear the better cause; for they do not like to confess that their pretense of knowledge has been detected—which is the truth; and as they are numerous and ambitious and energetic, and are drawn up in battle array and have persuasive tongues, they have filled your ears with their loud and inveterate calumnies. And this is the reason why my three accusers, Meletus and Anytus and Lycon, have set upon me; Meletus, who has a quarrel with me on behalf of the poets; Anytus, on behalf of the craftsmen and politicians; Lycon, on behalf of the rhetoricians: and, as I said at the beginning, I cannot expect to get rid of such a mass of calumny all in a moment. And this, O men of Athens, is the truth and the whole truth; I have concealed nothing, I have dissembled nothing. And yet, I know that my plainness of speech makes them hate me, and what is their hatred but a proof that I am speaking the truth? Hence has arisen the prejudice against me; and this is the reason of it, as you will find out either in this or in any future enquiry.

I have said enough in my defense against the first class of my accusers; I turn to the second class. They are headed by Meletus, that good man and true lover of his country, as he calls himself. Against these, too, I must try to make a defense:—Let their affidavit be read: it contains something of this kind: It says that Socrates is a doer of evil, who corrupts the youth; and who does not believe in the gods of the State, but has other new divinities of his own. Such is the charge; and now let us examine the particular counts. He says that I am a doer of evil, and corrupt the youth; but I say, O men of Athens, that Meletus is a doer of evil, in that he pretends to be in earnest when he is only in jest, and is so eager to bring men to trial from a pretended zeal and interest about matters in which he really never had the smallest interest. And the truth of this I will endeavor to prove to you.

Come hither, Meletus, and let me ask a question of you. You think a great deal about the improvement of youth?

Yes, I do.

Tell the judges, then, who is their improver; for you must know, as you have taken the pains to discover their corrupter, and are citing and accusing me before them. Speak, then, and tell the judges who their improver is.—Observe, Meletus, that you are silent, and have nothing to say. But is not this rather disgraceful, and a very considerable proof of what I was saying, that you have no interest in the matter? Speak up, friend, and tell us who their improver is.

The laws.

But that, my good sir, is not my meaning. I want to know who the person is, who, in the first place, knows the laws.

The judges, Socrates, who are present in court.

What do you mean to say, Meletus, that they are able to instruct and improve youth?

Certainly they are.

What, all of them, or some only and not others?

All of them.

By the goddess Here, that is good news! There are plenty of improvers, then. And what do you say of the audience,—do they improve them?

Yes, they do.

And the senators?

Yes, the senators improve them.

But perhaps the members of the assembly corrupt them?—or do they improve them?

They improve them.

Then every Athenian improves and elevates them; all with the exception of myself; and I alone am their corrupter? Is that what you affirm?

That is what I stoutly affirm.

I am very unfortunate if you are right. But suppose I ask you a question: How about horses? Does one man do them harm and all the world good? Is not the exact opposite the truth? One man is able to do them good, or at least not many;—the trainer of horses, that is to say, does them good, and others who have to do with them rather injure them? Is not that true, Meletus, of horses, or of any other animals? Most assuredly it is; whether you and Anytus say yes or no. Happy indeed would be the condition of youth if they had one corrupter only, and all the rest of the world were their improvers. But you, Meletus, have sufficiently shown that you never had a thought about the young: your carelessness is seen in your not caring about the very things which you bring against me.

And now, Meletus, I will ask you another question—by Zeus I will: Which is better, to live among bad citizens, or among good ones? Answer, friend, I say; the question is one which may be easily answered. Do not the good do their neighbors good, and the bad do them evil?

Certainly.

And is there any one who would rather be injured than benefited by those who live with him? Answer, my good friend, the law requires you to answer—does any one like to be injured?

Certainly not.

And when you accuse me of corrupting and deteriorating the youth, do you allege that I corrupt them intentionally or unintentionally?

Intentionally, I say.

But you have just admitted that the good do their neighbors good, and the evil do them evil. Now, is that a truth which your superior wisdom has recognized thus early in life, and am I, at my age, in such darkness and ignorance as not to know that if a man with whom I have to live is corrupted by me, I am very likely to be harmed by him; and yet I corrupt him, and intentionally, too—so you say; although neither I nor any other human being is ever likely to be convinced by you. But either I do not corrupt them, or I corrupt them unintentionally; and on either view of the case you lie. If my offense is unintentional, the law has no cognizance of unintentional offenses: you ought to have taken me privately, and warned and admonished me; for if I had been better advised, I should have left off doing what I only did unintentionally—no doubt I should; but you would have nothing to say to me and refused to teach me. And now you bring me up in this court, which is a place not of instruction, but of punishment.

It will be very clear to you, Athenians, as I was saying, that Meletus has no care at all, great or small, about the matter. But still I should like to know, Meletus, in what I am affirmed to corrupt the young. I suppose you mean, as I infer from your indictment, that I teach them not to acknowledge the gods which the State acknowledges, but some other new divinities or spiritual agencies in their stead. These are the lessons by which I corrupt the youth, as you say.

Yes, that I say emphatically.

Then, by the gods, Meletus, of whom we are speaking, tell

me and the court, in somewhat plainer terms, what you mean! For I do not as yet understand whether you affirm that I teach other men to acknowledge some gods, and therefore that I do believe in gods, and am not an entire atheist—this you do not lay to my charge,—but only you say that they are not the same gods which the city recognizes—the charge is that they are different gods. Or, do you mean that I am an atheist simply, and a teacher of atheism?

I mean the latter—that you are a complete atheist.

What an extraordinary statement! Why do you think so, Meletus? Do you mean that I do not believe in the godhead of the sun or moon, like other men?

I assure you, judges, that he does not: for he says that the sun is stone, and the moon earth.

Friend Meletus, you think that you are accusing Anaxagoras: and you have but a bad opinion of the judges, if you fancy them illiterate to such a degree as not to know that these doctrines are found in the books of Anaxagoras the Clazomenian, which are full of them. And so, forsooth, the youth are said to be taught them by Socrates, when there are not infrequently exhibitions of them at the theater[3] (price of admission one drachma at the most); and they might pay their money, and laugh at Socrates if he pretends to father these extraordinary views. And so, Meletus, you really think that I do not believe in any god?

I swear by Zeus that you believe absolutely in none at all.

Nobody will believe you, Meletus, and I am pretty sure that you do not believe yourself. I cannot help thinking, men of Athens, that Meletus is reckless and impudent, and that he has written this indictment in a spirit of mere wantonness and youthful bravado. Has he not compounded a riddle, thinking to try me? He said to himself:—I shall see whether the wise Socrates will discover my facetious contradiction, or whether I shall be able to deceive him and the rest of them. For he certainly does appear to me to contradict himself in the indictment as much as if he said that Socrates is guilty of not believing in the gods, and yet of believing in them—but this is not like a person who is in earnest.

I should like you, O men of Athens, to join me in examining what I conceive to be his inconsistency; and do you, Meletus, answer. And I must remind the audience of my request that they

---

[3]Probably in allusion to Aristophanes, who caricatured, and to Euripides, who borrowed the notions of Anaxagoras, as well as to other dramatic poets.

would not make a disturbance if I speak in my accustomed manner:

Did ever man, Meletus, believe in the existence of human things, and not of human beings? . . . I wish, men of Athens, that he would answer, and not be always trying to get up an interruption. Did ever any man believe in horsemanship, and not in horses? or in flute-playing, and not in flute-players? No, my friend; I will answer to you and to the court, as you refuse to answer for yourself. There is no man who ever did. But now please to answer the next question: Can a man believe in spiritual and divine agencies, and not in spirits or demigods?

He cannot.

How lucky I am to have extracted that answer, by the assistance of the court! But then you swear in the indictment that I teach and believe in divine or spiritual agencies (new or old, no matter for that); at any rate, I believe in spiritual agencies,—so you say and swear in the affidavit; and yet if I believe in divine beings, how can I help believing in spirits or demigods;—must I not? To be sure I must; and therefore I may assume that your silence gives consent. Now what are spirits or demigods? are they not either gods or the sons of gods?

Certainly they are.

But this is what I call the facetious riddle invented by you: the demigods or spirits are gods, and you say first that I do not believe in gods, and then again that I do believe in gods; that is, if I believe in demigods. For if the demigods are the illegitimate sons of gods, whether by the nymphs or by any other mothers, of whom they are said to be the sons—what human being will ever believe that there are no gods if they are the sons of gods? You might as well affirm the existence of mules, and deny that of horses and asses. Such nonsense, Meletus, could only have been intended by you to make trial of me. You have put this into the indictment because you had nothing real of which to accuse me. But no one who has a particle of understanding will ever be convinced by you that the same men can believe in divine and superhuman things, and yet not believe that there are gods and demigods and heroes.

I have said enough in answer to the charge of Meletus: any elaborate defense is unnecessary; but I know only too well how many are the enmities which I have incurred, and this is what will be my destruction if I am destroyed;—not Meletus, nor yet Anytus, but the envy and detraction of the world, which has been the death of many good men, and will probably be the death of many more; there is no danger of my being the last of them.

Some one will say: And are you not ashamed, Socrates, of a course of life which is likely to bring you to an untimely end? To him I may fairly answer: There you are mistaken: a man who is good for anything ought not to calculate the chance of living or dying; he ought only to consider whether in doing anything he is doing right or wrong—acting the part of a good man or of a bad. Whereas, upon your view, the heroes who fell at Troy were not good for much, and the son of Thetis above all, who altogether despised danger in comparison with disgrace; and when he was so eager to slay Hector, his goddess mother said to him, that if he avenged his companion Patroclus, and slew Hector, he would die himself—"Fate," she said, in these or the like words, "waits for you next after Hector"; he, receiving this warning, utterly despised danger and death, and instead of fearing them, feared rather to live in dishonor, and not to avenge his friend. "Let me die forthwith," he replies, "and be avenged of my enemy, rather than abide here by the beaked ships, a laughing stock and a burden of the earth." Had Achilles any thought of death and danger? For wherever a man's place is, whether the place which he has chosen or that in which he has been placed by a commander, there he ought to remain in the hour of danger; he should not think of death or of anything but of disgrace. And this, O men of Athens, is a true saying.

Strange, indeed, would be my conduct, O men of Athens, if I, who, when I was ordered by the generals whom you chose to command me at Potidaea and Amphipolis and Delium, remained where they placed me, like any other man, facing death—if now, when, as I conceive and imagine, God orders me to fulfil the philosopher's mission of searching into myself and other men, I were to desert my post through fear of death, or any other fear; that would indeed be strange, and I might justly be arraigned in court for denying the existence of the gods, if I disobeyed the oracle because I was afraid of death, fancying that I was wise when I was not wise. For the fear of death is indeed the pretense of wisdom, and not real wisdom, being a pretense of knowing the unknown; and no one knows whether death, which men in their fear apprehend to be the greatest evil, may not be the greatest good. Is not this ignorance of a disgraceful sort, the ignorance which is the conceit that a man knows what he does not know? And in this respect only I believe myself to differ from men in general, and may perhaps claim to be wiser than they are:—that whereas I know but little of the world below, I do not suppose that I know: but I do know that injustice and disobedience to a better, whether God or man, is evil and dishonorable, and I will never fear or avoid a possible good rather than a certain evil. And therefore if you let me go now, and are not convinced by Anytus, who said that since I had been prosecuted I must be put to death; (or if not that I ought never to have been prosecuted at all); and that if I escape now, your sons will all be utterly ruined by listening to my words—if you say to me, Socrates, this time we will not mind Anytus, and you shall be let off, but upon one condition, that you are not to enquire and speculate in this way any more, and that if you are caught doing so again you shall die;—if this was the condition on which you let me go, I should reply: Men of Athens, I honor and love you; but I shall obey God rather than you, and while I have life and strength I shall never cease from the practice and teaching of philosophy, exhorting any one whom I meet and saying to him after my manner: You, my friend,—a citizen of the great and mighty and wise city of Athens,—are you not ashamed of heaping up the greatest amount of money and honor and reputation, and caring so little about wisdom and truth and the greatest improvement of the soul, which you never regard or heed at all? And if the person with whom I am arguing, says: Yes, but I do care; then I do not leave him or let him go at once; but I proceed to interrogate and examine and cross-examine him, and if I think that he has no virtue in him, but only says that he has, I reproach him with undervaluing the greater, and overvaluing the less. And I shall repeat the same words to every one whom I meet, young and old, citizen and alien, but especially to the citizens, inasmuch as they are my brethren. For know that this is the command of God; and I believe that no greater good has ever happened in the State than my service to the God. For I do nothing but go about persuading you all, old and young alike, not to take thought for your persons or your properties, but first and chiefly to care about the greatest improvement of the soul. I tell you that virtue is not given by money, but that from virtue comes money and every other good of man, public as well as private. This is my teaching, and if this is the doctrine which corrupts the youth, I am a mischievous person. But if any one says that this is not my teaching, he is speaking an untruth. Wherefore, O men of Athens, I say to you, do as Anytus bids or not as Anytus bids, and either acquit me or not; but whichever you do, understand that I shall never alter my ways, not even if I have to die many times.

Men of Athens, do not interrupt, but hear me; there was an understanding between us that you should hear me to the end: I have something more to say, at which you may be inclined to cry out; but I believe that to hear me will be good for you, and therefore I beg that you will not cry out. I would have you know, that if you kill such an one as I am, you will injure yourselves more than you will injure me. Nothing will injure me, not Meletus nor yet Anytus—they cannot, for a bad man is not permitted to injure a better than himself. I do not deny that Anytus may, perhaps, kill him, or drive him into exile, or deprive him of civil rights; and he may imagine, and others may imagine, that he is inflicting a great injury upon him: but there I do not agree. For the evil of doing as he is doing—the evil of unjustly taking away the life of another—is greater far.

And now, Athenians, I am not going to argue for my own sake, as you may think, but for yours, that you may not sin against the God by condemning me, who am his gift to you. For if you kill me you will not easily find a successor to me, who, if I may use such a ludicrous figure of speech, am a sort of gadfly, given to the State by God; and the State is a great and noble steed who is tardy in his motions owing to his very size, and requires to be stirred into life. I am that gadfly which God has attached to the State, and all day long and in all places am always fastening upon you, arousing and persuading and reproaching you. You will not easily find another like me, and therefore I would advise you to spare me. I dare say that you may feel out of temper (like a person who is suddenly awakened from sleep), and you think that you might easily strike me dead as Anytus advises, and then you would sleep on for the remainder of your lives, unless God in his care of you sent you another gadfly. When I say that I am given to you by God, the proof of my mission is this:—if I had been like other men, I should not have neglected all my own concerns or patiently seen the neglect of them during all these years, and have been doing yours, coming to you individually like a father or elder brother, exhorting you to regard virtue; such conduct, I say, would be unlike human nature. If I had gained anything, or if my exhortations had been paid, there would have been some sense in my doing so; but now, as you will perceive, not even the impudence of my accusers dares to say that I have ever exacted or sought pay of any one; of that they have no witness. And I have a sufficient witness to the truth of what I say—my poverty.

Some one may wonder why I go about in private giving advice and busying myself with the concerns of others, but do not venture to come forward in public and advise the State. I will tell you why. You have heard me speak at sundry times and in divers places of an oracle or sign which comes to me, and is the divinity which Meletus ridicules in the indictment. This sign, which is a kind of voice, first began to come to me when I was a child; it always forbids but never commands me to do anything which I am going to do. This is what deters me from being a politician. And rightly, as I think. For I am certain, O men of Athens, that if I had engaged in politics, I should have perished long ago, and done no good either to you or to myself. And do not be offended at my telling you the truth: for the truth is, that no man who goes to war with you or any other multitude, honestly striving against the many lawless and unrighteous deeds which are done in a State, will save his life; he who will fight for the right, if he would live even for a brief space, must have a private station and not a public one.

I can give you convincing evidence of what I say, not words only, but what you value far more—actions. Let me relate to you a passage of my own life which will prove to you that I should never have yielded to injustice from any fear of death and that "as I should have refused to yield" I must have died at once. I will tell you a tale of the courts, not very interesting perhaps, but nevertheless true. The only office of State which I ever held, O men of Athens, was that of senator: the tribe Antiochis, which is my tribe, had the presidency at the trial of the generals who had not taken up the bodies of the slain after the battle of Arginusae; and you proposed to try them in a body, contrary to law, as you all thought afterwards; but at the time I was the only one of the Prytanes who was opposed to the illegality, and I gave my vote against you; and when the orators threatened to impeach and arrest me, and you called and shouted, I made up my mind that I would run the risk, having law and justice with me, rather than take part in your injustice because I feared imprisonment and death. This happened in the days of the democracy. But when the oligarchy of the Thirty was in power, they sent for me and four others into the rotunda, and bade us bring Leon the Salaminian from Salamis, as they wanted to put him to death. This was a specimen of the sort of commands which they were always giving with the view of implicating as many as possible in their crimes; and then I showed, not in word only but in deed, that, if I may be allowed to use such an expression, I cared not a straw for death, and that my great and only care was lest I should do an unrighteous or unholy thing. For the strong arm of that oppressive power did not frighten me into doing wrong; and when we came out of the rotunda the other four went to Salamis and fetched Leon, but I went quietly home. For which I might have lost my life, had not the power of the Thirty shortly afterwards come to an end. And many will witness to my words.

Now, do you really imagine that I could have survived all these years, if I had led a public life, supposing that like a good man I had always maintained the right and had made justice, as I ought, the first thing? No, indeed, men of Athens, neither I nor any other man. But I have been always the same in all my actions, public as well as private, and never have I yielded any base compliance to those who are slanderously termed my disciples, or to any other. Not that I have any regular disciples. But if any one likes to come and hear me while I am pursuing my mission, whether he be young or old, he is not excluded. Nor do I converse only with those who pay; but any one, whether he be rich or poor, may ask and answer me and listen to my words; and whether he turns out to be a bad man or a good one, neither result can be justly imputed to me; for I never taught or professed to teach him anything. And if any one says that he has ever learned or heard anything from me in private which all the world has not heard, let me tell you that he is lying.

But I shall be asked, Why do people delight in continually conversing with you? I have told you already, Athenians, the whole truth about this matter: they like to hear the cross-examination of the pretenders to wisdom; there is amusement in it. Now, this duty of cross-examining other men has been imposed upon me by God; and has been signified to me by oracles, visions, and in every way in which the will of divine power was ever intimated to any one. This is true, O Athenians; or, if not true, would be soon refuted. If I am or have been corrupting the youth, those of them who are now grown up and have become sensible that I gave them bad advice in the days of their youth should come forward as accusers, and take their revenge; or if they do not like to come themselves, some of their relatives, fathers, brothers, or other kinsmen, should say what evil their families have suffered at my hands. Now is their time. Many of them I see in the court. There is Crito, who is of the same age and of the same deme with myself, and there is Critobulus his son, whom I also see. Then again there is Lysanias of Sphettus, who is the father of Aeschines—he is present; and also there is Antiphon of Cephisus, who is the father of Epigenes; and there are the brothers of several who have associated with me. There is Nicostratus the son of Theosdotides, and the brother of Theodotus (now Theodotus himself is dead, and therefore he, at any rate, will not seek to stop him); and there is Paralus the son of Demodocus, who had a brother Theages; and Adeimantus the son of Ariston, whose brother Plato is present; and Aeantodorus, who is the brother of Apollodorus, whom I also see. I might mention a great many others, some of whom Meletus should have produced as witnesses in the course of his speech; and let him still produce them, if he has forgotten—I will make way for him. And let him say, if he has any testimony of the sort which he can produce. Nay, Athenians, the very opposite is the truth. For all these are ready to witness on behalf of the corrupter, of the injurer of their kindred, as Meletus and Anytus call me; not the corrupted youth only—there might have been a motive for that—but their uncorrupted elder relatives. Why should they too support me with their testimony? Why, indeed, except for the sake of truth and justice, and because they know that I am speaking the truth, and that Meletus is a liar.

Well, Athenians, this and the like of this is all the defense which I have to offer. Yet a word more. Perhaps there may be some one who is offended at me, when he calls to mind how he himself on a similar, or even a less serious occasion, prayed and entreated the judges with many tears, and how he produced his children in court, which was a moving spectacle, together with a host of relations and friends; whereas I, who am probably in danger of my life, will do none of these things. The contrast may occur to his mind, and he may be set against me, and vote in anger because he is displeased at me on this account. Now, if there be such a person among you,—mind, I do not say that there is,—to him I may fairly reply: My friend, I am a man, and like other men, a creature of flesh and blood, and not "of wood or stone," as Homer says; and I have a family, yes, and sons, O Athenians, three in number, one almost a man, and two others who are still young; and yet I will not bring any of them hither in order to petition you for an acquittal. And why not? Not from any self-assertion or want of respect for you. Whether I am or am not afraid of death is another question, of which I will not now speak. But, having regard to public opinion, I feel that such conduct would be discreditable to myself, and to you, and to the whole State. One who has reached my years, and who has a name for wisdom, ought not to demean himself. Whether this opinion of me be deserved or not, at any rate the world has decided that Socrates is in some way superior to other men. And if those among you who are said to be superior in wisdom and courage, and any other virtue, demean themselves in this way, how shameful is their conduct! I have seen men of reputation, when they have been condemned, behaving in the strangest manner: they seemed to fancy that they were going to suffer something dreadful if they died, and that they could be immortal if you only allowed them to live; and I think that such are a dishonor to the State, and that any stranger coming in would have said of them that the most eminent men of Athens, to whom the Athenians themselves give honor and command, are no better than women. And I say that these things ought not to be done by those of us who have a reputation; and if they are done, you ought not to permit them; you ought rather to show that you are far more disposed to condemn the man who gets up a doleful scene and makes the city ridiculous, than him who holds his peace.

But, setting aside the question of public opinion, there seems to be something wrong in asking a favor of a judge, and thus procuring an acquittal, instead of informing and convincing him. For his duty is, not to make a present of justice, but to give judgment; and he has sworn that he will judge according to the laws, and not according to his own good pleasure; and we ought not to encourage you, nor should you allow yourselves to be encouraged, in this habit of perjury—there can be no piety in that. Do not then require me to do what I consider dishonorable and impious and wrong, especially now, when I am being tried for impiety on the indictment of Meletus. For if, O men of Athens, by force of persuasion and entreaty I could overpower your oaths, then I should be teaching you to believe that there are no gods, and in defending should simply convict myself of the charge of not believing in them. But that is not so—far otherwise. For I do believe that there are gods, and in a sense higher than that in which any of my accusers believe in them. And to you and to God I commit my cause, to be determined by you as is best for you and me.

There are many reasons why I am not grieved, O men of Athens, at the vote of condemnation. I expected it, and am only surprised that the votes are so nearly equal; for I had thought that the majority against me would have been far larger; but now, had thirty votes gone over to the other side, I should have been acquitted. And I may say, I think, that I have escaped Meletus. I may say more; for without the assistance of Anytus and Lycon, any one may see that he would not have had a fifth part of the votes, as the law requires, in which case he would have incurred a fine of a thousand drachmae.

And so he proposes death as the penalty. And what shall I propose on my part, O men of Athens? Clearly that which is my due. And what is my due? What returns shall be made to the man who has never had the wit to be idle during his whole life; but has been careless of what the many care for—wealth, and family interests, and military offices, and speaking in the assembly, and magistracies, and plots, and parties. Reflecting that I was really too honest a man to be a politician and live, I did not go where I could do no good to you or to myself; but where I could do the greatest good privately to every one of you, thither I went, and sought to persuade every man among you that he must look to himself, and seek virtue and wisdom before he looks to his private interests, and look to the State before he looks to the interests of the State; and that this should be the order which he observes in all his actions. What shall be done to such an one? Doubtless some good thing, O men of Athens, if he has his reward; and the good should be of a kind suitable to him. What would be a reward suitable to a poor man who is your benefactor, and who desires leisure that he may instruct you? There can be no reward so fitting as maintenance in the Prytaneum, O men of Athens, a reward which he deserves far more than the citizen who has won the prize at Olympia in the horse or chariot race, whether the chariots were drawn by two horses or by many. For I am in want, and he has enough; and he only gives you the appearance of happiness, and I give you the reality. And if I am to estimate the penalty fairly, I should say that maintenance in the Prytaneum is the just return.

Perhaps you think that I am braving you in what I am saying now, as in what I said before about the tears and prayers. But this is not so. I speak rather because I am convinced that I never intentionally wronged any one, although I cannot convince you—the time has been too short; if there were a law at Athens, as there is in other cities, that a capital cause should not be decided in one day, then I believe that I should have convinced you. But I cannot in a moment refute great slanders; and, as I am convinced that I never wronged another, I will assuredly not wrong myself. I will not say of myself that I deserve any evil, or propose any penalty. Why should I? Because I am afraid of the penalty of death which Meletus proposes? When I do not know whether death is a good or an evil, why should I propose a penalty which would certainly be an evil? Shall I say imprisonment? And why should I live in prison, and be the slave of the magistrate of the year—of the Eleven? Or shall the penalty be a fine, and imprisonment until the fine is paid? There is the same objection. I should have to lie in prison, for money I have none, and cannot pay. And if I say exile (and this may possibly be the penalty which you will affix), I must indeed be blinded by the love of life, if I am so irrational as to expect that when you, who are my own citizens, cannot endure my discourses and words, and have found them so grievous and odious that you will have no more of them, others are likely to endure me. No, indeed, men of Athens, that is not very likely. And what a life should I lead, at my age, wandering from city to city, ever changing my place of exile, and always being driven out! For I am quite sure that wherever I go, there, as here, the young men will flock to me; and if I drive them away, their elders will drive me out at their request; and if I let them come their fathers and friends will drive me out for their sakes.

Some one will say: Yes, Socrates, but cannot you hold your tongue, and then you may go into a foreign city, and no one will interfere with you? Now, I have great difficulty in making you understand my answer to this. For if I tell you that to do as you say would be a disobedience to the God, and therefore that I cannot hold my tongue, you will not believe that I am serious; and if I say again that daily to discourse about virtue, and of those other things about which you hear me examining myself and others, is the greatest good of man, and that the unexamined life is not worth living, you are still less likely to believe me. Yet I say what is true, although a thing of which it is hard for me to persuade you. Also, I have never been accustomed to think that I deserve to suffer any harm. Had I money I might have estimated the offense at what I was able to pay, and not have been much the worse. But I have none, and therefore I must ask you to proportion the fine to my means. Well, perhaps I could afford a mina, and therefore I propose that penalty: Plato, Crito, Critobulus, and Apollodorus, my friends here, bid me say thirty minae, and they will be the sureties. Let thirty minae be the penalty; for which sum they will be ample security to you.

*   *   *

Not much time will be gained, O Athenians, in return for the evil name which you will get from the detractors of the city, who will say that you killed Socrates, a wise man; for they will call me wise, even although I am not wise, when they want to reproach you. If you had waited a little while, your desire would have been fulfilled in the course of nature. For I am far advanced in years, as you may perceive, and not far from death. I am speaking now not to all of you, but only to those who have condemned me to death. And I have another thing to say to them: You think that I was convicted because I had no words of the sort which would have procured my acquittal—I mean, if I had thought fit to leave nothing undone or unsaid. Not so; the deficiency which led to my conviction was not of words—certainly not. But I had not the boldness or impudence or inclination to address you as you would have liked me to do, weeping and wailing and lamenting, and saying and doing many things which you have been accustomed to hear from others, and which, as I maintain, are unworthy of me. I thought at the time that I ought not to do anything common or mean when in danger: nor do I now repent of the style of my defense; I would rather die having spoken after my manner, than speak in your manner and live. For neither in war nor yet at law ought I or any man to use every way of escaping death. Often in battle there can be no doubt that if a man will throw away his arms, and fall on his knees before his pursuers, he may escape death; and in other dangers there are other ways of escaping death, if a man is willing to say and do anything. The difficulty, my friends, is not to avoid death, but to avoid unrighteousness; for that runs faster than death. I am old and move slowly, and the slower runner has overtaken me, and my accusers are keen and quick, and the faster runner, who is unrighteousness, has overtaken them. And now I depart hence condemned by you to suffer the penalty of death,—they too go their ways condemned by the truth to suffer the penalty of villainy and wrong; and I must abide by my award—let them abide by theirs. I suppose that these things may be regarded as fated,—and I think that they are well.

And now, O men who have condemned me, I would fain prophesy to you; for I am about to die, and in the hour of death men are gifted with prophetic power. And I prophesy to you who are my murderers, that immediately after my departure punishment far heavier than you have inflicted on me will surely await you. Me you have killed because you wanted to escape the accuser, and not to give an account of your lives. But that will not be as you suppose: far otherwise. For I say that there will be more accusers of you than there are now; accusers whom hitherto I have restrained: and as they are younger they will be more inconsiderate with you, and you will be more offended at them. If you think that by killing men you can prevent some one from censuring your evil lives, you are mistaken; that is not a way of escape which is either possible or honorable; the easiest and the noblest way is not to be disabling others, but to be improving yourselves. This is the prophecy which I utter before my departure to the judges who have condemned me.

Friends, who would have acquitted me, I would like also to talk with you about the thing which has come to pass, while the magistrates are busy, and before I go to the place at which I must die. Stay then a little, for we may as well talk with one another while there is time. You are my friends, and I should like to show you the meaning of this event which has happened to me. O my judges—for you I may truly call judges—I should like to tell you of a wonderful circumstance. Hitherto the divine faculty of which the internal oracle is the source has constantly been in the habit of opposing me even about trifles, if I was going to make a slip or error in any matter; and now as you see there has come upon me that which may be thought, and is generally believed to be, the last and worst evil. But the oracle made no sign of opposition, either when I was leaving my house in the morning, or when I was on my way to the court, or while I was speaking, at anything which I was going to say; and yet I have often been stopped in the middle of a speech, but now in nothing I either said or did touching the matter in hand has the oracle opposed me. What do I take to be the explanation of this silence? I will tell you. It is an intimation that what has happened to me is a good, and that those of us who think that death is an evil are in error. For the customary sign would surely have opposed me had I been going to evil and not to good.

Let us reflect in another way, and we shall see that there is great reason to hope that death is a good; for one of two things—either death is a state of nothingness and utter unconsciousness, or, as men say, there is a change and migration of the soul from this world to another. Now, if you suppose that there is no consciousness, but a sleep like the sleep of him who is undisturbed even by dreams, death will be an unspeakable gain. For if a person were to select the night in which his sleep was undisturbed even by dreams, and were to compare with this the other days and nights of his life, and then were to tell us how many days and nights he had passed in the course of his life better and more pleasantly than this one, I think that any man, I will not say a private man, but even the great king will not find many such days or nights, when compared with the others. Now, if death be of such a nature, I say that to die is gain; for eternity is then only a single night. But if death is the journey to another place, and there, as men say, all the dead abide, what good, O my friends and judges, can be greater than this? If, indeed, when the pilgrim arrives in the world below, he is delivered from the professors of justice in this world, and finds the true judges who are said to give judgment there, Minos and Rhadamanthus and Aeacus and Triptolemus, and other sons of God who were righteous in their own life, that pilgrimage will be worth making. What would not a man give if he might converse with Orpheus and Musaeus and Hesiod and Homer? Nay, if this be true, let me die again and again. I myself, too, shall have a wonderful interest in there meeting and conversing with Palamedes, and Ajax the son of Telamon, and any other ancient hero who has suffered death through an unjust judgment; and there will be no small pleasure, as I think, in comparing my own sufferings with theirs. Above all, I shall then be able to continue my search into true and false knowledge, as in this world, so also in the next; and I shall find out who is wise, and who pretends to be wise, and is not. What would not a man give, O judges, to be able to examine the leader of the great Trojan expedition; or Odysseus or Sisyphus, or numberless others, men and women too! What infinite delight would there be in conversing with them and asking them questions! In another world they do not put a man to death for asking questions: assuredly not. For besides being happier than we are, they will be immortal, if what is said is true.

Wherefore, O judges, be of good cheer about death, and know of a certainty, that no evil can happen to a good man, either in life or after death. He and his are not neglected by the gods; nor has my own approaching end happened by mere chance. But I see clearly that the time had arrived when it was better for me to die and be released from trouble; wherefore the oracle gave no sign. For which reason, also, I am not angry with my condemners, or with my accusers; they have done me no harm, although they did not mean to do me any good; and for this I may gently blame them.

Still, I have a favor to ask of them. When my sons are grown up, I would ask you, O my friends, to punish them; and I would have you trouble them, as I have troubled you, if they seem to care about riches, or anything, more than about virtue; or if they pretend to be something when they are really nothing, —then reprove them, as I have reproved you, for not caring about that for which they ought to care, and thinking that they are something when they are really nothing. And if you do this, both I and my sons will have received justice at your hands.

The hour of departure has arrived, and we go our ways—I to die, and you to live. Which is better God only knows.

CRITO

Translated by F. J. Church

Socrates. Why have you come at this hour, Crito? Is it not still early?

Crito. Yes, very early.

Socrates. About what time is it?

Crito. It is just daybreak.

Socrates. I wonder that the jailer was willing to let you in.

Crito. He knows me now, Socrates; I come here so often, and besides, I have given him a tip.

Socrates. Have you been here long?

Crito. Yes, some time.

Socrates. Then why did you sit down without speaking? Why did you not wake me at once?

Crito. Indeed, Socrates, I wish that I myself were not so sleepless and sorrowful. But I have been wondering to see how soundly you sleep. And I purposely did not wake you, for I was anxious not to disturb your repose. Often before, all through your life, I have thought that your temperament was a happy one; and I think so more than ever now when I see how easily and calmly you bear the calamity that has come to you.

Socrates. Nay, Crito, it would be absurd if at my age I were disturbed at having to die.

Crito. Other men as old are overtaken by similar calamities, Socrates; but their age does not save them from being disturbed by their fate.

Socrates. That is so; but tell me why are you here so early?

Crito. I am the bearer of sad news, Socrates; not sad, it seems, for you, but for me and for all your friends, both sad and hard to bear; and for none of them, I think, is it as hard to bear as it is for me.

Socrates. What is it? Has the ship come from Delos, at the arrival of which I am to die?

Crito. No, it has not actually arrived, but I think that it will be here today, from the news which certain persons have brought from Sunium, who left it there. It is clear from their report that it will be here today; and so, Socrates, tomorrow your life will have to end.

Socrates. Well, Crito, may it end well. Be it so, if so the gods will. But I do not think that the ship will be here today.

Crito. Why do you suppose not?

Socrates. I will tell you. I am to die on the day after the ship arrives, am I not?[1]

Crito. That is what the authorities say.

Socrates. Then I do not think that it will come today, but tomorrow. I am counting on a dream I had a little while ago in the night, so it seems to be fortunate that you did not wake me.

Crito. And what was this dream?

Socrates. A fair and beautiful woman, clad in white, seemed to come to me, and call me and say, "O Socrates—

On the third day shall you fertile Phthia reach."[2]

Crito. What a strange dream, Socrates!

Socrates. But its meaning is clear, at least to me, Crito.

Crito. Yes, too clear, it seems. But, O my good Socrates, I beg you for the last time to listen to me and save yourself. For to me your death will be more than a single disaster; not only shall I lose a friend the like of whom I shall never find again, but many persons who do not know you and me well will think that I might have saved you if I had been willing to spend money, but that I neglected to do so. And what reputation could be more disgraceful than the reputation of caring more for money than for one's friends? The public will never believe that we were anxious to save you, but that you yourself refused to escape.

Socrates. But, my dear Crito, why should we care so much about public opinion? Reasonable men, of whose opinion it is worth our while to think, will believe that we acted as we really did.

Crito. But you see, Socrates, that it is necessary to care about public opinion, too. This very thing that has happened to you proves that the multitude can do a man not the least, but almost the greatest harm, if he is falsely accused to them.

---

[1] Criminals could not be put to death while the sacred ship was away on its voyage.

[2] Homer, *Iliad*, 9. 363.

Socrates. I wish that the multitude were able to do a man the greatest harm, Crito, for then they would be able to do him the greatest good, too. That would have been fine. But, as it is, they can do neither. They cannot make a man either wise or foolish: they act wholly at random.

Crito. Well, as you wish. But tell me this, Socrates. You surely are not anxious about me and your other friends, and afraid lest, if you escape, the informers would say that we stole you away, and get us into trouble, and involve us in a great deal of expense, or perhaps in the loss of all our property, and, it may be, bring some other punishment upon us besides? If you have any fear of that kind, dismiss it. For of course we are bound to run these risks, and still greater risks than these, if necessary, in saving you. So do not, I beg you, refuse to listen to me.

Socrates. I am anxious about that, Crito, and about much besides.

Crito. Then have no fear on that score. There are men who, for no very large sum, are ready to bring you out of prison into safety. And then, you know, these informers are cheaply bought, and there would be no need to spend much upon them. My fortune is at your service, and I think that it is adequate; and if you have any feeling about making use of my money, there are strangers in Athens whom you know, ready to use theirs; and one of them, Simmias of Thebes, has actually brought enough for this very purpose. And Cebes and many others are ready, too. And therefore, I repeat, do not shrink from saving yourself on that ground. And do not let what you said in the court—that if you went into exile you would not know what to do with yourself—stand in your way; for there are many places for you to go to, where you will be welcomed. If you choose to go to Thessaly, I have friends there who will make much of you and protect you from any annoyance from the people of Thessaly.

And besides, Socrates, I think that you will be doing what is unjust if you abandon your life when you might preserve it. You are simply playing into your enemies' hands; it is exactly what they wanted—to destroy you. And what is more, to me you seem to be abandoning your children, too. You will leave them to take their chance in life, as far as you are concerned, when you might bring them up and educate them. Most likely their fate will be the usual fate of children who are left orphans. But you ought not to bring children into the world unless you mean to take the trouble of bringing them up and educating them. It seems to me that you are choosing the easy way, and not the way of a good and brave man, as you ought, when you have been talking all your life long of the value that you set upon human excellence. For my part, I feel ashamed both for you and for us who are your friends. Men will think that the whole thing which has happened to you—your appearance in court to face trial, when you need not have appeared at all; the very way in which the trial was conducted; and then last of all this, the crowning absurdity of the whole affair—is due to our cowardice. It will look as if we had shirked the danger out of miserable cowardice; for we did not save you, and you did not save yourself, when it was quite possible to do so if we had been good for anything at all. Take care, Socrates, lest these things be not evil only, but also dishonorable to you and to us. Reflect, then, or rather the time for reflection is past; we must make up our minds. And there is only one plan possible. Everything must be done tonight. If we delay any longer, we are lost. Socrates, I implore you not to refuse to listen to me.

Socrates. My dear Crito, if your anxiety to save me be right, it is most valuable; but if not, the greater it is the harder it will be to cope with. We must reflect, then, whether we are to do as you say or not; for I am still what I always have been—a man who will accept no argument but that which on reflection I find to be truest. I cannot cast aside my former arguments because this misfortune has come to me. They seem to me to be as true as ever they were, and I respect and honor the same ones as I used to. And if we have no better argument to substitute for them, I certainly shall not agree to your proposal, not even though the power of the multitude should scare us with fresh terrors, as children are scared with hobgoblins, and inflict upon us new fines and imprisonments, and deaths. What is the most appropriate way of examining the question? Shall we go back first to what you say about opinions, and ask if we used to be right in thinking that we ought to pay attention to some opinions, and not to others? Were we right in saying so before I was condemned to die, and has it now become apparent that we were talking at random and arguing for the sake of argument, and that it was really nothing but playful nonsense? I am anxious, Crito, to examine our former argument with your help, and to see whether my present circumstance will appear to me to have affected its truth in any way or not; and whether we are to set it aside, or to yield assent to it. Those of us who thought at all seriously always used to say, I think, exactly what I said just now, namely, that we ought to respect some of the opinions which men form, and not others. Tell me, Crito, I beg you, do you not think that they were right? For you in all probability will not have to die tomorrow, and your judgment will not be biased by that circumstance. Reflect, then, do you not think it reasonable to say that we should not respect all the opinions of men but only some, nor the opinions of all men but only of some men? What do you think? Is not this true?

Crito. It is.

Socrates. And we should respect the good opinions, and not the worthless ones?

Crito. Yes.

Socrates. But the good opinions are those of the wise, and the worthless ones those of the foolish?

Crito. Of course.

Socrates. And what did we say about this? Does a man who is in training, and who is serious about it, pay attention to the praise and blame and opinion of all men, or only of the one man who is a doctor or a trainer?

Crito. He pays attention only to the opinion of the one man.

Socrates. Then he ought to fear the blame and welcome the praise of this one man, not of the multitude?

Crito. Clearly.

Socrates. Then he must act and exercise, and eat and drink in whatever way the one man who is his director, and who understands the matter, tells him; not as others tell him?

Crito. That is so.

Socrates. Good. But if he disobeys this one man, and disregards his opinion and his praise, and respects instead what the many say, who understand nothing of the matter, will he not suffer for it?

Crito. Of course he will.

Socrates. And how will he suffer? In what way and in what part of himself?

Crito. Of course in his body. That is disabled.

Socrates. You are right. And, Crito, to be brief, is it not the same in everything? And, therefore, in questions of justice and injustice, and of the base and the honorable, and of good and evil, which we are now examining, ought we to follow the opinion of the many and fear that, or the opinion of the one man who understands these matters (if we can find him), and feel more shame and fear before him than before all other men? For if we do not follow him, we shall corrupt and maim that part of us which, we used to say, is improved by justice and disabled by injustice. Or is this not so?

Crito. No, Socrates, I agree with you.

Socrates. Now, if, by listening to the opinions of those who do not understand, we disable that part of us which is improved by health and corrupted by disease, is our life worth living when it is corrupt? It is the body, is it not?

Crito. Yes.

Socrates. Is life worth living with the body corrupted and crippled?

Crito. No, certainly not.

Socrates. Then is life worth living when that part of us which is maimed by injustice and benefited by justice is corrupt? Or do we consider that part of us, whatever it is, which has to do with justice and injustice to be of less consequence than our body?

Crito. No, certainly not.

Socrates. But more valuable?

Crito. Yes, much more so.

Socrates. Then, my good friend, we must not think so much of what the many will say of us; we must think of what the one man who understands justice and injustice, and of what truth herself will say of us. And so you are mistaken, to begin with, when you invite us to regard the opinion of the multitude concerning the just and the honorable and the good, and their opposites. But, it may be said, the multitude can put us to death?

Crito. Yes, that is evident. That may be said, Socrates.

Socrates. True. But, my good friend, to me it appears that the conclusion which we have just reached is the same as our conclusion of former times. Now consider whether we still hold to the belief that we should set the highest value, not on living, but on living well?

Crito. Yes, we do.

Socrates. And living well and honorably and justly mean the same thing: do we hold to that or not?

Crito. We do.

Socrates. Then, starting from these premises, we have to consider whether it is just or not for me to try to escape from prison, without the consent of the Athenians. If we find that it is just, we will try; if not, we will give up the idea. I am afraid that considerations of expense, and of reputation, and of bringing up my children, of which you talk, Crito, are only the opinions of the many, who casually put men to death, and who would, if they could, as casually bring them to life again, without a thought. But reason, which is our guide, shows us that we can have nothing to consider but the question which I asked just now—namely, shall we be acting justly if we give money and thanks to the men who are to aid me in escaping, and if we ourselves take our respective parts in my escape? Or shall we in truth be acting unjustly if we do all this? And if we find that we should be acting unjustly, then we must not take any account either of death, or of any other evil that may be the consequence of remaining here, where we are, but only of acting unjustly.

Crito. I think that you are right, Socrates. But what are we to do?

Socrates. Let us examine this question together, my friend, and if you can contradict anything that I say, do so, and I shall be persuaded. But if you cannot, do not go on repeating to me any longer, my dear friend, that I should escape without the consent of the Athenians. I am very anxious to act with your approval and consent. I do not want you to think me mistaken. But now tell me if you agree with the premise from which I start, and try to answer my questions as you think best.

Crito. I will try.

Socrates. Ought we never to act unjustly voluntarily? Or may we act unjustly in some ways, and not in others? Is it the case, as we have often agreed in former times, that it is never either good or honorable to act unjustly? Or have all our former conclusions been overturned in these few days; and did we at our age fail to recognize all along, when we were seriously conversing with each other, that we were no better than children? Is not what we used to say most certainly the truth, whether the multitude agrees with us or not? Is not acting unjustly evil and shameful in every case, whether we incur a heavier or a lighter punishment as the consequence? Do we believe that?

Crito. We do.

Socrates. Then we ought never to act unjustly?

Crito. Certainly not.

Socrates. If we ought never to act unjustly at all, ought we to repay injustice with injustice, as the multitude thinks we may?

Crito. Clearly not.

Socrates. Well, then, Crito, ought we to do evil to anyone?

Crito. Certainly I think not, Socrates.

Socrates. And is it just to repay evil with evil, as the multitude thinks, or unjust?

Crito. Certainly it is unjust.

Socrates. For there is no difference, is there, between doing evil to a man and acting unjustly?

Crito. True.

Socrates. Then we ought not to repay injustice with injustice or to do harm to any man, no matter what we may have suffered from him. And in conceding this, Crito, be careful that you do not concede more than you mean. For I know that only a few men hold, or ever will hold, this opinion. And so those who hold it and those who do not have no common ground of argument; they can of necessity only look with contempt on each other's belief. Do you therefore consider very carefully whether or not you agree with me and share my opinion. Are we to start in our inquiry from the premise that it is never right either to act unjustly, or to repay injustice with injustice, or to avenge ourselves on any man who harms us, by harming him in return? Or do you disagree with me and dissent from my premise? I myself have believed in it for a long time, and I believe in it still. But if you differ in any way, explain to me how. If you still hold to our former opinion, listen to my next point.

Crito. Yes, I hold to it, and I agree with you. Go on.

Socrates. Then, my next point, or rather my next question, is this: Ought a man to carry out his just agreements, or may he shuffle out of them?

Crito. He ought to carry them out.

Socrates. Then consider. If I escape without the state's consent, shall I be injuring those whom I ought least to injure, or not? Shall I be abiding by my just agreements or not?

Crito. I cannot answer your question, Socrates. I do not understand it.

Socrates. Consider it in this way. Suppose the laws and the commonwealth were to come and appear to me as I was preparing to run away (if that is the right phrase to describe my escape) and were to ask, "Tell us, Socrates, what have you in your mind to do? What do you mean by trying to escape but to destroy us, the laws and the whole state, so far as you are able? Do you think that a state can exist and not be overthrown, in which the decisions of law are of no force, and are disregarded and undermined by private individuals?" How shall we answer questions like that, Crito? Much might be said, especially by an orator, in defense of the law which makes judicial decisions supreme. Shall I reply, "But the state has injured me by judging my case unjustly?" Shall we say that?

Crito. Certainly we will, Socrates.

Socrates. And suppose the laws were to reply, "Was that our agreement? Or was it that you would abide by whatever judgments the state should pronounce?" And if we were surprised by their words, perhaps they would say, "Socrates, don't be surprised by our words, but answer us; you yourself are accustomed to ask questions and to answer them. What complaint have you against us and the state, that you are trying to destroy us? Are we not, first of all, your parents? Through us your father took your mother and brought you into the world. Tell us, have you any fault to find with those of us that are the laws of marriage?" "I have none," I should reply. "Or have you any fault to find with those of us that regulate the raising of the child and the education which you, like others, received? Did we not do well in telling your father to educate you in music and athletics?" "You did," I should say. "Well, then, since you were brought into the world and raised and educated by us, how, in the first place, can you deny that you are our child and our slave, as your fathers were before you? And if this be so, do you think that your rights are on a level with ours? Do you think that you have a right to retaliate if we should try to do anything to you? You had not the same rights that your father had, or that your master would have had if you had been a slave. You had no right to retaliate if they ill-treated you, or to answer them if they scolded you, or to strike them back if they struck you, or to repay them evil with evil in any way. And do you think that you may retaliate in the case of your country and its laws? If we try to destroy you, because we think it just, will you in return do all that you can to destroy us, the laws, and your country, and say that in so doing you are acting justly—you, the man who really thinks so much of excellence? Or are you too wise to see that your country is worthier, more to be revered, more sacred, and held in higher honor both by the gods and by all men of understanding, than your father and your mother and all your other ancestors; and that you ought to reverence it, and to submit to it, and to approach it more humbly when it is angry with you than you would approach your father; and either to do whatever it tells you to do or to persuade it to excuse you; and to obey in silence if it orders you to endure flogging or imprisonment, or if it sends you to battle to be wounded or to die? That is just. You must not give way, nor retreat, nor desert your station. In war, and in the court of justice, and everywhere, you must do whatever your state and your country tell you to do, or you must persuade them that their commands are unjust. But it is impious to use violence against your father or your mother; and much more impious to use violence against your country." What answer shall we make, Crito? Shall we say that the laws speak the truth, or not?

Crito. I think that they do.

Socrates. "Then consider, Socrates," perhaps they would say, "if we are right in saying that by attempting to escape you are attempting an injustice. We brought you into the world, we raised you, we educated you, we gave you and every other citizen a share of all the good things we could. Yet we proclaim that if any man of the Athenians is dissatisfied with us, he may take his goods and go away wherever he pleases; we give that privilege to every man who chooses to avail himself of it, so soon as he has reached manhood, and sees us, the laws, and the administration of our state. No one of us stands in his way or forbids him to take his goods and go wherever he likes, whether it be to an Athenian colony or to any foreign country, if he is dissatisfied with us and with the state. But we say that every man of you who remains here, seeing how we administer justice, and how we govern the state in other matters, has agreed, by the very fact of remaining here, to do whatsoever we tell him. And, we say, he who disobeys us acts unjustly on three counts: he disobeys us who are his parents, and he disobeys us who reared him, and he disobeys us after he has agreed to obey us, without persuading us that we are wrong. Yet we did not tell him sternly to do whatever we told him. We offered him an alternative; we gave him his choice either to obey us or to convince us that we were wrong; but he does neither.

"These are the charges, Socrates, to which we say that you will expose yourself if you do what you intend; and you are more exposed to these charges than other Athenians." And if I were to ask, "Why?" they might retort with justice that I have bound myself by the agreement with them more than other Athenians. They would say, "Socrates, we have very strong evidence that you were satisfied with us and with the state. You would not have been content to stay at home in it more than other Athenians unless you had been satisfied with it more than they. You never went away from Athens to the festivals, nor elsewhere except on military service; you never made other journeys like other men; you had no desire to see other states or other laws; you were contented with us and our state; so strongly did you prefer us, and agree to be governed by us. And what is more, you had children in this city, you found it so satisfactory. Besides, if you had wished, you might at your trial have offered to go into exile. At that time you could have done with the state's consent what you are trying now to do without it. But then you gloried in being willing to die. You said that you preferred death to exile. And now you do not honor those words: you do not respect us, the laws, for you are trying to destroy us; and you are acting just as a miserable slave would act, trying to run away, and breaking the contracts and agreement which you made to live as our citizen. First, therefore, answer this question. Are we right, or are we wrong, in saying that you have agreed not in mere words, but in your actions, to live under our government?'' What are we to say, Crito? Must we not admit that it is true?

Crito. We must, Socrates.

Socrates. Then they would say, ''Are you not breaking your contracts and agreements with us? And you were not led to make them by force or by fraud. You did not have to make up your mind in a hurry. You had seventy years in which you might have gone away if you had been dissatisfied with us, or if the agreement had seemed to you unjust. But you preferred neither Sparta nor Crete, though you are fond of saying that they are well governed, nor any other state, either of the Greeks or the Barbarians. You went away from Athens less than the lame and the blind and the crippled. Clearly you, far more than other Athenians, were satisfied with the state, and also with us who are its laws; for who would be satisfied with a state which had no laws? And now will you not abide by your agreement? If you take our advice, you will, Socrates; then you will not make yourself ridiculous by going away from Athens.

''Reflect now. What good will you do yourself or your friends by thus transgressing and breaking your agreement? It is tolerably certain that they, on their part, will at least run the risk of exile, and of losing their civil rights, or of forfeiting their property. You yourself might go to one of the neighboring states, to Thebes or to Megara, for instance—for both of them are well governed—but, Socrates, you will come as an enemy to these governments, and all who care for their city will look askance at you, and think that you are a subverter of law. You will confirm the judges in their opinion, and make it seem that their verdict was a just one. For a man who is a subverter of law may well be supposed to be a corrupter of the young and thoughtless. Then will you avoid well-governed states and civilized men? Will life be worth having, if you do? Will you associate with such men, and converse without shame—about what, Socrates? About the things which you talk of here? Will you tell them that excellence and justice and institutions and law are the most valuable things that men can have? And do you not think that that will be a disgraceful thing for Socrates? You ought to think so. But you will leave these places; you will go to the friends of Crito in Thessaly. For there is found the greatest disorder and license, and very likely they will be delighted to hear of the ludicrous way in which you escaped from prison, dressed up in peasant's clothes, or in some other disguise which people put on when they are running away, and with your appearance altered. But will no one say how you, an old man, with probably only a few more years to live, clung so greedily to life that you dared to break the highest laws? Perhaps not, if you do not annoy them. But if you do, Socrates, you will hear much that will make you blush. You will pass your life as the flatterer and the slave of all men; and what will you be doing but feasting in Thessaly? It will be as if you had made a journey to Thessaly for a banquet. And where will be all our old arguments about justice and excellence then? But you wish to live for the sake of your children? You want to bring them up and educate them? What? Will you take them with you to Thessaly, and bring them up and educate them there? Will you make them strangers to their own country, that you may bestow this benefit of exile on them too? Or supposing that you leave them in Athens, will they be brought up and educated better if you are alive, though you are not with them? Yes, your friends will take care of them. Will your friends take care of them if you make a journey to Thessaly, and not if you make a journey to Hades? You ought not to think that, at least if those who call themselves your friends are worth anything at all.

"No, Socrates, be persuaded by us who have reared you. Think neither of children nor of life, nor of any other thing before justice, so that when you come to the other world you may be able to make your defense before the rulers who sit in judgment there. It is clear that neither you nor any of your friends will be happier, or juster, or more pious in this life, if you do this thing, nor will you be happier after you are dead. Now you will go away a victim of the injustice, not of the laws, but of men. But if you repay evil with evil, and injustice with injustice in this shameful way, and break your agreements and covenants with us, and injure those whom you should least injure, yourself and your friends and your country and us, and so escape, then we shall be angry with you while you live, and when you die our brothers, the laws in Hades, will not receive you kindly; for they will know that on earth you did all that you could to destroy us. Listen then to us, and let not Crito persuade you to do as he says."

Be sure, my dear friend Crito, that this is what I seem to hear, as the worshippers of Cybele seem, in their passion, to hear the music of flutes; and the sound of these arguments rings so loudly in my ears, that I cannot hear any other arguments. And I feel sure that if you try to change my mind you will speak in vain. Nevertheless, if you think that you will succeed, speak.

Crito. I have nothing more to say, Socrates.

Socrates. Then let it be, Crito, and let us do as I say, since the god is our guide.

EUTHYPHRO

Translated by R. E. Allen

Euthyphro. What happened, Socrates, to make you leave your accustomed pastimes in the Lyceum and spend your time here today at the King's Porch? You can hardly have a suit pending before the King, as I do.

Socrates. In Athens, Euthyphro, it is not called a suit, but an indictment.

Euthyphro. Really? Someone must have indicted you. For I will not suspect you of indicting someone else.

Socrates. Certainly not.

Euthyphro. But someone has indicted you?

Socrates. Yes.

Euthyphro. Who is he?

Socrates. I do not know the man well, Euthyphro; it appears to me that he is young and not prominent. His name, I think, is Meletus. He belongs to the deme of Pitthus, if you recall a Pitthean Meletus with lanky hair and not much beard, but a hooked nose.

Euthyphro. I have not noticed him, Socrates. But what is the charge?

Socrates. Charge? One that does him credit, I think. It is no small thing, young as he is, to be knowledgeable in so great a matter; for he says he knows how the youth are being corrupted and who is corrupting them. No doubt he is wise, and realizing that, in my ignorance, I corrupt his comrades, he comes to the city as to a mother to accuse me. He alone seems to me to begin his political career correctly; for the correct way to begin is to look after the young men of the City first, so that they will be as good as possible, just as a good farmer naturally looks after his young plants first and the rest later. So too with Meletus. He will perhaps first weed out those of us who blight the young shoots, as he claims; afterwards, he will obviously look after their elders and become responsible for many great blessings to the City, the natural result of so fine a beginning.

Euthyphro. I would hope so, Socrates, but I shudder for fear lest the opposite may happen. He seems, as it were, to be injuring the City from the start at its very hearth, in undertaking to wrong you. But tell me, what is it he says you do to corrupt the youth?

Socrates. It sounds a bit strange at first hearing, my friend. He says I am a maker of gods, and on the ground that I make new ones, and do not worship the old ones, he indicted me on their account, he says.

Euthyphro. I see, Socrates. It is because you say the divine sign comes to you from time to time. So he has indicted you for making innovations in religious matters, and hales you into court to slander you, knowing full well that such things are easily misrepresented to the multitude. Why I, even me, when I speak about religious matters in the Assembly, foretelling the future to them, why, they laugh at me as though I were mad. And yet nothing I ever predicted has failed to come true. Still, they are jealous of people like us. We must not worry about them, but face them boldly.

Socrates. My dear Euthyphro, being laughed at is perhaps a thing of little moment. The Athenians, it seems to me, do not much care if they think a man is clever, so long as they do not suspect him of teaching his cleverness to others; but if they think he makes others like himself, they become angry, whether out of jealousy as you suggest, or for some other reason.

Euthyphro. On that point I am not very anxious to test their attitude toward me.

Socrates. Perhaps they think you give yourself sparingly, that you are unwilling to teach your wisdom. But I fear my own generosity is such that they think me willing to pour myself out in speech to any man—not only without pay, but glad to pay myself if only someone will listen. So as I just said, if they were to laugh at me as you say they do you, it would not be unpleasant to pass the time in court laughing and joking. But if they are in earnest, how it will then turn out is unclear—except to you prophets.

Euthyphro. Perhaps it will not amount to much, Socrates. Perhaps you will settle your case satisfactorily, as I think I will mine.

Socrates. What about that, Euthyphro? Are you plaintiff or defendant?

Euthyphro. Plaintiff.

Socrates. Against whom?

Euthyphro. Someone I am again thought mad to prosecute.

Socrates. Really? He has taken flight?

Euthyphro. Far from flying. As a matter of fact, he is well along in years.

Socrates. Who is he?

Euthyphro. My father.

Socrates. Your own father, dear friend?

Euthyphro. Yes, indeed.

Socrates. But what is the charge? What is the reason for the suit?

Euthyphro. Murder, Socrates.

Socrates. Heracles! Surely, Euthyphro, the majority of people must be ignorant of what is right. Not just anyone would undertake a thing like that. It must require someone quite far gone in wisdom.

Euthyphro. By Zeus, very far indeed, Socrates.

Socrates. Was the man your father killed a relative? But, of course, he must have been—you would not be prosecuting him for murder in behalf of a stranger.

Euthyphro. It is laughable, Socrates, your thinking it makes a difference whether the man was a relative or not; the only thing to watch out for is whether his slayer was justified. If so, let him off. If not, prosecute him, even if he shares your hearth and table. For if you knowingly associate with a man like that and do not cleanse yourself, and him, by bringing action at law, the pollution is equal for you both. Now as a matter of fact, the dead man was a day-laborer of mine, and when we were farming in Naxos he worked for us for hire. Well, he got drunk and flew into a rage with one of our slaves and cut his throat. So my father bound him hand and foot, threw him in a ditch, and sent a man here to Athens to consult the religious adviser as to what should be done. In the meantime, my father paid no attention to the man he had bound; he neglected him because he was a murderer and it made no difference if he died. Which is just what he did. He died of hunger and cold and his bonds before the messenger got back. But even so, my father and the rest of my relatives are angry at me for prosecuting him for murder in behalf of a murderer. For he did not kill him, they claim, and even if he did, still, the fellow was a murderer, and it is wrong to be concerned in behalf of a man like that—and anyway, it is unholy for a son to prosecute his father for murder. They little know, Socrates, how things stand in religious matters regarding the holy and the unholy.

Socrates. But in the name of Zeus, Euthyphro, do you think you know so accurately how matters stand respecting divine law, and things holy and unholy, that with the facts as you declare, you can prosecute your father without fear that it is you, on the contrary, who are doing an unholy thing?

Euthyphro. I would not be much use, Socrates, nor would Euthyphro differ in any way from the majority of men, if I did not know all such things with strict accuracy.

Socrates. Well then, my gifted friend, I had best become your pupil. Before the action with Meletus begins I will challenge him on these very grounds. I will say that even in former times I was much concerned to learn about religious matters, but that now, in view of his claiming that I am guilty of loose speech and innovation in these things, I have become your pupil. "And if, Meletus," I shall say, "if you agree that Euthyphro is wise in such things, then accept the fact that I worship correctly and drop the case. But if you do not agree, then obtain permission to indict this my teacher in my place, for corrupting the old—me and his own father—by teaching me, and by correcting and punishing him." And if I can not persuade him to drop charges, or indict you in place of me, might I not then say the same thing in court I said in my challenge?

Euthyphro. By Zeus, if he tried to indict me, I would find his weak spot, I think, and the discussion in court would concern him long before it concerned me.

Socrates. I realize that, my friend. That is why I want to become your pupil. I know that this fellow Meletus, and no doubt other people too, pretend not even to notice you; but he saw through me so keenly and easily that he indicted me for impiety. So now in Zeus's name, tell me what you confidently claimed just now that you knew: what sort of thing do you say the pious and impious are, both with respect to murder and other things as well? Or is not the holy, itself by itself, the same in every action? And the unholy, in turn, the opposite of all the holy—is it not like itself, and does not everything which is to be unholy have a certain single character with respect to unholiness?

Euthyphro. No doubt, Socrates.

Socrates. Then tell me, what do you say the holy is? And what is the unholy?

Euthyphro. Well, I say the holy is just what I am doing now, prosecuting murder and temple theft and everything of the sort, whether it is a father or mother or anyone else who is guilty of it. And not prosecuting is unholy. Now, Socrates, examine the proof I shall give you that this is a dictate of divine law. I have offered it before to other people, to show that it is established right not to let off someone guilty of impiety, no matter who he happens to be. For these same people worship Zeus as the best and most righteous of the gods. And they agree that he put his own father in bonds for swallowing his children unjustly; yes, and that that father had in his turn castrated his father, for similar reasons. Yet me they are angry at for indicting my father for his injustice. So they contradict themselves: they say one thing about the gods and another about me.

Socrates. I wonder if this is why I am being prosecuted, Euthyphro, because when anyone says such things about the gods, I somehow find it difficult to accept? Perhaps that is why people will claim I transgress. But as it is, if even you who know such things so well accept them, people like me must apparently concede. What indeed are we to say, we who ourselves agree that we know nothing of them. But in the name of Zeus, the God of Friendship, tell me: do you truly believe that these things happened so?

Euthyphro. Yes, and things still more wonderful than these, Socrates, which the multitude does not know.

Socrates. Do you believe there is really war among the gods, and terrible enmities, and battles, and other things of the sort our poets tell, which embellish other things sacred to us through the work of our capable painters, but especially embellish the robe filled with embroidery that is carried to the Acropolis at the Great Panathenaea? Are we, Euthyphro, to say those things are so?

Euthyphro. Not only those, Socrates. As I just said, I shall explain many other things about religion to you if you wish, and you may rest assured that what you hear will amaze you.

Socrates. I should not be surprised. But explain them another time at your leisure; right now, try to answer more clearly the question I just asked. For, my friend, you did not sufficiently teach me before, when I asked you what the holy is: you said that the thing you are doing now is holy, prosecuting your father for murder.

Euthyphro. Yes, and I told the truth, Socrates.

Socrates. Perhaps. But, Euthyphro, are there not many other things you say are holy too?

Euthyphro. Of course there are.

Socrates. Do you recall that I did not ask you to teach me about some one or two of the many things which are holy, but about that characteristic itself by which all holy things are holy? For you agreed, I think, that it is by one character that unholy things are unholy and holy things holy. Or do you not recall?

Euthyphro. I do.

Socrates. Then teach me what this same character is, so that I may look to it and use it as a standard, which, should those things which you or someone else may do be of that sort, I may affirm that they are holy, but should they not be of that sort, deny it.

Euthyphro. Well if you wish it so, Socrates, so shall I tell you.

Socrates. I do indeed wish it.

Euthyphro. Then what is dear to the gods is holy, and what is not dear to them is unholy.

Socrates. Excellent, Euthyphro. You have now answered as I asked you to. Whether correctly, I do not yet know—but clearly you will now go on to teach me that what you say is true.

Euthyphro. Of course.

Socrates. Come then, let us examine what it is we are saying. The thing and the person dear to the gods is holy; the thing and the person hateful to the gods is unholy; and the holy is not the same as the unholy, but its utter opposite. Is that what we are saying?

Euthyphro. It is.

Socrates. Yes, and is it also well said?

Euthyphro. I think so, Socrates.

Socrates. Now, Euthyphro, we also said, did we not, that the gods quarrel and disagree with one another, and that there is enmity among them?

Euthyphro. We did.

Socrates. But what is the disagreement which causes enmity and anger about, my friend? Look at it this way: If you and I were to disagree about a question of number, about which of two sums is greater, would our disagreement cause us to become angry with each other and make us enemies? Or would we take to counting in a case like that, and quickly settle our dispute?

Euthyphro. Of course we would.

Socrates. So too, if we disagreed about a question of the larger and smaller, we would take to measurement, and put an end to our disagreement quickly?

Euthyphro. True.

Socrates. And we would go to the balance, I imagine, to settle a dispute about the heavier and lighter?

Euthyphro. Certainly.

Socrates. But what sort of thing would make us enemies, angry at each other, if we disagreed about it and were unable to arrive at a decision? Perhaps you cannot say offhand, but I suggest you consider whether it would not be the just and the unjust, beautiful and ugly, good and evil. Is it not these things, when we disagree about them, and cannot reach a satisfactory decision, concerning which we on occasion become enemies—you, and I, and all other men?

Euthyphro. Yes, Socrates. This kind of disagreement has its source there.

Socrates. What about the gods, Euthyphro? If they were to disagree, would they not disagree for the same reasons?

Euthyphro. Necessarily.

Socrates. Then by your account, my noble friend, different gods must believe that different things are just—and beautiful and ugly, good and evil. For surely they would not quarrel unless they disagreed on this. True?

Euthyphro. You are right.

Socrates. Now, what each of them believes to be beautiful and good and just they also love, and the opposites of those things they hate?

Euthyphro. Of course.

Socrates. Yes, but the same things, you say, are thought by some gods to be just and by others unjust. Those are the things concerning which disagreement causes them to quarrel and make war on one another. True?

Euthyphro. Yes.

Socrates. Then the same things, it seems, are both hated by the gods and loved by the gods, and would be both dear to the gods and hateful to the gods.

Euthyphro. It seems so.

Socrates. Then by this account, Euthyphro, the same things would be both holy and unholy.

Euthyphro. I suppose so.

Socrates. Then you have not answered my question, my friend. I did not ask you what same thing happens to be both holy and unholy; yet what is dear to the gods is hateful to the gods, it seems. And so, Euthyphro, it would not be surprising if what you are now doing in punishing your father were dear to Zeus, but hateful to Cronos and Uranus, and loved by Hephaestus, but hateful to Hera; and if any of the other gods disagree about it, the same will be true of them too.

Euthyphro. But Socrates, surely none of the gods disagree about this, that he who kills another man unjustly should answer for it.

Socrates. Really, Euthyphro? Have you ever heard it argued among *men* that he who kills unjustly, or does anything else unjustly, should not answer for it?

Euthyphro. Why, people never stop arguing things like that, especially in court. They do a host of wrongs, and then say and do everything to get off.

Socrates. Yes, but do they admit the wrong, Euthyphro, and, admitting it, still claim that they should not answer for it?

Euthyphro. No; they certainly do not do that.

Socrates. Then they do not do and say everything: for they do not, I think, dare to contend that if they in fact did a wrong they should not answer for it. Rather, I think, they deny they did wrong. Well?

Euthyphro. True.

Socrates. So they do not contend that those who do wrong should not answer for it, but rather, perhaps, about who it is that did the wrong, and what he did, and when.

Euthyphro. True.

Socrates. Now is it not also the same with the gods, if, as your account has it, they quarrel about what is just and unjust, and some claim that others do wrong, and some deny it? Presumably no one, god or man, would dare to claim that he who does a wrong should not answer for it.

Euthyphro. Yes, on the whole what you say is true, Socrates.

Socrates. But I imagine that those who disagree, Euthyphro—both men and gods, if indeed the gods disagree—disagree about particular things which have been done. They differ over given actions, some claiming that these have been done justly, and others unjustly. True?

Euthyphro. Certainly.

Socrates. Come now, my friend, teach me too and make me wiser. Where is your proof that all the gods believe that a man has been unjustly killed who, hired as a laborer, became a murderer, was bound by the master of the dead slave, and died of his bonds before the man who bound him could learn from the religious advisers what to do? Where is your proof that it is right for a son to indict and prosecute his father for murder in behalf of a man like that? Come, try to show me clearly that all the gods genuinely believe this action right. If you succeed, I shall praise you for your wisdom and never stop.

Euthyphro. Well, I can certainly do it, Socrates, but it is perhaps not a small task.

Socrates. I see. You think I am rather harder to teach than the judges; you will certainly make it clear to them that actions such as your father's are wrong, and that all the gods hate them.

Euthyphro. Very clear indeed, Socrates, if they listen to what I say.

Socrates. They will listen, if you seem to speak well. Here is something that occurred to me while you were talking. I asked myself, "Suppose Euthyphro were to teach me beyond any question that all the gods believe a death of this sort wrong. What more have I learned from Euthyphro about what the holy and the unholy are? The death, it seems, would be hateful to the gods. But what is holy and what is not proved, just now, not to be marked off by this; for what was hateful to the gods proved dear to the gods as well." So I let you go on that point, Euthyphro: if you wish, let all the gods believe your father's action wrong, and let all of them hate it. But is this the correction we are now to make in your account, that what *all* the gods hate is unholy, and what *all* the gods love is holy, but what some love and some hate is neither or both? Do you mean for us now to mark off the holy and the unholy in that way?

Euthyphro. What is to prevent it, Socrates?

Socrates. Nothing, at least as far as I am concerned, Euthyphro. But, examine your account to see whether, if you assume this, you will most easily teach me what you promised.

Euthyphro. But I would certainly say that the holy is what all the gods love, and that the opposite, what all the gods hate, is unholy.

Socrates. Well, Euthyphro, should we examine this in turn to see if it is true? Or should we let it go, accept it from ourselves or anyone else without more ado, and agree that a thing is so if only someone says it is? Should we consider what he who says this means?

Euthyphro. Of course. I believe, though, that this time what I say is true.

Socrates. Perhaps we shall learn better, my friend. For consider: is the holy loved by the gods because it is holy? Or is it holy because it is loved by the gods?

Euthyphro. I do not know what you mean, Socrates.

Socrates. Then I will try to put it more clearly. We speak of carrying and being carried, of leading and being led, of seeing and being seen. And you understand in such cases, do you not, that they differ from each other, and how they differ?

Euthyphro. Yes; I think I do.

Socrates. Now, is there such a thing as being loved, and is it different from loving?

Euthyphro. Of course.

Socrates. Then tell me: if a thing is being carried, is it being carried because of the carrying, or for some other reason?

Euthyphro. No, for that reason.

Socrates. And if a thing is being led, it is being led because of the leading? And if being seen, being seen because of the seeing?

Euthyphro. Certainly.

Socrates. Then it is not because a thing is being seen that the seeing exists; on the contrary, it is because of the seeing that it is being seen. Nor is it because a thing is being led that the leading exists; it is because of the leading that it is being led. Nor is it because a thing is being carried that the carrying exists; it is because of the carrying that it is being carried. Is what I mean quite clear, Euthyphro? I mean this: if something comes to be or something is affected in a certain way, it is not because it is a thing which is coming to be that the process of coming to be exists, but, because of the process of coming to be, it is a thing which is coming to be; it is not because it is affected that the affecting exists, but because of the affecting, the thing is affected. Do you agree?

Euthyphro. Yes.

Socrates. Now, if a thing is being loved, it is either something which is coming to be or something which is affected by something.

Euthyphro. Of course.

Socrates. And so it is as true of this as it was of the former: it is not because a thing is being loved that there is loving by those who love it; it is because of the loving that it is being loved.

Euthyphro. Necessarily.

Socrates. Then what are we to say about the holy, Euthyphro? Is it loved by all the gods, as your account has it?

Euthyphro. Yes.

Socrates. Because it is holy? Or for some other reason?

Euthyphro. No, for that reason.

Socrates. Then it is loved because it is holy, not holy because it is loved?

Euthyphro. It seems so.

Socrates. Moreover, what is loved and dear to the gods is loved because of their loving.

Euthyphro. Of course.

Socrates. Then what is dear to the gods is not (the same as) holy, Euthyphro, nor is the holy (the same as) dear to the gods, as you claim: the two are different.

Euthyphro. But why, Socrates?

Socrates. Because we agreed that the holy is loved because it is holy, not holy because it is loved.

Euthyphro. Yes.

Socrates. But what is dear to the gods is, because it is loved by the gods, dear to the gods by reason of this same loving; it is not loved because it is dear to the gods.

Euthyphro. True.

Socrates. But if in fact what is dear to the gods and the holy were the same, my friend, then, if the holy were loved because it is holy, what is dear to the gods would be loved because it is dear to the gods; but if what is dear to the gods were dear to the gods because the gods love it, the holy would be holy because it is loved. But as it is, you see, the opposite is true, and the two are completely different. For the one (what is dear to the gods) is of the sort to be loved *because* it is loved; the other (the holy), because it is of the sort to be loved, *therefore* is loved. It would seem, Euthyphro, that when you were asked what the holy is, you did not mean to make its nature and reality clear to me; you mentioned a mere affection of it—the holy has been so affected as to be loved by all the gods. But what it really is, you have not yet said. If you please, Euthyphro, do not conceal things from me: start again from the beginning and tell me what sort of thing the holy is. We will not quarrel over whether it is loved by the gods, or whether it is affected in other ways. But tell me in earnest: What is the holy and unholy?

Euthyphro. But, Socrates, I do not know how to tell you what I mean. Somehow everything I propose goes around in circles on us and will not stand still.

Socrates. Your words are like the works of my ancestor, Daedalus. If I had offered them, if I had put them forward, you would perhaps have laughed at me because my kinship to him makes my words run away and refuse to stay put. But as it is, you put them forward, and we must find another joke; it is for you that they refuse to stay, as you agree yourself.

Euthyphro. But, Socrates, the joke, I think, still tells. It is not me who makes them move around and not stay put. I think you are the Daedalus. If it had been up to me, they would have stayed where they were.

Socrates. Then apparently, my friend, I am even more skillful than my venerated ancestor, inasmuch as he made only his own work move, whereas I make mine move and other people's too. And certainly the most subtle feature of my art is that I am skilled against my will. For I want arguments to stand still, to stand fixed and immovable. I want that more than the wealth of Tantalus and the skill of Daedalus combined. But enough of this. Since you seem to be lazy and soft, I will come to your aid and help you teach me about the holy. Don't give up: ask yourself if you do not think that all the holy is necessarily just.

Euthyphro. I do.

Socrates. Then is all the just holy? Or is all the holy just, but not all the just holy—part of it holy, part something else?

Euthyphro. I don't follow you, Socrates.

Socrates. And yet you are as much wiser than I am as you are younger; as I said, you are lazy and soft because of your wealth of wisdom. My friend, extend yourself: what I mean is not hard to understand. I mean exactly the opposite of what the poet meant when he said that he was "Unwilling to insult Zeus, the Creator, who made all things: for where there is fear there is also reverence." I disagree with him. Shall I tell you why?

Euthyphro. Yes; certainly.

Socrates. I do not think that "where there is fear there is also reverence." I think people fear disease and poverty and other such things—fear them, but have no reverence for what they fear. Do you agree?

Euthyphro. Yes; certainly.

Socrates. Where there is reverence, however, there is also fear. For if anyone stands in reverence and awe of something, does he not at the same time fear and dread the imputation of wickedness?

Euthyphro. Yes; he does.

Socrates. Then it is not true that "where there is fear there is also reverence." But where there is reverence there is also fear, even though reverence is not in every place that fear is; fear is broader than reverence. Reverence is a part of fear just as odd is a part of number, and where there is number there is not also odd, but where there is odd there is also number. I imagine you follow me?

Euthyphro. Yes; I do.

Socrates. Well then, that is the sort of thing I had in mind when I asked if, where there is just, there is also holy. Or is it rather that where there is holy there is also just, but holy is not in every place that just is, the holy being a part of the just. Shall we say that, or do you think differently?

Euthyphro. No. I think you are right.

Socrates. Then consider the next point. If the holy is part of the just, it would seem that we must find out what part of the just the holy is. Now, to take an example we used a moment ago, if you were to ask me what part of number the even is, and what kind of number it is, I would say that it is number with equal rather than unequal sides. Do you agree?

Euthyphro. Yes; I do.

Socrates. Then try in the same way to teach me what part of the just is holy, so that I may tell Meletus to wrong me no longer, and not to indict me for impiety, since I have already learned from you what things are pious and holy and what are not.

Euthyphro. Well, Socrates, I think that that part of the just which is pious and holy is concerned with ministering to the gods, and the remaining part of the just is concerned with ministering to men.

Socrates. Excellently put, Euthyphro. But there is still one small point left: I do not yet understand what you mean by "ministering." You surely do not mean that ministering to the gods is like ministering to other things, though I suppose we do talk that way, as when we say that it is not everyone who knows how to minister to horses, but only the horse-trainer. That is true, is it not?

Euthyphro. Yes; certainly.

Socrates. Because horse-training takes care of horses.

Euthyphro. Yes.

Socrates. And it is not everyone who knows how to minister to dogs, but only the huntsman.

Euthyphro. True.

Socrates. Because huntsmanship takes care of dogs.

Euthyphro. Yes.

Socrates. And the same is true of herdsmanship and cattle?

Euthyphro. Yes; certainly.

Socrates. And holiness and piety minister to the gods, Euthyphro? Is that what you are saying?

Euthyphro. Yes; it is.

Socrates. Now, is not all ministering meant to accomplish

the same thing? I mean this: to take care of a thing is to aim at some good, some benefit, for the thing cared for, as you see horses benefited and improved when ministered to by horse-training. Or do you not agree?

Euthyphro. Yes; I do.

Socrates. And dogs are benefited by huntsmanship, and cattle by herdsmanship, and similarly with other things as well—or do you think ministering can work harm to what is cared for?

Euthyphro. No, by Zeus; not I.

Socrates. But must be beneficial?

Euthyphro. Of course.

Socrates. Now, does holiness, which is to be a kind of ministering, benefit the gods? Does it improve them? Would you agree that when you do something holy you are making some god better?

Euthyphro. No, by Zeus; not I.

Socrates. I did not think you meant that, Euthyphro. Far from it. That is why I asked you what you meant by ministering to the gods: I did not believe you meant such a thing as that.

Euthyphro. Yes; and you were right, Socrates. I did not mean that.

Socrates. Very well. But what kind of ministering to the gods is holiness?

Euthyphro. The kind, Socrates, with which slaves minister to their masters.

Socrates. I see. Holiness would, it seems, be a kind of service to gods.

Euthyphro. Quite so.

Socrates. Now, can you tell me what sort of product service to physicians would be likely to produce? Would it not be health?

Euthyphro. Yes.

Socrates. What about service to ship-builders? Is there not some product it produces?

Euthyphro. Clearly it produces a ship, Socrates.

Socrates. And service to house-builders produces a house?

Euthyphro. Yes.

Socrates. Then tell me, my friend: What sort of product would service to gods produce? Clearly you know, for you say you know better than anyone else about religious matters.

Euthyphro. Yes; and I am telling the truth, Socrates.

Socrates. Then in the name of Zeus, tell me: What is that fine product which the gods produce by using us as servants?

Euthyphro. They produce many things, Socrates, excellent things.

Socrates. So do generals, my friend, but still their work can be summed up quite easily. Generals produce victory in war. Not so?

Euthyphro. Of course.

Socrates. And farmers produce many excellent things, but still their work can be summed up as producing food from the earth.

Euthyphro. Yes; of course.

Socrates. But what about the many excellent things the gods produce? How does one sum up their production?

Euthyphro. I told you a moment ago, Socrates, that it is difficult to learn accurately how things stand in these matters. Speaking freely, however, I can tell you that if a man knows how to say and do things acceptable to the gods in prayer and sacrifice, those things are holy; and they preserve both families and cities and keep them safe. The opposite of what is acceptable to the gods is impious, and impiety overturns and destroys all things.

Socrates. You could have summed up the answer to my question much more briefly, Euthyphro, if you had wished. But you are not eager to instruct me; I see that now. In fact, you just came right up to the point and turned away, and if you had given me an answer, I would already have learned holiness from you. But as it is, the questioner must follow the answerer wherever he leads. But again, what do you say the holy and holiness is? Is it not knowledge of how to pray and sacrifice?

Euthyphro. It is.

Socrates. Now to sacrifice is to give to the gods, and to pray is to ask something from them?

Euthyphro. Exactly, Socrates.

Socrates. Then by this account, holiness is knowledge of how to ask from and give to the gods.

Euthyphro. Excellent, Socrates. You have followed what I said.

Socrates. Yes, my friend, for I am enamored of your wisdom and attend to it closely, so naturally what you say does not fall to the ground wasted. But tell me, what is the nature of this service we render the gods? You say it is to ask from them and give to them?

Euthyphro. Yes; I do.

Socrates. Now, to ask rightly is to ask for things we need from them?

Euthyphro. Certainly.

Socrates. And again, to give rightly is to give in return what they happen to need from us? For surely there would be no skill involved in giving things to someone that he did not need.

Euthyphro. You are right, Socrates.

Socrates. So the art of holiness would be a kind of business transaction between gods and men.

Euthyphro. Yes; if it pleases you to call it that.

Socrates. Why, nothing pleases me unless it happens to be true. But tell me, what benefit do the gods gain from the gifts they receive from us? It is clear to everyone what they give, for we have nothing good they have not given. But how are they benefited by what they get from us? Or do we claim the larger share in the transaction to such an extent that we get all good from them, and they nothing from us?

Euthyphro. But, Socrates, do you think the gods benefit from the things they receive from us?

Socrates. Why, Euthyphro, whatever would these gifts of ours to the gods then be?

Euthyphro. What do you suppose, other than praise and honor and as I just said, things which are acceptable?

Socrates. Then the holy is what is acceptable, Euthyphro, and not what is beneficial or loved by the gods?

Euthyphro. I certainly think it is loved by the gods, beyond all other things.

Socrates. Then, on the contrary, the holy is what is loved by the gods.

Euthyphro. Yes, that beyond anything.

Socrates. Will it surprise you if, in saying this, your words get up and walk? You call me a Daedalus. You say I make them walk. But I say that you are a good deal more skillful than Daedalus, for you make them walk in circles. Or are you not aware that our account has gone round and come back again to the same place? Surely you remember that, in what went before, the holy proved not to be the same as what is loved by the gods; the two were different. Do you recall?

Euthyphro. Yes; I recall.

Socrates. Then do you not now realize that you are saying that what is loved by the gods is holy? But that is in fact something other than dear to the gods, is it not?

Euthyphro. Yes.

Socrates. Then either we were wrong a moment ago in agreeing to that, or, if we were right in assuming it then, we are wrong now.

Euthyphro. It seems so.

Socrates. Let us begin again from the beginning, and ask what the holy is. For I shall not willingly give up until I learn. Please do not scorn me: bend every effort of your mind and now tell me the truth. You know it if any man does, and, like Proteus, you must not be let go before you speak. For if you did not know the holy and the unholy with certainty, you could not possibly undertake to prosecute your aged father for murder in behalf of a hired man. You would fear to risk the gods, lest your action be wrongful; and you would be ashamed before men. But as it is, I am confident that you think you know with certainty what is holy and what is not. So say it, friend Euthyphro. Do not conceal what it is you believe.

Euthyphro. Some other time, Socrates. Right now I must hurry somewhere and I am already late.

Socrates. What are you doing, my friend! You leave me and cast me down from my high hope, that I should learn from you what things are holy and what are not, and escape the indictment of Meletus by showing him that, due to Euthyphro, I am now wise in religious matters, that I no longer ignorantly indulge in loose speech and innovation, and most especially, that I shall live better the rest of my life.

PHAEDO

Translated by R. S. Bluck

Were you yourself with Socrates, Phaedo, on the day when he drank the poison in his prison? or did you hear the story from someone else?

I was there myself, Echecrates.

Well, what did he talk about just before his death? And how did he die? I would very much like to hear. The people of Phlius, you see, hardly ever go and stay at Athens nowadays, and no visitor has come to us from Athens for a long time past who might have been able to tell us something definite about it—apart, I mean, from the mere fact that he died by drinking poison. That was all the news that we could get.

You never heard, then, about the proceedings at the trial?

Yes, we did hear about them; and we couldn't understand why the execution took place, as it appears to have done, so long[1] after the trial. Why was that, Phaedo?

That was mere chance, Echecrates. The ship which the Athenians send on sacred mission to Delos had in fact had its prow decorated the day before the trial began.

What ship is this?

The ship in which, according to the Athenians, Theseus sailed with the famous fourteen, when he saved them and himself too.[2] It is said that they at that time prayed to Apollo, and vowed that if they were saved they would send a sacred embassy to Delos every year. As a result, they do so to this day, every year, in honor of the god; and when they send this embassy on its way, it is their practice during this period to keep the city free from bloodshed, and to hold no state executions until the ship

---

[1] Thirty days (Xenophon, *Mem.*, 4.8.2).

[2] Minos, king of Crete, compelled the Athenians to send seven youths and seven maidens every year, by way of tribute, to be devoured by the fabulous Minotaur in the Cretan labyrinth. Theseus killed the Minotaur.

has reached Delos and returned again to Athens; and sometimes this takes quite a while, when winds are against them. The embassy officially starts when the priest of Apollo decorates the ship's prow—and this happened, as I say, the day before the trial began. That is why Socrates was in prison for a considerable time after the trial before he was executed.

Tell me about his actual death, Phaedo. What did they say and do? and which of his friends were present at the time? or did the archons not allow any to attend—did he die without any friends by him?

Oh! no, there were some there—quite a number.

Do please tell us the whole story in detail, if you are not too busy.

I am quite free. I will try to give you an account of what happened. There is nothing I like better than thinking about Socrates, whether I am talking about him myself or listening to someone else.

Your present audience are like you in that, Phaedo; so try to give as detailed an account as you possibly can.

Well, when I arrived I had an extraordinary sensation. I did not feel *pity* as might have been expected of one who was present at the death of a friend. The man seemed to me to be wonderfully gifted, Echecrates, in temperament no less than in speech; he died so fearlessly and nobly. It struck me that even on the point of his departure for the other world Providence was guiding him, and that even when he reached it, if anyone there has ever enjoyed blessings, then he would. Consequently, I had none of the sensations of pity that you might expect a man to have on so sad an occasion. Nor again did I derive pleasure from the fact that we were engaged in our usual philosophical discussions—for that was the nature of the conversation. It was simply a rather strange feeling, an unusual mixture of pleasure and pain combined, which came over me when I reflected that in a very short while he was going to die. All of us who were present were affected in much the same way, sometimes laughing, at times crying—one of our number in particular, Apollodorus. I expect you know the man, and what he is like.

Of course.

Well, he was completely overcome in this way. I and the others present were very much distressed.

Who were present, Phaedo?

Of Athenians, there was this Apollodorus, and Critobulus and his father, and Hermogenes, Epigenes, Aeschines, and

Antisthenes. Then there was Ctesippus of the Paeanian deme, Menexenus, and other Athenians; but Plato, I believe, was ill.

Were any foreigners there?

Yes, Simmias the Theban, and Cebes and Phaedondes, and from Megara Euclides and Terpsion.

Weren't Aristippus and Cleombrotus present?

No: they were said to be in Aegina.

Was anyone else there?

I think that was about all.

Well now, how do you say the discussion went?

I will try to tell you everything, from the beginning. We had all been in the habit, during those last few days preceding the execution, of visiting Socrates, meeting for the purpose, at dawn, in the court in which the trial had taken place—it was near the prison. We used to wait until the prison opened, chatting among ourselves, for it didn't open very early. When it did open, we would go in and find Socrates, and spend most of the day with him. On this particular day we gathered together rather earlier than usual; for the previous day, when we left the prison in the evening, we had learnt that the ship had arrived back from Delos. We passed the word round that we should arrive as early as possible at the usual rendezvous. We duly arrived, and the warder who always opened the gates for us came out and told us to wait patiently, and not to go in until he gave the word. "The Eleven are freeing Socrates from his fetters," he said, "and are giving instructions that he is to die today."

However, after a brief interval he came and told us to go in. On entering, we found Socrates just released from his chains, and Xanthippe[3]—you know her—sitting beside him with his little son.[4] When Xanthippe saw us, she cried out, and said the sort of things that women always do—"Oh! Socrates, this is the last time that your friends will ever speak to you, or you to them." Socrates looked at Crito and said, "Crito, let someone take her home"; and some of Crito's retainers took her away, crying aloud and beating her breast.

Meanwhile Socrates, sitting down on the couch, bent his leg and rubbed it, and as he rubbed he said: "How strange would appear to be this thing that men call pleasure! and how curiously it is related to what is thought to be its opposite, pain! The two will never be found *together* in a man, and yet if you seek the one and obtain it, you are almost bound always to get the other

[3]Socrates' wife. She had apparently spent the night in the prison.
[4]Socrates had three sons: this was no doubt the youngest.

as well, just as though they were both attached to one and the same head. It seems to me that if Aesop had noticed them he would have written a fable about them, showing how God wanted to part them when they quarreled, but finding that he could not do so, joined their heads together: so that wherever the one is found, the other follows up behind. So, in my case, since I had pain in my leg as a result of the fetters, pleasure seems to have come to follow it up."

At this point Cebes broke in: "I say, Socrates, I am glad you reminded me. A number of people have asked me, and Euenus did just recently, about those poems which you have written, putting Aesop's tales into verse, and the hymn to Apollo, too; what was your intention in composing them when you came here, although you had never composed anything before? If you would like me to be able to give Euenus an answer next time he asks me—for I know that he will ask—tell me what I must say."

"Tell him the truth, Cebes," said Socrates, "that I did not compose them because I wanted to rival him or his works. I knew that that was not easy. I was trying to discover the meaning of some dreams, and I wrote the poems to clear my conscience, in case this was the sort of 'art' that I was told to pursue. It happened something like this: the same dream had kept on coming to me from time to time throughout my life, taking different forms at different times, but always saying the same thing: 'Socrates, pursue the arts, and work hard at them.' I formerly used to suppose that it was urging me to do what I was in fact doing, and trying to encourage me in the performance of that: that like those who shout encouragement to runners in a race, so the dream, when it urged me to 'pursue the arts,' was encouraging me in what I was doing; for philosophy is the greatest of all arts, and that was my pursuit. But then when the trial took place, and the god's festival prevented my execution, I thought that just in case the dream meant, after all, that I should follow this popular kind of 'art,' I ought to follow it and not disobey. It seemed safer not to depart before salving my conscience by the composition of poems in obedience to the dream. So I first wrote in honor of the god for whom the ceremonies were being held; and then, after the hymn, realizing that the 'poet,' if he was going to be a 'poet' or 'composer' at all, must compose not fact but fiction, and that I myself was not a story-teller, I used fables that were ready to hand, the fables of Aesop, which I knew—the first of them that I came across.

"So tell Euenus this, Cebes; and wish him good-bye, and

tell him, if he has any sense, to follow me as quickly as he can. I shall be taking my departure today, it seems; for such is the Athenians' will.''

"What a thing to advise Euenus to do, Socrates!" said Simmias. "I have often come across the man, and from what I have seen of him I should say that he will certainly not willingly take your advice.''

"But is he not a philosopher?" asked Socrates.

"I believe so," said Simmias.

"Well, Euenus or anyone who deserves to have anything to do with this business will be willing to do as I advise—though he will not, perhaps, commit suicide; for they say that that is wrong.'' As he said this, Socrates put his feet down on the ground and sat up, and remained in this position for the rest of the discussion.

Then Cebes asked him a question. "How do you mean, Socrates, that it is wrong to commit suicide, and yet that the philosopher would gladly follow one who was dying?''

"But surely, Cebes, you and Simmias have heard all about this when you have been with Philolaus?''[5]

"Not very clearly, Socrates.''

"Well, I myself am only speaking about it according to what I have heard; but what I have heard, I am quite ready to pass on. It is perhaps particularly appropriate that one who is about to make the journey to the next world should look fully into the matter, and tell stories about what we suppose to be the nature of our residence there. And after all, how else could we spend the time until sunset?''[6]

"Well, Socrates, what are the real reasons for saying that it is not right to take one's life? To answer the question you asked just now, I did indeed go to hear Philolaus, when he lived among us, and many others, who said that one should not commit suicide, but I have never heard any clear arguments from anyone on the subject.''

"Well, don't be despondent," he said, "and perhaps you will hear of some. And yet maybe it will seem surprising to you that while this alone of all things admits of no qualification, and

[5]This distinguished Pythagorean lived at Thebes after the expulsion of the Pythagoreans from Southern Italy. If Socrates is suggesting that Philolaus will have explained why death is desirable as well as why suicide is wrong, the inference surely is that Philolaus is not likely to have been the author of Simmias' view of the soul, which is incompatible with immortality; in this Simmias had departed from the earlier, orthodox Pythagoreanism. But Cebes seems to take the question to refer only to the matter of suicide.

[6]The time of execution.

it *never* happens (as with everything else) that death is preferable to life for man only on *some* occasions and in *some* cases, yet nevertheless—it seems surprising to you, perhaps—these human beings, for whom death is preferable, are *not* morally justified in doing themselves a good turn, but must wait for someone else to do it for them.

Cebes chuckled, and in his native dialect replied, "Goodness knows how that can be."

"Looked at in this way," said Socrates, "it might appear to be illogical. And yet it has, perhaps, some explanation. The story told about them *sub arcano* to the effect that we mortals are in a sort of prison, and that a man must not, apparently, free himself from it, or try to run away, seems to me a weighty argument and difficult to grasp; but the doctrine that gods are our guardians and that we men are one of the gods' possessions does seem to me to be a good one—don't you agree?"

"I do," said Cebes.

"Now if one of your possessions were to destroy itself, without your having indicated that you wanted it to perish, you would be annoyed with it, and if you could punish it, you would?"

"Certainly," he said.

"So perhaps in that case it is not unreasonable, the idea that one should refrain from bringing one's life to an end until God sends some necessity, such as the present one in my case."

"That is probably true," said Cebes. "But what you said just now, that the philosophers would readily agree to die, seems strange, Socrates, if what we have just agreed upon is true, that God is our guardian and we are his possessions. It is not reasonable that the wisest of men should, without demur, leave this tutelage, in which gods, the best of all possible guardians, watch over them. I don't suppose such a man imagines that he will do better when, free from their care, he has to look after himself. A fool might think that he should escape from his master—he might not realize that so far from trying to escape from the good master, he should stay with him as long as possible, and that it would be quite unreasonable to run away; but the man of sense would want, I imagine, always to remain with someone better than himself. And yet this seems to contradict what was said just now, if the wise are to dislike dying, and the foolish to delight in it."

At this Socrates seemed to me very pleased with Cebes' analysis, and looking at us he remarked, "Cebes is always hunting out arguments; he doesn't like immediately accepting just what anyone may say."

"Well, this time," said Simmias, "I too believe that there is something in what Cebes says. Why should men who are really wise try to escape from masters who are better than themselves, and lightly and readily free themselves from them? I believe that Cebes is aiming his argument at you, because you take it so lightly that you should be leaving us, and leaving also masters who, on your own admission, are good—I mean, the gods."

"Fair enough," he said. "I suppose you mean that I should defend myself against these arguments as though I were in court."

"Certainly," said Simmias.

"Well then," he said, "let me try to make my defense, and to convince you more than I did my judges. If I did not believe, Simmias and Cebes, that I shall go to other wise and good gods, and moreover to men now dead who are better than the men on earth, then indeed I should be wrong in not complaining at my death; but, as it is, you may be sure that I do hope to join a company of good men. I would not swear to this, but one thing I would maintain, as certain of it as I can be of anything—that I shall go to gods who are very good masters. So for this reason I grumble less; I have a strong hope that there is something left to those who have died, and a something (according to the old accounts) that is much better for the good than for the bad."

"Well, Socrates," said Simmias, "do you intend to depart keeping this idea to yourself, or would you share it with us? This benefit seems to me to belong to us also; and it will be your defense, too, if you convince us that what you say is true."

"I will try," he said. "But first let us enquire what it is that Crito, if I am not mistaken, has long been wanting to say."

"Only, Socrates," said Crito, "that the man who is going to give you the poison keeps on telling me that we should urge you to talk as little as possible. He says they get warmer through talking, and the poison mustn't come into contact with anything warm; otherwise, those who let that happen sometimes have to drink the draught two or three times over."

"Never mind him," said Socrates. "He, for his part, can just prepare to give it to me twice, or, if need be, three times over."

"I knew it!" cried Crito. "But he has kept on worrying me."

"Forget him," he said. "I want to render my account to

you as my judges now, showing that a man who has really spent his life in philosophy is naturally glad when he is on the point of dying, and hopeful that in the next world, when he is dead, he will enjoy great blessings. I will try to explain to you, Simmias and Cebes, how this could be so.

"It may be that the rest of mankind are not aware that those who apply themselves correctly to the pursuit of philosophy are in fact practicing nothing more nor less than dying and death. If this is so, it would indeed be strange that men who had throughout their lives sought precisely this, should grumble when it came—the very thing which they had, for so long, desired and rehearsed."

And Simmias laughed and said, "Well, Socrates, I was not in a mood for laughter just now, but you have certainly made me laugh. I think that most people, when they heard this, would consider your remarks most appropriate as applied to the philosophers—and our fellow-citizens,[7] I think, would very much agree—saying that philosophers are, in very fact, more dead than alive, and adding that they are well aware that they deserve to be."

"And they would be right in what they said, Simmias, except for their claim to be aware of it all; for they are *not* aware *in what sense* the true philosophers are more dead than alive, or *in what sense* they deserve death, or *what sort* of death they deserve. Now let us discuss the matter between ourselves, forgetting all about those others. Do we think that death is something definite and real?"

"Certainly," replied Simmias.

"Surely we think of it as separation of the soul from the body?—and of being dead as the independent state of the body in separation from the soul, and the independent state of the soul in separation from the body? Surely death can hardly be anything else?"

"Quite correct," he said.

"Then follow closely, my friend, and see if you reach the same opinions as I hold; for through these, I think, we shall achieve a better understanding of the object of our enquiry. Now do you think that a philosopher should concern himself greatly with the so-called pleasures of, for example, food and drink?"

"Certainly not, Socrates," said Simmias.

"Or of love-making?"

---

[7] I.e., the Thebans.

"No."

"Or do you think that such a man holds in high esteem any of the other ways of attending to the body?—for example, buying fine cloaks and shoes—or any of the other forms of showing-off in connection with the body; do you think that the philosopher regards these pursuits as honorable, or as worthless—except in so far as he *has* to concern himself with them?"

"The true philosopher regards them as worthless, in my opinion," he said.

"Then the philosopher *qua* philosopher, it seems, does not concern himself with the body, but so far as he can separates himself from it, and concentrates upon the soul?"

"Yes."

"Then is it not clear, to begin with, in such cases, that the philosopher far more than anyone else is freeing his soul, as much as possible, from association with the body?"

"It seems so."

"And the man who finds no pleasure in any of these things, and takes no part in them, for him, I suppose, the majority of men think that life is not worth living; he who pays no heed to the pleasures of the body seems already to border upon the state of death."

"What you say is very true."

"Now how about the acquisition of wisdom? Is the body a hindrance, or is it not, if you use it as an accessory in the search? What I mean is, do sight and hearing provide men with any true knowledge, or are even the poets always trying to tell us something like this, that nothing that we hear or see is accurate? And yet if *these* bodily senses are not accurate or reliable, the others are hardly likely to be—for all the others are inferior, I suppose, to these. Don't you think so?"

"I do indeed," he said.

"When, then, does the soul attain to truth?" he went on. "When it tries to investigate anything with the help of the body, the body quite clearly deceives it."

"True."

"So it is only through reasoning, if at all, that any part of reality can be plainly understood?"

"Yes."

"And the soul reasons best, presumably, when none of these things worries her—neither hearing, nor sight, nor pain, nor any pleasure; when she is, so far as may be, alone and by herself, forgetting all about the body, and when she strives after truth having no more communication with the body nor contact with it than is absolutely necessary."

"That is so."

"So here again the philosopher's soul has no respect for the body, and shuns it, seeking rather to be independent of it?"

"It appears so."

"Well, now, what about things of this sort—do we say that there is such a thing as the Just Itself or not?"

"We certainly do."

"And a Beautiful and a Good also?"

"Certainly."

"Well, have you ever seen any thing of this sort with your eyes?"

"No, indeed," he said.

"Then have you ever grasped them with any other form of bodily perception? I am talking about everything, for example Tallness, Health, Strength, and, in fact, the real nature of *everything* else as well—what each thing really is: is the truth about them perceived by means of the body, or is it rather thus—whoever among us aims at fixing his mind most carefully and precisely on each thing *in and by itself*—whatever it may be that he is considering—he would come nearest to having knowledge of that thing?"

"That is the case."

"Then he would reach the purest truth in this procedure who approached each thing with the intellect itself alone, not bringing in sight to aid his thinking, nor dragging in any other sense to supplement his reason: he who should try to track down each item of reality, alone by itself, in its pure essence, by using pure thought, alone by *its* self—disregarding, so far as was possible, eyes and ears, and practically all the body, on the ground that it caused confusion, and whenever it played any part, would not allow the soul to acquire truth and wisdom; is not this the man, Simmias, who, if anyone, is likely to reach truth?"

"You are absolutely right, Socrates," said Simmias.

"And so," he said, "it follows from all these considerations that some such notion as this is bound to present itself to the genuine philosophers, and they are bound to talk like this to one another: 'It looks as though a sort of narrow path will bring us out on to the trail, because so long as we use the body as well as reason in our search, and our soul is tainted with that sort of blemish, we will never fully attain to what we want—namely, the truth. The body presents us with innumerable distractions, because of the necessity of looking after it; and again, if any illnesses assail it, they too hamper us in our pursuit of truth. The body fills us with emotions of love, desire, and fear, with all kinds of phantasy and nonsense, so that in very truth it really doesn't give us a chance, as they say, ever to think of anything at all. In fact, wars and strife and battles are all due simply to the body and its desires. All wars take place because of the acquisition of property, and property we are compelled to acquire simply because of the body—we are slaves in its service; and so, for all these reasons, we have no time for philosophy. And, lastly, even if we do get some time off from looking after it, and turn to some investigation, it keeps on turning up everywhere in our search, and causes disturbance and confusion, and thoroughly dumbfounds us, so that because of it we cannot catch a glimpse of truth; it really is proved to us that if we are ever going to have pure knowledge of anything, we must get rid of the body and survey things alone in themselves by means of the soul herself alone; *then*, it seems, we shall have our heart's desire, that of which we claim to be lovers, even wisdom—when we die, as the argument indicates, but not so long as we live. For if it is not possible to have pure knowledge of anything so long as we are with the body, then one of two things must be true: either it is nowhere possible to acquire knowledge, or only after death—for then, but not till then, the soul will be independent, free from the body. So long as we are alive, it seems likely that we shall come nearest to having knowledge if we do our utmost to have no contact or association with the body except in so far as is absolutely necessary, and do not infect ourselves with its nature, but purify ourselves of it, until God himself gives us final release; and if we are thus purified and freed from the foolishness of the body, we shall probably be in the company of the pure, and through our very selves come to have knowledge of all that is unsullied—that is, I suppose, of truth; for it is, perhaps, not lawful for the impure to attain to that which is pure.'

"That is the sort of thing, Simmias, that all true lovers of learning are bound, I think, to say to each other, and the sort of view that they are bound to hold. Don't you agree?"

"Most certainly, Socrates."

"And so," said Socrates, "if all this is true, my friend, there is every hope that when a man has arrived at the destination to which I am journeying, he may there, if anywhere, satisfactorily obtain what has, throughout our lives past, been the object of our great endeavors; so that I may make the journey now enjoined upon me with good hopes, as may anyone else who feels that his mind has been purified, as it were, and thereby duly prepared.''

''That is so,'' said Simmias.

''And purification—isn't it just what it has long been said to be, according to the old accounts, the separation (so far as is possible) of the soul from the body, and the attempt to habituate her to collecting herself up and gathering herself together, away from the body, into herself—and to living, so far as is possible, both now and in the future, alone by herself, freeing herself from the body as though from bonds?''

''Quite so,'' he said.

''Then this is what is called death, a freeing or separation of soul from body?''

''Certainly,'' he said.

''And we say that the true philosophers in particular, or rather alone, are always eager to free her, and that this very thing is the philosopher's occupation, a freeing or separation of soul from body. Isn't that the case?''

''It seems to be.''

''So, as I said to begin with, it would be absurd for a man who was training himself throughout his life to live as closely as possible to death to grumble when death came to him?''

''Absurd, of course.''

''In fact, then, those who are really philosophers practice dying, and death has less terror for them than for anyone else. Look at it in this way: if they altogether hate the body, and want to have their souls independent—if, when this were coming about, they were to be afraid and object, would it not be very illogical?—if, that is, they were not glad to go to the place where, on their arrival, they might hope to get what throughout their lives they longed for—namely, wisdom—and to be completely free from association with that which they had hated. When lovers or wives or sons, who are merely human, have died, many have been ready and gladly willing to go to Hades in search of them, in the hope of seeing them there and being with those for whom they yearned; can it be, when one is truly in love with wisdom, and conceives exactly this same expectation, that he will never meet it (in a worthwhile manner) anywhere except in Hades, that he will grumble when he is dying, and not go gladly to that very place? The idea of it, my friend, if he is really a philosopher!—for he will think precisely this, that he will never meet wisdom in all its purity anywhere else but there. And if this is so, as I said just now, would it not be very unreasonable if such a man were afraid of death?"

"Very unreasonable," he said.

"Then if ever you see a man grumbling when on the point of death, isn't this sufficient proof that he has not been a lover of wisdom, but merely a lover of the body? And this same man is also, I suppose, a lover of wealth and of honor—of either, or of both."

"It is exactly as you say," he said.

"Then again, Simmias, surely what men call courage is particularly appropriate to those whose outlook is such as I have described?"

"Certainly," he said.

"Then temperance too—even the popular conception of temperance, not to be agog with desires, but to be above such things, and moderate in one's ways—does not this also belong to these men alone, who regard the body as of very little account and live the philosophic life?"

"It must," he said.

"If you like to consider," he said, "the courage or the temperance of the rest,[8] you will find it strange."

"How do you mean, Socrates?"

"You know," he said, "that all the rest count death as one of the worst of ills."

"Yes, indeed," he said.

"Then when the brave endure death, they do so simply through fear of greater evils?"

"That is so."

"Then all except the philosophers are brave simply because they are afraid, simply through fear?"

"Quite so."

"What about the moderate among them? Is it not just the same with them? They are temperate because of a sort of licentiousness. We say, of course, that this is impossible, but their condition which they naïvely regard as temperance does appear to be something of the sort. They are afraid of being deprived of one lot of pleasures, and desire them, and so they refrain from some pleasures simply because they are overcome by others. Being dominated by pleasures they call licentiousness; but in fact

---

[8]I.e., non-philosophers who try to practice their own conception of virtue.

they themselves are masters over some only because they are dominated by others; and this is more or less what we said a minute ago, that in a way they are temperate because of licentiousness."

"Yes, it seems so."

"Perhaps, my most excellent Simmias, this is not the right method of purchasing virtue, to exchange pleasures for pleasures and pains for pains and fear for fear, greater for smaller, as though these things were coins; perhaps the only coin of real value for which we ought to part with all these things is wisdom, and if they are all bought and sold for this, or with this, then that really does constitute courage and temperance and justice, and in short true virtue—*if* wisdom is present—whether pleasures and fears and all the rest of such things come also or are lost; but if they are divorced from wisdom, and are exchanged merely one for another, perhaps this may be called a sort of impressionistic imitation of virtue, in reality mean and sordid with nothing sound or true about it. Perhaps really, in actual fact, temperance and justice and courage are a sort of consummated purification of all such sensations, and wisdom itself is a sort of purificatory rite; and it may be that even those fellows who established our Mysteries are not to be despised—they have in fact long been saying in their riddles that whoever reaches Hades without having begun or without having completed his initiation into the rites will lie in the Slough, but that when a man arrives there purified and fully initiated, he will dwell with gods. As those who have to do with the Mysteries say, there are 'many who carry the mystic wand, but few are truly inspired': these, in my view, are none other than the true philosophers—and I, so far as I have been able, have striven by every means—leaving nothing undone at any time in my life—to become one of them. If I have striven correctly, if we have achieved anything, we will know, I think, for certain, if God be willing, when we get there not long hence.

"This, then, Simmias and Cebes, is my defense, which I hope will show that I have every reason for not grumbling or complaining at leaving you and my masters here, because I believe that there too, no less than here, I shall meet good masters and friends. I only hope that in my defense I have convinced you somewhat more than I convinced the Athenians' judges."

When Socrates had finished his speech, Cebes answered: "Socrates, I agree with you in everything else, but what you say about the soul leaves room for a good deal of apprehension: men may still be afraid that when the soul is separated from the body it may exist nowhere any more—that on that day on which the man dies it may be destroyed and perish: immediately on being separated from the body, even as it issues forth, it may be scattered like vapor or smoke and disappear, wafted away completely, and have no existence anywhere any more. If it *did* exist anywhere all by itself, as a unified entity, separated from these evils which you have just enumerated, there would be every reason to hope, Socrates, that your account might be true; but of this, I am afraid, a good deal of convincing reassurance may be needed—when you say that on the man's death his soul lives on and still has some powers and intelligence left.''

"True, Cebes," said Socrates, "but what are we to do? Would you have us go on with the story, dealing with these very points and seeing whether it is likely that this is the case or not?''

"I would certainly much like to hear," said Cebes, "what your opinion is on these matters.''

"Well, I don't think," said Socrates, "that anyone who should hear me now, even if he were a comic poet, could say that I was prattling and talking about matters that did not concern me; so, if you like, let's continue the enquiry.

"Let us consider the matter in this way, by asking whether, when men die, their souls really are in Hades or not. There is an ancient doctrine, which we have recalled, that they exist in the other world, when they have got there from this one, and that they come back here again and are born from the dead; and if this is so, if the living are born again from the dead, our souls will surely exist in the other world? I presume that they could not be born again if they had no existence, and that this would be sufficient proof of these contentions, if it really could be made plain that the living are born from the dead and from nowhere else; if this is not so, we should need some other argument.''

"Quite so," said Cebes.

"Do not," he said, "regard the question only as it affects human beings, if you want to understand it readily, but also as it applies to all animals and plants, and, in fact, to everything that is 'born'—let us consider in every case whether things are not all born simply from their opposites—everything, that is, which *has* an opposite, in the way in which the beautiful is opposite to the ugly, and just to unjust, and so on. Let us consider, I say, whether all things which have an opposite are not born simply from their opposites. For example, when something "larger" comes into being, it must, I suppose, become 'larger' after having previously been 'smaller.' ''

"Yes."

"Then similarly if it becomes 'smaller,' it will only become 'smaller' after having formerly been 'larger'?"

"Yes," he said.

"And again, that which is 'weaker,' after having been 'stronger,' and that which is 'quicker' after having been 'slower'?"

"Certainly."

"Again, if anything becomes 'worse,' does it not do so *after having been* 'better'? or if 'juster,' *after having been* 'more unjust'?"

"Of course."

"Then we are satisfied," he said, "that in every instance, generation is of opposites *from* opposites?"

"Yes."

"Well, perhaps we may say something of this sort about them, that between every pair of opposites there are two processes of 'coming into being'—from the one into the other, and then from the other back again into the former. When a thing becomes larger or smaller, there is increase or decrease, and we call these processes 'increasing' and 'decreasing.' ''

"Yes," he said.

"So separating and combining, growing cold and growing hot, and all such processes, even if we haven't got names for some of them, must nevertheless in fact always be in the same case: they must always arise out of each other, and there must always be a process of generation from the one into the other."

"Certainly," he said.

"Well," he said, "has 'living' an opposite, in the same sense as 'sleeping' is the opposite of 'being awake'?"

"Certainly," he said.

"And what is it?"

"Being dead," he said.

"Then these things are generated from each other, inasmuch as they are opposites, and there are two processes of generation between the two opposites?"

"Of course."

"Well, I will tell you about one of the pairs I mentioned just now," said Socrates, "and I'll name the appropriate processes. You do the same for the other pair. I say that sleeping and being awake are distinct, that 'being awake' follows on 'sleeping,' and *vice versa*; and I say that the intervening 'processes' are 'going to sleep' and 'waking up.' Do you think that adequate, or not?''

"I do."

"Then tell me in your turn," he said, "about life and death. Don't you say that being dead is the opposite of being alive?''

"I do."

"And that these two states arise out of each other?''

"Yes."

"And what is it that arises out of the living?''

"The dead."

"And from the dead?''

"One must admit that the answer is 'the living.' ''

"Then all living men and all living things are born from the dead?''

"It appears so," he said.

"Then our souls," he said, "exist in Hades."

"It seems so."

"Well, one of the two processes concerned is also clear, surely? Dying is clear enough, I presume?''

"Certainly," he said.

"What shall we do then?" he said. "Shall we not posit, for the sake of balance, the existence of the opposite process, or will nature be lame in this respect? Surely we must allow that there is a process opposite to dying?''

"Most certainly," he said.

"What is it then?''

"Coming to life again."

"Then," he said, "if there is such a thing as coming to life again, this 'coming to life again' will be a process of generation by which one leaves the dead to join the living?''

"Yes."

"We are agreed then, that in this way the living have been born from the dead no less than the dead have been 'born' from the living? And we decided, I think, that if this is true there is sufficient evidence that the souls of the dead must exist somewhere—in some place, I mean, from which to be born again.''

"In view of what we have agreed, Socrates, I think this must be so."

"And in my opinion, Cebes, we were quite right too in what we agreed upon. Just consider: if the one set of opposites did not make continual restitution for the other by coming into

being—coming round in a circle, as it were—if, instead, generation were a one-way process, simply from one thing into its
opposite, with no turning-back[9] into the original or veering-
round—do you realize that everything would end up by having
the same shape, undergoing the same experience, and ceasing to
be born?''

"How do you mean?'' he said.

"What I am getting at is not at all difficult to grasp. For
example, if there were such a thing as 'going to sleep,' but
'waking up' did not make compensation by coming into being
from the sleeping state, you may be sure that eventually everything would put Endymion[10] in the shade—in fact, he would be
nowhere—because *everything* else would do the same as he
did—namely, *sleep*. And if everything were being combined,
and nothing separated out, very soon Anaxagoras' notion would
be realized, 'Everything all together.'[11] Now in the same way,
dear Cebes, if everything that has a share in life were to die, and
when dead were to remain in this state—'the dead'—and not
come to life again, then surely in the end everything would
necessarily die, and nothing would live? If 'the living' were to
be born from the other world, and the living were dying all the
time, what would there be to prevent everything being used up in
death?''

"Nothing, Socrates,'' said Cebes. "I think you are quite
right.''

"I think, Cebes, that it is bound to be so, and that we are
not being misled in reaching these conclusions, but that in actual
fact there is such a thing as coming to life again as well, and that
the living are born from the dead, and that the souls of the dead
have real existence.''

"Yes,'' replied Cebes, "and then there is that argument,
Socrates, which you are often putting forward, that our learning
is simply recollection—that argument, also, if it is sound, proves
that we must have learned what we now recollect at some previous
time; and that would be impossible unless our souls had existed
somewhere before appearing in this human frame—so that according to this argument as well, the soul seems to be something
immortal.''

---

[9]A metaphor from the racecourse, which was shaped like a narrow U.

[10]For attempting to make love to Hera, he was condemned to eternal sleep; but
according to the poem of John Keats, he was loved by the goddess of the moon, and she
made him sleep.

[11]This was how Anaxagoras described the state of chaos which existed before,
according to his doctrine, "Mind arranged everything" (Diogenes Laertius II, 6).

"But what are the grounds of these arguments, Cebes?" put in Simmias. "Remind me, for at the moment I can't quite recollect."

"I can give you one excellent reason," said Cebes. "When people are asked something, if the question is well put, they themselves explain everything—and yet if they hadn't got knowledge and a right account of the matter stored away inside them, they couldn't do that; and if you next take them to the figures of geometry or something else of that sort, it is then as clear as could possibly be that this is the case."

"But if you are not convinced by this, Simmias," said Socrates, "look at the matter in this way, and see if you agree. You doubt whether what is called learning can be recollection?"

"I am not *doubting*," said Simmias, "but I need to do just what we are talking about, to *recollect*. I almost remember and almost believe as a result of Cebes' explanation; but I shall be none the less glad to hear how you have explained it."

"This is my method," he said. "We agree, I suppose, that if a man remembers something, he must have *known* it at some time previously."

"Yes," he said.

"And do we also agree that when a man gets knowledge in this sort of way, that is recollection? *How* do I mean? Well, if a man sees or hears or otherwise perceives something, and not only recognizes that particular thing, but thinks of *something else*—of a thing that is the object of *different* knowledge—isn't it right that we should say that he has *recollected* this thing of which he has suddenly thought?"

"How do you mean?"

"For example, our knowledge of a man is different from our knowledge of a lyre."

"Of course."

"Now you know that when lovers see a lyre or cloak or something else that their loved ones are accustomed to use, what they experience is this: they recognize the lyre and form a mental image of the boy who owns the lyre. This is recollection—just as when people see Simmias they are often reminded of Cebes; and there will be hundreds of other examples."

"Hundreds, yes," said Simmias.

"Surely, then, this sort of thing is a kind of recollection—especially when the experience is concerned with those things which you have forgotten through lapse of time, and through not having seen them."

"Certainly."

"Again," he said, "is it possible to see a picture of a horse or of a lyre and to be reminded of a man, or to see a picture of Simmias and to remember Cebes?"

"Yes, indeed."

"And even, seeing a picture of Simmias, to remember Simmias?"

"It is," he said.

"And does it not follow from all this that the recollection can be caused *either* by what is like[12] *or* by what is unlike?"[13]

"Yes."

"But when you are reminded of something by what is like it, are you not bound also to notice whether this similar thing falls short or not in any way in its resemblance to the thing of which you have been reminded?"

"Necessarily," he said.

"Now consider whether this is true. We say, I think, that there is a thing which is *Equal*—I don't mean a particular piece of wood that is like another, or a stone that is like another, or anything of that sort, but something over and above all these, the Equal Itself. Are we to agree that there is such a thing, or not?"

"Yes, certainly," said Simmias, "most assuredly."

"And do we really know what its essential nature is?"

"Yes," he said.

"Then where did we get the knowledge of it *from*? Surely we got that conception from the things we were talking about just now, from seeing pieces of wood or stones or any other things equal, although it is different from these; or don't you think that it is different? Consider it in this way: do not stones that are equal, or pieces of wood, very often seem—the self-same objects—to one man, equal, to another, unequal?"

"Certainly."

"Well, have the things that are *really* equal ever seemed to you to be unequal? or has Equality seemed the same as Inequality?"

"Never, Socrates."

"Then these so-called equal things and the Equal Itself are not the same."

"Definitely not, in my opinion, Socrates."

"Yet from these equal things, which are different from that 'Equal,' you have conceived and acquired your knowledge of it?"

---

[12]E.g., as a picture of Simmias reminds us of Simmias.

[13]E.g., a picture of Simmias that reminds us of Cebes.

"True," he said.

"Presumably either because it is like them, or else because it is unlike?"[14]

"Yes."

"But it makes no difference," he said. "So long as from seeing one thing you form mental images of another, whether this other thing be similar or dissimilar, the process must be recollection."

"Certainly."

"Now when we have to do with the pieces of wood and the equal things we were talking about just now, do they seem to us to be equal in the same way as that which is essentially and perfectly equal, or do they, perhaps, fall short of that, in point of resemblance to what is equal?"

"They fall short a great deal," he said.

"Then we agree that when a man sees a thing, and tells himself that 'the thing I am now looking at wants to be like some other thing,' but that it falls short and cannot be like that—that it is, in fact, inferior—the man who gets this notion must, I suppose, have previous knowledge of that thing to which he says that he sees a real but imperfect resemblance."

"He must."

"Well, isn't that the case with us, so far as the so-called equal things and the Equal Itself are concerned?"

"Absolutely."

"Then we must have had knowledge of the Equal *before* that time when we first saw the things that are 'equal' and conceived the idea that all these things were trying to be like the Equal, but fell short."

"That is so."

"But we also agree that we derived the conception from no other source—to do so, indeed, would not be possible—than from sight or touch or from some other one of the senses. I count all of them as the same."

"Yes, Socrates, they are all one so far as the present discussion is concerned."

"Then it is through the senses that we must reach the conclusion that all the objects of sense which are 'equal' aim at that which really *is* Equal, but fall short of it. Or what is our verdict?"

"Just that."

---

[14]I.e., because they resemble it, or because they are associated with it only in thought.

"I suppose, then, that we must have acquired knowledge of the nature of the Equal Itself before we began to see and to hear and to use our other senses, if we were going to refer to that criterion things that appeared to the senses equal, on the ground that they all do their best to be like it, though they are inferior."

"We must have, in view of what we have admitted already, Socrates."

"And did we not begin to see and to hear and to enjoy our other faculties of sense the moment we were born?"

"Certainly."

"But we say that we must have acquired our knowledge of the Equal before these?"

"Yes."

"So that we must have acquired it before we were born?"

"It seems so."

"So if we acquired it before birth and then were born with it, both before birth and the very moment after birth we had knowledge not only of the Equal and the Greater and the Smaller, but of all such things?—for our discussion now is concerned with the Beautiful Itself and the Good Itself and the Just and the Holy, no less than with the Equal; in fact, as I say, it is concerned with all those things to which, in our questions and answers, we attach as a sort of hall-mark of identification the words 'that which *is*, all by itself.' We must, then, have acquired our knowledge of all these things before being born."

"That is so."

"And unless, after acquiring it, we have on each occasion forgotten it, we must always be born in full possession of knowledge, and always *know* throughout life; for surely knowing is just this, having acquired knowledge of a thing, to have it and not to have lost it? And by 'forgetting' surely what we mean is loss of knowledge?"

"Quite, Socrates," he said.

"But if, I suppose, having acquired it before birth, we lost it while being born, and later by applying the senses to the things in question we recover that knowledge which once, formerly, we possessed—then surely what we call 'learning' will be the recovery of knowledge which is our own? And we should be right in calling this 'recollection'?"

"Yes."

"It seemed possible, on perceiving something by means of sight or hearing or some other sense, to think, as a result of this, of something else—something similar or dissimilar, but anyhow in some way related—which had been forgotten; so that, as I say, we are faced with two alternatives, either all of us are born with knowledge of these things and know them throughout life, or else those whom we describe as learning simply *recollect* later on; and learning will be *recollection.*"

"That is certainly so, Socrates."

"Which then, do you choose, Simmias?—that we are born in possession of knowledge, or that we recollect later on things of which we had acquired knowledge before."

"I can't decide for the moment, Socrates."

"Well, can you decide this, or how do you feel about it?—my question is, Would a man who had knowledge be able to give an account of the things he knew about, or not?"

"Necessarily, Socrates," he said.

"Do you think everyone can give an account of the things we were talking about just now?"

"I wish they could," said Simmias, "but I am afraid that this time tomorrow there may be no one any longer able to do this adequately."

"You don't think, then, Simmias, that everyone does know them?"

"No."

"They recollect, then, what they once learned."

"They must."

"When did our souls acquire the knowledge of them? Not presumably during the time that we have been human beings?"

"No, indeed."

"Earlier, then?"

"Yes."

"Our souls, then, Simmias, existed earlier on, before inhabiting human form; they existed apart from bodies, and they had intelligence."

"Unless, of course, we acquire this knowledge at the very time of birth, Socrates; this time is still left as a possibility."

"Perhaps, my friend; but at whatever other time did we lose it?—for we are not born already in possession of it, as we agreed just now—or do we lose it at the very same time as we acquire it? or can you suggest any other time?"

"No, Socrates. I was talking rubbish; I didn't realize it."

"Is this, then, how the matter stands, in our opinion, Simmias? If the things we are always talking about do exist—a Beautiful and Good and all reality of that kind; and if we refer all the data of the senses to this reality, discovering that it existed previously and belonged to us, and compare these sense-data with that reality—then our souls must exist no less than these things before we are born. But if these things do *not* really exist, then our discussion will have been to no purpose? Is this how the matter stands, and is it equally necessary that these things and our souls must have existed before we were born—if the former did not, then neither did the latter?''

"It seems to me quite clear, Socrates," said Simmias, "that there is the same necessity in either case, and it is very satisfactory that the argument should lead us to this, that our souls and the reality of which you are now speaking both equally exist before we are born. Nothing is so clear to me as this, that all these things really do have full and complete existence—Beautiful, Good, and all the other things you mentioned just now. It seems to me to have been sufficiently proved."

"What about Cebes?" said Socrates. "We must convince Cebes too."

"It's enough for him too, I think," said Simmias, "though he is the most stubborn of men when it comes to mistrusting arguments; but I think he has been fully convinced that our souls existed before we were born. On the other hand, I myself don't think it has been proved, Socrates, that they will still exist when we die. We have still to face the popular theory that Cebes was talking about just now, the fear that when the man dies the soul is simultaneously dispersed, and that that is the end of it. What is there to prevent it from coming into being and taking shape from some other source, and existing before entering a human body, but then, after it has entered it and again been released from it, itself coming to an end and perishing?"

"You are right, Simmias," said Cebes. "Only half of the necessary proof seems to have been given. We see that our souls existed before we were born, but if the proof is to be complete we need to prove in addition that they will exist after we are dead also, no less than before we were born."

"It has already been proved, Simmias and Cebes," said Socrates, "if you will combine this argument with our earlier admission that all that is alive comes into being from the dead. If our soul has previous existence, and when coming to the land of the living and being born must necessarily be generated from death and the state of deadness, surely it must exist even after death, since it has got to be born again? The point you raise has already been proved. Nevertheless, it appears to me that you and Simmias would like to deal with this matter, too, even further and more thoroughly, and that you are afraid, as children are, that the wind may disperse it and scatter it as it leaves the body, particularly if a man dies when the weather is far from calm and a high wind is blowing.''

And Cebes chuckled and said, ''Try to convince us, then, Socrates, on the assumption that we are afraid; or rather, not as though *we* are afraid—perhaps there is a child inside us that is apprehensive in this way. So try to persuade *him* not to be afraid of the bogey Death.''

''You must sing charms over him,'' said Socrates, ''every day, until you have charmed the fear out of him.''

''Where, Socrates,'' he said, ''shall we find a good charmer to charm away such fears, since you are leaving us?''

''Hellas is wide, Cebes,'' he said, ''and in it there are, I suppose, many good men; and many, too, are the tribes of barbarians. Among all of these you must enquire diligently in your search for such a charmer, sparing neither money nor toil, since there is nothing on which you could spend your money to better purpose. You should search, too, by yourselves, with the help of one another; for perhaps it would be difficult for you to find anyone more capable of doing this than you are.''

''This shall be done,'' said Cebes. ''But let us resume the argument at the point where we left it, if you are agreeable.''

''I am indeed, of course.''

''Good,'' he said.

''Then,'' said Socrates, ''we should ask ourselves something of this sort—what sort of thing it is appropriate should experience this 'scattering,' so that we might reasonably fear that it will do so; and again, what sort of thing is not likely to be 'scattered.' After that we should consider to which class soul belongs; and then we can feel secure or apprehensive regarding our souls according to the results of these enquiries. Don't you think so?''

''True enough,'' he said.

''Then is it fitting that what has been compounded and what is composite by nature should undergo this experience, being decomposed in the same way as it was compounded? But if there is anything incomposite, is it appropriate that this alone, before all else, should be exempt from decomposition?''

''I think you are right,'' said Cebes.

''Now that which is always constant and invariable is likely to be the incomposite, while that which is in a different state at different times and never constant will be composite?''

"I think so."

"Let us turn again," he said, "to the things that we were discussing just now. The absolute reality the essence of which we try to define in our questions and answers—is it always invariable and constant, or is it in a different state, at different times?—the Equal Itself, the Beautiful Itself, everything in itself, that which *is*—do these things ever admit of any change whatever? Doesn't the essential nature of each of them, being of single form when taken by itself, remain invariable and constant, never admitting any variation at any point in any way?"

"It must remain invariable and constant, Socrates," said Cebes.

"But what about the many particular instances of beauty—human beings, horses, cloaks, or any other beautiful things you like to mention—or particular equal things, or all the things that are named after those archetypes? Are they constant, or, quite the opposite of those archetypes, are they hardly ever to be found bearing the same relationship to themselves or to each other?"

"That is so: they are always changing."

"These, then, you might touch or see or perceive with the other senses, but the things that are constant you could never grasp except by the reasoning of the mind; such things are invisible, and not seen?"

"You are quite right," he said.

"Do you want us, then," he said, "to lay it down that there are two kinds of existents, the one kind seen, the other invisible?"

"Let us do that," he said.

"And that the invisible kind is always constant, while the seen is never constant?"

"That too," he said.

"Now then," he said, "surely we ourselves are composed of body and of soul?"

"Yes," he said.

"To which class, then, do we consider that the body will be more similar in its form, and more akin?"

"Quite clearly to the seen," he said.

"And what about the soul? Is it seen, or invisible?"

"Not visible to men, anyway, Socrates," he said.

"But we meant what was seen or not seen by human faculties—or do you think that any other kind of faculty is concerned?"

"No."

"What do we say about soul, then? Is it seen, or not seen?"

"Not seen."

"Invisible, then?"

"Yes."

"Then soul is more similar than body to the invisible, while body is more like that which is seen."

"That must be so, Socrates."

"Again, we said this some time ago, that when the soul makes use of the assistance of the body for the study of something, by using sight or hearing or some other sense—for this is the bodily method, the study of something through sense—it is dragged by the body toward what is never constant, and it vacillates, and is confused, and dithers as though it were drunk, because it is in contact with things that are in that sort of state?"

"Yes."

"But when it makes enquiry all by itself, it goes off there to what is pure and everlasting and deathless and invariable, and as though akin to it always remains with that kind of being, whenever it is by itself and can do so; it ceases to vacillate and is always constant and invariable in its relationship with those realities, because it is in contact with things that are themselves constant and invariable. And this condition of it is called contemplation. Isn't that so?"

"Well said, Socrates; you are quite right," he said.

"To which class, then, in view of our former and our present statements, does soul seem to you to be more like and akin?"

"It seems to me, Socrates," he said, "that everyone—even the dullest wit—would agree on the strength of this investigation that soul is altogether more like that which is always invariable."

"And what about the body?"

"That is like the other class."

"Consider the matter again from this point of view. Whenever soul and body are together, the nature of the body bids it be subservient and ruled over, while the soul's nature bids it rule and dominate. Here again, which of the two do you think is like the divine, and which is like the mortal?—or don't you think that it is the nature of the divine to rule and to lead, and of the mortal to be ruled over and to serve?"

"I do."

"To which class, then, is soul similar?"

"Clearly, Socrates, the soul is like the divine, the body like the mortal."

"Then consider, Cebes," he said, "whether this is our conclusion as a result of all that has been said, that soul is very like that which is divine and deathless and intelligible and uniform and indissoluble and always invariable and constant, while body is very like that which is human and mortal and manifold, incomprehensible to the intelligence, always liable to dissolution, never constant. Can we bring forward any argument against these statements, dear Cebes, to show that they are false?"

"We can't."

"Well, this being so, surely it belongs to body to be disrupted quickly, but to soul to be completely indissoluble, or anyhow nearly so?"

"Of course."

"You observe then," he said, "that when the man dies, the visible part of him, situated in the visible realm—that is to say, the body, which we call a 'corpse,' which must be disrupted and decomposed and dissipated by the winds—does not suffer any of these experiences straightway, but remains as it is for quite a long while. Even if a man dies when his body is in fine condition, and at a fine season of the year, it lasts for a very long time; in fact, when the body is withered, and is embalmed—as in the case of those who have been embalmed in Egypt—it remains almost entire for an amazing length of time; and even if the body corrupts, some parts of it—bones and sinews and all such things—are practically everlasting. Isn't that so?"

"Yes."

"But the soul, the invisible part which has gone to a place which resembles itself in being fine and pure and invisible—quite literally to the Unseen World—to the good and wise God—to which place, if God wills, my soul too must go very shortly; does our soul, I say, which is of such a form and nature, really get blown away and perish in the very moment of being separated from the body, as most men say? Far from it, dear Cebes and Simmias. The facts are rather these: let us suppose that it is *pure* when separated, dragging nothing of the body with it, as having (wilfully anyhow) had no dealings with the body during its lifetime, but having shunned it and kept itself to itself, making that its constant aim and practice—which simply means, in fact, pursuing philosophy in the correct manner, and in very truth readily practicing death; or wouldn't you call this a 'practice of death'?"

"Certainly."

"Then in this state it goes away to the place which is like

itself, invisible, to that which is divine and deathless and wise, and when it arrives there it is its lot to be happy, freed from uncertainty and folly and fears and wild desires and all the other ills from which man suffers, and (as is said of those who have been initiated into the Mysteries) in very truth spending the rest of time in company with gods? Is that to be our account of the matter, Cebes, or something different?"

"That, most certainly," said Cebes.

"But, I suppose, if it is polluted and impure when separated from the body, as having always consorted with the body and cherished and loved it—having been bewitched by it, by its desires and its pleasures, to such an extent as to think nothing real but what is of bodily form, whatever one may touch or see or eat or drink or use for the purpose of sexual satisfaction—and having, moreover, accustomed itself to hate and fear and shun that which is hidden from the eyes and invisible, to be grasped only by the intelligence and by philosophy: do you think that a soul in this condition will depart by itself pure and unalloyed?"

"By no means," he said.

"Shot through, rather, I suppose, with the corporeal, which the association and intercourse of the body, through continual intimacy and habituation over a long period, have implanted and made to grow up as part of it."

"Yes."

"We must suppose, my friend, that this corporeal element is burdensome and heavy and earthy and visible; and when such a soul possesses this, it is weighed down and dragged back into the visible realm, and through fear of what is not seen and of the Unseen World it haunts, as men say, monuments and tombs; by these have been seen shadowy forms of souls, apparitions such as souls of this kind provide when they are separated from the body in an impure state, still partaking of the visible, which is what causes them to be seen."

"That is probable, Socrates."

"It is certainly probable, Cebes; and that they are the souls not of the good, but of the bad—souls which are compelled to wander about such places, paying the penalty for their former wicked way of life. And they wander about until, through the desires of that which follows about with them, the corporeal element, they are imprisoned again in a body; and they are probably imprisoned in creatures of whatever sort of character they have cultivated during their lives."

"What sort of characters do you mean, Socrates?"

"Those who have practiced gluttony, for example, and outrage and drunkenness, and have exercised no restraint, will probably enter into asses and beasts of that sort. Don't you think so?"

"What you say is very probable."

"And those who have chosen to commit acts of injustice, or play the tyrant or the robber, will probably become wolves and hawks or kites. Or where else can we say that such souls will go?"

"Certainly they will enter into beasts of that sort," said Cebes.

"And it is clear," he said, "that the way every other class also would go depends upon the nature of their previous practices?"

"It is, of course," he said.

"And among these, again, they are happiest and likely to go to the best place, who have aimed at 'popular' or 'civic' virtue, at what they call temperance and justice—such virtue as is the result of habit and of practice, but not of philosophy or of the activity of the mind?"

"Why are these happiest?"

"Because it is probable that they will go into creatures similar to themselves, sociable and peaceful—bees, perhaps, or wasps or ants, and back into human beings again, and that law-abiding men will appear from among them."

"Yes, that is probable."

"But it is not lawful to join the gods without having pursued philosophy, without departing absolutely pure. Only the lover of learning may go there. For this reason, dear Simmias and Cebes, the true philosophers abstain from all the lusts of the body, and instead of surrendering themselves, exercise will-power—not because they are afraid of wasting their substance and becoming poor, which is the reason of the avaricious mob, nor because they fear the ill-repute and disgrace that accompany wickedness, like those who abstain from those lusts because they love power and honor."

"That would not be proper, Socrates," said Cebes.

"Certainly it would not," he said. "So those who have any regard for their souls, Cebes, and do not live for the body, cultivating only that, part company with all these worldlings who don't know where they are going, and take a very different course: believing that they should do nothing to hinder philosophy and the release and purification that it gives, they follow philosophy, taking the path along which philosophy leads them."

"How do you mean, Socrates?"

"I will tell you," he said. "The lovers of learning find that philosophy takes their souls in hand—for their souls are simply bound and glued in the body, and compelled to survey reality through the body as through a prison wall, instead of freely by themselves, and they are wallowing, moreover, in utter ignorance; and philosophy sees that the body-prison in its cunning works through desire, contriving to make the prisoner aid and abet his own imprisonment as much as possible. The lovers of learning, then, as I say, find that philosophy, taking over their souls in this condition, gently soothes and tries to free them, pointing out that the evidence of the eyes and of the ears and of the other organs of sense is thoroughly misleading, and urging them to withdraw from the use of the senses except when such use is inevitable. It encourages the soul to gather itself up into itself, all alone, and to put trust in nothing but itself—to trust only such realities as it may discern in their essential nature by its own essential nature; whatever it sees by the use of something else, things appearing variously *in various other things,* it should count in no way real. Such things are objects of sense and visible, while what the soul sees *by itself* is an object of thought and invisible. The soul of the true philosopher, simply because it believes that it should not oppose this release, abstains from pleasures and desires and pains so far as it can, reckoning that whenever you experience intense pleasure or fear or desire you do not suffer any such slight evil through these things as you might suppose—illness, for example, or reduction of capital, as a result of your desires; you suffer the greatest and worst of all evils, and yet fail to take it into account."

"What is this worst of all evils, Socrates?" asked Cebes.

"That the soul of every man is compelled, through experiencing some extreme pleasure or pain, to imagine that whatever most strongly arouses such feelings is most vivid and real—although, of course, it is not; and these things are chiefly the things that can be seen. Isn't that so?"

"Yes."

"Then the soul is more particularly bound fast by the body when undergoing this sort of experience?"

"How do you mean?"

"Every pleasure and pain fastens it as with a nail to the body, and pins it down, and makes it similar to the body, since it imagines to be true whatever the body declares to be so. From holding the same opinions as the body and taking delight in the same things it is forced, I suppose, to acquire the same sort of habits and to take the same sort of nourishment, and to become such that it can never reach the other world in a state of purity; it must always depart contaminated by the body, and quickly fall back again into another body, and grow there like a seed that has been sown, and as a result be deprived of the privilege of dwelling with what is divine and pure and of single nature."

"True, Socrates," said Cebes.

"This, then, Cebes, is why the true lovers of learning are moderate and manly; it is not for the reasons that most men suppose—or do you think it is?"

"No, I don't."

"No, indeed. The soul of a philosopher would judge as we have said, and realizing that it was philosophy's job to work for its release, it would not think it right, while philosophy was in the very process of doing so, wilfully to give itself up again to those pleasures and pains to bind once more in the body, thus performing a fruitless task of Penelope—when she *un*wove a web; it would aim at acquiring rest from these emotions, and follow reason, and always occupy itself with that, fixing its gaze on what is true and divine, the object not of opinion but of knowledge, and nourishing itself on that; it believes that this is how it should live so long as it is alive, and that when the end comes and it arrives at what is akin to itself and such as we have described, it is then released from all human ills. After such nurture, Simmias and Cebes, there is no danger of its being afraid that it may be rent apart at the time when it is freed from the body, dispersed by the winds, and that flying away it may disappear and have no existence anywhere any more."

Silence ensued for some time after Socrates finished speaking. Socrates himself was absorbed in consideration of the foregoing argument, to judge from his appearance, and so were most of us. Cebes and Simmias continued to talk to each other, in a low voice. Socrates, noticing them, asked, "Can it be that our account of the matter doesn't seem to you to be adequate? There certainly are many good grounds for doubt, and many ways of attacking what has been said, if the matter is to be fully explored. If it is something else that you are considering, no matter; but if you have some difficulty connected with what we have said, don't hesitate to put it forward and to explain it, if you think it would be better that it should be stated; and don't hesitate to call me in, too, if you think that I can help at all to get you out of your difficulty."

And Simmias said: "Well, Socrates, I will tell you the truth. We both of us have difficulties, and for some time have been urging and telling each other to question you—for we want to hear your answer, but shrink from causing trouble, in case it may be distasteful to you in your present misfortune."

Socrates laughed quietly at this and said, "For shame, Simmias! I shall certainly find it difficult to convince the rest of the world that I *don't* regard the present situation as a misfortune, if I can't convince even you, and you are afraid that I am more irritable now than I used to be. I must seem to you to be a poorer prophet than the swans who, when they see that they must die, sing longer and more sweetly than they have ever sung before, because they are delighted that they are going to depart to the god whose servants they are. Mankind, because of their own fear of death, malign the swans, and say that they are bewailing their death, and that they are singing a departing song of sorrow because they are distressed. They don't take into account the fact that no bird sings when it is hungry or cold or experiencing any other sort of pain—not even the nightingale or swallow or the hoopoe,[15] birds which are reputed to sing songs of sorrow in distress. I don't think that these birds *do* sing through distress, or that the swans do either—but simply that the swans are prophetic (as belonging, I suppose, to Apollo[16]), and foresee the good things awaiting them in the other world, and that *that* is why they sing; they are filled with joy that day in a higher degree than ever in their lives before. And I think that I myself am a fellow-servant with the swans and a priest of the same god, and that I no less than they have the gift of prophecy from the master, and that I am leaving this life no more sorrowfully than they do. So far as this is concerned, then, you should say and ask whatever you like, so long as the Athenians' eleven magistrates permit."

"Excellent," said Simmias. "I will tell you my difficulty, and Cebes will tell you why he can't accept the arguments put forward. I think, Socrates, as perhaps you do too, that in these matters certain knowledge is impossible, or very difficult, to attain during life, but that nevertheless to fail to test the theories concerning them in every possible way, or to give up doing so before you have made a thorough and exhaustive examination, shows a very poor spirit. You must do one or other of these

---

[15]There is an allusion to the legend of Philomela, Procne, and Tereus, who were said to have been transformed, respectively, into a swallow, a nightingale, and a hoopoe.

[16]The god of prophecy.

things—either learn from another or discover for yourself how things are, or, if this is impossible, accept the best of human arguments, the hardest to refute, and risk riding on this raft, as it were, in the voyage through life—if you should not be able to travel more surely and safely on a more reliable raft, some divine explanation. Now I for my part shall not be ashamed to put my question, since you tell me to, and I shall not reproach myself in time to come for having failed to express my thoughts on this occasion. In *my* opinion, Socrates—and I have been going over the arguments not only in my own mind but also with Cebes—we haven't quite got to the bottom of the matter yet.''

"Perhaps you are right, my friend," said Socrates. "Tell me how you mean."

"It is like this. In the case of a lyre and its strings, you might put forward this same argument, that the attunement of the tuned lyre is something invisible and bodiless and very beautiful and divine, while the lyre itself and the strings are bodies and of bodily form and composite and earthy and akin to what is mortal. So, when you break the lyre or cut and sever the strings, suppose the same argument were to be put forward as you have used, that that attunement cannot perish but must still exist; for certainly it couldn't happen that when the string had been broken both the lyre and the strings, which are of mortal kind, should still exist, while the attunement, which is related and akin to the divine and the immortal, perished—dying before that which is mortal. Suppose it were to be affirmed that the attunement itself must still exist somewhere, and that the pieces of wood and the string would corrupt before anything happened to that; for I imagine, Socrates, that you for your part have realized that we suppose the soul to be something of this sort: that our body is in tension, as it were, and held together by hot and cold, and dry and moist, and such things as that, and that our soul is a mixture and an attunement of these same things, when they are suitably blended with each other in moderate proportions. If, then, the soul is a sort of attunement, it is clear that whenever our body is 'loosened' or 'tightened' too much through diseases or other ills, the soul must at once die, divine though it be, just like the other kinds of attunement—those of musical notes and those of all the works of craftsmen—while what is left of the body in every instance remains with us for a long time, either until it is cremated or until it decays. Consider what we shall say in reply to this argument, if anyone supposes that the soul is a blending of the elements of the body, and that therefore it is the first thing to be destroyed at the time of what is called death.''

Socrates, staring with his usual stare, and with a smile on his face, said, ''Simmias' objection is fair enough. If any one of you is better off for an answer than I am, let him give it; for Simmias seems to handle the argument in no unskillful manner. But I think that before giving our reply we should first hear what fault Cebes has to find with the argument, so that in the intervening time we may consider what we shall say. Then, when we have heard him, we should agree with them, if it appears that they are 'hitting the right note,' or else defend our argument against them then. Come, Cebes,'' he said, ''tell us what has been troubling you.''

''I will,'' said Cebes. ''It seems to me that the argument has got us no further, and is open to the same criticism as we made earlier on. I do not retract my admission that it has been very well—and, if it is not overdoing it to say so, quite sufficiently—proved that our souls did exist before entering this human frame. It's just that I don't think the same about its survival after our death. As a matter of fact, I don't agree with Simmias' objection in so far as he maintains that soul is not stronger and more long-lived than body, for I think that it is far superior in all these respects. 'Well,' the argument might retort, 'since you can see that the weaker part survives after the man's death, why do you still disbelieve? And don't you think that that which is longer-lived must still be preserved during this period?' See now whether there is anything in my reply to these questions.

''I think that like Simmias I need an analogy. It seems to me that there is no more justification in the argument than there would be if an old weaver were to die, and someone were to put forward this argument, that the man has not died, but still exists safe and sound, and as evidence were to point to the fact that the home-made coat that he wore is still safe and sound and has not perished; and then, whenever anyone doubted him, he were to ask, 'Which lives longer, a man, or a coat that is used and worn?' and when the reply came, 'Man, by far,' he considered it proved that the man was definitely safe, since that which was shorter-lived has not perished. But I don't think this is so, Simmias. Just reflect on this point. Anyone could see that this is a silly argument; for this weaver wears out and weaves many such coats, and dies *after* them, many as they are, though naturally before the *last* one; and this does not mean that man is of less account or weaker than a coat, I think that this particular analogy may be applied to the relationship between soul and body, and I would think it fair enough if anyone were to say just the same about them, that the soul is long-lived, while the body is weaker and shorter-lived. He might say that 'each soul wears out many bodies, especially if it lives for many years, for if the body is decaying and perishing while the man continues to live, yet the soul is always weaving anew that which is being worn out'—but nevertheless, when the soul should come to die, it would be bound to do so while in possession of its last 'web,' and to die before this single one; 'and when the soul does die, then the body,' he would say, 'at last reveals the nature of its weakness, and soon corrupts and disappears. Therefore, there is no good reason, on the strength of this argument, to be confident that our souls exist after death. For even if one were to grant still more to the champion of the argument than *you* say, and grant him not only that our souls exist in the period before we are born, but also that there is nothing to prevent some people's souls still existing even after death, and that they will continue to exist and will be born and will die again several times over—a soul being a thing *so* strong by nature that it survives several births; if one were to grant that, but still refuse to allow that it doesn't *suffer* during these many births, and doesn't finally, at one of its deaths, perish utterly—and were to say, moreover, that no one knows this death and dissolution of the body which brings destruction to the soul, it being impossible for any one of us to distinguish it'—and if this is so, then anyone who has no concern about death must be a fool, unless he can prove that soul is wholly immortal and indestructible; and if he can't, then our objector might conclude that 'the man who is on the point of death must always be afraid that at its present separation from the body his soul may perish utterly.' ''

When Cebes and Simmias had put their objections we were all very despondent at what we had heard, as we later admitted to each other, because whereas we had been thoroughly convinced by the earlier argument, it seemed that they had again confused us and made us inclined to mistrust not only what had been said already, but also what might be said later; we began to be afraid that we were not capable of judging anything correctly, or even that the matter itself might prove not to admit of any certainty.

Echecrates. Good gracious, Phaedo, I can excuse you for that. I myself, who have just been listening to you now, feel inclined to say to myself something like, ''What argument *shall* we believe now? How completely convincing Socrates' argument was, and yet it is no longer trusted." I am and always have been thoroughly taken with the argument that our souls are attunements, and when you expounded it I was reminded, as it were, that I myself had already reached that conclusion. I certainly want to start all over again with some other argument that will convince me that the soul of the man who has died does not die with him. Tell me then, please, how did Socrates pursue the question? and did it appear that he too was disconcerted at all, as you say that you were, or did he come calmly to the rescue? And was his aid sufficient, or not? Please tell us all, as accurately as you can.

Phaedo. Well, Echecrates, I had often admired Socrates, but was never more pleased with him than on that occasion. It is not surprising, perhaps, that he should have had an answer to give, but I was astonished, first, at the glad and kindly and admiring way in which he listened to the young men's view, then, at the keen manner in which he perceived the effect that these arguments had had on us; and then again at the skillful way in which he treated us, and, as though we were a defeated army in flight, rallied us, and got us to follow with him and to reconnoiter the position together.

How so?

I will tell you. I happened to be sitting on his right, beside the couch, on a stool; and he was on one much higher than mine. Putting his hand on my head and clasping the hair on my neck—it was his way, sometimes, to play with my hair—he said, "Tomorrow, perhaps, Phaedo, you will cut off this beautiful hair."[17]

"Probably, Socrates," I said.

"You won't, if you take my advice."

"What should I do then?" I asked.

"You will cut off your hair today, and I will mine, if our argument meets its doom and we aren't able to revive it. If I were you, and the argument were to evade me, I should swear an oath, like the Argives,[18] not to grow my hair again until I had fought back and overcome the argument of Simmias and Cebes."

"But," I replied, "it is said that not even Heracles[19] could fight against two."

---

[17] The regular token of mourning.

[18] The Argives, according to Herodotus (1.82), swore an oath not to grow their hair again until they had recovered a town which the Spartans had captured.

[19] In the course of his labors Hercules (Heracles) fought the Lernean hydra, and while doing so was attacked by a large crab. He then called in the assistance of Iolaus.

"Then call me in," he said, "to play the Iolaus, while it is still light."

"I do ask your aid," I said, "but not as though I were Heracles—rather as though I were Iolaus, calling in Heracles."

"It will make no difference," he said. "But first let us take care not to make a mistake."

"What sort of mistake?" I asked.

"To become haters of reason," he said, "in the way in which some become misanthropists. There is no worse evil that a man could suffer than this—hating arguments. Misology and misanthropy spring from the same source. Misanthropy comes from putting complete confidence in someone without having understanding, and supposing that the fellow is absolutely true and sound and trustworthy, and then a little later on finding that he is bad and untrustworthy—and then doing the same with someone else; and when you have experienced this several times, and particularly at the hands of those whom you might consider your nearest and dearest friends, you finally, after many rebuffs, come to hate all men and to suppose that there is nothing sound in anyone at all. Haven't you ever noticed this happening?"

"Yes, I have," I said.

"Then is it not wrong," he said, "and clear that such a person is trying to deal with his fellow-men without being an expert in human nature? If he had been an expert, he would have held the correct view, that there are few perfectly good men and few utterly bad, but very many in between."

"How do you mean?" I asked.

"As with what is extremely small," he said, "or extremely big. Don't you think it is rather rare to find an extremely big or extremely small man, or dog, or anything? or, for that matter, one who is extremely fast or extremely slow or base or noble or white or black? Haven't you noticed, in regard to all of these qualities, that the extremes at both ends are rare and few, but that the in-between types are plentiful and common?"

"Yes," I said.

"Then don't you think," he said, "that if there were to be instituted a contest in villainy, there too the winners would be few?"

"That is probable," I said.

"It is," he said. "But it is not that arguments are like men in that respect—you led me to digress, and I followed—the analogy lies rather in this: you may believe that an argument is true without being an expert in arguments, and then a little later on decide that the argument is false—sometimes it is, and sometimes it isn't—and again the same happens with another and yet another. In particular, those who concern themselves with contentious arguments end up, you know, by considering themselves very clever, and supposing that they alone have discovered that there is nothing sound or reliable in any thing or in any argument, and that all things are simply carried this way and that exactly as in the Euripus,[20] and never remain fixed for a single moment.''

"You are quite right," I said.

"Now suppose, Phaedo," he said, "that there should be a true and reliable argument, one that could be comprehended, but that a man had come up against arguments like these present ones, which sometimes seem true and at other times false. Wouldn't it be a pity if in these circumstances, instead of blaming himself and his own lack of expertise, the man finally, in his distress, gladly transferred the blame from himself to the arguments, and so continued for the rest of his life hating and abusing the arguments, and never acquired truth and knowledge concerning reality?''

"It would indeed be a pity," I said, "most certainly."

"So let us in the first place," he said, "beware of this, and let us not admit that there is likely to be nothing sound in our arguments concerning the soul, but far rather that we are not yet in a sound and healthy condition. We must fight hard and use all our energy to become sound—you and the others for the sake of the rest of your lives, and I because of my very death; for at the moment on this very question I look like being not philosophically-minded, but, like the utterly uneducated, merely contentious. When they quibble about something, they do not consider the true facts concerning the object of their discussion, but are merely anxious that their own views may prevail with the assembled company. It seems to me that at the moment I differ from them only in this: I shall not be endeavoring to prove the truth of my contention to the assembled company (except, perhaps, incidentally), but to prove it, so far as possible, to myself. I reckon, my dear friend—see, how greedy!—that if what I say is true, then so much the better for my convictions; while if there is nothing for a man when he is dead, at any rate during this period just before my death I shall not cause more distress to those present by lamentations, and this folly of mine will not continue

---

[20]The narrow strait between Euboea and Boeotia, with strong and very frequently changing currents.

to exist with me—that would be bad—but will come to an end not long from now.

"I come to face the argument, Simmias and Cebes," he said, "thus fully prepared. And you, if you take my advice, will regard Socrates as of little account, but the truth as of much more, and if you think that anything I say is true, then agree with me, but if not, resist every argument, taking care that in my eagerness I do not deceive you as well as myself, and depart like a bee, leaving my sting behind me.

"Well, let us begin," he said. "First remind me of what you said, if I have obviously forgotten. Simmias, I think, has doubts, and fears that the soul, though it is more divine and noble than the body, may yet perish before it, because it is a sort of attunement. Cebes, I thought, seemed to agree with me in this, that soul is longer-lived than body, but he held that it was not clear to anyone whether the soul, after wearing out many bodies many times over, might not leave behind its last body and now die itself; and whether death might be just this, destruction of soul, since body is perishing all the time, and never stops. Isn't this what we have got to consider, Simmias and Cebes?"

They both agreed that this was so.

"Do you reject, then," he said, "*all* our former arguments, or only some?"

"Only some," they said.

"Well, what," he said, "have you to say about that argument in which we said that learning was recollection, and that this being so our souls must exist somewhere before being bound inside the body?"

"I was thoroughly convinced by that argument at the time, and I still hold to it now, more strongly than to any other," said Cebes.

"It's the same with me," said Simmias, "and I should be very surprised if I were ever to think at all differently about that."

"Well," said Socrates, "you must think differently, Theban friend, if you still stick to this opinion of yours that an attunement is something composite, and that soul is an attunement composed of the elements strung throughout the body. I don't suppose you will admit, though you say it yourself, that an attunement existed before those elements of which it must have been composed; or will you?"

"Certainly not, Socrates," he said.

"You see, then," he said, "that this is what you are in fact saying, when you affirm that the soul existed before entering the form and body of a man, but that it was composed of those things which did not yet exist? An attunement, in fact, is *not* like that with which you compare it. The lyre and the strings and the notes come into being before it, as yet unattuned, and the attunement appears last of all, and dies first. How, then, will this statement harmonize with that other?"

"It won't," said Simmias.

"And yet," he said, "if any theory should be harmonized, certainly the one which is concerned with attunement should."

"It should," said Simmias.

"Well," he said, "this one doesn't harmonize. Which theory do you choose, that learning is recollection, or that soul is an attunement?"

"The former, Socrates," he said, "most decidedly. This other one was founded not on any proof, but only on likelihood and what seemed plausible, which is why most people believe in it; but I know that arguments which rest only upon likelihood are frauds, and that if you are not on your guard against them they completely deceive you, in geometry or in anything else. But the theory about learning and recollection was based on a premise that has every right to be accepted. We said, I think, that our souls' existence before they enter the body is as certain as is the fact that the reality to which we refer by adding the words 'in its essential nature' belongs to them; and I am satisfied that my acceptance of this premise is justified and correct. It seems, therefore, that I cannot possibly accept the proposition, whether I myself have suggested it, or anyone else, that soul is an attunement."

"And look at it in this way, Simmias," he said. "Do you think that the condition of an attunement or of any other composite thing can fail to be determined by the condition of those elements of which it is composed?"

"No."

"Nor, I suppose, that any such thing can affect anything else, or be affected, differently from those elements?"

He admitted that it couldn't.

"An attunement, then, cannot *lead* the things of which it is made; it will simply follow."

He accepted the conclusion.

"Certainly an attunement would not cause vibrations or give forth sounds that were incompatible with the nature of its component parts, or in any other way oppose them."

"Certainly not," he said.

"Well then, doesn't the character of every attunement depend upon the manner of the tuning?"

"I don't understand," he said.

"Isn't it the case," he said, "that only if a thing be brought into tune *more* or *to a greater extent*—just supposing that this is possible—could there be more and greater attunement?—or if less and to a slighter extent, then a lesser and slighter attunement?"

"Certainly."

"Well, is this possible with soul then, that one soul can, even in the slightest degree, be what it is—*be soul*—more and to a greater extent, or less and to a lesser extent, than another?"

"Definitely not," he said.

"Now come," he said, "please tell me this: do we say that some souls have intelligence and virtue, and are good, while others contain folly and wickedness and are bad? And are we right in speaking like that?"

"We are."

"Then what will any one of those who hold that soul is an attunement say these qualities are that exist in our souls—virtue and vice? Will he say that they are another kind of attunement, and lack of attunement? that the good soul has been brought into tune, and contains within itself (which is an attunement) another attunement, while the untuned soul is just itself, and contains no other attunement within itself?"

"I cannot say," said Simmias. "But clearly the man who held that theory would say *something* of the sort."

"We have already agreed," he said, "that no soul is more or less a soul than any other; and this agreement means that no attunement is more or to a greater extent an attunement, or less or to a slighter extent an attunement, than any other. Isn't that so?"

"Yes."

"But that which is neither more nor less an attunement has not been brought into tune either more or less? Is this correct?"

"It is."

"And can that which has not been brought into tune either more or less enjoy a share of attunement that is at all greater or smaller, or will it have the same share?"

"The same."

"Since, in fact, no soul is ever either more or less a soul than any other, soul has never, presumably, been brought into tune either more or less?"

"That is so."

"And that being so, it will never have a greater share of attunement or lack of attunement?"

"It will not."

"And that being so, will one be more wicked or virtuous than another—on the assumption that virtue is attunement, and wickedness lack of attunement?"

"No."

"Or rather, Simmias, to be accurate, no soul will be at all vicious, if it is an attunement; for if an attunement is just this, an attunement, it will never, I suppose, be at all out of tune?"

"No."

"And so a soul, just because it is a soul, will never be wicked."

"It couldn't be, in view of what we have said."

"So according to this argument we find that all souls of all living creatures will be equally good, since all souls are souls equally as much as each other."

"I agree, Socrates," he said.

"Do you think we are right in saying this?" he asked, "or that the argument would come to this if the premise had been sound, that soul is an attunement?"

"Decidedly not," he said.

"Now," he said, "is there in your opinion anything, of all that man possesses, that *rules* him, except his soul—especially if it is a wise one?"

"No."

"And does it accord with the emotions of the body, or does it oppose them? I mean, for example, if the body is hot and thirsty, forcing the man to do the opposite of what he desires, compelling him not to drink; or when he's hungry, not to eat—and surely there are hundreds of other ways in which we see the soul opposing the body, aren't there?"

"Yes, indeed."

"And didn't we agree before that soul if it were indeed an attunement, could never possibly be at discord with the tension or relaxation or vibration of its component parts, but would follow them and never lead?"

"We did," he said, "most certainly."

"Well, doesn't it seem now to be doing exactly the reverse, *leading* all those elements of which it is said to be composed, and opposing them in almost everything throughout life, and lording it over them in almost every conceivable way—sometimes cruelly, punishing them and causing pain (in gymnastics and in medicine), sometimes more gently, and sometimes using threats, sometimes admonition, holding converse with the desires and passions and fears, as though it were something quite distinct? Homer too, I suppose, has represented this same sort of thing, in the *Odyssey*,[21] where he says of Odysseus: 'And he smote his breast and rebuked his heart thus: "Be strong, my heart; you have endured worse ere now." ' Do you think that he wrote this with the idea that the soul was an attunement, the sort of thing to be led by the emotions of the body? or that it was something capable of leading them and of ruling over them, a thing much more divine than such as should merit comparison with a mere attunement?"

"I should certainly say that was his idea, Socrates."

"Then it is quite wrong, my friend, for us to say that soul is an attunement. If we did we should be disagreeing with the divine poet Homer and contradicting ourselves."

"That is so," he said.

"Well now," said Socrates, "the Theban Harmonia[22] has become fairly propitious toward us, it seems, as we take our leave of her; but what about Cadmus, Cebes?" he said, "how shall we propitiate him? what argument shall we use?"

"I think you will find one," said Cebes. "This argument of yours about attunement, at any rate, I found most surprising and unexpected. When Simmias was speaking, when he had a difficulty, I very much wondered whether anyone would be able to deal with his argument; so that it struck me as very odd when it did not withstand the very first onset of your remarks. I wouldn't be surprised if the same should happen to Cadmus' argument."

"My friend," said Socrates, "do not boast, in case some evil influence should put to flight the remarks that are going to be made. But that will be as God wills. Like Homer's heroes, we will come to grips, and see if there really is any truth in your argument. What you may be summed up thus: you think that it should be proved that our souls are indestructible and immortal, if the confidence of a philosopher on the point of death is not to be merely unintelligent and stupid, when he confidently holds the belief that after death he will fare much better, in the next world, than if the life he is ending had been lived in a

---

[21]Homer, *Odyssey*, 20.17.

[22]Harmonia (the word means "attunement") was the daughter of Aphrodite and wife of Cadmus, legendary founder of Thebes. There was a cult of both Harmonia and Cadmus in Thebes, the native town of Simmias and Cebes.

different way. As for our showing that the soul is something strong and divine, and that it existed before we became human beings, you say that there is no reason why this shouldn't indicate, not immortality, but only that the soul is long-lived, and existed somewhere an unimaginably long time ago, and knew and did all sorts of things, but that nevertheless it was not immortal—that its very arrival in human body was, in fact, the beginning of its destruction, a sort of disease: it lives this life in anguish, and finally, at what is called death, it perishes. You say that it makes no difference whether it enters into a body once or many times, so far as the fears of each one of us is concerned. It is natural that a man should be afraid, if he had any sense, if he did not know and could not prove that it is immortal. That, I think, is roughly your argument, Cebes. I purposely repeat it several times, so that it may not escape us, and so that if you like you may add to it or subtract."

"Well, I don't want to add or subtract anything now," said Cebes. "That is my argument."

So after a long pause and considerable reflection, Socrates began: "You are asking for quite a lot, Cebes. We must deal very thoroughly with the causes of generation and destruction in general. I will tell you, if you like, of my own experiences in relation to these questions. Then, if you think that in anything I say there is something to help you, you will use it to support your argument."

"Well, I do like," said Cebes.

"Then listen, and I will tell you. When I was young, Cebes," he said, "I became very keen on this learning which they call 'physical' philosophy. It seemed to me a wonderful sort of study, to know the causes of everything, why each thing comes into being and why it perishes and why it exists. And as I considered it I often turned over in my mind first of all such questions as these: 'Are living creatures nurtured when the hot and the cold undergo putrefaction, as some people used to say? and is it the blood that we do our thinking with, or the air or the fire? or is it none of these, but the brain which provides the sensations of hearing and seeing and smelling—and did memory and opinion come from these, and from memory and opinion (when it had acquired stability) did knowledge come into being? —and, again, when I considered the decay of these things, and the phenomena of the sky and of the earth, it finally seemed to me that I was the most stupid creature in the world, so far as this sort of investigation was concerned. I will give you ample evidence of this: what I had at first definitely known, in my own opinion and in that of others, I was so completely blinded by this sort of enquiry as to *un*learn—even what I had formerly thought I knew, on many subjects, and particularly why a man grows. I had formerly thought that it was clear to everyone that he grew through eating and drinking; that when, through food, new flesh and bones came into being to supplement the old, and thus in the same way each kind of thing was supplemented by new substances proper to it, only then did the mass which was small become large, and in the same way the small man big. That was my opinion. Don't you think it was reasonable?''

"I do,'' said Cebes.

"Consider this too. I used to think that I was justified in my conclusion, whenever a big man standing by a short one appeared to be taller 'just by the head'—and a horse taller than a horse in the same way; and there are still clearer examples of this—ten seemed to me to be greater than eight because of the addition of two, and the two-cubit measure to be greater than the one-cubit because it exceeded it by half its own length.''

"And what,'' said Cebes, "is your opinion about them now?''

"That I am very far,'' he said, "from thinking that I know the cause of any of these things, since I can't admit, when one is added to one, either that the one to which it is added has become two, or that that which is added *and* the original one to which it is added have become two, simply by the addition of the one to the other. I am surprised that while the two were separate, each was just one and no 'two' existed, and then when they came into contact with each other, this should be the cause of the generation of the 'two'—the combination formed by their juxtaposition. Again, if you cut one thing in half, I can no longer be convinced that this, the division, has been the cause of the generation of two; for there is a cause of the generation of 'two' opposite to that of the former instance. First it was because they were brought together alongside of each other, and one was added to another, and next it was because one was taken away and separated from another. Nor can I still persuade myself that I know how a unit comes into being at all, nor, to be brief, how anything else comes into being or perishes or exists—by *this kind* of reckoning, that is; I make up a sort of wild jumble of a method of my own, but I certainly don't want *this* one.

"I once heard someone reading from a book, which he said was by Anaxagoras, and saying that Mind was what arranged everything and caused everything. I was delighted with this 'cause,' and it seemed to me to be somehow rather appropriate that mind should be responsible for everything, and I supposed that if this were so, the ordering Mind ordered everything and placed each thing severally as it was best that it should be; so that if anyone wanted to discover the cause of anything, how it came into being or perished or existed, he simply needed to discover what kind of existence was *best* for it, or what it was best that it should do or have done to it. According to this line of reasoning, the only thing that man needed to consider in regard to that particular question or any other was simply what was best. And this same man was bound to know also what was *worse*, for this was included in that same knowledge.

"In view of this I was delighted to think that I had found an instructor in the cause of things after my own mind—Anaxagoras—and that he would show me first of all whether the earth was flat or round, and then, when he had shown me, would go on to explain the reason and the necessity of its being as it was, telling me what was *better*, and that it had been better that it should be like this; and if he said that it was in the middle of the universe, I thought that he would explain further that it had been better that it should be in the middle; and if he proved that to me, I was prepared to require no further cause of any kind. Further, I was prepared to make similar enquiry about the sun and moon, and the stars too, about their relative speed and their solstices and the other things that happened to them, how it was better that each should do and experience the things that it did. I never thought that Anaxagoras, when he said that they were ordered by Mind, would bring in any *other* cause *as well* to explain them, *apart* from the fact that it was best that they should be as they were. I supposed that in assigning the cause to each severally and to all *en bloc* he would go on to explain what was best in each case and what was good for all combined. I would not have sacrificed my hopes for a fortune: I eagerly got hold of his books and read for all I was worth, so as to know as soon as I could what was best and what was worse.

"High indeed were the hopes, my friend, from which I was parted, when, as I continued on my course of reading, I saw a man making no use of Mind and not making it in any way responsible for the ordering of things, simply accounting mists and air and water and many other strange things causes. It seemed to me that it was just as if someone were to say that all that Socrates does is to be attributed to his mind, and then, undertaking to state the causes of all that I do, were to say first of all that the reason for my sitting here now is that my body is composed of bones and muscles, and that the bones are hard and have joints between them, while the muscles are such as can be stretched or relaxed, and together with the flesh and skin which keeps them all together are laid about the bones; and as the bones swing loosely in their sockets, it is the muscles, which relax them or make them taut, that enable me now to bend my limbs, and that *that* is why I sit here now in this bent posture. And he might give you other such causes to explain my talking to you, accounting voice and air and hearing and hundreds of other such things responsible, neglecting to give the *real* reasons—that, as the Athenians have decided that it is better to condemn me, I for my part have thought it better to sit here, and more right and proper not to run away, but to undergo whatever penalty they may impose. Indeed, by the dog! these muscles and bones would long ago have been, I think, in the region of Megara or Boeotia, borne by an opinion of what was best, did I not think it right and honorable to undergo whatever punishment the city should prescribe, rather than to escape and run away.

"But to call such things causes is quite absurd. If you were to say that *without having such things*—bones and sinews and all the other things that I have got—I wouldn't be able to carry out my decisions, you would be right; but to say that my actions are *caused* by these (and that too although I 'act because of Mind'!), rather than simply by the choice of what is best, would be an utterly slip-shod sort of argument. Fancy not being able to see that the real cause is very different from the mere *sine qua non* of any cause! Yet that is what most people, groping, as it were, in the dark, seem to call 'cause,' using a name that doesn't belong to it. And so one[23] man encompasses the earth with a vortex, and claims that it is kept in its place by the heavens, while another[24] puts the air underneath it as a support, as though it were a sort of broad kneading-trough. But they don't even look for the force that causes things to be now arranged in the best manner in which they possibly could be arranged, nor do they think that this force has any divine power; they think that they might at some time find an Atlas stronger than this one[25] and more immortal and better able to hold all together, and do not suppose

---

[23]Empedocles.

[24]Anaximenes, Anaxagoras, Democritus.

[25]Atlas was a mythical giant who supported the heavens on his shoulders. Socrates means that the real "Atlas" is the power that arranges things as is best.

that that which is really good and 'fitting' can fit or hold anything together. I would very much like to learn about such a cause from someone—anyone you please; but since I have been denied this, and have not been able to find out about it for myself or learn it from anyone else, would you like me to demonstrate, Cebes, how I have busied myself with the second line of approach toward the search for the cause?''

"There is nothing that I should like better," he said.

"I decided after this," he said, "when I had failed in my study of *things*, that I must beware of experiencing what those who look at and study the sun during an eclipse experience. Some of them are dazzled and blinded if they don't look at its reflection in water or something of that sort. That was roughly my idea; I was afraid that my soul might be utterly blinded if I regarded things with the eyes and tried to grasp them with each of the senses. I decided that I should take refuge with *definitions*, and study the truth of things by means of them. (Perhaps my analogy is in a way not quite right: for I don't altogether admit that he who studies things by means of definitions is using images more than he who studies things by means of physical examples.) Anyhow, this was my procedure: taking as my starting-point in every instance the definition that I judge to be most reliable, I assume to be genuine whatever seems to me to be in accordance with it—both in regard to causation and in regard to everything else. Whatever doesn't seem to harmonize, I assume to be untrue. But I want to make my meaning clearer, for I don't think you understand at present.''

"I'm afraid I don't," said Cebes, "not completely."

"Well," he said, "what I mean is this. It is nothing new, but simply what I have always been talking about, in our present discussion as well as constantly at other times. I am going to undertake to expound to you the kind of cause with which I am concerned, and I will return once more to those much-talked-of things and take my start from them—making it my premise that there is a Beautiful in the absolute and a Good and a Great and so on. If you grant me this and agree that they exist, I hope to expound the cause to you, and reveal that soul is immortal.''

"I do agree," said Cebes, "so please go straight on."

"Consider," he said, "what follows next and see if you agree with me. It seems to me that if there is anything *else* beautiful besides the Beautiful Itself, it is so purely and simply because it partakes of that 'Beautiful.' The same is true, in my opinion, of every kind of thing. Do you agree with this sort of 'cause'?''

"I do," he said.

"I no longer learn about, and cannot understand," he said, "these other subtle 'causes,' but if anyone tells me that anything is beautiful, as having a bright color or a special shape or anything of that sort, I dismiss the other 'reasons'—all the others confuse me—and purely and simply and perhaps naïvely keep to this, that the only thing that makes it beautiful is the presence of or its participation in—or whatever the relationship may be—that 'Beautiful.' I do not now insist upon any particular relationship, but only that all beautiful things are beautiful simply *because* of the Beautiful. This, I think, is the safest answer to give myself or anyone else, and I think that if I cling to this I shall not fall, and that it is safe for me or anyone else to answer that the beautiful things are beautiful simply because of the Beautiful. Don't you agree?''

"Yes, I do.''

"And the large things are large and the larger are larger because of largeness, and the smaller are smaller because of smallness?''

"Yes.''

"So you too wouldn't accept the statement, if anyone were to say that one person was taller than another by a head, and that the shorter person was shorter by reason of this same thing. You would testify that you for your part simply affirm that anything larger than anything else is larger only because of Largeness—that this is the reason of its being larger, its largeness; and that which is smaller is smaller simply because of Smallness—this is the reason of its being smaller, its smallness. You would be afraid, I expect, that if you said someone was taller and someone shorter by a head, you might come up against an opponent who would say that the taller is then taller and the shorter is shorter by reason of the same thing—and moreover that the bigger is bigger by reason of the head, which is a small thing; and that this is extraordinary, that someone should be big by reason of something small! Wouldn't you be afraid of this retort?''

Cebes laughed and said, "Yes, I would.''

"Then," he said, "you would be afraid to say that ten is more than eight by two—that it exceeds eight on account of this cause, rather than by reason of Quantity, and simply on account of that? and that the two-cubit length is greater than the cubit by a half, rather than by reason of Size? There would be the same fear, I imagine."

"Yes," he said.

"Then you would beware of saying that when one is added to one the addition is the cause of two, or that when one is separated off from one the division is the cause? And you would shout loudly that you don't know of anything coming into being in any other way than by coming to participate in the particular reality of each thing in which it comes to participate, and that in these instances you have no other reason to give for the generation of two than the participation in Duality (Twoness), and that what is going to be two *must* participate in this, while whatever is going to be one must participate in Oneness; but these divisions and additions and all the other niceties of this sort you would disregard, leaving them to those wiser than yourself to make use of in reply. You, yourself, in your reply, shying at your own shadow, as they say, and your inexperience—would cling to the safety of your 'hypothesis.' If anyone were to fasten upon the hypothesis itself, you would disregard him and not reply until you had considered whether its consequences agreed with each other or not; and when you *should* have to give an account of the hypothesis itself, you would do so in just the same way, positing a further hypothesis, whichever seemed best of those more ultimate—until you came to something sufficient for your purpose. And you would not jumble up the two together like the eristics, talking about the basic hypothesis and its consequences in one and the same breath, if you wanted to discover any truth. The eristics are perhaps not in the least interested in or concerned with *this*: they are so clever that they are quite capable of making a complete muddle of everything without disturbing their own self-satisfaction. But you, I think, if you are a philosopher, will proceed in the manner which I am describing."

"That is correct," said Simmias and Cebes simultaneously.

Echecrates. Certainly, Phaedo, and with good reason too. I should say that what he said is clear enough even to a man of very little intelligence.

Phaedo. Yes, Echecrates, that's what all those who were present thought.

Echecrates. I am not surprised, as we do who were not there, but only hear now what he said, at second hand. But what was said after that?

Phaedo. I think that when he had got their consent to this, and it was agreed that each of the Forms really existed, and that everything else, participating in them, was named after them, he went on to ask next: "Well, if this is your opinion, surely when you say that Simmias is taller than Socrates, but shorter than Phaedo, you are then saying that both these things, both tallness and shortness, exist in Simmias?"

"Yes."

"But," he said, "you agree that 'Simmias surpassing Socrates' is not really what the words might suggest? You would say, wouldn't you, that it is not an essential attribute of Simmias that he should surpass Socrates—that he doesn't do so simply because he is Simmias—but rather that he does so simply by reason of the tallness that he happens to possess? Nor would you say that he surpasses Socrates because Socrates is Socrates, but rather because Socrates has shortness, compared with the tallness of Simmias?"

"True."

"Nor would you say that Simmias is surpassed by Phaedo because Phaedo is Phaedo, but rather because Phaedo has tallness compared with the shortness of Simmias?"

"That is so."

"And so Simmias is said to be both short and tall, and is, in fact, between the two—submitting his *shortness* to be surpassed by the *tallness* of Phaedo, and presenting his tallness which surpasses the shortness of Socrates." As he said this, Socrates smiled and said, "It looks as though I shall be talking like a professor! Anyway, that's how things are, I imagine."

He agreed.

"I am saying this because I want you to reach the same conclusions as I have. It seems to me that Tallness Itself will never be tall *and* short at one and the same time, and what is more that *that tallness which is in us* never admits the short and will not be overcome by it; one of two things must happen—either it flees and beats a retreat whenever its opposite, the short, approaches it, or else, when that comes, it has perished. It refuses to hold its ground and admit the shortness and to be different from what it was before. If I, for example, have received and admitted shortness, and am still the person I really am, then I, this same person, am short; but that tallness, being tall, has not dared to be short. In the same way 'the short' that is in us will never become or be tall, nor will any one of the opposites, while still retaining its identity, become and be the opposite at the same time: either it departs or it perishes, when this happens to it."

"That is exactly my view," said Cebes.

One of those who were present, hearing this—who he was I don't clearly remember—said, "Good Heavens, in what we said earlier on, didn't we agree to exactly the reverse of what we are saying now—that the greater *does* come into being from the smaller, and the smaller from the greater, and in a word that this *is* generation where opposites are concerned—that they are generated from their opposites? But now it seems to me that we are saying that this could never happen."

Socrates turned his head and listened and said, "Bravo! Thank you for reminding me. But you don't realize the difference between what we are talking about now and what we were then. *Then* it was said that an opposite thing is generated from the opposite thing, but *now* that the opposite *itself* could never be opposite to itself—either that which exists in us or that which exists in nature. *Then* we were talking about the things which *possess* the opposites, calling them by the same name as the opposites themselves have, but now we are talking about those opposites themselves which, by their presence, give their names to the things called after them; and we say that they themselves would never submit to becoming one another." Saying this he glanced at Cebes and said, "And you then, Cebes, have you been troubled by any of these difficulties that he has raised?"

"No, I haven't," said Cebes, "not this time; but I don't deny that many things are troubling me."

"We have simply agreed," he said, "that the opposite will never be opposite to itself."

"Quite," he said.

"Now please consider this too, and see if you will agree. Do you talk about 'hot' and 'cold'?"

"Yes."

"As being the same as snow and fire?"

"No, certainly not."

" 'Hot' is different from fire, and 'cold' from snow?"

"Yes."

"But I think you believe that snow, if it admits heat, will, as we said earlier on, no longer be what it was before—snow *and* hot at the same time; at the approach of heat it will either make way for it, or perish."

"Yes."

"And that fire, when the cold approaches it, will either make way for it or perish; it will never dare to receive the coldness and still remain what it was before, fire—*and* be cold as well.''

"That's right," he said.

"Then it is the case with some of these things that not only is the Form itself entitled for ever to the name that is given to it, but also something else which, while not the same thing as that Form, nevertheless always, in every instance, presents the manifestation of it. Perhaps this will make my meaning clearer: the Odd, I suppose, always deserves this name which we give to it, doesn't it?''

"Yes."

"Now is this the only thing—this is my question—or is there something else as well, different from the Odd, to which we must always apply the term 'odd,' because its essential nature is such that it is inseparable from the Odd? I mean by this the sort of thing that is true—to mention one instance out of many—in the case of the number three. Don't you think that it must always be entitled not only to its own name, but also to the term 'odd'— even though the Odd is not the same thing? Such is the nature of 'three' and 'five,' a whole half of the number-series, that while they are different from the Odd, each one of them is, always, odd. Similarly, 'two' and 'four' and the whole of the other series of numbers, while being different from the Even, are nevertheless, each one of them, always even. Do you agree, or not?''

"Of course," he said.

"Consider, then, what I want to point out," he said. "It is this: not only, it seems, do these opposites refuse to admit each other, but also those things that are not opposite to each other, but always contain the opposites, will not admit that character which is opposite to the character that they contain—instead, when it attacks, they either perish or retreat. Shall we not say that 'three' will perish or suffer anything rather than stand its ground and, while still remaining three, become even?''

"Certainly," said Cebes.

"Again," he said, "two is not opposite to three?''

"No."

"Not only, then, do opposite Forms refuse to stand firm at each other's attack, but certain other things refuse to withstand the opposites when they attack."

"Very true," he said.

"Would you have us then," he said, "determine what sort of things these are?''

"Yes."

"Well, Cebes," he said, "won't they be those things which compel anything they take possession of to have not only its own character, but also in every case the character of some opposite?"

"How do you mean?"

"What we were saying just now. You know, I suppose, that whatever the character of 'three' takes hold of must be not only 'three' but also 'odd'?"

"Yes."

"And the character which is opposed to that quality, whatever it may be, that brings this about will never assail such a thing?"

"It won't."

"But the odd brought this about?"

"Yes."

"And the opposite of this is the character of the Even?"

"Yes."

"So the character of the Even will never come against 'three'?"

"No, indeed."

" 'Three' has no share in the Even. 'Three,' then, is *un*even."

"Yes."

"Now what I said we have to determine is, what sort of things, not themselves opposite to a thing, nevertheless refuse to admit that opposite—as in the present case 'three,' which is not opposite to the even, but nevertheless refuses to admit it, since 'three' always brings into the field the opposite of the even; and 'two' brings with it the opposite of the odd, fire the opposite of the cold, and so on. See now whether this is your definition—that not only will an opposite refuse to admit its opposite, but also anything which brings with itself something opposite to that which it attacks never itself admits the opposite of what is thus brought. Let me remind you once again; there is no harm in hearing several times. 'Five' will not admit the character of the Even, nor 'ten,' which is the double of 'five,' that of the Odd. Again, 'double' itself *is* opposite to something *else*, yet it will not admit the character of the Odd; nor will 'once-and-a-half,' or such things as that (the *half* of something) admit the character of the Whole—nor will a 'third,' or any such thing as that, if you follow and agree with what I say?"

"Most certainly I agree," he said, "and follow."

"Tell me, then," he said, "from the beginning; and do not answer simply in the terms of my question, but copy what I do now—I say this because, as a result of what we have just been saying, I can see, beside that safe sort of answer that I talked about at first, another way of safety. If you were to ask me what, when present in its body, will always make a thing hot, I shall not give you that safe, foolish answer 'heat,' but, after what we have just said, a more subtle answer, 'fire.' And if you ask what, when present in a body, will always make it ill, I shall say not 'illness' but 'fever'; and if you ask what, when present in a number, will always make it odd, I shall answer not 'oddness,' but 'oneness,' and so on. Does that give you a full enough understanding of what I want?"

"Quite," he said.

"Answer me, then," he said: "what, when present in a body, will always make it alive?"

"Soul," he said.

"And this is *always* so?"

"Of course," he said.

"Then soul always brings life with it when it approaches whatever it takes hold of?"

"It does," he said.

"Has 'life' an opposite, or not?"

"It has," he said.

"What is that opposite?"

"Death."

"Then it follows from our previous admissions that soul will never admit the opposite of what it brings with it?"

"Certainly," said Cebes.

"Well, what did we just now call that which will not receive the character of the Even?"

"Uneven," he said.

"And that which doesn't admit justice—and that which doesn't admit culture?"

"Uncultured," he said, "and unjust."

"Well, and what do we call that which doesn't admit death?"

"Deathless," he said.

"And soul does not admit death?"

"Quite."

"Then soul is deathless."

"It is."

"Well," he said, "may we say that this has been proved, or what do you think?"

"Thoroughly, Socrates."

"How about you, Cebes?" he said. "If the 'uneven' had

necessarily to be indestructible, is it not the case that 'three' would be indestructible?''

"Definitely."

"And if 'that which cannot be heated' had necessarily to be indestructible, whenever anyone brought 'hot' up against snow, the snow would retreat safe and unmelted? It would not have perished, nor again would it have stood its ground and admitted the heat.''

"True," he said.

"In the same way, I suppose, if 'what cannot be cooled' were indestructible, whenever something cold approached fire, the fire would not be quenched and perish, but retreat and depart safe and sound.''

"Necessarily," he said.

"Then mustn't we say the same about what is deathless? If that which will not admit death is also incapable of admitting destruction, it is impossible for soul, when death assails it, to perish; for according to our agreements it will not admit death or pass into a state of being dead, just as 'three' will not become even, as we said, any more than the odd will—and fire will not become cold, any more than the heat in the fire will. 'But,' someone may say, 'although the odd may not become even at the approach of the even, what is there to prevent it from *perishing* and *in that way* ceasing to be odd, and becoming even?' If someone says this we will not be able to prove that it doesn't perish; for that which will not admit the even is not incapable of admitting destruction. If we *had* admitted *that*, we could easily prove that at the approach of the even the odd and 'threeness' depart and withdraw; and the same applies to fire and 'hot,' and all the rest—we could give similar proofs in regard to them, couldn't we?''

"Yes, indeed."

"And so now, in the case of that which will not admit death, if we are agreed that it is also incapable of admitting destruction, then *soul*, in addition to being incapable of admitting death, will be incapable of admitting destruction also; if we are not so agreed, then we shall need some other argument.''

"So far as that is concerned," he said, "we need no other argument; if that which cannot admit death, although everlasting, will admit destruction, I don't see how anything else could resist it.''

"But I suppose," said Socrates, "that it will be agreed by

everyone that God, and the Form itself of Life, and anything else
that cannot admit death, never perishes."

"Yes, by everyone, most certainly," he said, "both by
men and—even more emphatically, I imagine—by gods."

"Then since what cannot admit death is also incapable of
admitting destruction, surely soul, if it is incapable of admitting
death, is incapable of admitting destruction also."

"Inevitably."

"So when death assails the man, the mortal part of him, it
seems, dies, but the deathless part withdraws, and goes away
safe and uncorrupted, giving place to death."

"It appears so."

"Then soul, Cebes," he said, "is certainly deathless and
indestructible, and our souls really will exist in the other world."

"For my part, Socrates," he said, "I have nothing more to
say against this, and I cannot doubt what you say. But if
Simmias here, or anyone else, has anything to say, it is best
that he should not keep silent; because if anyone wants to say or
hear anything about matters of this sort, I don't know of any
time to which he might postpone it that would be more suitable
than the present."

"Well, I have no ground for doubt either," said Simmias,
"so far as the argument goes. But in view of the weightiness of
the subject, and my poor opinion of human frailty, I am bound
still to have doubts inside me about what has been said."

"Quite, Simmias," said Socrates: "you are right in saying
that, and you should examine our primary hypotheses still more
thoroughly, even if you do trust them; and if you have analysed
them satisfactorily, you will, I suppose, be guided by the argument so far as it is humanly possible to follow it up; and then if
this much itself becomes clear, you will seek no more than
that."

"True," he said.

"But it is right, my friends," he said, "to bear in mind that
if the soul is immortal, we need to care for it, not only for the
sake of this period to which belongs what we call life, but also
for the sake of all time; and now it will be clear that if we are
going to neglect it, we shall be running a great risk. If death
were separation from everything, it would be a godsend to the
wicked to be freed when they died, together with the soul, from
the body and from their own wickedness; but as it is, since soul
is seen to be immortal, there will be no escape nor any salvation
except through becoming as good and as wise as possible. The

only thing the soul takes with it to the other world is its education and culture, which are said to be the greatest help or the greatest hindrance that the dead man can have, from the moment when he starts on his journey to that region.

"The story goes that when a man dies his guardian deity, to whose lot it fell to watch over the man while he was alive, undertakes to conduct him to some place where those who gather must submit their cases to judgment before journeying to the other world; and this they do with the guide to whom the task has been assigned of taking them there. When they have there met with their appropriate fates and waited the appropriate time, another guide brings them back here again, after many long cycles of time.[26] The journey, then, is not as Aeschylus' Teleph describes it: he says that a single track leads to the other world, but I don't think that it is 'single' or 'one' at all. If it were, there would be no need of guides; no one would lose the way, if there were only one road. As it is, there seem to be many partings of the way and places where three roads meet. I say this, judging by the sacrifices and rites that are performed here. The orderly and wise soul follows on its way and is not ignorant of its surroundings; but that which yearns for the body, as I said before, after its long period of passionate excitement concerning the body and the visible region, departs only after much struggling and suffering, taken by force, with great difficulty, by the appropriate deity. When it arrives where the others are, the unpurified soul, guilty of some act for which atonement has not been made, tainted with wicked murder or the commission of some other crime which is akin to this and the work of a kindred soul, is shunned and avoided by everyone, and no one will be its fellow-traveler or guide, but all by itself it wanders, the victim of every kind of doubt and distraction, until certain periods of time have elapsed, and when they are completed, it is carried perforce to its appropriate habitation. But that soul which has spent its life in a pure and temperate fashion finds companions and divine guides, and each dwells in the place that is suited to it. There are many wonderful places in the world, and the world itself is not of such a kind or so small as is supposed by those who generally discourse about it; of that a certain person has convinced me."

"How do you mean, Socrates?" asked Simmias. "I too

---

[26]According to the *Republic* the period spent in Hades is a thousand years, since every soul must be punished or rewarded, as the case may be, ten times over for its good or evil deeds.

have heard a great deal about the world, but not the doctrine that has found favor with you. I would much like to hear about it."

"Well, I don't think it requires the skill of a Glaucus to relate my theory; but to prove that it is true would be a task, I think, too difficult for the skill of Glaucus. In the first place I would probably not even be capable of proving it, and then again, even if I did know how to, I don't think my lifetime would be long enough for me to give the explanation. There is, however, no reason why I should not tell you about the shape of the earth as I believe it to be, and its various regions."

"That will certainly do," said Simmias.

"I am satisfied," he said, "in the first place, that if it is spherical and in the middle of the universe, it has no need of air or any other force of that sort to make it impossible for it to fall; it is sufficient by itself to maintain the symmetry of the universe and the equipoise of the earth itself. A thing which is in equipoise and placed in the midst of something symmetrical will not be able to incline more or less toward any particular direction; being in equilibrium, it will remain motionless. This is the first point," he said, "of which I am convinced."

"And quite rightly so," said Simmias.

"And again, I am sure that it is very big," he said, "and that we who live between the Phasis river and the pillars of Hercules inhabit only a small part of it, living round the coast of the sea like ants or frogs by a pond, while many others live elsewhere, in many similar regions. All over the earth there are many hollows of all sorts of shape and size, into which the water and mist and air have collected. The earth itself is a pure thing lying in the midst of the pure heavens, in which are the stars; and most of those who generally discourse about such things call these heavens the 'ether.' They say that these things I have mentioned are the precipitation of the 'ether' and flow continually into the hollows of the earth. We do not realize that we are living in the earth's hollows, and suppose that we are living up above on the top of the earth—just as if someone living in the middle of the sea-bed were to suppose that he was living on the top of the sea, and then, noticing the sun and the stars through the water, were to imagine that the sea was sky; through sluggishness and weakness he might never have reached the top of the sea, nor by working his way up and popping up out of the sea into this region have observed how much purer and more beautiful it is than theirs; nor even heard about it from anyone who had seen it. That is exactly what has happened to us: we live in a hollow in the earth, but suppose that we are living on top of it; and we call the air sky, as though this were the sky, and the stars moved across it. But the truth of the matter is just the same—through weakness and sluggishness we are not able to pass through to the limit of the air. If anyone could climb to the air's surface, or grow wings and fly up, then, as here the fishes of the sea pop their heads up and see our world, so he would pop his head up and catch sight of that upper region; and if his nature were such that he could bear the sight, he would come to realize that *that* was the real sky and the real light and the real earth. This earth of ours, and the stones, and all the region here is corrupted and corroded, just as the things in the sea are corroded by the brine; and in the sea nothing worth mentioning grows, and practically nothing is perfect—there are just caves and sand and indescribable mud and mire, wherever there is earth too, and there is nothing in any way comparable with the beautiful things of our world; but those things in the upper world, in their turn, would be seen far to surpass the things of our world. If it is a good thing to tell a story, then you should listen, Simmias, and hear what the regions on the earth beneath the sky are really like.''

"We should certainly very much like to hear this story, Socrates,'' said Simmias.

"In the first place, then, my friend, the true earth is said to appear to anyone looking at it from above like those balls which are made of twelve pieces of leather, variegated, a patchwork of colors, of which the colors that we know here—those that our painters use—are samples, as it were. There the whole earth is made up of such colors, and of colors much brighter and purer than these: part of it is purple, of wondrous beauty, and part again golden, and all that part which is white is whiter than the whiteness of chalk or snow; and it is made up of all the other colors likewise, and of even more numerous and more beautiful colors than those that we have seen. Indeed these very hollows of the earth, full of water and of air, are said to present a kind of color as they glitter amid the variety of all the other colors, so that the whole appears as one continuous variegated picture. And in this colorful world the same may be said of the things that grow up—trees and flowers and all the fruits; and in the same way again the smoothness and transparency and colors of the mountains and of the stars are more beautiful than in *our* world. Our little stones, these highly prized ones, sards and jaspers and emeralds and so on, are but fragments of those there; there, they say, *everything* is like this, or even more beautiful than these stones that we possess. The reason is that the stones there are pure, and not corroded or corrupted, as ours are, by rust and brine, as a result of all that has collected here, bringing ugliness and diseases to stones and to soil, and to animals and to plants besides. The earth itself, they say, is ornamented with all these things, and moreover with gold and silver and all things of that sort. They are exposed to view on the surface, many in number and large, all over the earth, so that the earth is a sight for the blessed to behold. There are many living creatures upon it, including men; some live inland, some live round about the borders of the air as we do on the coasts of the sea, while others again live on islands encompassed by air near the mainland. In a word, what the water and the sea are to us, for our purposes, the air is to them; and what the air is to us, the 'ether' is to them. Their climate is such that they are free from illnesses, and live much longer than the inhabitants of our world, and surpass us in sight and hearing and wisdom and so on, by as much as the pureness of air surpasses that of water, and the pureness of 'ether' surpasses that of air. Moreover they have groves and temples sacred to the gods, in which the gods really dwell, and utterances and prophesies and visions of the gods; and other such means of intercourse are for them direct and face to face. And they see the sun and moon and stars as they really are, and their blessedness in other respects is no less than in these.

"This is the nature of the earth as a whole, and of the regions round about it, and in the earth, in the cavities all over its surface, are many regions, some deeper and wider than that in which we live, others deeper but with a narrower opening than ours, while others again are shallower than this one and broader. All of these are connected with each other by underground passages, some narrower, some wider—bored through in many different places; and they have channels along which much water flows, from one region to another, as into mixing-bowls; and they have, too, enormous ever-flowing underground rivers and enormous hot and cold springs, and a great deal of fire, and huge rivers of fire, and many rivers also of wet mud, some clearer, some denser, like the rivers of mud that flow before the lava in Sicily, and the lava itself; and they fill the several regions into which, at any given time, they happen to be flowing. They are all set in motion, upwards and downwards, by a sort of pulsation within the earth. The existence of this pulsation is due to something like this: one of the chasms of the earth is not only the biggest of them all, but is bored *right through* the earth—the one that Homer meant, when he said that it is 'very far off, where is the deepest abyss of all below the earth.' Homer elsewhere—and many other poets besides—have called this Tartarus. Now into this chasm all the rivers flow together, and then they all flow back out again; and their natures are determined by the sort of earth through which they flow. The reason why all these streams flow out of here and flow in is this, that this fluid has no bottom or resting-place: it simply pulsates and surges upwards and downwards, and the air and the wind round about it does the same; they follow with it, whenever it rushes to the far side of the earth, and again whenever it rushes back to this side, and as the breath that men breathe is always exhaled and inhaled in succession, so the wind pulsates in unison with the fluid, creating terrible, unimaginable blasts as it enters and as it comes out. Whenever the water withdraws to what we call the lower region, the streams flow into the regions on the farther side of the earth and fill them, like irrigating canals; and whenever it leaves those parts and rushes back here, it fills the streams here afresh, and they when filled flow through their several channels and through the earth, and as each set of streams arrives at the particular regions to which its passages lead, it creates seas and marshes and rivers and springs; and then, sinking back again down into the earth, some encircling larger and more numerous regions, others fewer and smaller, these streams issue back into Tartarus again—some of them at a point much lower down than that from which they were emitted, others only a little lower, but all flow in *below* the place from which they poured forth. Some flow into the same part of Tartarus from which they sprang, some into the part on the opposite side; and others again go right round in a circle, coiling themselves round the earth several times like snakes, before descending as low as possible and falling back again.

"It is possible to descend in either direction as far as the center, but not beyond, for the ground on either side begins then to slope *upwards* in the face of *both* sets of streams.

"There are many large streams of every sort, but among these many there are four that I would mention in particular. The largest, the one which flows all round in a circle furthest from the center, is that which is called Oceanus; over against this, and flowing in the opposite direction, is Acheron, which flows through many desert places and finally, as it flows under the earth, reaches the Acherusian lake, where the souls of most of the dead arrive and spend certain appointed periods before being sent back

again to the generations of living creatures. The third of these
rivers issues forth between these two, and near the place where it
issues forth it falls into a vast region burning with a great fire,
and forms a marsh that is larger than our sea, boiling with water
and mud. Thence it makes its way, turbulent and muddy, and as
it coils its way round inside the earth it arrives, among other
places, at the borders of the Acherusian lake, but it does not mix
with the water of the lake; and having coiled round many times
beneath the earth, it flows back at a lower point in Tartarus. This
is the river they call Pyriphlegethon, and volcanoes belch forth
lava from it in various parts of the world. Over against this,
again, the fourth river flows out, into a region that is terrible and
wild, all of a steely blue-grey color, called the Stygian region;
and the marsh which the river forms as it flows in is called the
Styx. After issuing into this marsh and receiving terrible powers
in its water, it sinks down into the earth, and coiling itself round
proceeds in the opposite direction to that of Pyriphlegethon, and
then meets it coming from the opposite way at the Acherusian
lake. The water of this river likewise mixes with no other, but
itself goes round in a circle and then flows back into Tartarus
opposite to Pyriphlegethon; and the name of this river, according
to the poets, is Cocytus.

"Such is the nature of the world; and when the dead reach
the region to which their divine guides severally take them, they
first stand trial, those who have lived nobly and piously, as well
as those who have not. And those who are found to have lived
neither particularly well nor particularly badly journey to Acheron,
and embarking on such vessels as are provided for them arrive in
them at the lake. There they dwell and are purified; paying due
penalties, they are absolved from any sins that they have committed, and receive rewards for their good deeds, each according
to his merits. Those who are judged incurable because of the
enormity of their crimes, having committed many heinous acts of
sacrilege or many treacherous and abominable murders or crimes
of that magnitude, are hurled by their fitting destiny into Tartarus,
whence they never more emerge. Those who are judged to be
guilty of crimes that are curable but nevertheless great—those,
for example, who having done some act of violence to father or
mother in anger live the rest of their lives repenting of their
wickedness, or who have killed someone in other circumstances
of a similar nature—must fall into Tartarus; but when they have
fallen in and stayed there a year, the wave casts them forth—the
murderers along Cocytus, those who have struck their fathers or

mothers along Pyriphlegethon; and when they are being carried past the Acherusian lake, they shout and cry out to those whom they have murdered or outraged, and calling upon them beg and implore them to let them come out into the lake, and to receive them; and if they can prevail upon them, they come out and cease from their woes, but if not, they are carried again into Tartarus, and from there once more into the rivers, and they do not stop suffering this until they can prevail upon those whom they have wronged, for such is the sentence that the judges have pronounced upon them. Lastly, those who are found to have lived exceptionally good lives are released from these regions within the earth and allowed to depart from them as from a prison, and they reach the pure dwelling place up above and live on the surface of the earth; and of these, those who have sufficiently purified themselves by means of philosophy dwell free from the body for all time to come, and arrive at habitations even fairer than these, habitations that it is not easy to describe; and there is no time to make the attempt now. But for these reasons, Simmias, which we have discussed, we should do all in our power to achieve some measure of virtue and of wisdom during our lives, for great is the reward, and great the hope.

"No man of sense should affirm decisively that all this is exactly as I have described it. But that the nature of our souls and of their habitations is either as I have described or very similar, since the soul is shown to be immortal—that, I think, is a very proper belief to hold, and such as a man should risk: for the risk is well worthwhile. And one should repeat these things over and over again to oneself, like a charm, which is precisely the reason why I have spent so long in expounding the story now.

"For these reasons, then, a man should have no fears about his soul, if throughout his life he has rejected bodily pleasures and bodily adornments, as being alien to it and doing more harm than good, and has concentrated on the pleasures of learning, and having adorned his soul with adornments that are not alien to it, but appropriate—temperance and justice and courage and freedom and truth—continues to wait, thus prepared, for the time to come for him to journey to the other world. As for you, Simmias and Cebes and all you others, you will make your several journeys later, at an appointed time; but in my case, as a character in a tragedy might put it, Destiny is already summoning me; and it is almost time for me to go to the bath. I think it is better to have a bath before drinking the poison, and not to give the women the trouble of washing a corpse.''

When he had finished saying this, Crito said: ''Well, Socrates, what instructions have you for me or for these others about your children, or anything else—anything that you would particularly like us to do?''

''My usual request, Crito,'' he said, ''nothing out of the ordinary: if you will look after yourselves, you will be doing a service to me and to mine and also to yourselves, in whatever you do—even if you don't give any undertaking now; but if you neglect yourselves, and refuse to live following in the track marked out, as it were, in our present and past discussions, then however much you may now undertake to do, and however earnestly, you will not be doing any good.''

''We will try hard, then, to do as you say,'' he said. ''And how are we to bury you?''

''Anyhow you like,'' he said, ''if you can catch me, and I don't elude you.'' And chuckling quietly and glancing at us he said, ''I can't persuade Crito, my friends, that I am Socrates here, the person who is talking to you now, and setting out each of these arguments. He thinks that I am the person he will be looking at shortly as a corpse, and so he asks how he should bury me. As for my lengthy arguments to show that when I drink the poison I shall no longer remain with you, but take my leave of you and go off to some 'joys of the blessed,' I think that my words are of no avail so far as he is concerned, although I was trying to console both you and myself as well. Be surety for me with Crito,'' he said, ''for exactly the opposite of what he went surety for with the judges at the trial. *He* swore that I would stay: but *you* should swear that I will not stay when I die, but will leave you and go off. Then Crito will bear things better, and when he sees my body being burnt or buried he will not be disturbed on my behalf, thinking that I am suffering terribly, and won't say at the funeral that he's laying out or following to the grave or burying *Socrates*. You may be sure, dear Crito,'' he said, ''that inaccurate language is not only in itself a mistake: it implants evil in men's souls. But you should have no fear; you should say that it is my body that you are burying, and you should bury it just as you like, and as seems to you to conform best to custom.''

When he had said this, he got up and went into a room to bathe; and Crito followed him, but he told us to wait. We waited, therefore, chatting amongst ourselves and reviewing the discussion that we had had, and then again speaking of the magnitude of our misfortune. It was as though we were losing a father, and we felt that when he had gone we should be living the rest of our lives as orphans. After he had had his bath, when his children were brought to him—he had two little sons, and one older—and those womenfolk of his had come, he talked with them in Crito's presence and gave his instructions, and then asked the women and the children to go away, and came over to us. It was now almost sunset, for he had been a long time inside. He came and sat down, fresh from his bath, and did not say much after that. Then the servant of the Eleven came and stood by him and said, "Socrates, I shall not have to reproach you, as I do others, for being angry with me and cursing me when, on the instructions of the archons, I tell you to drink the poison. I have found you during this period the noblest and most kindly and best man who has ever come here; and now, I am sure, you are not angry with *me*, but with those who you know are responsible. So now—you know what I have come to tell you—good-bye, and try to bear the inevitable as easily as you can." He burst into tears, turned round, and went away.

And Socrates looked up at him and said, "Good-bye to you too. We will do as you say"; and to us he said, "What a fine fellow! He always used to come and visit me, and sometimes would chat with me, and was the best of men; and now, how good of him to weep for me! But now, Crito, let us do as he asks, and let the poison be brought, if it has been prepared. If not, let the pounding be done."

"I think, Socrates," said Crito, "that the sun is still on the mountains; it hasn't set yet. What's more, I know that others drink the poison very late after they have been told to, after a good dinner and a good deal of drinking, and even after intercourse, in some cases, with their lovers. Don't be in a hurry; there is still time left."

"It is natural, Crito," said Socrates, "that those whom you mention should do this—they think they gain something by doing it; and it is natural, too, that I should not do this, for in my opinion the only thing I shall gain, if I drink a little later, will be to make myself a laughing-stock in my own eyes—clinging to life and being sparing with it when my cup has been drained to the dregs. Come now," he said, "do as I say, please."

At this Crito nodded to the boy who was standing near; and the boy went out and after some while returned with the man who was going to administer the poison, which he brought ready-pounded in a cup. Socrates, when he saw the fellow, said, "Well, my friend, you know all about these things, what do I have to do?"

"Simply drink it," he said, "and then walk about until a heaviness comes over your legs; then lie down. Then it will do the work itself." With this, he handed Socrates the cup. Socrates took it, Echecrates, and said—quite serenely, and without any trembling, or any change in color or countenance, but glancing up from under his brows with his usual quizzical, bull-like look: "What do you say," he said, "about pouring a libation to anyone from this cup? Is it permitted, or not?"

"We only prepare, Socrates," he said, "what we think is enough for the dose."

"I understand," he said; "but no doubt I may offer a prayer to the gods—and that I should do—that my journey from this world to the next may be accompanied by good fortune. That is my prayer and may it be fulfilled." And as soon as he had said that, he raised the cup to his lips, and showing not the least distaste, quite unperturbed, he drained the draught. Most of us had till then been more or less able to restrain our tears, but when we saw him drinking and then that he had drunk it, we could do so no longer. For my part, despite my efforts I found that the tears flooded down my cheeks; I wrapped my face in my cloak and wept for my misfortune—not for his, but for my own, to think what a friend I had lost. Crito had got up and gone away even before me, unable to restrain his tears. Apollodorus even before this had been weeping ceaselessly, and then he burst out crying aloud, and distressed us so much that he made everyone present break down, except Socrates himself.

"What are you doing, strange fellows?" he said. "That was my chief reason for sending the women away, so that they shouldn't make this mistake; I have heard that it is better to die in silence. Please remain quiet, and be brave."

At this we felt ashamed, and checked our weeping. Socrates walked about, and when he said his legs felt heavy, he lay down on his back—as the fellow told him to; and after a while, this man who had given the poison felt him, examining his feet and his legs, and then pinching his foot hard he asked if he felt it, and Socrates replied, "No." After that, the man did the same to his shins; and then, passing upwards in this way, he showed us that he was becoming numbed and rigid. And he himself continued to feel him, and said that when the coldness reached his heart, then he would be gone.

The region about the groin was now becoming more or less numb, and uncovering his head (for it had been covered up), he said—and these were the last words he uttered: "Crito, we owe a cock to Asclepius[27]; please pay it—do not neglect it."

"It shall be done," said Crito. "Is there anything else?"

Socrates gave no reply to this question, but after a little while he made a movement, and the man uncovered him, and his eyes had become fixed. Seeing this, Crito closed his lips and his eyes.

Such, Echecrates, was the end of our friend—the best man of his time, in our opinion, that we had ever come across, and in general the wisest, and the most just.

---

[27]The god of healing. A cock was the customary offering in gratitude for a cure. Socrates regards death as release from all human ills.

PROTAGORAS

Translated by B. A. F. Hubbard
and E. S. Karnofsky

Friend. Socrates, where have you appeared from? As if it weren't obvious: you've been on a hunt, haven't you; chasing the youthful Alcibiades? And I certainly did think him a *beautiful* young man when I saw him the other day; but a man for all that, Socrates, and, strictly between ourselves, already beginning to sprout a beard.

Socrates. Well, and what of that? Don't you agree with Homer when he says that the most charming age is that of early manhood—the age Alcibiades is now?

Friend. And today? Have you, in fact, been with him? How is the young man disposed toward you?

Socrates. Oh, pretty well, I think, and especially today. He spoke up in my defense several times, and indeed I have only just now left him. But actually, I have something rather odd to tell you: though he was there, I paid him no attention and several times I quite forgot about him.

Friend. How could such a thing possibly happen between you two? You didn't, I take it, encounter a greater *beauty* in the city?

Socrates. Very much so, yes.

Friend. What? A citizen or a foreigner?

Socrates. A foreigner.

Friend. Where from?

Socrates. Abdera.

Friend. And this foreigner, whoever he is; you found him so *beautiful* that he actually seemed *fairer* to you than Cleinias' son?

Socrates. But my dear fellow, is not the *greatest wisdom* likely to be the greater *beauty*?

Friend. Then you have come from some *wise man*, Socrates?

137

Socrates. Yes indeed. The wisest of any living, if, that is, you think Protagoras is the wisest.

Friend. What's that you say? Protagoras has come to town?

Socrates. Two days ago, yes.

Friend. And you have just been conversing with him?

Socrates. Indeed so, having said and heard many things.

Friend. Well then, why don't you give us the whole story of your conversation? Make this slave give up his seat, and sit down—if you have no other business, that is.

Socrates. Certainly: in fact you will be doing me a kindness by listening.

Friend. And you us, by giving us the story.

Socrates. Then the kindness will be mutual. Well now, listen.

Early this morning, when it was still pitch dark, Hippocrates, Apollodorus' boy, the brother of Phason, started hammering at my door with his staff; and when someone opened up, he came rushing straight in and said at the top of his voice: "Socrates, are you awake or asleep?" And recognizing his voice I said: "Oh, it's Hippocrates. Nothing up, is there?"

"Nothing but good," he said.

"That," I said, "really would be good news. But what is it, and why have you come round at this hour?"

"Protagoras has come," he said, standing beside me.

"Yes," I said, "the day before yesterday. Have you only just found that out?"

"Of course," he said; "well, yesterday evening, that is." And groping for my camp bed, he sat down by my feet and said: "Yes, in the evening, rather late actually, after I got back from Oenoe. Satyrus, my slave, was on the run, you see, and I was going to tell you that I was after him, when something came up and put it out of my head. And after dinner, when we were off to bed, my brother tells me Protagoras has come. And even then I set out to tell you straight away, but then it occurred to me that it was too late. But as soon as I had slept off my fatigue, I got straight up and was on my way here, as you see."

Knowing how bold and volatile he is, I remarked: "But what has this got to do with you? You don't have some charge to bring against Protagoras, do you?"

"Indeed I do, Socrates," he laughed: "that he alone is *wise*, but is not making me wise."

"Oh yes he will, by Zeus," I said; "if you give him money and persuade him, he will make you wise too."

"Oh by Zeus and all the gods, if it were just a question of money," he said, "I should spare none of my own or my friends' possessions. But that is just what I came to see you about—to get you to talk to him for me. I am rather young, and I have never seen Protagoras before, or ever heard anything he has said. I was still a child when he was last in town. But after all, Socrates, everyone is praising him and saying that he is very *clever* at speaking. But why don't we go there so that we can catch him in? He is staying with Callias, the son of Hipponicus, so I've heard. Come on."

And I said: "Let's not go there yet, my dear fellow; it's still early. Let's get up instead and go out into the courtyard where we can take a few turns until it gets light. Then we can go. After all, Protagoras spends much of his time indoors; so you needn't worry; we shall probably catch him in."

At this we got up and strolled about the courtyard. And to put Hippocrates to the test I gave him a searching look and said: "Tell me, Hippocrates, you are taking it upon yourself to go to Protagoras and to pay him a fee on your own behalf in his capacity as a . . . what? With the expectation of becoming . . . what? For instance, suppose you have a mind to go to your namesake, Hippocrates of Cos, the servant of Asclepius, and to pay him a fee on your own behalf. If someone were to ask you 'Tell me, Hippocrates, you mean to pay Hippocrates a fee in his capacity as a . . . what?', what answer would you give?"

"I should say, as a doctor," he said.

"With a view to becoming . . . what?"

"A doctor," he said.

"Or suppose you intend," I said, "to go to Polycleitus of Argos, or Pheidias of Athens, and pay him a fee on your own behalf: if someone were to ask 'You are intending to hire Polycleitus or Pheidias as . . . what?', what would your answer be?"

"I should say, as sculptors," he said.

"With a view to becoming . . . what?"

"A sculptor, obviously."

"Well then," I said, "we are prepared, you and I, to go to Protagoras and pay him money on your behalf; and if we have enough money, to use that to persuade him, or, if that fails, to use our relatives' money as well. So if, seeing us so eager, someone should ask us: 'Tell me, Socrates and Hippocrates, you are intending to pay Protagoras a fee in his capacity as a . . . what?', what should we reply to him? What other name do we

hear used of Protagoras? In the case of Pheidias it is the name
of 'sculptor,' or, in the case of Homer, the name of 'poet.'
What similar type of name do we hear applied to Protagoras?''

"Well, a *sophist* is what they call the man, Socrates."

"So it is as a sophist then that we are going to pay him the
money?"

"Certainly."

"Then if someone went on to ask you 'And what about
you; you are going to Protagoras with a view to becoming . . .
what?' ''

And then, with a blush—for it was just growing light
enough for me to see him clearly—he said: "Well, if it is like
the other examples, obviously I would expect to become a
sophist."

"But for heaven's sake!" I said, "wouldn't you be ashamed
to make yourself known among the Greeks as a sophist?"

"Yes, of course, Socrates, if I must give my own opinion."

"But in that case, Hippocrates, perhaps it is not this kind of
instruction which you expect from Protagoras, but rather the kind
which you received from your instructors in letters or music or
athletics? Under each of these you were instructed so that you
could acquire not some *skill* or profession, but the kind of liberal
education suitable for a free man of independent means."

"I think instruction under Protagoras is more like that," he
said; "yes."

"Well, do you know what you are about to do, or don't you
realize?" I said.

"How do you mean?"

"That you are about to place your own *mind* in the care of a
man who is, as you say, a sophist; although I should be amazed
if you knew just what a sophist might be. And yet if you don't
know that, you don't know whether the thing to which you have
entrusted your mind is *good* or *bad*."

"I think I know," he said.

"All right, tell me: what do you consider a sophist to be?"

"So far as I am concerned," he said, "he is what the word
implies: someone who has knowledge of *wise things*."

"Well, it is possible to say as much of painters and builders, that they have 'knowledge of wise things.' But should
someone ask us 'What wise things are painters knowledgeable
about?', I suppose we should tell him that it was the production
of paintings, and so on. But what if someone were to ask 'Yes,
but what about the sophist; what wise things is he knowledgeable

about?', what would our answer be? In relation to what productive activity is he knowledgeable?''

"What should we say, Socrates? That he knows how to make a man clever at speaking?''

"And our answer might possibly be true, too,'' I said, "but not sufficient. For the answer raises a further question as to what the sophist makes a man clever at speaking about. For example, the lyrist presumably makes people clever at speaking on the subject about which he makes them knowledgeable—yes?''

"Yes.''

"Very well, what about the sophist? What does he make people clever at speaking about?''

"Obviously the subject about which he makes them knowledgeable.''

"No doubt. But what is this subject about which, being knowledgeable himself, the sophist makes his student knowledgeable as well?''

"Oh dear,'' he said, "now I have nothing left to say.''

At this I said: "What's this? You do know what a risk you are about to take with your *mind*? If you had to place your body in somebody's care at the risk of its becoming good or bad, you would make a thorough inquiry to establish whether it was advisable or not, and consult the opinions of your friends and relations, and spend several days considering it; but now that something is at stake which you value more highly than your body—your *mind*—by which your entire welfare is determined, depending on whether your mind turns out good or bad—you didn't consult your father, or your brother, or any of your friends, including me, as to whether you should place your mind in the care of this foreigner who has just arrived, but instead, after hearing of it in the evening, as you tell me, first thing in the morning you turn up, without giving any account of him or asking for any advice about whether you ought to place yourself in his hands or not, and you are ready to spend both your own money and that of your friends, as though you had already arrived at the considered judgment that association with Protagoras was an absolute must, when you neither know him, as you yourself told me, nor have you ever spoken with him before, but you call him a sophist, and yet, asked what a sophist is, you show manifest ignorance, though you mean to put yourself in his hands.''

"It does rather look like that, Socrates,'' he replied, "judging from what you've been saying.''

"Well, Hippocrates, isn't the sophist in reality a sort of merchant or dealer in wares by which the *mind* is fed? Certainly he seems to me to be something of the kind."

"Yes, but by what is a mind fed, Socrates?"

"By *learning*, presumably," I said. "And take care, my friend, that the sophist doesn't take us in with his advertisements as do the merchant and dealer in food for the body. For they too do not know which of the wares they peddle are good for the body and which bad, any more than their customers do—unless one of them happens to be an expert in physical fitness or medicine. And yet they promote all their wares equally. The same applies to those who hawk their *courses of instruction* round the various cities, flogging them to anyone who happens to want them; they give equal promotion to everything they have for sale, though it may well be the case, my excellent friend, that some of these men also do not know which of their wares are good for the mind and which bad, unless one of them happens to be an expert in the care of the mind; and the same holds true for their customers. So in your case, if you happen to know which of these courses of instruction are good for the mind and which bad, you can safely purchase them from Protagoras or from anyone you please. But if not, beware, my dear boy; you may be dicing with your dearest possession. In fact, where the purchase of *instruction* is concerned, the danger is much greater. For when we buy food and drink from a dealer or merchant, we can take them away in other containers and, before we allow them to enter our system by eating or drinking them, we can take them home, put them away and take the advice of an expert as to which we should eat or drink and which we should not, and in what quantities and upon what occasions, so that the purchase itself carries no great risk. But with a course of instruction we cannot take it away in any other container, but are compelled to put down our money and go away after we have *learned* and let the course enter our very mind, whether to its benefit or detriment. So let's examine these courses and take the advice of our elders, for we are still a little young to exercise discretion over such an important issue. All the same, let's go now, as we planned, and listen to the man. Then, after we have heard him let's join the company of some others. After all, Protagoras isn't the only one there, but Hippias of Elis as well, and Prodicus of Ceos too, I think, and many other wise men."

This agreed, we set off; but when we reached the porch we stayed a while, continuing a discussion which had arisen between us on our way. So, preferring to complete it before going in, rather than break off in the middle, we continued our conversation in the porch until we arrived at a mutually acceptable conclusion. And I suppose the doorman, a eunuch, must have been listening to us; and what with the number of sophists in the house and the resulting stream of visitors, I fear he was fed up. At all events, when we knocked he opened the door, took one look at us and said, "Huh! Sophists! Master's busy," and promptly used both his hands to slam the door as hard as he could.

We knocked again and he answered through the door—locked by now.

"Hey, you," he said, "didn't you hear me say Master's busy?"

"But my good fellow," I said, "we haven't come to see Callias. And we aren't sophists either—don't worry. It's Protagoras we've come to see, so show us in." And at last the man grudgingly opened the door.

We entered to find Protagoras walking up and down the portico, while walking up and down with him were, in order, on one side Callias the son of Hipponicus, his maternal step-brother Paralus the son of Pericles, and Charmides the son of Glaucon, and, on the other side, Pericles' other son Xanthippus, Philippides the son of Philomelus and Antimoerus of Mende, who is Protagoras' star pupil and is studying to acquire the art and become a sophist. And of those who followed behind, listening in on their discourse, the majority seemed to be foreigners. Protagoras draws these people from every city he visits, enchanting them, like Orpheus, with his voice, while they follow after his voice spellbound. But there were also a few native Athenians in the chorus. I particularly enjoyed the spectacle of this chorus and the splendid care they took never to be in Protagoras' way or get in front of him. Each time he and his companions turned about, his audience parted ranks in good order, this way and that, and so, circling about, returned each time to their positions in the rear: magnificent!

"After him I beheld" (as Homer says) Hippias of Elis seated in state in the portico opposite, while about him, on benches, sat Eryximachus the son of Acumenus, Phaedrus the Myrrhinusan, and Andron the son of Androtion, together with some foreigners from his own native city, and some others. As it appeared, they were plying Hippias with questions about natural science and astronomy while he, from his chair of state, was

deciding any arguments which arose and giving lengthy exposi-
tions in answer to their questions.

"Tantalus then I espied" (as Homer also says); for Prodicus
of Ceos was in town as well. He was in a chamber which
Hipponicus had previously used as a storeroom; but because of
the number of guests, Callias had cleared this room out and
turned it into a guest-room for his visitors. Anyway, Prodicus
was still in bed, wrapped in sheepskins and blankets—a considerable quantity, to judge from his appearance. Sitting beside him
on the nearby couches were Pausanias from Cerameis, and with
Pausanias a young stripling, of good breeding, I think, and
extremely good looking. I heard his name as Agathon, I think,
and I shouldn't be surprised if he isn't actually Pausanias' boy-
friend. Anyway, there was this lad, the two Adeimantuses, one
the son of Cepis and the other the son of Leucolophides, and
apparently some others. But from where I was standing, outside,
I was unable to discover what they were discussing, though I
was eager to hear Prodicus. For I think he is a very wise man
indeed—wonderfully so. But his voice was so deep that the
reverberation of the room made his words indistinct.

We had only just come in when behind us came Alcibiades—
the beautiful, as you call him, and I agree—together with Critias
the son of Callaeschrus.

So we came on in. But still we hung back a little while,
taking in the scene before us. Then we went up to Protagoras.

"Excuse me, Protagoras," I said. "Hippocrates here and I
have come to see you."

"Do you want to speak with me in private," he said, "or in
front of the others?"

"So far as we are concerned," I said, "it makes no difference. You can decide for yourself when you have heard the
purpose of our visit."

"Well," he said, "what is the purpose of your visit?"

"Hippocrates here is a native of this town. His father is
Apollodorus and he comes from an important and prosperous
family. He is, moreover, temperamentally disposed to compete
with other young men of his age, and I think he desires a name
in the *community*. This he thinks he would be most likely to
achieve by associating himself with you. So now with this in
mind, decide whether you prefer to discuss all this in private or
in front of the others."

"Your consideration for me is very proper, Socrates," he
said. "For when a man visits great *cities* as a foreigner, and in

those cities persuades the best of their young men to forsake the company of all others, whether of family or of friends, old or young, and to associate with him alone, expecting by that very association to become better men—when, I say, a man is engaged in such activities, he must take precautions. For this kind of activity causes considerable unpopularity and even a variety of malicious conspiracies. However, I myself declare that the sophistic *art* itself has a long-standing tradition, whereas its practitioners in former times were intimidated by its unpopularity, and therefore concealed it behind specious façades. Thus there are some, like Homer, Hesiod or Simonides, who have hidden it behind a façade of poetry, while others made use of mystery cults or prophecy, as did the Orphics and the followers of Musaeus. Similarly I have perceived some such use of physical training: Iccus of Taras, for example, and even today Herodicus of Selymbria, formerly of Megara, is as able a sophist as any. Then there was your own Agathocles who presented himself to the public as a practitioner of music, though he was in fact a great sophist, and Pythocleides of Ceos and many more besides. All these men, I say, fearing unpopularity, used these *arts* as window-dressing. But I differ from all of them. I consider that they failed to accomplish their objective: for they did not pass undetected by those men who played a leading part in their *communities*, and for whose benefit they put up these façades in the first place; after all, the *masses* notice hardly anything for themselves, merely acclaiming whatever these leading citizens pronounce. For a man to run for cover, and not only to fail to get away but actually to make himself conspicuous in the process is in itself sheer stupidity; besides which it will inevitably make people even more hostile, since they regard that sort of man as unprincipled into the bargain. Which is why I have taken precisely the opposite course from these men and openly admit to being a sophist and an educator, thinking it a better precaution to admit to it openly than to be caught denying it. And in addition to this I have taken other precautions which, with the help of God, ensure that I can openly admit, without any unpleasant consequences, that I am a sophist. And yet I have been practicing the art for many years now; indeed I have been alive for a great many years—indeed, I am old enough to be the father of any one of you. So if there is something you want, much the most agreeable course for me would be to talk it over in front of all the other visitors to this house.''

Now I had a suspicion that he wanted to show off to

Prodicus and Hippias, and parade the fact that the new arrivals were admirers of his. So I said: "Well then, why don't we call Prodicus and Hippias and their companions? They can listen in on our conversation as well."

"Certainly," said Protagoras.

"Do you want us to arrange the seating in a circle so that you can be seated for your conversation?" said Callias. It was agreed, and in our eagerness to hear these *wise men* we all set to and actually shifted the benches and sofas ourselves, arranging them by Hippias as the benches were already over there. Meanwhile Callias and Alcibiades brought Prodicus over with his companions, after helping him up off his bed.

When we were all assembled Protagoras began: "Now, Socrates, perhaps you could repeat, for the benefit of these people here, the matter which you outlined to me just now on behalf of the young man."

And I said: "I shall begin as before, Protagoras, with my reason for coming. It so happens that Hippocrates here desires to associate with you. So he wishes to learn what, if he does associate with you, the outcome of his studies will be. That is all we have to say."

"If you associate with me, young man," said Protagoras in reply, "then you will be able, at the end of your first day in my company, to go away a better man; and the same will happen on the next day, and each day after that you will continue to grow better and improve."

At this I said: "There is nothing surprising in what you say so far, Protagoras; in fact it is what I should expect. Even in your case, despite your seniority and wisdom, were someone to give you instruction on a subject about which, by some chance, you knew nothing, you too would grow better. But that is not what I meant. Think of it this way: suppose Hippocrates here were suddenly to change his mind and set his heart on associating with that young man who is in town at the moment— Zeuxippus, from Heraclea, I mean—and came to him, just as he has come to you, and heard him say just what he has heard from you: that each day on which he associates with him he will grow better and make progress; and suppose someone were to ask Zeuxippus the further question, 'At what are you saying he will grow better, and toward what will he make progress?' Zeuxippus would say at painting. Or suppose that in company with Orthagoras of Thebes he heard what he has heard from you, and were again to ask at what he would be better each day by his association with him; he would say at playing the flute. Well, in the same way, Protagoras, tell the young lad and me (since I am asking the question on his behalf) the following: If Hippocrates here associates with Protagoras, he will go away better on the first day and will make progress every day after that—but toward what, Protagoras, and in relation to what?"

"You ask a good question, Socrates," said Protagoras, hearing me say this, "and I'm always pleased to reply to a good question. If Hippocrates comes to me he won't have the same experience as he would have had by associating with one of the other sophists. These others are a curse on young men. Just when they have escaped from *technical subjects*, they bring them unwillingly back and throw them once again into technical subjects—arithmetic, astronomy, geometry, music"—this with a pointed look at Hippias—"but with me he will learn only the subject which he came to learn and no other. The course of instruction is *good planning* both of his own affairs, to the end that he would best manage his personal estate, and of the *city*'s, to the end that he would be in the strongest position to conduct, in speech and action, the common business of the city."

"Am I following you correctly?" I said. "It seems to me that the technical subject of which you speak is *citycraft*, and that you are promising to make men *good members of their city*."

"That, Socrates," he said, "is precisely the declaration which I am making."

"Well," I said, "this is a fine *technique* you have acquired, if indeed you have acquired it. For you will get from me nothing less than my honest opinion. That is, Protagoras, I didn't think that this was something which could be taught. But now that you say it is, I don't know what to do but take your word for it. Still, it's only right that I should say why I do consider that it can be neither taught nor passed on by one man to another. You see, I, in common with all other Greeks, call the Athenians *wise*. And I observe that whenever we convene in the *assembly*, and the city has some business related to building, it is the builders who are summoned as *advisers* about the buildings; or again, if ship construction is involved, it is the shipwrights, and the same for every other matter which they consider is capable of being both learned and taught. And if someone else attempts *to give them advice*, whom they don't consider a skilled professional, be he *handsome* and wealthy and well-born, they will have none of him, for all that, but laugh and jeer at him until this man who has ventured to speak either stands down of his own accord, discouraged by the uproar, or is dragged from the platform by the police or removed on the order of the presidents. That is what they do when they consider a *technical skill* to be at issue. But when they come to *deliberate* political issues, then a builder can get up and *give advice*, or, equally, smith or cobbler, merchant or shipper, rich or poor, high-born or low, without distinction. And nobody heckles them, as they do in the previous instances, with shouts of 'You didn't learn about it anywhere. No qualified instructor trained you, and now you try to give us advice!' And the reason is plainly that they don't consider that it can be taught.

"But it isn't just that the common affairs of the city are conducted like that. Even in private life our best and wisest citizens are unable to pass on this *excellence* to others. Take Pericles, the father of these two young men here. In all the fields which fall within the competence of teachers, he has had them excellently educated. But in the one field in which he is himself *wise*, he neither educates them himself nor does he put them in someone else's hands. No, he lets them roam free, like sacred flocks, in the hope that they will somehow stumble upon this excellence of their own accord. Or take Cleinias, if you like, the younger brother of Alcibiades here. This same man, Pericles, is his guardian, and he was concerned that Alcibiades might have a corrupting influence upon him. So he dragged him away from the company of Alcibiades, and placed him in Ariphon's household to be educated. But not six months had passed before he returned him to his brother, not knowing what to do with him. And there are many others I could cite who, for all their good qualities, have never yet made anyone better, be it their own or anyone else's sons. It is with this in view, Protagoras, that I don't consider that *excellence* can be taught. But when I hear the suggestion coming from you, I begin to have second thoughts and to think that you must have a point, since I consider you to be a man of wide experience who has acquired extensive knowledge both from learning and from your own researches. If, therefore, you can give us a clearer demonstration that excellence can be taught, please don't stint us, but give a demonstration."

"Of course I shan't stint you, Socrates," he said. "But shall I present my demonstration in the manner of an elder to younger men, by telling a story, or shall I expound an argument?"

Several of the assembled company interrupted and told him to use whichever method he pleased.

"In that case," said Protagoras, "I think it will be more congenial if I tell you a story.

"There once was a time when there were gods, but no
mortal creatures. And when the time came which was decreed by
fate for their creation also, the gods figured them within the
earth, compounding them of earth and of fire, and of everything
which is mixed with fire and earth. And when they were ready to
lead them toward the light, they charged Prometheus and
Epimetheus that they should furnish and distribute powers to
each as it should be fitting. But Epimetheus begged Prometheus
and asked that he might himself make distribution, saying, 'Let
me first distribute; afterward examine my work.' And when he
had persuaded him with these words he began to make distribution. And as he distributed, to some he added strength without
speed, while the weaker he furnished with swiftness. And some
he armed, while to others he gave an unarmed nature, devising
for them instead some other power for their safety. For whichsoever he confined and made small of stature, to these he distributed a refuge of wings or a dwelling under the earth; but
whichsoever he made great of stature, by their very greatness he
kept them safe. And so, in like manner, he made just and equal
distribution, devising these things as a precaution lest any kind
might vanish from the earth.

"But when for each he had prepared a refuge from the others
against destruction, next he devised comfort against the seasons
sent by Zeus, clothing them about with thick fur and tough hide
sufficient to keep out the winter and able to resist the scorching
sun, and in order also that when they took themselves to their
rest, these things might supply to each its own natural covering
for the night. And some he shod with hooves, and others with
tough and bloodless hide. Next he supplied for them varied
nourishment—to some the plants of the earth, to others the fruit
of trees, and to others roots. And to some he granted other
creatures for their sustenance, adding to these meagerness of
progeny, but to their prey abundant fruitfulness, supplying their
kind with a means for their preservation.

"But because Epimetheus was not exceeding wise, he ex-
hausted all the powers upon the brute beasts and noticed it not.
Yet still humankind was left unfurnished, so that he was perplexed what he should do. And being thus perplexed behold
there came to him Prometheus to examine his distribution. And
he found the other animals diligently provided for, but man
without clothing, without shoes, without coverings for the night,
without weapons. And already the allotted day was at hand in
which man must come out of the earth into the light. Being thus

sore perplexed as to what safety he should find for man,
Prometheus stole from Hephaestus and Athene *practical wisdom*
together with fire—for without fire no man may acquire or make
use of this—and he bestowed them upon man. In this way man
acquired *wisdom* for his sustenance, but he did not have *citycraft*.
For it lay with Zeus. Nor was it any longer permitted to Prometheus
to approach the citadel where Zeus had his habitation; and
moreover the guardians of Zeus were fearsome. But he came in
stealth to the common habitation of Hephaestus and Athene, in
which they practiced their *skill*, and stealing the *skills* of
Hephaestus—which is working with fire—and of Athene, he
gave them to men, so that it came to pass that man had abundant
means for his sustenance. Afterward Prometheus was charged
with theft, as it is told, because of Epimetheus.

"Since there was a part of man which was divine, he alone
of all living things began, because of his kinship with the gods,
to believe in gods and to build altars and images of gods. And
then soon, by his skill, he began to speak and to use words; he
invented dwellings and clothing and shoes, coverings for the
night and nourishment from the earth. Being thus equipped, men
were scattered at the beginning, and there were no cities, so
that they were destroyed by wild animals because they were
weaker in all things. And though the skill of their hands was
sufficient for their sustenance, for warring against the beasts it
was not sufficient. For they did not yet have *citycraft*, of which
warcraft is a part. At first they sought to gather together for their
safety by founding cities. But when they were gathered together,
they *committed injury* one upon another, since they had not the
skill of citycraft, so that they were scattered anew and began
once more to perish. Whereupon Zeus, being afraid concerning
our kind, that it might perish utterly, sent Hermes unto mankind
with *justice* and a *sense of shame*, to bring order to their cities
and common bonds of amity. And Hermes asked Zeus in what
manner he ought to give justice and a sense of shame to men,
saying: 'Am I to distribute them even as the practical skills have
been distributed? For thus have they been distributed: one man
skilled in medicine is sufficient unto many who have not the
skill, as it is also with other men of skill. Am I in like manner to
distribute justice and a sense of shame among men, or am I to
distribute among all?' 'Among all,' Zeus replied, 'and let all
have them in common. For there could be no cities if but a few
had them, as it is with the other skills. And lay down this law
from me: if any man be not able to share justice and a sense of

shame even as other men do, they must kill him as a pestilence
to the city.'

"That, Socrates, is why the Athenians—as indeed everyone
else—hold the view that when their deliberations require excellence at building and other such practical skills, only a restricted
group of men should contribute advice, and so they refuse to
tolerate advice from anyone outside that group, as you say (naturally so, I would add); and that is why, on the contrary, when
their deliberations involve *political excellence*, and must be conducted entirely on the basis of *justice* and *moderation* they quite
naturally tolerate everyone. For they believe that all men must
have this excellence in common, since otherwise there could be
no *cities*. That is the reason for this, Socrates.

"And in case you should think I am deceiving you when I say
that all men really do believe that *justice*, along with the rest of
political excellence, is something which every single individual
has in common, here is further evidence. In the case of the other
excellences it is true, as you say, that if someone claims to be
good at some such *skill* as flute-playing when in fact he isn't,
people treat him with derision or annoyance, while his family
and friends take him on one side and warn him that he is out of
his mind; but where justice and the rest of political excellence is
concerned, if a man truthfully accuses himself in public of being
unjust, even in cases where he is actually known to be *unjust*,
then that very truthfulness, which in the former case was regarded as *moderation*, in this case they treat as madness, and say
that everyone should claim to be *just*, whether he is or not, and
that the man who doesn't put up some show of being just is out
of his mind, in the belief that no one can fail to have at least
some share of justice, or he would not be human.

"So much, then, for my claim that it is natural for them to
recognize all men as competent to give advice on questions
related to this excellence, in consequence of their belief that all
men have it in common. That they consider it to be a teachable
thing possessed in every case as a result rather of teaching and
practice than of chance or birth, I shall now try to show. Where
a man's failings are thought to be the result of chance or birth,
he doesn't become the object of anger, admonition, correction or
punishment, nor of any attempt to alter him. He is the object,
rather, of pity. Who, for example, would be so foolish as to
attempt any such thing with the ugly or small or puny? For men
know, I think, that such things as beauty and its opposite are due
either to birth or to chance. But when it comes to those human

excellences which are generally regarded as the products of
training or practice or teaching, if someone lacks these and has
the opposite failings, why then it is that anger, punishment and
admonition are brought into play; and among these failings are
injustice, impiety, and, all in all, the complete opposite of
political excellence. Where men grow angry with one another
and admonish one another, it is clear that they do so in the belief
that this is an excellence which can be acquired by practice and
instruction. For consider, if you will, Socrates, the influence of
punishment upon those who *commit injustice*, and the institution
itself will show you that men regard excellence as something
which can be acquired. For no one punishes anyone because of
the mere fact that he has committed an injustice and with that
alone in mind, unless he is inflicting unreasoned punishment as
one might upon a brute beast. No, the man who exacts reasoned
punishment does so not because of the past injustice—the past
cannot be undone—but for the sake of the future: to deter him,
or another who sees him punished, from committing a further
injustice. And since he has this belief, it follows that he believes
that excellence can be inculcated; deterrence is, after all, his
purpose in inflicting punishment. This, then, is the opinion of all
those who impose punishment, whether on their own or on the
city's account; punishment and correction are in fact imposed by
all men, and foremost among them the Athenians, your fellow-
citizens, upon those they believe guilty of injustice. It follows,
therefore, on this argument, that the Athenians are also among
those who believe that excellence is something which can be
inculcated and taught. So, Socrates, you have had a sufficient
demonstration, as it seems to me, that it is quite natural for your
fellow-citizens to recognize both smith and cobbler as competent
to give advice on political questions, and that they take the view
that excellence can be taught and acquired.

"There remains the difficulty you experience in relation to
good men, as to why it might be that in subjects which are the
province of teachers, they teach their own sons and make them
wise, while at that very excellence in which they are themselves
outstanding, they make them no better than anyone else. For this
question I shall dispense with parables, Socrates, and give you
an argument. Consider: Is there or is there not some single thing
which all citizens must possess if a city is to exist at all? In this
question alone lies the solution to your difficulty. For if there is,
and if this single thing is not skill at building or metalwork or
pottery, but *justice*, *moderation*, being *holy* or, in short, what I

call manly *excellence*; if this is the excellence which all men
must have in common; and if every man, whatever else he
wishes to learn or to do, must act in accordance with it and must
not act without it, since otherwise whoever lacks it, whether
child, man or woman, must either be taught or punished until he
improves under punishment, while whoever refuses to respond to
punishment and instruction, being regarded as incurable, must be
expelled from his city or killed; if all this is so, and if, given
that this is its nature, good men teach their sons every subject but
this one, think what strange creatures good men must be. For we
have already shown that they think it can be taught in both its
public and its private aspects; yet although it can be taught and
nurtured, all those other subjects, of which their sons can afford
to be ignorant without incurring the death penalty they teach
them; but when it comes to the very subject which may bring
execution or exile upon their sons if they aren't educated and
brought up to excellence, and in addition to execution the confis-
cation of their property and, in short, the total ruin of their
households, are we then to say that they fail to teach it and
don't, on the contrary, devote to it every care? Of course they
do, Socrates. They both teach and admonish them from their
earliest childhood throughout their whole lives. As soon as the
infant can understand what is said to it, nurse, mother, tutor and
father himself vie with each other to ensure that the child will
develop the best possible character, so that, whatever it does or
says, they instruct it, pointing out that 'this is just, that is
unjust; this is *fine*, that is *base*; this is holy, that is unholy; do
this, don't do that.' And if he shows a ready obedience, well
and good; if not, then like a warped and twisted plank they
straighten him with threats and blows. Next, when they send him
to school, they are much more insistent that his teachers should
pay attention to the children's seemly conduct than to the lyre
and to the alphabet. So the teachers see to this, and when, in turn,
the children have learned their letters and are beginning to
understand the written, as before the spoken, word, they seat
them on benches and set them the works of good poets to read
and learn by heart, works containing much good advice, stories,
and praises and eulogies of good men of old, so that the child
may eagerly imitate and strive to be like such men. Then again
the lyre-teachers cultivate in them *self-discipline*, and ensure that
young men do not go wrong in this respect. Moreover, once they
have learned to play the lyre, their tutors teach them the works of
good lyric poets, to the accompaniment of the lyre, and mold

the minds of the children to their rhythms and melodies so that, by becoming more calm, graceful and harmonious, they may acquire more facility both of speech and action: for rhythm and harmony are essential to every aspect of a man's life. And then, in addition to all this, they send them to the trainer so that they can have a better physique to put at the service of their good character, and not be forced to act like a coward, whether in war or any other enterprise, because they are in poor physical condition.

"And this is done above all by those in the best position to do so—the very rich. They send their sons to school earliest in childhood and keep them under instruction longest. Moreover, when children are released from schooling, the city compels them to learn the *laws*, and to model their lives on them, so that they may not follow the random dictates of personal inclination, but, just as the writing instructor guides those children who aren't yet good at writing by drawing lines with the pen and then handing the slate to the pupil and making him follow the guidance of the lines, so the city gives laws, which were invented by good lawgivers of olden times, as outlines, and compels him to govern and be governed in accordance with these, while it punishes anyone who strays outside them. And this punishment, both in your city and in many others besides, has the name 'correction,' since justice corrects. Given, then, that both individuals and the state as a whole take such pains over excellence, are you really surprised or puzzled that it should be teachable, Socrates? There is no need for surprise: it would be far more surprising if it were not teachable.

"Why is it, then, that many good fathers have good-for-nothing sons? Let me explain this too. There is nothing strange, if I was correct in my previous claim that in this thing—excellence, that is—no one must be a layman if a city is to exist at all. For if it is as I say—as it most assuredly is—consider any other pursuit or study you choose. If a city couldn't exist unless we are all, say, flute-players to the best of our abilities, and if everyone taught each other both in private and public life, using reproof against incompetent players instead of keeping the skill to themselves, just as today no one makes a jealously guarded secret of the just and the *lawful* as they do with the other skills—because, I think, the justice and excellence of our relations with each other profits us: which is why we are all so eager to argue and expound our views on issues of justice and the law; if, in short, we exhibited the same total and unstinting enthusiasm for mutual instruction in flute-playing, do you think, Socrates," he said, "that the sons of good flute-players would show any greater tendency to become good flute-players than the sons of the incompetent? I think not. Rather it would be the son most naturally gifted at flute-playing, irrespective of his origins, who would grow up to acquire a great reputation, while the ungifted would, irrespective of his origins, remain unknown. As it is, it frequently happens that the son of a good flute-player turns out to be useless, while the son of a useless player turns out to be good. Even so, they would all be good enough performers in comparison with laymen and those with no knowledge of the flute whatever. Similarly in our present case, take whomsoever you consider to be the most unjust of those who are brought up in the society of men with *laws* and you would find him just and expert in this matter, if you had to judge him by comparison with men who have neither education nor *law-courts* nor *laws* nor any compulsion of any kind to make them care consistently for excellence—men like the savages which the poet Pherecrates presented last year at the Lenaea. If you found yourself among such men as the man-haters in that chorus, then you would be delighted to fall in with Eurybatus or Phrynondas, and would moan with misery and long for the viciousness of your fellow men here. As it is, you are spoiled, Socrates: because each and every man teaches excellence as well as he is able, you think that no one does. Yet no more would you find one man who teaches people to speak their native Greek, if you were to look for one. No more would you succeed, if you were to try to establish which individual man teaches the sons of our craftsmen, when they have learned from their fathers and from their fathers' fellow-craftsmen all teaching as well as they are able. I do not think it is easy, Socrates, to single out any one of these as the teacher, though it is quite easy to identify their teachers as a group from among the whole populace. And such is the case with excellence and with everything else.

"So that if any one of us is even marginally better at advancing people along the path to excellence, he should be welcomed. I believe that I am one of these, being better than others at helping men on their way to becoming *noble and excellent*, worthy of my fee, if not more, as my pupils agree. That is why I have adopted the following method of charging. Any student may, if he wishes, pay me my fee in cash. But if not, he can go to a temple, make a sworn declaration of what he believes to be the true value of my instruction, and deposit that sum.

"There now, Socrates," he said, "I have given you both parable and argument. I have shown you that excellence can be taught, that the Athenians believe it to be so, and that it isn't surprising that the sons of good fathers turn out to be good-for-nothings—after all, even the sons of Polycleitus, who are contemporaries of Paralus and Xanthippus here, bear no comparison with their father, any more than the sons of other craftsmen do; but it is still too early to find fault with them over this; there is still hope for them: for they are young."

Such was Protagoras' demonstration which he now brought to an end. And for a long time I went on gazing at him, mesmerized, expecting him to continue, hanging on his words. But when I realized that he really had finished, I recovered, with some difficulty, my presence of mind, and turned to speak to Hippocrates:

"Son of Apollodorus, I thank you most sincerely for having prevailed upon me to come here. To have heard what I have just heard from Protagoras has been invaluable to me. For till now I had been of the opinion that it was not by any human effort that *good men* become good. But now he has convinced me.

"Except, that is, for one small difficulty which I am sure Protagoras will easily explain, now that he has already explained so many other points. For indeed, if you went and discussed these very matters with one of our political orators, be it Pericles or another of our competent speakers, you might hear much the same arguments from them. Yet if one of these is asked a further question, they are like books, incapable of returning an answer or asking a question; ask them the slightest question about what they have said and just as bronze vessels, once struck, ring on and on till someone puts a hand to them, so orators, asked the smallest question, spin out a marathon speech. But Protagoras here is equally competent at delivering long and splendid speeches, as we have heard for ourselves, and at answering a question briefly, and, when he has asked a question himself, at waiting to hear other people's replies—a rare attainment.

"So now, Protagoras, I shall have all I need if you would answer me just this. You say that excellence can be taught, and you of all men should be able to convince me. But one thing you said I found strange, and I should like you to satisfy my mind on the point. You were saying that Zeus sent *justice* and a sense of shame to man, and again at several points in your speech you were speaking of *justice* and *moderation* and *holiness* and so on, as though they amounted to a single thing: *excellence*. This is the point on which I need a precise explanation. Is it the case that excellence is some single thing, while justice, moderation and holiness are parts of it, or is it that all these things which I mentioned just now are names for one and the same single thing? That is what I still need from you.''

"Well, that is an easy question to answer, Socrates," he said. "Excellence is a single thing, and the things about which you ask are parts of it.''

"Do you mean," I said, "as the parts of the face—mouth, nose, eyes and ears—are parts, or are they like the parts of a lump of gold, indistinguishable from each other and from the whole except in size?''

"The former, I think, Socrates. They are related to excellence as the parts of the face are related to the whole face.''

"In that case," said I, "is it also true that, when men come to have these parts of excellence in common, some have one part and others another, or is it that if a man acquires one he has them all?''

"Certainly not," he said. "Many men are *courageous* but *unjust*; and many are *just* but not *wise*.''

"So these are also parts of excellence," I said, "*wisdom*, I mean, and *courage*?''

"Oh, most certainly so," he said. "And wisdom is the greatest of all the parts.''

"And in each case one part is one thing and another is something distinct?''

"Yes.''

"And is it the case that each of them has a unique capacity? Take, for example, the parts of the face: the eye isn't the same kind of thing as the ears, nor does it have the same capacity; nor is any one of the other parts the same kind of thing as any other part, either in its capacity or in any other respect. Is this also true of the parts of excellence; and is it the case that no one part is the same kind of thing as another part, either in itself or in its capacity? It must be, mustn't it, if it conforms to the analogy?''

"It is indeed so, Socrates," he said. And I said:

"So none of the other parts of excellence is the same kind of thing as *knowledge*, and similarly for *justice*, for *courage*, for *moderation*, and for *holiness*?''

He agreed.

"Well, now," I said, "let us examine together what kind of thing each of them is, beginning with this. Is *justice* some thing or no thing at all? I think it is; what about you?''

"I think so too," he said.

"Very well. Then if someone were to ask me and you, 'Tell me, Protagoras and Socrates, this thing, as you just termed it, justice: is it itself *just* or *unjust*?', my reply would be that it is just. Which way would you vote: the same as me, or otherwise?"

"The same," he said.

"Then in answer to the question, I should say that justice is a just kind of thing; wouldn't you?"

"Yes," he said.

"So that if he should then ask, 'Don't you also say that holiness is something?' I assume we should say yes."

"Yes," he said.

"And if he added, 'And don't you agree that this also is a thing?' we should say yes, shouldn't we?"

He agreed to this as well.

" 'But do you say that the thing itself is essentially an *unholy* kind of thing, or a *holy* kind of thing?' For myself I should be indignant and say: 'Mortal, guard thy tongue! There could hardly be anything else which is holy if holiness itself is not holy.' What about you? I take it you would give the same answer?"

"Absolutely," he said.

"Then if he went on to ask us: 'But what was it you were claiming a moment ago? I suppose I heard you correctly? I thought you were saying that the parts of excellence are so related that no one of them can be the same kind of thing as any other.' For my part, I should say: 'You heard quite correctly, except for your impression that it was I who said it; here you misheard. It was Protagoras here who was making the statement, in reply to my questions.' If he were to respond by saying: 'Is it true what this man says, Protagoras? Do you in fact maintain that no part of excellence is the same kind of thing as any other? Is this indeed your position?' How would you reply?"

"I should have to agree, Socrates," he said.

"And now that we are agreed on this point, Protagoras, what shall we say if he persists with his questions and says: 'So holiness is not a just kind of thing, nor justice a holy kind of thing, but rather of such a kind as not to be holy; while holiness is of such a kind as not to be just, but, in consequence, unjust, and justice unholy'? How should we reply? For if I were to speak for myself, I should say both that justice is holy and that holiness is just; indeed, I should give the same reply on your behalf as well, if you would permit it: that is, that justice is the same as holiness, or as similar as it can be, and above all that justice is the same kind of thing as holiness, and *vice versa*. But consider whether you would prevent me from making this reply for you, or whether you share the same view.''

"Not exactly, Socrates,'' he said. ''I don't think it is just a simple matter of agreeing that justice is holy and holiness just. I think there is a difference there. Still, what does it matter?'' he said. ''If you like, we can take it that justice is holy and holiness just.''

"Oh no I can't,'' I said; ''it isn't this 'if you like' or 'if you think so' I want to examine, but me and you. I say 'me and you' because I believe that the question will best be examined without the 'if.' ''

"Very well,'' he said, ''there is a certain similarity between justice and holiness; indeed there could be a certain similarity between anything and virtually anything else. There could be, for example, a certain similarity between black and white, or hard and soft, and so on; though one would say that they were absolute opposites. Thus to return to the previous point, that the parts of the face have each a distinct capacity, and that no one of them is the same kind of thing as any other, there is, nevertheless, a sense in which they are alike and in which one is like another. So by this method you could, if you chose, maintain that they are all alike. But it isn't fair to call things similar merely on the grounds that they bear some one point of similarity, however minor, any more than it is fair to call them dissimilar merely because they have some single dissimilarity.''

Surprised at this, I said: ''Oh, is that how you see the relationship between justice and holiness—as having only a minor similarity?''

"Not quite that,'' he said, ''but not as you seem to suppose, either.''

"Never mind,'' I said; ''since you appear to be unhappy with that line of argument, let's leave it there and examine one of your other points. Is there something which you call *folly*?''

He assented to this.

"And isn't the absolute opposite of this thing *wisdom*?''

"So I believe,'' he said.

"Now when men act *correctly* and *advantageously*, do you then say that they are *controlling their actions*, or the opposite?''

"They are controlling their actions,'' he said.

"And do they not control their actions under the influence of *self-control*?''

"Necessarily," he said.

"And is it the case that those who don't act correctly act *foolishly*, and in so doing are not controlling their actions?"

"Yes, I think so," he said.

"So acting foolishly is the opposite of acting *in a self-controlled manner*?"

He said it was.

"And is it the case that what is done foolishly is done under the influence of *folly*, and that what is done in a self-controlled manner is done under the influence of self-control?"

He agreed.

"And if something is done under the influence of strength it is done strongly and if under the influence of weakness, weakly?"

So he thought.

"And if with quickness, quickly, and if with slowness, slowly?"

It was.

"So whatever is done thus and so, is done under the influence of thus and such a thing, and similarly for its opposite?"

He agreed.

"Now," I said, "is there such a thing as the *noble*?"

"Yes."

"And does it have any opposite but the *base*?"

"No."

"And such a thing as the *good*?"

"Yes."

"Having any opposite but the *bad*?"

"No."

"What about high pitch: is there such a thing?"

He said yes.

"Does it have any opposite but low?"

He said no.

"So," I said, "for each of the opposites there is one single opposite and no more?"

He continued to agree.

"Come now," I said, "let us reckon up what we have agreed so far. We are agreed that for each thing there is one single opposite and no more?"

"We are."

"And that what is done in an opposite manner is done under the influence of an opposite?"

He said yes.

"And we are agreed that what is done *foolishly* is done in

an opposite manner from what is done *in a self-controlled manner?*"

He said yes.

"And that what is done *in a self-controlled manner* is done under the influence of *self-control*, while what is done foolishly is done under the influence of *folly?*"

He agreed.

"And since they are done in an opposite manner, they would each be done under the influence of an opposite?"

"Yes."

"And one is done under the influence of *self-control* while the other is done under the influence of *folly?*"

"Yes."

"In an opposite manner?"

"Absolutely."

"Under the influence of opposites?"

"Yes."

"So that folly is the opposite of self-control?"

"Apparently."

"Well, do you recall our earlier agreement that folly is the opposite of *wisdom?*"

He did.

"And that to one thing there is one single opposite and no more?"

"I agree."

"In that case, Protagoras, which of our two statements are we to give up: that one thing is the opposite of only one thing, or the claim that wisdom is a thing distinct from self-control, and that each is a part of excellence, and that in addition to being distinct they are also dissimilar both in themselves and in relation to their capacities, as with the parts of the face? Which are we to give up? The two statements are not in unison; they don't chime in well-tuned harmony together. How could they, when one thing can have only one opposite and no more, while wisdom and self-control are each the opposite of folly, itself a single thing? That is how it is, isn't it, Protagoras; or would you have it otherwise?"

He agreed, though with great reluctance.

"Then wouldn't wisdom and self-control be one and the same thing? And what's more, we have already discovered that justice and holiness are more-or-less the same thing.

"Come now, Protagoras," I continued; "let us not falter till we have completed our investigation. Would you ever say that a man who *commits an injustice acts soundly* in committing that injustice?''

"For my part, Socrates," he said, "I should be ashamed to make such an admission. But many people say so."

"And shall I address myself to them," I said, "or to you?"

"If you like," he said, "address yourself first to the popular view."

"It's all the same to me," I said, "whether the view is your own or not, just so long as you are giving the answers. For it is the view itself which I shall be testing; though it may turn out that it's both I who ask and you who answer who are being tested."

At first Protagoras tried to make excuses, and claimed that it was a complicated question. Finally, however, he agreed to answer.

"Come," I said, "let's go back to the beginning. Would you say that some men who *commit injustice act soundly*?"

"We shall assume so."

"And when you say *act soundly*, you mean that they *exercise good sense*?"

"Yes."

"And when you say *good sense*, you mean that they *plan well* by committing those injustices?"

"Let us say that."

"If they *do well* in committing it, or if they do badly?"

"If they do well."

"Do you call some things *good*?"

"I do."

"And what you call good," I said, "are things which are *beneficial* to men?"

"Whether they are beneficial to men or not, by Zeus," he said, "I still call them good."

It was obvious that Protagoras was riled and spoiling for a fight, setting out his answers in battle array. Realizing this, I continued with more caution and asked gently: "Are you referring to things which are beneficial to no man, Protagoras, or to things which are not beneficial at all? Is that what you call good?"

"Not at all," he said. "I know plenty of things which are not beneficial to men—foods, drinks, drugs, thousands of things—and plenty which are beneficial. But there are many other things which are neither beneficial nor harmful to men but are beneficial to horses. Again there are some things which are beneficial only to cattle or to dogs; or to none of these, but to trees; or good for the roots of trees but bad for the shoots. Dung, for example, is good for all plants when applied to the roots, but utterly destructive when applied to the shoots and young branches. The same is true of olive oil, which is thoroughly bad for all plants and most inimical to the hair of all animals but man; in the case of man, however, it benefits the hair and the whole body. Indeed goodness is such a diverse and complex thing that even in this case the same thing can be good for a man when applied externally, but very bad when taken internally. That is why doctors forbid sick patients to add more than the smallest quantity of oil to the food which they are to eat—just sufficient to overcome the unpleasantness that arises from food and savories, and affects the senses through the nostrils.''

This point was greeted by general applause, as well made. And I said: ''Being, as it happens, a rather forgetful sort of person, Protagoras, I tend to forget, faced with a lengthy statement, the original point of the argument. Now, suppose I happened to be hard of hearing: if you meant to hold a conversation with me, you would think it necessary to speak more loudly than normal; so now that you are faced by a man with a poor memory, please cut your answers down and make them short enough for me to follow.''

''What do you mean, 'make my answers short'? Am I to make them shorter than is necessary?'' he said.

''Certainly not,'' I said.

''As short as is necessary, then?'' he said.

''Yes,'' I said.

''Am I then to make my answers as short as I think necessary, or as short as you think necessary?''

''They do tell me,'' I said, ''that you are adept both as an exponent and as a teacher of the art of speaking either at length, if you choose, so that you never run dry, or briefly, so much so that no one could be more concise. So if you want to hold a discourse with me, please use the second technique—the brief one.''

''Socrates,'' he said, ''I have debated against many men in my time; and if I had argued by the rules of debate laid down by my opponent, as you demand, I should have proved no better than the next man, and the name of Protagoras would not be celebrated throughout Greece.''

Well I realized that he was dissatisfied with his performance so far, and would be reluctant to continue the discussion as answerer. So I decided that there was no longer any place for me in these proceedings, and said: "Very well, Protagoras, I don't insist on holding a discussion on what you consider unsatisfactory terms. But I will only converse with you when you are prepared to talk in a way which I can follow. For you, so they say, are equally competent at conversing briefly or at length: after all, you are *wise*. I, on the other hand, am no good at these long speeches, however much I might wish it otherwise. But it was for you, who are good at both, to make a concession to me, and adopt the method suited to both of us, to make the conversation possible; as it is, since you aren't prepared to do so, and I have other business, and I am not able to wait while you spin out your long speeches—I have an urgent appointment, you see—so I am going. Otherwise I might not have been unwilling to listen even to your speeches."

With these words I got up to leave. And as I was getting up Callias seized my hand with his right hand, this old coat of mine with his left, and said:

"We shan't let you go, Socrates; our discussion will not be the same if you leave. Do stay, I beg you. There is no one I should rather hear than Protagoras and you arguing it out. Please let us all have our way in this."

And I said—on my feet by now, and ready to leave: "Son of Hipponicus, I have always admired your love of wisdom, and I certainly praise and love you for it now; so I should willingly let you have your way if your request were a possible one to fulfill. But as it is you might as well beg me to keep up with Crison, the runner from Himera, in his peak form, or to match the speed of some long-distance or marathon runner. I should reply that, never mind you, I myself wish I could keep up with runners like these. But I can't. If for some reason it is necessary to watch me running in the same race as Crison, beg him to slow down: for I can't run fast, but he can run slowly. So if you desire to listen to Protagoras and me, beg him to answer briefly and to confine himself to the questions asked, as he did earlier. Otherwise, what basis for discussion can there be between us? For my part, I used to think there was a difference between a companionable discussion and a public harangue!"

"But Socrates," he said, "you must see that Protagoras is quite justified in asking for the same right to argue his points in the manner he chooses as you yourself are."

At this Alcibiades interrupted and said, "You're wrong, Callias. Socrates admits that he doesn't share Protagoras' aptitude for speaking at length, and defers to him; but when it comes to debate and skill in deploying and understanding an argument I should be surprised if he came off second to any man. If, therefore, Protagoras in turn admits that he is inferior to Socrates in debate, Socrates is content. If, on the other hand, he pretends otherwise, let him discuss the issue by means of question and answer instead of spinning out long speeches in response to every question, and avoiding the argument by refusing to give a reasoned account of his own position, and instead going on and on until most of his audience have forgotten the point of the question in the first place—except Socrates, that is: I have a suspicion he won't forget, in spite of his little joke about having a poor memory. So in my opinion Socrates' position is the fairer—after all, everyone must express his own point of view."

After Alcibiades, the next to speak, as I recall, was Critias, who turned to Prodicus and Hippias and said:

"In my opinion, Callias is highly biased toward Protagoras, while Alcibiades is always concerned to get his way in any enterprise. But we shouldn't take sides with Socrates or Protagoras in their jealous rivalry but beg them both equally not to break up our meeting."

At these words Prodicus said: "I quite agree, Critias. Those who are present at such discussions ought to give a hearing to both sides equally but not give both sides an equal hearing. There is a distinction: one must hear both sides equally yet not give equal weight to both, but more to the wiser and less to the more ignorant. My opinion, Protagoras and Socrates, is that you should agree to argue the topic and not to debate it: for whereas argument is conducted amicably among friends, debate takes place between antagonists and adversaries. The former will be the most proper atmosphere for our discourse. For you, by speaking in this spirit, will win our respect, not praise (respect being the sincerely felt disposition of us, your audience, as opposed to praise, which is a frequently insincere verbal expression of regard); while we, by listening, shall experience delight, not pleasure (delight being an intellectual feeling experienced by one engaged in the activity of thought and learning, as opposed to pleasure, which is an agreeable sensation accompanying such purely physical activities as eating)."

When Prodicus had finished, a large number of the company agreed with him. But after him the wise Hippias spoke:

"Gentlemen," he said, "I believe that all of us here are brothers, friends and compatriots, not by *convention* but by *nature*. For by nature it is affinity which makes us brothers, whereas convention, that tyrant of humanity, often violates nature by compulsion. What ignominy it is, then, that we should know the nature of things and yet, when we assemble together, we the *leading experts* of Hellas, in this sacred hearth of Hellenic *knowledge*, and in that very city's greatest and most magnificent household, in pursuit of that very knowledge—that we should have nothing to show worthy of this noble renown but fall to bickering among ourselves like the most vulgar of mankind. I therefore urge and implore you, Protagoras and Socrates, to be reconciled through our mediating arbitration. Socrates, do not insist on this rigorous and excessively brief form of discourse, if it displeases Protagoras, but ease off and hold a looser rein on your discussions and so make them grander and more elegant; Protagoras, do not spread all sail to the wind and take refuge on an ocean of words, concealing dry land from view. Take a middle course, both of you. Do as I suggest and choose someone to be umpire, chairman and president who can ensure a moderate length of argument on the part of each of you.''

The gathering approved of this proposal and everyone praised Hippias. Moreover Callias insisted that he would not let me go, while everyone begged me to select a chairman. So I pointed out that it would be invidious to appoint a referee over the arguments, ''since,'' I said, ''the man you appoint will either be inferior to us, in which case he will be in no position to judge between the better and the worse, or he will be our equal, in which case he will still be in no position to judge: for our equal will do the same as we do, so that his appointment will be otiose. 'Ah,' you may say, 'but we shall appoint a man who is your superior.' But in my opinion it is in fact impossible to choose anyone wiser than Protagoras, whereas if you select a man who is no better and claim that he is, this too will be a personal affront to Protagoras, as though you were appointing someone to preside over a nobody, though for myself I shouldn't mind at all. But I should like to adopt the following procedure to enable us to conduct the meeting and discussion which you desire. If Protagoras doesn't wish to be the answerer, then let him ask the questions while I give the answers; and at the same time I shall try to give him an illustration of what I consider to be the correct way to reply to questions. Then, when I have answered as many questions as he chooses to ask, let him likewise in his turn submit to my cross-questioning. In that case, if it turns out that he is reluctant to answer the actual question asked, I can join with you in begging him not to break up our gathering, just as you did with me a moment ago. Moreover this procedure needs no single presiding officer, since you will all be presiding together."

This proposal was accepted, and although Protagoras was very reluctant, he was forced to agree first to be the questioner and then when he had asked enough questions, to take his turn at giving only brief replies.

Protagoras began his questioning something like this:

"I believe, Socrates," he said, "personally, that the greatest mark of education in a man is his skill at discussing verses; that is to say, his ability to discriminate what is sound from what is unsound in a poet's writings, and to give a reasoned account in reply to questions. Indeed my question still concerns the topic which you and I were discussing just now—excellence, that is—but transferred to the context of poetry; that will be the only difference. Simonides, in a poem addressed to Scopas the son of Creon of Thessaly, says:

> To *be* a good man in truth, *I admit*,
> is *hard*—a man in mind and frame
> a flawless minting foursquare struck.

Do you know the lyric, or shall I recite the whole thing for you?"

And I said: "There's no need. Not only do I know the song, it so happens that I have made a detailed study of it."

"Good," he said. "Then do you find it well and soundly composed, or not?"

"Most excellently and soundly," I said.

"But do you think that a poem in which the poet contradicts himself is well composed?"

"No," I said.

"Then look," he said, "more closely."

"But my dear fellow," I said, "I have looked quite closely enough."

"Then you will be aware," he said, "that a little later in the poem he says:

> *Yet* Pittacus' familiar words, I find, do not
> ring true, though they come from a wise man;
> It is *hard*, he said, to *be* noble.

You realize that it is the same man who both says this and wrote the previous lines?''

"I know," I said.

"Then do you think," he said, "that the second statement is consistent with the first?"

"So it seems to me," I said, although I feared he might have a point. "Why, doesn't it seem so to you?"

"How can the man who makes both these statements appear to be consistent, when he begins with the premise that it is hard to be a good man in truth, and then a little further on in the poem forgets, and criticizes Pittacus, who says the same as he does, that it is hard to be noble, and refuses to accept his statement which is identical with his own? Yet when he criticizes the man who says the same as he does, he evidently criticizes himself, so that either his first or his second statement is not sound."

These words produced general applause and praise among the audience. And at first, like a man struck by a skillful boxer, my eyes went dim and my head reeled at his words and at the applause of the others. Then—and to be perfectly candid with you, I was trying to gain time to think out what the poet did mean—I turned and called on Prodicus.

"Prodicus," I said, "Simonides is a fellow-citizen of yours; so you are the right person to come to the man's assistance. So I think I shall call upon you. As the river Scamander called upon the Simoeis, in Homer, when it was beset by Achilles, with the words 'Dear brother, let us together check his mighty onslaught,' so I call upon you: let not Protagoras reduce Simonides to ruins. For now, you see, Simonides' rescue requires the art of which you gave such a fine demonstration just now: that of drawing distinctions between such things as 'wishing' and 'desiring.' See if you agree with me on this point. Simonides does not seem to be contradicting himself. But first, Prodicus, give me your opinion: do you think to *become* is the same as to *be*, or different?"

"Oh surely different," said Prodicus.

"And at the beginning Simonides gave his own opinion when he said that to *become* a good man was in truth hard?"

"That's right," said Prodicus.

"And when he criticizes Pittacus," I said, "he does not, as Protagoras supposes, thereby criticize the same statement as he himself had made, but a different one. For Pittacus' statement was not that it is hard to *become* good, as Simonides stated, but that it is hard to *be* good. But as Prodicus here says, Protagoras, to *become* and to *be* aren't the same thing. And if to *be* and to *become* aren't the same, it follows that Simonides doesn't contradict himself. Indeed, perhaps Prodicus and many others besides would agree that it is hard to be*come* good. As Hesiod says: 'The gods have placed sweat on the path to virtue; but when virtue's summit is mounted it is thenceforth an easy attainment, though it was hard to gain.' "

Prodicus approved my words; but Protagoras said: "The rescue is worse than the error from which you seek to rescue him, Socrates."

"Then I have done harm, Protagoras," I replied, "and I am, it seems, an absurd physician, whose treatment has aggravated the disease."

"I'm afraid that's so," he said.

"Why?" I asked.

"The poet must be exceedingly foolish," he replied, "if he thinks that excellence is so trivial a thing as to be regarded as an easy attainment when it is the hardest of all, as everyone agrees."

And I said: "By Zeus, what a happy coincidence that Prodicus should be here for our discussion. You see, Protagoras, I suspect that Prodicus' *knowledge* is both divine and ancient—going back to Simonides or perhaps even further. Yet it would seem that you yourself, learned as you are in many other fields, are not familiar with this one—not as familiar as I who have studied under Prodicus here. For in the present case I don't think you appreciate that Simonides didn't understand by '*hard*' in this context what you understand. Take the word '*terrible*'; each time I use the word to praise someone like yourself and say that 'Protagoras is a terribly wise man,' Prodicus corrects me and asks if I'm not ashamed to call bad what is good. For what is terrible, he says, is bad. At any rate no one speaks ever of 'terrible wealth' or 'terrible peace' or 'terrible healthiness,' but of 'terrible illness' and 'terrible war' and 'terrible poverty,' since what is terrible is bad. Thus perhaps by 'hard' Simonides and other Ceians understand 'bad' or something like that, without your realizing it. Let's ask Prodicus—for it's fair to ask him about Simonides' dialect. What did Simonides mean by 'hard,' Prodicus?"

" 'Bad,' " he said.

"And so presumably, Prodicus," I said, "that's why he criticized Pittacus for saying 'It's hard to be noble,' as though he understood him to mean that it's bad to be noble."

"Why, what else do you think Simonides means, Socrates," he said. "He's attacking Pittacus for the fact that being from Lesbos and educated in a barbarous dialect he was incapable of properly distinguishing the meanings of words."

"You hear Prodicus," I said to Protagoras. "What do you have to say to that?"

"That's quite wrong, Prodicus," he said. "I know perfectly well that Simonides meant by 'hard' precisely what everyone else means: not 'bad' but 'that which is not easy and is accomplished only with great effort.' "

"In my opinion, Protagoras," I said, "not only is that what Simonides meant, but Prodicus knows it was, and is joking and wants to see if you are capable of rescuing your own argument. For there is strong evidence that Simonides didn't mean 'bad' by 'hard' in the passage which immediately follows, where he says 'A god alone could have that privilege.' He would hardly say that it's bad to be noble, and go on to say that nobility belongs to the god alone, and so confine this privilege to the god alone: if so, Prodicus would be accusing Simonides, a fellow Ceian, of villainy. But if you really want to make the discussion of verses the test, as you claim, of my ability, I should like to explain what I think Simonides means in his lyric; or if you wish I shall listen to you."

Now Protagoras, hearing me say this, said, "If you want, Socrates." But Prodicus and Hippias and the others warmly urged me to go ahead.

"Well now," I said, "I shall try to expound my interpretation of the lyric. In all Greece, philosophy has the strongest and most long-established tradition in Crete and Lacedaemon [Sparta]; and it is there that the largest number of sophists is to be found. But, like the men whom Protagoras was calling sophists, they deny this and pretend to be uneducated, in order to prevent people from finding out that their dominance in Greece is due to their *wisdom*, and they prefer to give the impression that it is due to their military superiority and courage. For they think that if people found out the secret of their power then everyone would cultivate wisdom. And their deceit has quite fooled laconizers [pro-Spartans] in the Greek cities who, in their attempts to copy them, sport cauliflower ears and don boxing gloves, indulge in physical training and wear short cloaks, under the impression that such things have made Sparta a power among the Greeks. Now when the Spartans are tired of discoursing with their sophists in secret and wish to do so openly, they put an expulsion order on all foreigners in the country, including the laconizers among them, and consort with their sophists without the knowledge of any foreigner. Moreover, like the Cretans, they forbid their young to travel abroad in case they should unlearn all that they themselves have taught them at home. Indeed, in Sparta and Crete it is not only men who take pride in their education, but women as well.

"And here is how you can tell that I am right and that the Spartans are the best-trained in philosophy and argument. Anyone who talks even to the dullest Spartan will find that while for most of the time he seems rather dull in his speech, at some point in the conversation he will throw out a striking aphorism, short and pithy, like a crack shot, and make his companion look like a mere child. And some people, both now and in the past, have realized that laconizing was a matter of the pursuit not of good physique but of wisdom, knowing that the ability to make this kind of saying is the mark of a truly educated man. Among these are numbered Thales of Miletus, Pittacus of Mytilene, Bias of Priene, our own Solon, Cleobulus of Lindos, Myson of Chen, and, seventh, the Spartan Chilon. All these men admired, emulated and studied the Spartan form of education. If you want proof that their wisdom consisted of short memorable sayings, remember that they went to Delphi together and, on the temple there, dedicated to Apollo the first fruits of their wisdom in the sayings 'Know thyself' and 'Nothing in excess.'

"Why am I telling you all this? Because this literally laconic terseness was the traditional style of philosophy. And this saying of Pittacus, 'It's hard to be noble,' was privately circulated among the wise men and highly praised by them. Now Simonides, anxious for a reputation for wisdom, realized that if he attacked this saying and defeated it, then, just as if he had defeated a famous athlete, he would become famous in his own time. So I think he wrote the entire poem as an attack on this saying of Pittacus in order to discredit it.

"Let's study it together and see if I am right. And straight away the opening of the poem would obviously be mad if he meant to say that it is hard to *become* good but qualified it with 'I *admit*.' This qualification seems complete nonsense unless you take it to be directed at Pittacus' words, and assume that Simonides is speaking contentiously, saying, as it were, in reply to Pittacus' claim that 'it's hard to *be* noble,' 'No it isn't Pittacus; it's *becoming* good that's truly hard'—not, notice, truly good: it isn't that word to which the word 'truth' belongs, as though he meant that among all good things some were truly good while others

were good but not truly so; that would be too naïve for
Simonides. Rather we must understand the position of the words
'in truth' as a hyperbaton; thus we may imagine Pittacus' words
coming first, as if he were speaking them himself, and then
Simonides replying. First Pittacus: 'O mortals, it is hard to *be*
noble.' Then Simonides: 'O Pittacus, that isn't true. Not to *be*
good, but to *become* good, in mind and frame a flawless minting
foursquare struck—*that* is the hard thing in truth.' Thus, it
becomes clear that the insertion of 'I *admit*' makes sense and the
words 'in truth' find their correct position at the end. Moreover
what follows proves that this is his meaning. Indeed I could
provide abundant proofs of the poem's excellent composition at
each point; it is both carefully constructed and full of charm.
Since, however, it would take too long to go through the entire
poem in that way, let us examine its general character and
meaning to see how above all it is in its entirety a rebuttal of
Pittacus' saying. A little further on he says, if we imagine him
developing an argument, that whereas it is truly hard to become
a good man but possible for a short while, 'yet according to you,
Pittacus, having once reached that state, to remain in it and *be* a
good man is impossible and superhuman since "A god alone
could have that privilege,"

> . . . while a man
> can not escape *being* bad
> dragged down by helpless circumstance.

Now who is dragged down by helpless circumstance in the
command of a ship? Not the private passenger evidently, since
he already was down in the first place: you cannot cast down
someone who is already on the ground; it is the man who is on
his feet that can be cast down and put on the ground, not the man
who already is on the ground. In the same way it is only the
resourceful who can be dragged down by helpless circumstance,
not the man who already is helpless. So too the onset of a great
storm might render a steersman helpless, or the advent of a bad
season might leave a farmer helpless, or similarly in the case of a
doctor. For it is possible for the noble to become bad, as is
shown by these words from another poet:

> But a good man is bad sometimes
> as well as noble at others.

But for the bad man, not only is it impossible for him to become bad; of necessity he already is continuously bad. Thus when helpless circumstance drags down the resourceful, wise and excellent man, he cannot escape being bad. But you claim, Pittacus, that it is hard to be noble, whereas in fact *becoming* noble is hard (but possible), but to *be* noble is impossible:

> For if he does well, any man is good,
> but bad if he does badly.

Now of what does doing well at letters consist, and what makes a man do well at letters? Clearly, the knowledge of letters. Or in what respect does a man do well to be a good doctor? Clearly the knowledge of healing the sick. 'But bad if he does badly': now who could become a bad doctor? Clearly the man who has the property first of being a doctor, then, in addition, of being a good doctor. For such a man can in turn become bad, whereas we laymen could never by doing badly become doctors, builders or anything of the sort; and a man who cannot become a doctor by doing badly clearly cannot become a bad doctor either. Thus, while the good man might become bad as a result of time or overwork or illness or some similar misfortune (for this is the only respect in which a man can do badly—by deprivation of knowledge) the bad man could never become bad, because he already was bad in the first place; if, then, he is to become bad, he will first have to become good. So this part of the poem is to the same purpose, that while to be a good man (in the sense of persistently good) is not possible, becoming good is possible, and similarly for badness: 'While best for longest are those whom the gods love.'

"And it is not only these remarks which are directed at Pittacus. The following passages in the lyric would make the point even more clearly. He says:

> So I'll not waste my lifetime's meager ration
> on an empty dream, in search of what can never
> ever *become*: that flawless man
> among us who for our living
> toil in the broad earth;
> Should I find one I'll let you know.

Thus throughout the poem he inveighs against Pittacus' saying:

> I praise and love all men
> who do no *evil* willingly;
> even the gods
> do not combat necessity.

This too makes the same point. For Simonides was not so untutored as to declare his praise of everyone who *willingly* does no *evil*, as though there were people who willingly do evil. For I suspect no wise man thinks that any man willingly goes astray or willingly acts badly and disgracefully. They know perfectly well that all who do what is *shameful* and *bad* do so against their will. So in Simonides' case, he is not saying he praises anyone who does not do evil willingly, but is rather applying the word 'willingly' to himself. For he considered that a *noble man* frequently finds himself in the position of having to force himself to love and praise someone—say, an estranged mother or father, or country, or whatever it may be. So when bad men found themselves in this position, he believed, they observed with glee the wickedness of their parents or mother country and critically pointed out and condemned it, in the hope of avoiding opprobrium for neglecting them, so that they even redoubled their rebukes, and willingly added enmities to those they couldn't avoid; the good, on the other hand, are forced to cover up and praise them, and should they be indignant at some wrong inflicted by their parents or their state, they calm and soothe their own anger and compel themselves to love and praise their own kin. Now Simonides too, I think, frequently felt that he was eulogizing a tyrant or someone of that kind, not willingly but under compulsion. Thus in Pittacus' case, he tells him: 'Pittacus, my reason for blaming you is not that I'm a harsh judge, since "good enough for me the man who's not all bad,"

> nor lawless to excess,
> who knows the worth of justice, bastion of cities;
> a sound man: I'll find no fault with him.

For I'm not a fault-finding kind of man.

> Without number the breed of fools.

So if anyone does take delight in criticizing, let him find fault, to his heart's content, with them.

You see, all things are *noble*
which bear not *evil's* taint.'

Now he says this not as one might say 'All things are white
which bear no taint of black.' That would be silly in many ways.
Rather, he means that he tolerates without censure the middle
course. 'I am not seeking,' he is saying,

'that flawless man
among us who for our living
toil in the broad earth;
Should I find one I'll let you know.

Therefore I shan't actually praise anyone. Good enough for me
the man who finds the middle way and does nothing bad because:

I praise and love all men . . .'

. . . here, by the way, he has employed the Mytilenean dialect as
though it were for Pittacus' benefit that he said 'I praise and love
all men willingly'—it is here with this clause that we must take
the word 'willingly'—with 'I praise and love'—'though there
are some whom I praise and love against my will. As for you,
Pittacus, if your words had even been moderately reasonable and
true, I should never have criticized you. But as it is, you have
the reputation of being right on a most serious matter though
what you say is profoundly wrong; and because of that I do
criticize you.'

"That, Prodicus and Protagoras, is what, in my view,
Simonides meant in this poem."

Here Hippias spoke up. "A good account of the poem,
Socrates," he said. "And I," he added, "also have a rather good
interpretation of it myself which I will expound, if you like."

"Yes, Hippias," said Alcibiades, "some other time, perhaps. But right now it is time for Protagoras' and Socrates'
agreement to be fulfilled; Protagoras must either ask questions
for Socrates to answer or, if he wants to answer Socrates'
questions he must let Socrates do the questioning."

"I leave Protagoras to choose whichever course he finds the
more agreeable," I said. "With his permission let us give up
songs and poetry, but I should be delighted to complete our
mutual examination of the questions I raised with you, Protagoras,
a while ago. Intellectual discourse on poetry, it seems to me, is

very like the drinking parties of common unsophisticated types
who, because of their inability to provide their own voices or
their own conversation while they drink—such is their lack of
education—bid up the price of flute-girls, and pay large fees to
hire the extraneous voice of the flute and so accompany their
evening with its voice to compensate for their own lack of
conversation. But when the companions are *well-bred* and educated you won't find flute-girls, dancing girls or female acrobats:
they are capable of entertaining themselves by the use of their
own voices, without silly fun and games of that sort, taking their
turns at speaking and listening in good order even after they have
drunk deeply. So it should be in the case of gatherings like this,
with men of the sort most of us claim to be; there is no need for
an extraneous voice or for poets, who cannot be asked to explain
their meaning, while the vulgar introduce them into their conver-
sations and offer varying explanations of a poet's meaning, since
they are discussing a subject in which they aren't open to refutation. No, they leave such debates alone and provide each other
with their own entertainment through the medium of their own
discourse, testing and being tested by each other. Such are the
people you and I should emulate, in my view: we should set
aside the poets and hold discourse directly with one another,
putting ourselves to the test of truth. And I am willing to
continue to submit to your questions if that is what you prefer;
or, if you like, you can submit to my questions, in a thorough
and complete investigation of the matters we broke off just
now.''

These, and more to the same effect, were my words; and
when Protagoras would give no clear sign of what he meant to
do, Alcibiades turned to Callias and said:

''Do you approve of Protagoras' conduct in refusing to
make it clear whether he will take up the argument or not? I
certainly don't. Let him either take up the discussion or say that
he doesn't want to do so; then we shall all know, and Socrates
can debate with someone else, or else two others can take up the
argument.''

Protagoras seemed to me to be stung by this, because at
these words of Alcibiades, and with Callias and most of the
others adding their pleas, he reluctantly agreed to take up the
discussion and told me that I could ask the questions while he
answered.

So I said: ''Protagoras, you mustn't think I'm arguing with
you for any other purpose than the investigation of questions by

which I myself am constantly puzzled. Homer made an important point, in my view, when he said:

When two go in company, one sees before the other.

I suppose that in this way we are all more inventive in every enterprise, discussion and conception; but 'if one sees by himself' then he immediately goes round looking for a man with whom he can share his discovery and confirm it, until he finds someone. Which is why I should rather hold a discussion with you than with any other man. For I think you are the best man to examine important matters suitable for rational inquiry, and particularly *excellence*. After all, who better? Not only do you consider yourself a *noble and excellent man*, a quality which you share with others who, although they are decent men themselves, nevertheless cannot also make other men good, but you are both good yourself and are able to make other men good. And such is your confidence in yourself that where others conceal this skill, you publicly advertise yourself to the whole of Greece, call yourself a sophist, declare yourself a teacher of education and excellence, and were the first to charge a fee for this. Mustn't I therefore invite you to investigate these matters, and ask questions and consult with you? Of course I must.

"But now, to return to the subject of my earlier questions, I should like you to go back to the beginning and refresh my memory about some points, and to join with me in the investigation of others. My question, as I recall, was this: *wisdom, moderation, courage, justice*, and *holiness* are five names; but do they name the same thing, or does some distinct essence or thing uniquely correspond with each of them, such that each has its own unique capacity, and that no one of them is the same kind of thing as any other? To this you replied that they are not names for a single thing, but that each of these names uniquely denotes a distinct thing, and that all these are parts of excellence; not, however, as the parts of gold which are like each other and the whole of which they are parts, but as the parts of a face, both unlike the whole of which they are parts and unlike each other, each having its own unique capacity. If you are of the same opinion as before, say so; if of a different opinion, explain it precisely. I'm not holding you to any view, if you now say something else; for I shouldn't be surprised if you were just trying me out when you said that."

"My reply to you, Socrates," he said, "is that these are

indeed all parts of excellence, and that while four of them are tolerably close to each other, *courage* is absolutely different from all of them. You can see the truth of my words in this way: you will find many men who are utterly *unjust, unholy,* unruly, and *ignorant* who are nevertheless exceedingly *courageous.*"

"Come," I said, "your point deserves investigation. Do you call the courageous *daring,* or something else?"

"Oh, daring," he said; "and they readily go to meet what many fear to face."

"Well now," I said, "do you agree that excellence is something *admirable* and that you offer yourself as a teacher of it, assuming it to be something admirable?"

"Oh, the most admirable," he said, "unless I'm mad."

"Then is part of it *base,*" I said, "and part of it admirable, or is it all admirable?"

"Oh, obviously all admirable—as admirable as can be."

"Then you know that some men dive into wells *daringly?*"

"Yes, I do: divers."

"Because of their *knowledge,* or for some other reason?"

"Because of their knowledge."

"And who are daring at fighting on horseback? Is it the ones who have horsemanship or the ones without horsemanship?"

"The ones who have horsemanship."

"And what about fighting with light shields? Is it the experienced light infantrymen or not?"

"The experienced light infantrymen. And in general, if that's what you want to know," he said, "those who have knowledge are more daring than those who don't, while they themselves are more daring after acquiring it than they were before they acquired it."

"And," said I, "have you never come across people with no knowledge of any of these things, who are nevertheless daring at all of them?"

"Oh yes," he said, "only too daring."

"And are these daring men also courageous?"

"Well, in that case," he said, "courage would be a *despicable thing*: such men are crazy."

"So what do you mean by the *courageous?*" I said. "Didn't you say they were the *daring?*"

"I still do," he said.

"And isn't it clear," I said, "that men who are daring in this way are not courageous but crazy? And again that the *wisest* are the most daring? And being the most daring, the most

courageous? And that, according to this argument, *wisdom* would
be *courage*?"

"You haven't correctly recalled what I was saying in answer to your questions, Socrates," he said. "When you asked if
the courageous were daring, I agreed; but you did not ask if the
daring were courageous. If you had asked me at the time, I
should have said not always: but you have nowhere proved that
when I agreed that the courageous were daring, my statement
was wrong. What you in fact proved was that those with knowledge are more daring both than they themselves would otherwise
have been, and than others who lack knowledge, and you therefore think courage and wisdom are the same thing. This would,
by analogy, lead you to suppose that *strength* is wisdom. For if,
going on, you began by asking me if the *strong* are *powerful*, I
should say yes. Next you would ask if those who have knowledge of wrestling have greater physical power than those with
none, and are more powerful after learning to wrestle than
before, and I should agree. Armed with these admissions you
would then be in a position to say, advancing exactly the same
proofs, that on my own admission strength is wisdom. But
nowhere do I concede even in this last instance that the
physically powerful are the strong, but only that the strong are
physically powerful. For physical power and strength aren't the
same, since power can be the result equally of knowledge or
madness and rage, whereas strength comes from *nature* and
proper physical training. Similarly in our case I can say that
daring and courage aren't the same thing; so it follows that the
courageous are daring but the daring aren't always courageous.
For men acquire their daring both from skill and from anger or
madness, like their physical power, but courage comes from
nature, and the *proper training of the mind*."

"And you agree, Protagoras," I said, "that some men *live
well* and others *badly*?"

He did.

"Well, do you think a man would be living well if he lived
in pain and misery?"

He didn't.

"What about the man who lived out his life *pleasantly*? I
suppose you think that, in that case, he would have lived well?"

"It seems so to me," he said.

"Then living *pleasantly* is good and living unpleasantly is
bad?"

"If, that is, the things one *enjoyed* in life were *worthy of respect*," he said.

"What's this, Protagoras? Surely you don't agree with *ordinary people* that some *pleasant things* are *bad* and some *painful things* are *good*; I mean, insofar as things are *pleasant* are they not, *qua* pleasant, good, disregarding any possible consequences? And similarly with painful things: are they not, *qua* painful, bad?"

"Socrates," he said, "I'm not sure I ought to give the unqualified response your question invites and say that the *desirable* is always good and the painful always bad. Rather, bearing in mind not only your present question but also my life as a whole, I think it would be safest to reply that some things which are *desirable* aren't good, that some painful things aren't bad while others are good, and that there is a third group which is neither good nor bad."

"You mean by '*desirable*,' " I said, "involving or producing *pleasure*?"

"Quite," he said.

"I mean this," I said. "Insofar as they are *desirable* are they not *good*—in other words, isn't *pleasure* itself good?"

"As you keep saying," he said, "let us examine the question, and if our thesis seems reasonable and the pleasant turns out to be the same as the good, we shall agree; if not, then will be the time to disagree."

"In that case," I said, "do you wish to lead the inquiry, or am I to take the lead?"

"You are the proper one to take the lead," he said; "after all, you raised the question."

"Well," I said, "perhaps it would become clear in this way. Suppose a man were examining someone for health or some similar bodily function; he might look at the face and hands and then say: 'Now undress and show me your chest and back as well, so that I can examine you more thoroughly.' I desire to do something like that in the case of our inquiry. Now that I have examined you for your disposition in relation to the *pleasant* and the *good*, and have found it to be as you say it is, I want to say something like this: 'Come now, Protagoras, show me your attitude to this: what is your disposition in relation to *knowledge*? Do you agree with the general opinion, or do you disagree? For the general opinion about knowledge is more or less as follows: it isn't a strong or guiding or controlling element. And not only do people have this opinion about knowledge, but they also believe that in many cases where knowledge is present in a man, it is not the knowledge that controls him, but something else—now anger, now pleasure, now pain, now love, often fear—thinking of knowledge just as one does of a slave, as something dragged along behind all the other elements. Now is this the sort of view you have of it, or do you think knowledge is admirable and capable of controlling a man, such that if a man knew what is good and bad, nothing could overpower this knowledge or force the man to do anything other than what it dictates, since his intelligence provides the man with sufficient support?''

"I agree with what you say," he said. "Indeed, it would be *shameful* if I of all people didn't agree that wisdom or knowledge is the most powerful of all human qualities.''

"An admirable and correct reply," I said. "You know that most people don't agree with us; they say that there are many who know what is best and are in a position to do it, but nevertheless refuse to do so and do otherwise. And whenever I ask people how on earth they account for this, they say they behave in this way because they're overcome by pleasure, or pain, or one of the things I mentioned.''

"Yes, Socrates," he said, "but people are mistaken about many other subjects too.''

"Very well, join me in the attempt to persuade and teach people the nature of this experience of being overcome by pleasure and consequently of not doing what is best although they know it to be what is best. For when we say to them, 'What you say is not true; you are wrong,' they might ask us: 'Protagoras and Socrates, if this experience isn't that of being overcome by desire, what, pray, is it? What do you say it is?' ''

"But Socrates, why do we have to examine the opinion of the mass of mankind who say the first thing that comes into their head?''

"I think," I said, "that it will help us in our inquiry into courage and the relation between it and the other parts of excellence. So if you wish to abide by your previous agreement that I should lead the way on whatever path I think most likely to lead us to the truth about courage, which I think would be the best way of discovering the answer, then you follow. Or if you don't wish to . . . if it suits you, I'll drop the whole question.''

"You're right," he said. "Continue as you began.''

"Suppose," I said, "they went on to ask: 'What, then, according to you, is this phenomenon which we call being overcome by *desire*?' My own answer would be: 'Listen, while Protagoras and I try to tell you. Do you agree that the phenomenon you describe is quite simply the common experience of doing what we know to be bad, overcome by pleasures like food, drink or sex?' They would agree. You and I should then continue with our questions: 'In what respect do you say such things are undesirable? Is it because each of them causes immediate short-term *pleasure* and is *pleasant* only in the short term, or because they store up illness, poverty and such like for the future? Or would they still be bad even if they held no trouble in store and produced nothing but pleasure, no matter how or why?' Do we expect, Protagoras, that they would give any other answer than that they are bad, not in virtue of their immediate propensity to induce pleasure, but rather because of the ensuing illnesses and so on?"

"For myself," said Protagoras, "I think this would be most people's answer."

"And asked if such things cause suffering by causing illness and poverty, they would agree, I imagine?"

Protagoras assented.

" 'So you can see,' we should continue, 'that just as Protagoras and I were saying, they are bad merely because they result either in suffering or deprivation of other pleasure.' Would they agree?"

We both thought they would agree.

"Why don't we proceed to ask them the converse: 'You men who also claim that some unpleasant things are good—aren't you thinking of things like physical training and military service, and medical treatments which involve cautery, surgery, drugs and starvation diets, and of the fact that they are good but unpleasant?' They would say yes?"

He agreed.

" 'Very well, and is your reason for calling them good the fact that their immediate result is extreme pain and suffering, or isn't it the fact that at a later time they result in cures, and physical health, and the safety of the city, and power over others, and wealth?' They would say yes, I think."

He agreed.

" 'Then are these things good for any other reason than because they lead in the end to pleasure and release from, or prevention of, pain? Or is there any end result other than pleasure and pain to explain why you call things good?' They would say they couldn't, I think."

"I don't think they could either," agreed Protagoras.

" 'Therefore you seek pleasure as being good, while you avoid pain as being bad?' "

He agreed.

" 'In that case by bad you must mean painful, and by good, pleasant, since you say that even enjoyment is bad when it either deprives people of greater pleasure than it produces or causes pain greater than the pleasure it provides; after all, if you had some other aspect or consequence of pleasure in mind when you called it bad, you could tell us what it was: but you can't.' "

"No indeed they can't," agreed Protagoras.

" 'And conversely the same argument applies to suffering pain, I suppose. You call pain good either when it frees people from greater pain than it induces, or when it causes greater pleasure than pain? For if, when you call suffering good, you have some consequence in mind other than the one I have just mentioned, you can tell us what it is. But you won't be able to do so.' "

"You're right," said Protagoras.

" 'To continue,' " I said, " 'if you were to ask me "What on earth has all this rigmarole got to do with the question?" I should reply: "Pardon me, in the first place it isn't easy to explain what exactly it is that you mean by being overcome by pleasure, and secondly my entire argument hinges on this point." But even now you may make a different move if you have some way of maintaining that the good is something other than pleasure, or that the bad is something other than pain—or are you satisfied to live out your life pleasantly and free from pain? If, on the other hand, you are satisfied and have no other account of good and bad to offer which does not amount in the end to this one, I shall tell you what follows. I declare that in view of this fact, your statement has become absurd: I mean when you say that often a man, knowing the bad for what it is, still does it, led on and thrown into confusion by pleasure; and again when you say that a man refuses to do what he knows to be good, overcome by the pleasure of the moment.

" 'The absurdity will become clear if we give up using several words at the same time—pleasant, painful, *good, bad*— and since they amount to only two things, let us call them by two names: first of all, good and *evil*, and then pleasure and pain. Making this substitution let us say that the man, knowing bad for what it is, still does it. But if someone asks why, we shall say: "Because he is overcome." "By what?" he will ask us. But it will no longer be possible for us to say "By pleasure": for another word has been substituted for pleasure—the good. So let us now say in reply that he has been overcome. . . . "By what?" he will say. . . . "By the good," we shall reply, "by Zeus!" And if our questioner turns out to be rude, he will laugh and say: "How ludicrous to suggest someone does something bad knowing it to be bad, when there is no need to do it, because he has been overcome by the good! Is this," he will say, "because the good proves not to outweigh the bad in you, or because it does?" Obviously we shall reply that "It does not"; otherwise the man whom we say was overcome by pleasure would not have gone astray. "But in virtue of what," he will say, "can it be said that the bad outweighs the good or the good the bad? Can it be in virtue of anything other than the fact that the one is greater and the other smaller? Or because the one is more and the other less?" We shall be unable to offer any alternative. "So obviously," he will say, "by being overcome you mean choosing greater *ills* in preference to lesser good." So far so good.

" 'Now let us go back and substitute the words *"pleasant"* and *"painful"* in the same propositions: where before we said that a man does something bad, let us now say that he does what is painful, knowing it to be painful, overcome by pleasure, although obviously the pleasure does not outweigh the pain. And surely the only way in which pleasure can fail to outweigh the pain must lie in their relative excess or deficiency? That is, in their being mutually greater or smaller, more or less, stronger or weaker. Now if someone says: "But there is all the difference, Socrates, between immediate and postponed pleasure and pain," I should say: "Not, surely, a difference of anything other than pleasure and pain?" For it cannot involve anything else. So like a man who is good at weighing, take all the pleasures together, and all the pains together, and making allowance in the scales for their relative proximity or distance, tell us which is greater. Thus if you are weighing pleasures against pleasures it is always the more and the greater which must be chosen; but if you are weighing pain against pain, the less and smaller is to be preferred; if, however, you are weighing pleasure against pain, then if the pleasure outweighs the pain, be this a case of the more distant outweighing the more immediate or *vice versa*, then we must undertake that action which entails that pleasure; but if the pleasure is outweighed by the pain, we must not undertake it. Could it possibly be otherwise,' I should say. I know they could not disagree."

To this he agreed.

" 'That being so, answer me this,' I shall say: 'Do not some sizes appear larger from close up and smaller from a distance when you look at them?' They will agree. 'And similarly for width and quantity; and the same sound seems louder from nearby and fainter at a distance?' They would agree. 'Well, if doing well depended on our ability in practice to choose the larger and avoid the smaller with respect to physical size, what would safeguard our lives: the *art of measurement* or the power of appearances over us? Or is it not this power exerted by appearance which often confuses us and makes us change our minds back and forth about the same things when we set about the practical choice between great and small, whereas the art of measurement would have rendered this illusion powerless and in showing the truth would have kept our minds steadily on the truth without confusion, and thus guarded our lives?' Would men agree that it is the art of measurement, rather than any other art, which preserves us?"

"The art of measurement," he agreed.

" 'And what about this? Suppose that safety in life depended on our choosing between odd and even, whenever it was necessary to choose more and whenever it was necessary to choose less, whether independently or relatively, disregarding proximity and distance: what would it be that preserved our lives? Wouldn't it be *knowledge*? Moreover would it not be some kind of quantitative knowledge, since it is a skill concerned with excess and deficiency? And since we are concerned in particular with odd and even, must not that knowledge be mathematics?' Would men agree with us, or not?"

Protagoras agreed that they would.

" 'Well then, gentlemen: since it has become clear to us that our safety in life depends on the correct choice between pleasure and pain, involving as it does the consideration of more and less, greater and smaller, nearer and more remote, is not the inquiry in the first place about measurement, since it is concerned with excess, deficiency and equality?' "

"Inevitably."

" 'And since it is quantitative then necessarily, I take it, it is a *skill* and a *science*?' They will agree. 'In that case, we shall investigate at some other time the question of what kind of skill or science it is, although the mere fact that it is a science satisfies the requirement of proof which you asked Protagoras and me to give. Your question, if you remember, arose when Protagoras and

I were agreeing that there was nothing stronger than *knowledge*, and that wherever knowledge is present, it is always stronger than pleasure or anything else; but you claimed that pleasure is frequently too strong for the man who knows better, and it was at that point, when we were disagreeing with you, that you asked: ''Protagoras and Socrates, if what happens to us in such a case is not that we are overcome by pleasure, then what does happen to us, and what do you say happens to us? Explain.'' Now if at that point we had immediately said that it was ignorance, you would have laughed at us; but if you laugh at us now, you will be laughing at yourselves as well. You have admitted that men go wrong in choosing between pleasure and pain—that is to say, good and bad—because of a deficiency of knowledge; and not only of knowledge but, as you have already agreed, of quantitative knowledge. And you presumably realize that an error brought about by a lack of knowledge is caused by ignorance. Therefore, that is what being overcome by pleasure is: supreme ignorance. And it is of this ignorance that Protagoras here claims to be the physician, along with Prodicus and Hippias. But you, because of your belief that it is something other than ignorance, refuse to send your sons to these teachers of this subject, these sophists, and refuse to visit them yourselves, on the assumption that it cannot be taught; and because you prefer to hoard your money rather than pay it to them you do badly both individually and as a community.'

''So much for our reply to the *general public*. But now, Hippias and Prodicus, let me ask you as well as Protagoras this question, so that you can all be involved in the answers: do you think the view I have expressed is true or false?''

They all fell over themselves to agree that what had been said was correct.

''Then you agree,'' I said, ''that pleasure is good and pain is bad. . . . I beg leave to waive Prodicus' semantic distinctions; whether you call it pleasure, or enjoyment, or gratification, or whatever else you prefer to call it, my dear Prodicus, please answer to my intended meaning.''

Prodicus laughed and the others agreed.

''Well then, gentlemen,'' I said, ''what about this? Are not all actions which are directed at a pleasant and painless life *admirable*? And is not an admirable action *good* and *beneficial*?''

It was agreed.

''Then if,'' I said, ''a pleasure is good and someone knows or thinks that some course of action open to him is better than the course of action in which he is engaged, he will never proceed to the inferior course when he could have adopted the better. Nor can 'being overcome by oneself' be anything other than ignorance or overcoming oneself be anything but *wisdom*.''

They all agreed.

"What now? Do you agree that ignorance is having a false opinion and being mistaken about matters of importance?''

This too they all agreed.

"Furthermore,'' I said, "nobody willingly goes to face *evil* or what he thinks is *bad*, nor is it in human nature, apparently, for a man to seek what he thinks is bad in preference to the good; and when compelled to choose one of two *evils*, no one chooses the greater where the less is open to him?''

We were in complete agreement.

"Very well, then,'' I said. "Do you recognize the existence of terror and fear, and define it in the same way I do? I am addressing myself to you in particular, Prodicus. I define it as the expectation of something bad, whether you call it fear or terror.''

Protagoras and Hippias thought this was the definition both of terror and fear, while Prodicus held that it was the definition of terror but not of fear.

"No matter, Prodicus,'' I said, "provided you agree to this: if our former statements are true, no man will be prepared to face a situation which terrifies him when it is open to him to avoid it, will he? Is that not impossible on the basis of the points we have agreed so far? For we have agreed that a man is terrified by what he conceives as bad; and that no man willingly either faces or chooses what he conceives as bad.''

Everyone agreed to that too.

"Then with all these points established, Prodicus and Hippias, how can Protagoras defend the truth of his original reply—and by that I do not mean the first of all, when he said that there were five parts of excellence of which no one was like any other, each having its unique capacity—that's not the statement I mean, but the one he made later, when he said that while four of them were tolerably close to each other, one of them was very different from the rest, namely *courage*, and I should be able, so he claimed, to see the truth of his words in this way: 'You will find, Socrates,' he said, 'men who are utterly unholy, unjust, lawless and ignorant who are nevertheless exceedingly courageous; and from this you will realize that courage is very different from the other parts of excellence.' And for my part, even then I was amazed at his reply, though all the more so now, since I have covered all these points with you. I asked him, therefore, if he called courageous men daring, and he said 'yes, who readily go to meet what many fear to face.' You do remember giving these replies, Protagoras," I said.

He admitted it.

"Very well," I said, "tell me what it is that they readily go to meet: the same thing as cowards?"

"No," he said.

"Something else then?"

"Yes," he said.

"Isn't it true that cowards head for safety while courageous men head for *the terrible*?"

"So they say, Socrates."

"Perfectly true," I said, "but that wasn't my question; I wanted to know what you yourself think the courageous head for. Do they head for *the terrible* in the belief that it is terrible, or for the opposite?"

"Well, on your previous arguments, Socrates, this was shown to be impossible," he said.

"Right again," I said. "If therefore these arguments were sound, no one goes to meet what he conceives to be terrible, since being overcome by oneself was found to be ignorance."

He conceded this.

"But in that case, everyone, courageous and cowardly alike, heads for whatever makes him feel secure, from which it follows that cowards and courageous men head for the same things."

"But look here, Socrates," he said, "the coward and the courageous man head for completely opposite things: for example, courageous men are willing to go to war, the cowards are not."

"And do they do so," I said, "because they consider war to be *admirable* or because they consider it *contemptible*?"

"Oh, admirable," he said.

"And has not our previous discussion committed us to the view that if it is admirable it must be *good*? For we agreed that all admirable deeds are also good."

"What you say is true," he said, "and I still hold that view."

"Quite right too," I said. "But which group is it that you claim do not wish to go to war, although it is admirable and good?"

"The cowards," he said.

"And if it is admirable and good," I said, "is it also *desirable*?"

"Well, that's what we've agreed," he said.

"And are the cowards consciously unwilling to make for what is more admirable and better and more desirable?"

"By admitting that we shall be completely destroying our previously agreed conclusions," he said.

"What about the man of courage? Does he not make for what is more admirable and better and more desirable?"

"I must necessarily concede the point."

"Then all in all, isn't it true that the courageous are not susceptible to *contemptible* fears, when they do feel fear, nor do they derive their sense of security, when they do feel safe, from anything which is contemptible?"

"Correct," he said.

"If not contemptible, then *admirable*?"

He conceded the point.

"And if admirable, then also good?"

"Yes."

"And is it not true that the cowardly and the daring and the mad are on the contrary susceptible to contemptible fears and derive their sense of security from what is contemptible?"

He conceded the point.

"And do they thus feel secure in what is contemptible and bad through anything but untutored *ignorance*?"

"No, they don't," he said.

"Well then," I said, "this thing which makes cowards cowardly, do you call it courage or cowardice?"

"I would say, cowardice," he said.

"But has it not emerged that they are cowards in virtue of their ignorance of what is *terrible*?"

"Certainly," he said.

"So they are cowards in virtue of this kind of ignorance?"

He conceded the point.

"And you have admitted that what makes them cowards is cowardice?"

He agreed.

"Then wouldn't ignorance of what is and is not terrible be cowardice?"

He nodded.

"But now," I said, "courage is the opposite of cowardice."

He agreed.

"And is not the *knowledge* of what is and is not terrible the opposite of ignorance of those things?"

Here too he nodded.

"But ignorance of these things is cowardice?"

With great reluctance, once again, he nodded.

"Therefore *knowledge* of what is and is not terrible is *courage*, whose opposite is the ignorance of these things?"

By now he was no longer prepared even to nod, and sat silent. So, I said:

"Protagoras, why don't you answer my question, yes or no?"

"Finish the job yourself," he said.

"I have only one question left to ask you," I said. "Are you still of the opinion that there are some people who are utterly *ignorant* yet very courageous?"

"You seem utterly determined to get your way and have me giving the answers, Socrates," he said. "Still if it makes you happy. I shall say that on the basis of what we have agreed, I do consider this impossible."

"But my only motive for this whole line of questioning," I said, "has been my desire to investigate the general subject of excellence, and what excellence itself is. For I know that once this matter has been clarified, we shall be best able to settle the truth of the question which gave rise to this whole lengthy discussion; I refer to my claim that excellence is not teachable, and yours that it is teachable. And it seems to me that the outcome of our discussion is like someone pointing an accusing finger and laughing; and could he but speak he would say: 'What a pair you are, Socrates and Protagoras! You, Socrates, who were originally maintaining that excellence is not teachable, are now eagerly turning yourself inside out attempting to prove that all things are knowledge, including justice, moderation, and courage, which would make it obvious that excellence must be teachable. For if excellence were anything other than knowledge, as Protagoras was attempting to maintain, it obviously could not be teachable; but now, if it turns out to be entirely a matter of knowledge, as you are so eager to maintain, Socrates, it would be amazing if it were not teachable. But Protagoras, on the other hand, after committing himself to the view that it is teachable, is now apparently rushing off to the opposite extreme and trying to show it to be almost anything rather than knowledge, in which case it could not possibly be teachable.' So when I survey this terrible confusion and chaos, Protagoras, I have a burning desire to make sense of it. And I would like us to give a thorough account of this subject until we can emerge with an understanding of what excellence is, and only then return to attack the question of whether it can or cannot be taught. For otherwise I am afraid that old Epimetheus [Afterthought] may lead us into many errors in our inquiry, just as he was negligent toward us in your story, when he allotted the various capacities. I must say I preferred Prometheus [Forethought] to Epimetheus in the story. For I am making use of him, and taking forethought for my entire life when I concern myself with all these questions. And as I said at the beginning, I should much prefer to investigate the question with your help, should you be willing."

To which Protagoras replied:

"For my part, Socrates, I admire both your enthusiasm and skill with arguments. I do not regard myself as a bad man, certainly not one to be envious of others. For I have often spoken of you, since of all those I have met, particularly those of your generation, you are the man I most admire; and let me say that I should not be surprised if you became one of the great men of *wisdom*. Let us indeed return to our examination of these questions on some other occasion, whenever you please. But now it is about time to turn to something else."

"As you please," I said. "As a matter of fact the time of the appointment I mentioned is long gone; I only stayed behind to please the noble Callias."

Having said and heard these things, we went away.

MENO

Translated by Benjamin Jowett

Meno. Can you tell me, Socrates, whether virtue is acquired by teaching or by practice; or if neither by teaching nor practice, then whether it comes to man by nature, or in what other way?

Socrates. O Meno, there was a time when the Thessalians were famous among the other Hellenes only for their riches and their riding; but now, if I am not mistaken, they are equally famous for their wisdom, especially at Larissa, which is the native city of your friend Aristippus. And this is Gorgias' doing; for when he came there, the flower of the Aleuadae, among them your admirer Aristippus, and the other chiefs of the Thessalians, fell in love with his wisdom. And he has taught you the habit of answering questions in a grand and bold style, which becomes those who know, and is the style in which he himself answers all comers; and any Hellene who likes may ask him anything. How different is our lot! my dear Meno. Here at Athens, there is a dearth of the commodity, and all wisdom seems to have emigrated from us to you. I am certain that if you were to ask any Athenian whether virtue was natural or acquired, he would laugh in your face and say: "Stranger, you have far too good an opinion of me if you think that I can answer your question. For I literally do not know what virtue is, and much less whether it is acquired by teaching or not." And I myself, Meno, living as I do in this region of poverty, am as poor as the rest of the world, and I confess with shame that I know literally nothing about virtue; and when I do not know the "*quid*" of anything, how can I know the "*quale*"? How, if I knew nothing at all of Meno, could I tell if he was fair or the opposite of fair; rich and noble, or the reverse of rich and noble? Do you think that I could?

Meno. No, indeed. But are you in earnest, Socrates, in

saying that you do not know what virtue is? And am I to carry back this report of you to Thessaly?

Socrates. Not only that, my dear boy, but you may say further that I have never known of any one else who did, in my judgment.

Meno. Then you have never met Gorgias when he was at Athens?

Socrates. Yes, I have.

Meno. And did you not think that he knew?

Socrates. I have not a good memory, Meno, and therefore I cannot now tell what I thought of him at the time. And I dare say that he did know, and that you know what he said: please, therefore, do remind me of what he said; or, if you would rather, tell me your own view; for I suspect that you and he think much alike.

Meno. Very true.

Socrates. Then as he is not here, never mind him, and do you tell me: By the gods, Meno, be generous and tell me what you say that virtue is; for I shall be truly delighted to find that I have been mistaken, and that you and Gorgias do really have this knowledge, although I have been just saying that I have never found anybody who had.

Meno. There will be no difficulty, Socrates, in answering your question. Let us take first the virtue of a man—he should know how to administer the state, and in the administration of it to benefit his friends and harm his enemies; and he must also be careful not to suffer harm himself. A woman's virtue, if you wish to know about that, may also be easily described: her duty is to order her house and keep what is indoors, and obey her husband. Every age, every condition of life, young or old, male or female, bond or free, has a different virtue: there are virtues numberless, and no lack of definitions of them; for virtue is relative to the actions and ages of each of us in all that we do. And the same may be said of vice, Socrates.

Socrates. How fortunate I am, Meno! When I ask you for one virtue, you present me with a swarm of them, which are in your keeping. Suppose that I carry on the figure of the swarm, and ask of you, What is the nature of the bee? and you answer that there are many kinds of bees, and I reply: But do bees differ as bees because there are many and different kinds of them; or are they not rather to be distinguished by some other quality, as, for example, beauty, size, or shape? How would you answer me?

Meno. I should answer that bees do not differ from one another, as bees.

Socrates. And if I went on to say: That is what I desire to know, Meno; tell me what is the quality in which they do not differ, but are all alike—would you be able to answer?

Meno. I should.

Socrates. And so of the virtues, however many and different they may be, they have all a common nature which makes them virtues; and on this he who would answer the question, "What is virtue?" would do well to have his eye fixed; do you understand?

Meno. I am beginning to understand; but I do not as yet take hold of the question as I could wish.

Socrates. When you say, Meno, that there is one virtue of a man, another of a woman, another of a child, and so on, does this apply only to virtue, or would you say the same of health, and size, and strength? Or is the nature of health always the same, whether in man or woman?

Meno. I should say that health is the same, both in man and woman.

Socrates. And is not this true of size and strength? If a woman is strong, she will be strong by reason of the same form and of the same strength subsisting in her which there is in the man—I mean to say that strength, as strength, whether of man or woman, is the same. Is there any difference?

Meno. I think not.

Socrates. And will not virtue, as virtue, be the same, whether in a child or in a grown-up person, in a woman or in a man?

Meno. I cannot help feeling, Socrates, that this case is different from the others.

Socrates. But why? Were you not saying that the virtue of a man was to order a state, and the virtue of a woman was to order a house?

Meno. I did say so.

Socrates. And can either house or state or anything be well ordered without temperance and without justice?

Meno. Certainly not.

Socrates. Then they who order a state or a house temperately or justly order them with temperance and justice?

Meno. Certainly.

Socrates. Then both men and women, if they are to be good

men and women, must have the same virtues of temperance and justice?

Meno. True.

Socrates. And can either a young man or an elder one be good if they are intemperate and unjust?

Meno. They cannot.

Socrates. They must be temperate and just?

Meno. Yes.

Socrates. Then all men are good in the same way, and by participation in the same virtues?

Meno. Such is the inference.

Socrates. And they surely would not have been good in the same way unless their virtue had been the same?

Meno. They would not.

Socrates. Then now that the sameness of all virtue has been proven, try and remember what you and Gorgias say that virtue is.

Meno. Will you have one definition of them all?

Socrates. That is what I am seeking.

Meno. If you want to have one definition of them all, I know not what to say but that virtue is the power of governing mankind.

Socrates. And does this definition of virtue include all virtue? Is virtue the same in a child and in a slave, Meno? Can the child govern his father, or the slave his master; and would he who governed be any longer a slave?

Meno. I think not, Socrates.

Socrates. No, indeed; there would be small reason in that. Yet once more, fair friend; according to you, virtue is "the power of governing"; but do you not add "justly and not unjustly"?

Meno. Yes, Socrates; I agree there; for justice is virtue.

Socrates. Would you say "virtue," Meno, or "a virtue"?

Meno. What do you mean?

Socrates. I mean as I might say about anything; that a round, for example, is "a figure" and not simply "figure," and I should adopt this mode of speaking, because there are other figures.

Meno. Quite right; and that is just what I am saying about virtue—that there are other virtues as well as justice.

Socrates. What are they? Tell me the names of them, as I would tell you the names of the other figures if you asked me.

Meno. Courage and temperance and wisdom and magnanimity are virtues; and there are many others.

Socrates. Yes, Meno; and again we are in the same case: in searching after one virtue we have found many, though not in the same way as before; but we have been unable to find the common virtue which runs through them all.

Meno. Why, Socrates, even now I am not able to follow you in the attempt to get at one common notion of virtue as of other things.

Socrates. No wonder; but I will try to get nearer if I can, for you know that all things have a common notion. Suppose now that someone asked you the question which I asked before: Meno, he would say, what is figure? And if you answered "roundness," he would reply to you, in my way of speaking, by asking whether you would say that roundness is "figure" or "a figure"; and you would answer "a figure."

Meno. Certainly.

Socrates. And for this reason—that there are other figures?

Meno. Yes.

Socrates. And if he proceeded to ask, What other figures are there? you would have told him.

Meno. I should.

Socrates. And if he similarly asked what color is, and you answered whiteness, and the questioner rejoined, Would you say that whiteness is color or a color? you would reply, A color, because there are other colors as well.

Meno. I should.

Socrates. And if he had said, Tell me what they are? —you would have told him of other colors which are colors just as much as whiteness.

Meno. Yes.

Socrates. And suppose that he were to pursue the matter in my way, he would say: Ever and anon we are landed in particulars, but this is not what I want; tell me then, since you call them by a common name and say that they are all figures, even when opposed to one another, what is that common nature which you designate as figure—which contains straight as well as round, and is no more one than the other—that would be your mode of speaking?

Meno. Yes.

Socrates. And in speaking thus, you do not mean to say that the round is round any more than straight, or the straight any more straight than round?

Meno. Certainly not.

Socrates. You only assert that the round figure is not more a figure than the straight, or the straight than the round?

Meno. Very true.

Socrates. To what then do we give the name of figure? Try and answer. Suppose that when a person asked you this question either about figure or color, you were to reply, Man, I do not understand what you want, or know what you are saying; he would look rather astonished and say: Do you not understand that I am looking for the "*simile in multis*"? And then he might put the question in another form: Meno, he might say, what is that "*simile in multis*" which you call "figure," and which includes not only round and straight figures, but all? Could you not answer that question, Meno? I wish that you would try; the attempt will be good practice with a view to the answer about virtue.

Meno. I would rather that you answer, Socrates.

Socrates. Shall I indulge you?

Meno. By all means.

Socrates. And then you will tell me about virtue?

Meno. I will.

Socrates. Then I must do my best, for there is a prize to be won.

Meno. Certainly.

Socrates. Well, I will try and explain to you what figure is. What do you say to this answer?—Figure is the only thing which always follows color. Will you be satisfied with it, as I am sure that I should be if you would let me have a similar definition of virtue?

Meno. But, Socrates, it is such a simple answer.

Socrates. Why simple?

Meno. Because, according to you, figure is that which always follows color.

(*Socrates*. Granted.)

Meno. But if a person were to say that he does not know what color is, any more than what figure is—what sort of answer would you have given him?

Socrates. I should have told him the truth. And if he were a philosopher of the eristic and antagonistic sort, I should say to him: You have my answer, and if I am wrong, your business is to take up the argument and refute me. But if we were friends, and were talking as you and I are now, I should reply in a milder strain and more in the dialectician's vein; that is to say, I should not only speak the truth, but I should make use of premises which the person interrogated would be willing to admit. And this is the way in which I shall endeavor to approach you. You will acknowledge, will you not, that there is such a thing as an end, or termination, or extremity?—all which words I use in the same sense, although I am aware that Prodicus might draw distinctions about them; but still you, I am sure, would speak of a thing as ended or terminated—that is all which I am saying—not anything very difficult.

Meno. Yes, I should; and I believe that I understand your meaning.

Socrates. And you would speak of a surface and also of a solid, as for example in geometry.

Meno. Yes.

Socrates. Well then, you are now in a condition to understand my definition of figure. I define figure to be that in which the solid ends; or, more concisely, the limit of solid.

Meno. And now, Socrates, what is color?

Socrates. You are outrageous, Meno, in thus plaguing a poor old man to give you an answer, when you will not take the trouble of remembering what is Gorgias' definition of virtue.

Meno. When you have told me what I ask, I will tell you, Socrates.

Socrates. A man who was blindfolded has only to hear you talking, and he would know that you are a fair creature and have still many lovers.

Meno. Why do you think so?

Socrates. Why, because you always speak in imperatives; like all beauties when they are in their prime, you are tyrannical; and also, as I suspect, you have found out that I have a weakness for the fair, and therefore to humor you I must answer.

Meno. Please do.

Socrates. Would you like me to answer you after the manner of Gorgias, which is familiar to you?

Meno. I should like nothing better.

Socrates. Do not he and you and Empedocles say that there are certain effluences of existence?

Meno. Certainly.

Socrates. And passages into which and through which the effluences pass?

Meno. Exactly.

Socrates. And some of the effluences fit into the passages, and some of them are too small or too large?

Meno. True.

Socrates. And there is such a thing as sight?

Meno. Yes.

Socrates. And now, as Pindar says, "read my meaning": color is an effluence of form, commensurate with sight, and palpable to sense.

Meno. That, Socrates, appears to me to be an admirable answer.

Socrates. Why, yes, because it happens to be one which you have been in the habit of hearing: and your wit will have discovered, I suspect, that you may explain in the same way the nature of sound and smell, and of many other similar phenomena.

Meno. Quite true.

Socrates. The answer, Meno, was in the orthodox solemn vein, and therefore was more acceptable to you than the other answer about figure.

Meno. Yes.

Socrates. And yet, O son of Alexidemus, I cannot help thinking that the other was the better; and I am sure that you would be of the same opinion if you would only stay and be initiated, and were not compelled, as you said yesterday, to go away before the mysteries.

Meno. But I will stay, Socrates, if you will give me many such answers.

Socrates. Well then, for my own sake as well as for yours, I will do my very best; but I am afraid that I shall not be able to give you very many as good; and now, in your turn, you are to fulfill your promise, and tell me what virtue is in the universal; and do not make a singular into a plural, as the facetious say of those who break a thing, but deliver virtue to me whole and sound, and not broken into a number of pieces; I have given you the pattern.

Meno. Well then, Socrates, virtue, as I take it, is when he, who desires the honorable, is able to provide it for himself; so the poet says, and I say, too—

Virtue is the desire of things honorable and the power of attaining them.

Socrates. And does he who desires the honorable also desire the good?

Meno. Certainly.

Socrates. Then are there some who desire the evil and

others who desire the good? Do not all men, my dear sir, desire good?

Meno. I think not.

Socrates. There are some who desire evil?

Meno. Yes.

Socrates. Do you mean that they think the evils which they desire to be good; or do they know that they are evil and yet desire them?

Meno. Both, I think.

Socrates. And do you really imagine, Meno, that a man knows evils to be evils and desires them notwithstanding?

Meno. Certainly I do.

Socrates. And desire is of possession?

Meno. Yes, of possession.

Socrates. And does he think that the evils will do good to him who possesses them, or does he know that they will do him harm?

Meno. There are some who think that the evils will do them good, and others who know that they will do them harm.

Socrates. And, in your opinion, do those who think that they will do them good know that they are evils?

Meno. Certainly not.

Socrates. Is it not obvious that those who are ignorant of their nature do not desire them; but they desire what they suppose to be goods although they are really evils; and if they are mistaken and suppose the evils to be goods, they really desire goods?

Meno. Yes, in that case.

Socrates. Well, and do those who, as you say, desire evils, and think that evils are hurtful to the possessor of them, know that they will be hurt by them?

Meno. They must know it.

Socrates. And must they not suppose that those who are hurt are miserable in proportion to the hurt which is inflicted upon them?

Meno. How can it be otherwise?

Socrates. But are not the miserable ill fated?

Meno. Yes, indeed.

Socrates. And does anyone desire to be miserable and ill fated?

Meno. I should say not, Socrates.

Socrates. But if there is no one who desires to be miserable, there is no one, Meno, who desires evil; for what is misery but the desire and possession of evil?

Meno. That appears to be the truth, Socrates, and I admit that nobody desires evil.

Socrates. And yet, were you not saying just now that virtue is the desire and power of attaining good?

Meno. Yes, I did say so.

Socrates. But if this be affirmed, then the desire of good is common to all, and one man is no better than another in that respect?

Meno. True.

Socrates. And if one man is not better than another in desiring good, he must be better in the power of attaining it?

Meno. Exactly.

Socrates. Then, according to your definition, virtue would appear to be the power of attaining good?

Meno. I entirely approve, Socrates, of the manner in which you now view this matter.

Socrates. Then let us see whether what you say is true from another point of view; for very likely you may be right—you affirm virtue to be the power of attaining goods?

Meno. Yes.

Socrates. And the goods which you mean are such as health and wealth and the possession of gold and silver, and having office and honor in the state—those are what you would call goods?

Meno. Yes, I should include all those.

Socrates. Then, according to Meno, who is the hereditary friend of the great king, virtue is the power of getting silver and gold; and would you add that they must be gained piously, justly, or do you deem this to be of no consequence? And is any mode of acquisition, even if unjust and dishonest, equally to be deemed virtue?

Meno. Not virtue, Socrates, but vice.

Socrates. Then justice or temperance or holiness, or some other part of virtue, as would appear, must accompany the acquisition, and without them the mere acquisition of good will not be virtue.

Meno. Why, how can there be virtue without these?

Socrates. And the non-acquisition of gold and silver in a dishonest manner for oneself or another; or, in other words, the want of them may be equally virtue?

Meno. True.

Socrates. Then the acquisition of such goods is no more virtue than the non-acquisition and want of them, but whatever is accompanied by justice or honesty is virtue, and whatever is devoid of justice is vice.

Meno. It cannot be otherwise, in my judgment.

Socrates. And were we not saying just now that justice, temperance, and the like, were each of them a part of virtue?

Meno. Yes.

Socrates. And so, Meno, this is the way in which you mock me.

Meno. Why do you say that, Socrates?

Socrates. Why, because I asked you to deliver virtue into my hands whole and unbroken, and I gave you a pattern according to which you were to frame your answer; and you have forgotten already and tell me that virtue is the power of attaining good justly, or with justice; and justice you acknowledge to be a part of virtue.

Meno. Yes.

Socrates. Then it follows from your own admissions that virtue is doing what you do with a part of virtue; for justice and the like are said by you to be parts of virtue.

Meno. What of that?

Socrates. What of that! Why, did not I ask you to tell me the nature of virtue as a whole? And you are very far from telling me this, but declare every action to be virtue which is done with a part of virtue, as though you had told me and I must already know the whole of virtue, and this, too, when frittered away into little pieces. And, therefore, my dear Meno, I fear that I must begin again and repeat the same question: What is virtue? for otherwise I can only say that every action done with a part of virtue is virtue; what else is the meaning of saying that every action done with justice is virtue? Ought I not to ask the question over again; for can anyone who does not know virtue know a part of virtue?

Meno. No; I do not say that he can.

Socrates. Do you remember how, in the example of figure, we rejected any answer given in terms which were as yet unexplained or unadmitted?

Meno. Yes, Socrates; and we were quite right in doing so.

Socrates. But then, my friend, do not suppose that we can explain to anyone the nature of virtue as a whole through some unexplained portion of virtue, or anything at all in that fashion;

we should only have to ask over again the old question, What is virtue? Am I not right?

Meno. I believe that you are.

Socrates. Then begin again, and answer me. What, according to you and your friend Gorgias, is the definition of virtue?

Meno. O Socrates, I used to be told, before I knew you, that you were always doubting yourself and making others doubt; and now you are casting your spells over me, and I am simply getting bewitched and enchanted, and am at my wits' end. And if I may venture to make a jest upon you, you seem to me both in your appearance and in your power over others to be very like the flat torpedo fish, who torpifies those who come near him and touch him, as you have now torpified me, I think. For my soul and my tongue are really torpid, and I do not know how to answer you; and though I have been delivered of an infinite variety of speeches about virtue before now, and to many persons—and very good ones they were, as I thought—at this moment I cannot even say what virtue is. And I think that you are very wise in not voyaging and going away from home, for if you did in other places as you do in Athens, you would be cast into prison as a magician.

Socrates. You are a rogue, Meno, and had all but caught me.

Meno. What do you mean, Socrates?

Socrates. I can tell why you made a simile about me.

Meno. Why?

Socrates. In order that I might make another simile about you. For I know that all pretty young gentlemen like to have pretty similes made about them—as well they may—but I shall not return the compliment. As to my being a torpedo, if the torpedo is torpid as well as the cause of torpidity in others, then indeed I am a torpedo, but not otherwise; for I perplex others, not because I am clear, but because I am utterly perplexed myself. And now I know not what virtue is, and you seem to be in the same case, although you did once perhaps know, before you touched me. However, I have no objection to join with you in the inquiry.

Meno. And how will you inquire, Socrates, into that which you do not know? What will you put forth as the subject of inquiry? And if you find what you want, how will you ever know that this is the thing which you did not know?

Socrates. I know, Meno, what you mean; but just see what a tiresome dispute you are introducing. You argue that a man cannot inquire either about that which he knows, or about that which he does not know; for if he knows, he has no need to inquire; and if not, he cannot; for he does not know the very subject about which he is to inquire.

Meno. Well, Socrates, and is not the argument sound?

Socrates. I think not.

Meno. Why not?

Socrates. I will tell you why: I have heard from certain wise men and women who spoke of things divine that—

Meno. What did they say?

Socrates. They spoke of a glorious truth, as I conceive.

Meno. What was it and who were they?

Socrates. Some of them were priests and priestesses who had studied how they might be able to give a reason of their profession; there have been poets also who spoke of these things by inspiration, like Pindar and many others who were inspired. And they say—mark now and see whether their words are true— they say that the soul of man is immortal, and at one time has an end, which is termed dying, and at another time is born again, but is never destroyed. And the moral is that a man ought to live always in perfect holiness. "For in the ninth year Persephone sends the souls of those from whom she has received the penalty of ancient crime back again from beneath into the light of the sun above, and these are they who become noble kings and mighty men and great in wisdom and are called saintly heroes in after-ages." The soul, then, as being immortal, and having been born again many times, and having seen all things that exist, whether in this world or in the world below, has knowledge of them all; and it is no wonder that she should be able to call to remembrance all that she ever knew about virtue and about everything; for as all nature is akin, and the soul has learned all things, there is no difficulty in her eliciting, or as men say "learning," out of a single recollection, all the rest, if a man is strenuous and does not faint; for all inquiry and all learning is but recollection. And therefore we ought not to listen to this sophistical argument about the impossibility of inquiry; for it will make us idle, and is sweet only to the sluggard; but the other saying will make us active and inquisitive. In that confiding, I will gladly inquire with you into the nature of virtue.

Meno. Yes, Socrates; but what do you mean by saying that we do not learn, and that what we call learning is only a process of recollection? Can you teach me how this is?

Socrates. I told you, Meno, just now that you were a rogue, and now you ask whether I can teach you, when I am saying that there is no teaching, but only recollection; and thus you imagine that you will involve me in a contradiction.

Meno. Indeed, Socrates, I protest that I had no such intention. I only asked the question from habit; but if you can prove to me that what you say is true, I wish that you would.

Socrates. It will be no easy matter, but I will try to please you to the utmost of my power. Suppose that you call one of your numerous attendants, that I may demonstrate on him.

Meno. Certainly. Come hither, boy.

Socrates. He is Greek, and speaks Greek, does he not?

Meno. Yes, indeed; he was born in the house.

Socrates. Attend now to the questions which I ask him, and observe whether he learns of me or only remembers.

Meno. I will.

Socrates. Tell me, boy, do you know that a figure like this is a square?

Boy. I do.

Socrates. And you know that a square figure has these four lines equal?

Boy. Certainly.

Socrates. And these lines which I have drawn through the middle of the square are also equal?

Boy. Yes.

Socrates. A square may be of any size?

Boy. Certainly.

Socrates. And if one side of the figure be of two feet, and the other side be of two feet, how much will the whole be? Let me explain: if in one direction the space was of two feet, and in the other direction of one foot, the whole would be of two feet taken once?

Boy. Yes.

Socrates. But since this side is also of two feet, there are twice two feet?

Boy. There are.

Socrates. Then the square is of twice two feet?

Boy. Yes.

Socrates. And how many are twice two feet? Count and tell me.

Boy. Four, Socrates.

Socrates. And might there not be another square twice as large as this, and having like this the lines equal?

Boy. Yes.

Socrates. And of how many feet will that be?

Boy. Of eight feet.

Socrates. And now try and tell the length of the line which forms the side of that double square: this is two feet—what will that be?

Boy. Clearly, Socrates, it will be double.

Socrates. Do you observe, Meno, that I am not teaching the boy anything, but only asking him questions; and now he fancies that he knows how long a line is necessary in order to produce a figure of eight square feet; does he not?

Meno. Yes.

Socrates. And does he really know?

Meno. Certainly not.

Socrates. He only guesses that because the square is double, the line is double.

Meno. True.

Socrates. Observe him while he recalls the steps in regular order. (*To the Boy.*) Tell me, boy, do you assert that a double space comes from a double line? Remember that I am not speaking of an oblong, but of a figure equal every way, and twice the size of this—that is to say of eight feet; and I want to know whether you still say that a double square comes from a double line?

Boy. Yes.

Socrates. But does not this line become doubled if we add another such line here?

Boy. Certainly.

Socrates. And four such lines will make a space containing eight feet?

Boy. Yes.

Socrates. Let us describe such a figure: Would you not say that this is the figure of eight feet?

Boy. Yes.

Socrates. And are there not these four divisions in the figure, each of which is equal to the figure of four feet?

Boy. True.

Socrates. And is not that four times four?

Boy. Certainly.

Socrates. And four times is not double?

Boy. No, indeed.

Socrates. But how much?

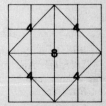

Boy. Four times as much.

Socrates. Therefore the double line, boy, has given a space, not twice, but four times as much.

Boy. True.

Socrates. Four times four are sixteen—are they not?

Boy. Yes.

Socrates. What line would give you a space of eight feet, as this gives one of sixteen feet—do you see?

Boy. Yes.

Socrates. And the space of four feet is made from this half line?

Boy. Yes.

Socrates. Good; and is not a space of eight feet twice the size of this, and half the size of the other?

Boy. Certainly.

Socrates. Such a space, then, will be made out of a line greater than this one, and less than that one?

Boy. Yes, I think so.

Socrates. Very good; I like to hear you say what you think. And now tell me, is not this a line of two feet and that of four?

Boy. Yes.

Socrates. Then the line which forms the side of eight feet ought to be more than this line of two feet, and less than the other of four feet?

Boy. It ought.

Socrates. Try and see if you can tell me how much it will be.

Boy. Three feet.

Socrates. Then if we add a half to this line of two, that will be the line of three. Here are two and there is one; and on the other side, here are two also and there is one: and that makes the figure of which you speak?

Boy. Yes.

Socrates. But if there are three feet this way and three feet that way, the whole space will be three times three feet?

Boy. That is evident.

Socrates. And how much are three times three feet?

Boy. Nine.

Socrates. And how much is the double of four?

Boy. Eight.

Socrates. Then the figure of eight is not made out of a line of three?

Boy. No.

Socrates. But from what line?—tell me exactly; and if you would rather not reckon, try and show me the line.

Boy. Indeed, Socrates, I do not know.

Socrates. Do you see, Meno, what advances he has made in his power of recollection? He did not know at first, and he does not know now, what is the side of a figure of eight feet; but then he thought that he knew, and answered confidently as if he knew, and had no difficulty; now he has a difficulty, and neither knows nor fancies that he knows.

Meno. True.

Socrates. Is he not better off in knowing his ignorance?

Meno. I think that he is.

Socrates. If we have made him doubt, and given him the "torpedo's shock," have we done him any harm?

Meno. I think not.

Socrates. We have certainly, as would seem, assisted him in some degree to the discovery of the truth; and now he will wish to remedy his ignorance, but then he would have been ready to tell all the world again and again that the double space should have a double side.

Meno. True.

Socrates. But do you suppose that he would ever have inquired into or learned what he fancied that he knew, though he was really ignorant of it, until he had fallen into perplexity under the idea that he did not know, and had desired to know?

Meno. I think not, Socrates.

Socrates. Then he was the better for the torpedo's touch?

Meno. I think so.

Socrates. Mark now the further development. I shall only ask him, and not teach him, and he shall share the inquiry with me; and do you watch and see if you find me telling or explaining anything to him, instead of eliciting his opinion. Tell me, boy, is not this a square of four feet which I have drawn?

Boy. Yes.

Socrates. And now I add another square equal to the former one?

Boy. Yes.

Socrates. And a third, which is equal to either of them?

Boy. Yes.

Socrates. Suppose that we fill up the vacant cor

Boy. Very good.

Socrates. Here, then, there are four equal space

Boy. Yes.

Socrates. And how many times larger is this space than this other?

Boy. Four times.

Socrates. But it ought to have been twice only, as you will remember.

Boy. True.

Socrates. And does not this line, reaching from corner to corner, bisect each of these spaces?

Boy. Yes.

Socrates. And are there not here four equal lines which contain this space?

Boy. There are.

Socrates. Look and see how much this space is.

Boy. I do not understand.

Socrates. Has not each interior line cut off half of the four spaces?

Boy. Yes.

Socrates. And how many spaces are there in this section?

Boy. Four.

Socrates. And how many in this?

Boy. Two.

Socrates. And four is how many times two?

Boy. Twice.

Socrates. And this space is of how many feet?

Boy. Of eight feet.

Socrates. And from what line do you get this figure?

Boy. From this.

Socrates. That is, from the line which extends from corner to corner of the figure of four feet?

Boy. Yes.

Socrates. And this is the line which the learned call the diagonal. And if this is the proper name, then you, Meno's slave, are prepared to affirm that the double space is the square of the diagonal?

Boy. Certainly, Socrates.

Socrates. What do you say of him, Meno? Were not all these answers given out of his own head?

Meno. Yes, they were all his own.

Socrates. And yet, as we were just now saying, he did not know?

Meno. True.

Socrates. But still he had in him those notions of his—had not?

Meno. Yes.

Socrates. Then he who does not know may still have true notions of that which he does not know?

Meno. He has.

Socrates. And at present these notions have just been stirred up in him, as in a dream; but if he were frequently asked the same questions, in different forms, he would know as well as anyone at last?

Meno. I dare say.

Socrates. Without anyone teaching him he will recover his knowledge for himself, if he is only asked questions?

Meno. Yes.

Socrates. And this spontaneous recovery of knowledge in him is recollection?

Meno. True.

Socrates. And this knowledge which he now has must he not either have acquired or always possessed?

Meno. Yes.

Socrates. But if he always possessed this knowledge he would always have known; or if he has acquired the knowledge he could not have acquired it in this life unless he has been taught geometry; for he may be made to do the same with all geometry and every other branch of knowledge. Now, has any one ever taught him all this? You must know about him if, as you say, he was born and bred in your house.

Meno. And I am certain that no one ever did teach him.

Socrates. And yet he has the knowledge?

Meno. The fact, Socrates, is undeniable.

Socrates. But if he did not acquire the knowledge in this life, then he must have had and learned it at some other time?

Meno. Clearly he must.

Socrates. Which must have been the time when he was not a man?

Meno. Yes.

Socrates. And if there have been always true thoughts in him, both at the time when he was and was not a man, which only need to be awakened into knowledge by putting questions to him, his soul must have always possessed this knowledge, for he always either was or was not a man?

Meno. Obviously.

Socrates. And if the truth of all things always existed in the soul, then the soul is immortal. Wherefore be of good cheer and try to recollect what you do not know, or rather what you do not remember.

Meno. I feel, somehow, that I like what you are saying.

Socrates. And I, Meno, like what I am saying. Some things I have said of which I am not altogether confident. But that we shall be better and braver and less helpless if we think that we ought to inquire than we should have been if we indulged in the idle fancy that there was no knowing and no use in seeking to know what we do not know—that is a theme upon which I am ready to fight, in word and deed, to the utmost of my power.

Meno. There again, Socrates, your words seem to me excellent.

Socrates. Then, as we are agreed that a man should inquire about that which he does not know, shall you and I make an effort to inquire together into the nature of virtue?

Meno. By all means, Socrates. And yet I would much rather return to my original question, Whether in seeking to acquire virtue we should regard it as a thing to be taught, or as a gift of nature, or as coming to men in some other way?

Socrates. Had I the command of you as well as of myself, Meno, I would not have inquired whether virtue is given by instruction or not, until we had first ascertained "what it is." But as you think only of controlling me who am your slave, and never of controlling yourself—such being your notion of freedom—I must yield to you, for you are irresistible. And therefore I have now to inquire into the qualities of a thing of which I do not as yet know the nature. At any rate, will you condescend a little and allow the question "Whether virtue is given by instruction, or in any other way," to be argued upon hypothesis? As the geometrician, when he is asked whether a certain triangle is capable of being inscribed in a certain circle,[1] will reply: "I cannot tell you as yet, but I will offer a hypothesis which may assist us in forming a conclusion. If the figure be such that when you have produced a given side of it,[2] the given area of the triangle falls short by an area corresponding to the part produced,[3] then one consequence follows, and if this is impossible, then some other; and therefore I wish to assume a hypothesis before I tell you whether this triangle is capable of being inscribed in the circle"—that is a geometrical hypothesis.

---

[1] Or: whether a certain area is capable of being inscribed as a triangle in a certain circle.

[2] Or: when you apply it to the given line, i.e., the diameter of the circle.

[3] Or: similar to the area so applied.

And we too, as we know not the nature and qualities of virtue, must ask whether virtue is or is not taught, under a hypothesis: as thus, if virtue is of such a class of mental goods, will it be taught or not? Let the first hypothesis be that virtue is or is not knowledge—in that case will it be taught or not, or, as we were just now saying, "remembered"? For there is no use in disputing about the name. But is virtue taught or not, or rather, does not everyone see that knowledge alone is taught?

Meno. I agree.

Socrates. Then if virtue is knowledge, virtue will be taught?

Meno. Certainly.

Socrates. Then now we have made a quick end of this question: if virtue is of such a nature, it will be taught; and if not, not?

Meno. Certainly.

Socrates. The next question is whether virtue is knowledge or of another species?

Meno. Yes, that appears to be the question which comes next in order.

Socrates. Do we not say that virtue is a good?—This is a hypothesis which is not set aside.

Meno. Certainly.

Socrates. Now, if there be any sort of good which is distinct from knowledge, virtue may be that good; but if knowledge embraces all good, then we shall be right in thinking that virtue is knowledge?

Meno. True.

Socrates. And virtue makes us good?

Meno. Yes.

Socrates. And if we are good, then we are profitable; for all good things are profitable?

Meno. Yes.

Socrates. Then virtue is profitable?

Meno. That is the only inference.

Socrates. Then now let us see what are the things which severally profit us. Health and strength, and beauty and wealth—these, and the like of these, we call profitable?

Meno. True.

Socrates. And yet these things may also sometimes do us harm, would you not think so?

Meno. Yes.

Socrates. And what is the guiding principle which makes

them profitable or the reverse? Are they not profitable when they are rightly used, and harmful when they are not rightly used?

Meno. Certainly.

Socrates. Next, let us consider the goods of the soul: they are temperance, justice, courage, quickness of apprehension, memory, magnanimity, and the like?

Meno. Surely.

Socrates. And such of these as are not knowledge, but of another sort, are sometimes profitable and sometimes hurtful; as, for example, courage wanting prudence, which is only a sort of confidence? When a man has no sense he is harmed by courage, but when he has sense he is profited?

Meno. True.

Socrates. And the same may be said of temperance and quickness of apprehension; whatever things are learned or done with sense are profitable, but when done without sense they are hurtful?

Meno. Very true.

Socrates. And in general, all that the soul attempts or endures, when under the guidance of wisdom, ends in happiness; but when she is under the guidance of folly, in the opposite?

Meno. That appears to be true.

Socrates. If then virtue is a quality of the soul, and is admitted to be profitable, it must be wisdom or prudence, since none of the things of the soul are either profitable or hurtful in themselves, but they are all made profitable or hurtful by the addition of wisdom or of folly; and therefore, if virtue is profitable, virtue must be a sort of wisdom or prudence?

Meno. I quite agree.

Socrates. And the other goods, such as wealth and the like, of which we were just now saying that they are sometimes good and sometimes evil, do not they also become profitable or hurtful, accordingly as the soul guides and uses them rightly or wrongly; just as the things of the soul herself are benefited when under the guidance of wisdom, and harmed by folly?

Meno. True.

Socrates. And the wise soul guides them rightly, and the foolish soul wrongly?

Meno. Yes.

Socrates. And is not this universally true of human nature? All other things hang upon the soul, and the things of the soul herself hang upon wisdom, if they are to be good; and so wisdom is inferred to be that which profits—and virtue, as we say, is profitable?

Meno. Certainly.

Socrates. And thus we arrive at the conclusion that virtue is either wholly or partly wisdom?

Meno. I think that what you are saying, Socrates, is very true.

Socrates. But if this is true, then the good are not by nature good?

Meno. I think not.

Socrates. If they had been, there would assuredly have been discerners of characters among us who would have known our future great men; and on their showing we should have adopted them, and when we had got them, we should have kept them in the citadel out of the way of harm, and set a stamp upon them far rather than upon a piece of gold, in order that no one might tamper with them; and when they grew up they would have been useful to the state?

Meno. Yes, Socrates, that would have been the right way.

Socrates. But if the good are not by nature good, are they made good by instruction?

Meno. There appears to be no other alternative, Socrates. On the supposition that virtue is knowledge, there can be no doubt that virtue is taught.

Socrates. Yes, indeed; but what if the supposition is erroneous?

Meno. I certainly thought just now that we were right.

Socrates. Yes, Meno; but a principle which has any soundness should stand firm not only just now, but always.

Meno. Well; and why are you so slow of heart to believe that knowledge is virtue?

Socrates. I will try and tell you why, Meno. I do not retract the assertion that if virtue is knowledge it may be taught; but I fear that I have some reason in doubting whether virtue is knowledge; for consider now and say whether virtue, and not only virtue but anything that is taught, must not have teachers and disciples?

Meno. Surely.

Socrates. And conversely, may not the art of which neither teachers nor disciples exist be assumed to be incapable of being taught?

Meno. True; but do you think that there are no teachers of virtue?

Socrates. I have certainly often inquired whether there were any, and taken great pains to find them, and have never succeeded; and many have assisted me in the search, and they were the persons whom I thought the most likely to know. Here at the moment when he is wanted we fortunately have sitting by us Anytus, the very person of whom we should make inquiry; to him then let us repair. In the first place, he is the son of a wealthy and wise father, Anthemion, who acquired his wealth, not by accident or gift, like Ismenias the Theban (who has recently made himself as rich as Polycrates), but by his own skill and industry, and who is a well-conditioned, modest man, not insolent, or overbearing, or annoying; moreover, this son of his has received a good education, as the Athenian people certainly appear to think, for they choose him to fill the highest offices. And these are the sort of men from whom you are likely to learn whether there are any teachers of virtue, and who they are. Please, Anytus, to help me and your friend Meno in answering our question, Who are the teachers? Consider the matter thus: If we wanted Meno to be a good physician, to whom should we send him? Should we not send him to the physicians?

Anytus. Certainly.

Socrates. Or if we wanted him to be a good cobbler, should we not send him to the cobblers?

Anytus. Yes.

Socrates. And so forth?

Anytus. Yes.

Socrates. Let me trouble you with one more question. When we say that we should be right in sending him to the physicians if we wanted him to be a physician, do we mean that we should be right in sending him to those who profess the art rather than to those who do not, and to those who demand payment for teaching the art and profess to teach it to anyone who will come and learn? And if these were our reasons, should we not be right in sending him?

Anytus. Yes.

Socrates. And might not the same be said of flute-playing and of the other arts? Would a man who wanted to make another a flute-player refuse to send him to those who profess to teach the art for money, and be plaguing other persons to give him instruction, who are not professed teachers and who never had a single disciple in that branch of knowledge which he wishes him to acquire—would not such conduct be the height of folly?

Anytus. Yes, by Zeus, and of ignorance, too.

Socrates. Very good. And now you are in a position to advise with me about my friend Meno. He has been telling me, Anytus, that he desires to attain that kind of wisdom and virtue by which men order the state or the house, and honor their parents, and know when to receive and when to send away citizens and strangers, as a good man should. Now, to whom should he go in order that he may learn this virtue? Does not the previous argument imply clearly that we should send him to those who profess and avouch that they are the common teachers of all Hellas, and are ready to impart instruction to anyone who likes, at a fixed price?

Anytus. Whom do you mean, Socrates?

Socrates. You surely know, do you not, Anytus, that these are the people whom mankind call Sophists?

Anytus. By Heracles, Socrates, forebear! I only hope that no friend or kinsman or acquaintance of mine, whether citizen or stranger, will ever be so mad as to allow himself to be corrupted by them; for they are a manifest pest and corrupting influence to those who have to do with them.

Socrates. What, Anytus? Of all the people who profess that they know how to do men good, do you mean to say that these are the only ones who not only do them no good, but positively corrupt those who are entrusted to them, and in return for this disservice have the face to demand money? Indeed, I cannot believe you; for I know of a single man, Protagoras, who made more out of his craft than the illustrious Phidias, who created such noble works, or any ten other statuaries. How could that be? A mender of old shoes, or patcher-up of clothes, who made the shoes or clothes worse than he received them, could not have remained thirty days undetected, and would very soon have starved; whereas, during more than forty years, Protagoras was corrupting all Hellas and sending his disciples from him worse than he received them, and he was never found out. For, if I am not mistaken, he was about seventy years old at his death, forty of which were spent in the practice of his profession; and during all that time he had a good reputation, which to this day he retains: and not only Protagoras, but many others are well spoken of; some who lived before him, and others who are still living. Now, when you say that they deceived and corrupted the youth, are they to be supposed to have corrupted them consciously or unconsciously? Can those who were deemed by many to be the wisest men of Hellas have been out of their minds?

Anytus. Out of their minds! No, Socrates, the young men who gave their money to them were out of their minds; and their relations and guardians who entrusted their youth to the care of these men were still more out of their minds, and most of all, the cities who allowed them to come in, and did not drive them out, citizen and stranger alike.

Socrates. Has any of the Sophists wronged you, Anytus? What makes you so angry with them?

Anytus. No, indeed, neither I nor any of my belongings has ever had, nor would I suffer them to have, anything to do with them.

Socrates. Then you are entirely unacquainted with them?

Anytus. And I have no wish to be acquainted.

Socrates. Then, my dear friend, how can you know whether a thing is good or bad of which you are wholly ignorant?

Anytus. Quite well; I am sure that I know what manner of men these are, whether I am acquainted with them or not.

Socrates. You must be a diviner, Anytus, for I really cannot make out, judging from your words, how, if you are not acquainted with them, you know about them. But I am not inquiring of you who are the teachers who will corrupt Meno (let them be, if you please, the Sophists); I only ask you to tell him who there is in this great city who will teach him how to become eminent in the virtues which I was just now describing. He is the friend of your family, and you will oblige him.

Anytus. Why do you not tell him yourself?

Socrates. I have told him whom I supposed to be the teachers of these things; but I learn from you that I am utterly at fault, and I dare say that you are right. And now I wish that you, on your part, would tell me to whom among the Athenians he should go. Whom would you name?

Anytus. Why single out individuals? Any Athenian gentleman, taken at random, if he will mind him, will do far more good to him than the Sophists.

Socrates. And did those gentlemen grow of themselves; and without having been taught by anyone, were they nevertheless able to teach others that which they had never learned themselves?

Anytus. I imagine that they learned of the previous generation of gentlemen. Have there not been many good men in this city?

Socrates. Yes, certainly, Anytus; and many good statesmen also there always have been, and there are still, in the city of Athens. But the question is whether they were also good teachers of their own virtue—not whether there are, or have been, good men in this part of the world, but whether virtue can be taught, is the question which we have been discussing. Now, do we mean to say that the good men of our own and of other times knew how to impart to others that virtue which they had themselves; or is virtue a thing incapable of being communicated or imparted by one man to another? That is the question which I and Meno have been arguing. Look at the matter in your own way: Would you not admit that Themistocles was a good man?

Anytus. Certainly; no man better.

Socrates. And must not he then have been a good teacher, if any man ever was a good teacher, of his own virtue?

Anytus. Yes, certainly—if he wanted to be so.

Socrates. But would he not have wanted? He would, at any rate, have desired to make his own son a good man and a gentleman; he could not have been jealous of him, or have intentionally abstained from imparting to him his own virtue. Did you never hear that he made his son Cleophantus a famous horseman; and had him taught to stand upright on horseback and hurl a javelin, and to do many other marvelous things; and in anything which could be learned from a master he was well trained? Have you not heard from our elders of him?

Anytus. I have.

Socrates. Then no one could say that his son showed any want of capacity?

Anytus. Very likely not.

Socrates. But did anyone, old or young, ever say in your hearing that Cleophantus, son of Themistocles, was a wise or good man, as his father was?

Anytus. I have certainly never heard anyone say so.

Socrates. And if virtue could have been taught, would his father Themistocles have sought to train him in these minor accomplishments, and allowed him who, as you must remember, was his own son, to be no better than his neighbors in those qualities in which he himself excelled?

Anytus. Indeed, indeed, I think not.

Socrates. Here was a teacher of virtue whom you admit to be among the best men of the past. Let us take another—Aristides, the son of Lysimachus; would you not acknowledge that he was a good man?

Anytus. To be sure I should.

Socrates. And did not he train his son Lysimachus better than any other Athenian in all that could be done for him by the help of masters? But what has been the result? Is he a bit better than any other mortal? He is an acquaintance of yours, and you see what he is like. There is Pericles, again, magnificent in his wisdom; and he, as you are aware, had two sons, Paralus and Xanthippus.

Anytus. I know.

Socrates. And you know, also, that he taught them to be unrivaled horsemen, and had them trained in music and gymnastics and all sorts of arts—in these respects they were on a level with the best—and had he no wish to make good men of them? Nay, he must have wished it. But virtue, as I suspect, could not be taught. And that you may not suppose the incompetent teachers to be only the meaner sort of Athenians and few in number, remember again that Thucydides had two sons, Melesias and Stephanus, whom, besides giving them a good education in other things, he trained in wrestling, and they were the best wrestlers in Athens: one of them he committed to the care of Xanthias, and the other to Eudorus, who had the reputation of being the most celebrated wrestlers of that day. Do you remember them?

Anytus. I have heard of them.

Socrates. Now, can there be a doubt that Thucydides, whose children were taught things for which he had to spend money, would have taught them to be good men, which would have cost him nothing, if virtue could have been taught? Will you reply that he was a mean man, and had not many friends among the Athenians and allies? Nay, but he was of a great family, and a man of influence at Athens and in all Hellas, and, if virtue could have been taught, he would have found out some Athenian or foreigner who would have made good men of his sons if he could not himself spare the time from cares of state. Once more, I suspect, friend Anytus, that virtue is not a thing which can be taught.

Anytus. Socrates, I think that you are too ready to speak evil of men: and, if you will take my advice, I would recommend you to be careful. Perhaps there is no city in which it is not easier to do men harm than to do them good, and this is certainly the case at Athens, as I believe that you know.

Socrates. O Meno, I think that Anytus is in a rage. And he may well be in a rage, for he thinks, in the first place, that I am defaming these gentlemen; and in the second place, he is of opinion that he is one of them himself. But some day he will know what is the meaning of defamation, and if he ever does, he will forgive me. Meanwhile I will return to you, Meno; for I suppose that there are gentlemen in your region, too?

Meno. Certainly there are.

Socrates. And are they willing to teach the young, and do they profess to be teachers, and do they agree that virtue is taught?

Meno. No, indeed, Socrates, they are anything but agreed; you may hear them saying at one time that virtue can be taught, and then again the reverse.

Socrates. Can we call those "teachers" who do not acknowledge the possibility of their own vocation?

Meno. I think not, Socrates.

Socrates. And what do you think of these Sophists, who are the only professors? Do they seem to you to be teachers of virtue?

Meno. I often wonder, Socrates, that Gorgias is never heard promising to teach virtue; and when he hears others promising he only laughs at them, but he thinks that men should be taught to speak.

Socrates. Then do you not think that the Sophists are teachers?

Meno. I cannot tell you, Socrates; like the rest of the world, I am in doubt, and sometimes I think that they are teachers, and sometimes not.

Socrates. And are you aware that not you only and other politicians have doubts whether virtue can be taught or not, but that Theognis the poet says the very same thing?

Meno. Where does he say so?

Socrates. In these elegiac verses:

> Eat and drink and sit with the mighty, and make yourself agreeable to them; for from the good you will learn what is good, but if you mix with the bad, you will lose the intelligence which you already have.[4]

Do you observe that here he seems to imply that virtue can be taught?

Meno. Clearly.

Socrates. But in some other verses he shifts about and says:[5]

---

[4]Hesiod, *Theog*., 33 ff.
[5]*Ibid*. 435 ff.

> If understanding could be created and put into a
> man, then they [who were able to perform this feat]
> would have obtained great rewards.

And again:

> Never would a bad son have sprung from a good
> sire, for he would have heard the voice of instruction;
> but not by teaching will you ever make a bad man into
> a good one.

And this, as you may remark, is a contradiction of the other.

Meno. Clearly.

Socrates. And is there anything else of which the professors
are affirmed not only not to be teachers of others, but to be
ignorant themselves, and bad at the knowledge of that which
they are professing to teach; or is there anything about which
even the acknowledged "gentlemen" are sometimes saying that
"this thing can be taught," and sometimes the opposite? Can
you say that they are teachers in any true sense whose ideas are
in such confusion?

Meno. I should say, certainly not.

Socrates. But if neither the Sophists nor the gentlemen are
teachers, clearly there can be no other teachers?

Meno. No.

Socrates. And if there are no teachers, neither are there
disciples?

Meno. Agreed.

Socrates. And we have admitted that a thing cannot be
taught of which there are neither teachers nor disciples?

Meno. We have.

Socrates. And there are no teachers of virtue to be found
anywhere?

Meno. There are not.

Socrates. And if there are no teachers, neither are there
scholars?

Meno. That, I think, is true.

Socrates. Then virtue cannot be taught?

Meno. Not if we are right in our view. But I cannot believe,
Socrates, that there are no good men; and if there are, how did
they come into existence?

Socrates. I am afraid, Meno, that you and I are not good for much, and that Gorgias has been as poor an educator of you as Prodicus has been of me. Certainly we shall have to look to ourselves, and try to find someone who will help in some way or other to improve us. This I say, because I observe that in the previous discussion none of us remarked that right and good action is possible to man under other guidance than that of *knowledge*—and indeed if this be denied, there is no seeing how there can be any good men at all.

Meno. How do you mean, Socrates?

Socrates. I mean that good men are necessarily useful or profitable. Were we not right in admitting this? It must be so.

Meno. Yes.

Socrates. And in supposing that they will be useful only if they are true guides to us of action—there we were also right?

Meno. Yes.

Socrates. But when we said that a man cannot be a good guide unless he has understanding, in this we were wrong.

Meno. What do you mean by the word "right"?

Socrates. I will explain. If a man knew the way to Larisa, or anywhere else, and went to the place and led others thither, would he not be a right and good guide?

Meno. Certainly.

Socrates. And a person who had a right opinion about the way, but had never been and did not know, might be a good guide also, might he not?

Meno. Certainly.

Socrates. And while he has true opinion about that which the other knows, he will be just as good a guide if he thinks the truth, as he who knows the truth?

Meno. Exactly.

Socrates. Then true opinion is as good a guide to correct action as knowledge; and that was the point which we omitted in our speculation about the nature of virtue, when we said that knowledge only is the guide of right action; whereas there is also right opinion.

Meno. True.

Socrates. Then right opinion is not less useful than knowledge?

Meno. The difference, Socrates, is only that he who has knowledge will always be right; but he who has right opinion will sometimes be right, and sometimes not.

Socrates. What do you mean? Can he be wrong who has right opinion, so long as he has right opinion?

Meno. I admit the cogency of your argument, and therefore,

Socrates, I wonder that knowledge should be preferred to right opinion—or why they should ever differ.

Socrates. And shall I explain this wonder to you?

Meno. Do tell me.

Socrates. You would not wonder if you had ever observed the images of Daedalus; but perhaps you have not got them in your country?

Meno. What have they to do with the question?

Socrates. Because they require to be fastened in order to keep them, and if they are not fastened, they will play truant and run away.

Meno. Well, what of that?

Socrates. I mean to say that they are not very valuable possessions if they are at liberty, for they will walk off like runaway slaves; but when fastened, they are of great value, for they are really beautiful works of art. Now this is an illustration of the nature of true opinions: while they abide with us they are beautiful and fruitful, but they run away out of the human soul, and do not remain long, and therefore they are not of much value until they are fastened by the tie of the cause; and this fastening of them, friend Meno, is recollection, as you and I have agreed to call it. But when they are bound, in the first place, they have the nature of knowledge; and, in the second place, they are abiding. And this is why knowledge is more honorable and excellent than true opinion, because fastened by a chain.

Meno. What you are saying, Socrates, seems to be very like the truth.

Socrates. I, too, speak rather in ignorance; I only conjecture. And yet that knowledge differs from true opinion is no matter of conjecture with me. There are not many things which I profess to know, but this is most certainly one of them.

Meno. Yes, Socrates; and you are quite right in saying so.

Socrates. And am I not also right in saying that true opinion leading the way perfects action quite as well as knowledge?

Meno. There again, Socrates, I think you are right.

Socrates. Then right opinion is not a whit inferior to knowledge, or less useful in action; nor is the man who has right opinion inferior to him who has knowledge?

Meno. True.

Socrates. And surely the good man has been acknowledged by us to be useful?

Meno. Yes.

Socrates. Seeing then that men become good and useful to

states, not only because they have knowledge, but because they have right opinion, and that neither knowledge nor right opinion is given to man by nature or acquired by him—(do you imagine either of them to be given by nature?

Meno. Not I.)

Socrates. Then if they are not given by nature, neither are the good by nature good?

Meno. Certainly not.

Socrates. And nature being excluded, then came the question whether virtue is acquired by teaching?

Meno. Yes.

Socrates. If virtue was wisdom [or knowledge], then, as we thought, it was taught?

Meno. Yes.

Socrates. And if it was taught, it was wisdom?

Meno. Certainly.

Socrates. And if there were teachers, it might be taught; and if there were no teachers, not?

Meno. True.

Socrates. But surely we acknowledged that there were no teachers of virtue?

Meno. Yes.

Socrates. Then we acknowledged that it was not taught, and was not wisdom.

Meno. Certainly.

Socrates. And yet we admitted that it was a good?

Meno. Yes.

Socrates. And the right guide is useful and good?

Meno. Certainly.

Socrates. And the only right guides are knowledge and true opinion—these are the guides of man; for things which happen by chance are not under the guidance of man; but the guides of man are true opinion and knowledge.

Meno. I think so, too.

Socrates. But if virtue is not taught, neither is virtue knowledge.

Meno. Clearly not.

Socrates. Then of two good and useful things, one, which is knowledge, has been set aside and cannot be supposed to be our guide in political life.

Meno. I think not.

Socrates. And therefore not by any wisdom, and not because they were wise, did Themistocles and those others of whom Anytus spoke govern states. This was the reason why they were unable to make others like themselves—because their virtue was not grounded on knowledge.

Meno. That is probably true, Socrates.

Socrates. But if not by knowledge, the only alternative which remains is that statesmen must have guided states by right opinion, which is in politics what divination is in religion; for diviners and also prophets say many things truly, but they know not what they say.

Meno. So I believe.

Socrates. And may we not, Meno, truly call those men "divine" who, having no understanding, yet succeed in many a grand deed and word?

Meno. Certainly.

Socrates. Then we shall also be right in calling divine those whom we were just now speaking of as diviners and prophets, including the whole tribe of poets. Yes, and statesmen above all may be said to be divine and illumined, being inspired and possessed of the god, in which condition they say many grand things, not knowing what they say.

Meno. Yes.

Socrates. And the women, too, Meno, call good men divine—do they not? And the Spartans, when they praise a good man, say "that he is a divine man."

Meno. And I think, Socrates, that they are right, although very likely our friend Anytus may take offense at the word.

Socrates. I do not care; as for Anytus, there will be another opportunity of talking with him. To sum up our inquiry—the result seems to be, if we are at all right in our view, that virtue is neither natural nor acquired, but an instinct given by God to the virtuous. Nor is the instinct accompanied by reason, unless there may be supposed to be among statesmen someone who is capable of educating statesmen. And if there be such a one, he may be said to be among the living what Homer says that Tiresias was among the dead, "he alone has understanding; but the rest are flitting shades"; and he and his virtue in like manner will be a reality among shadows.

Meno. That is excellent, Socrates.

Socrates. Then, Meno, the conclusion is that virtue comes to the virtuous by divine dispensation. But we shall never know the certain truth until, before asking how virtue is given, we inquire into the actual nature of virtue. I fear that I must go away, but do you, now that you are persuaded yourself, persuade our friend Anytus. And do not let him be so exasperated; if you can conciliate him, you will have done good service to the Athenian people.

SYMPOSIUM

Translated by Seth Benardete

Apollodorus. In my own opinion, I am not unprepared for what you ask about; for just the other day—when I was on my way up to town from my home in Phaleron—one of my acquaintances spotted me a long way off from behind and called, playing with his call: "Phalerian," he said. "You there, Apollodorus, aren't you going to wait?" And I stopped and let him catch up. And he said, "Apollodorus, why, it was just recently that I was looking for you; I had wanted to question you closely about Agathon's party—the one at which Socrates, Alcibiades, and the others were then present at dinner together—to question you about the erotic speeches. What were they? Someone else who had heard about the party from Phoenix the son of Philippus was telling me about it, and he said that you too knew. As a matter of fact, there wasn't anything he could say with certainty. So *you* tell me, for it is most just that you report the speeches of your comrade. But first," he said, "tell me, were you yourself present at this party or not?" And I said, "It really does seem as if there were nothing certain in what your informant told you, if you believe that this party which you are asking about occurred so recently that I too was present." "That is indeed what I believed," he said. "But how could that be, Glaucon?" I said. "Don't you know that it has been many years since Agathon resided here, but that it is scarcely three years now that I have been spending my time with Socrates and have made it my concern on each and every day to know whatever he says or does? Before that, I used to run round and round aimlessly, and though I believed I was doing something of importance, I was more miserable than anyone in the world (no less than you are at this moment), for I believed that everything was preferable to philosophy." And he said, "Don't mock me now, but tell me when this party did occur." And I said, "When we were still boys, at the time of Agathon's victory with his first tragedy, on the day after he and his choral dancers celebrated the victory sacrifice." "Oh," he said, "a very long time ago, it seems. But who told you? Was it Socrates himself?" "No, by Zeus," I said, "but the same one who told Phoenix. It was a certain Aristodemus, a Kydathenean, little and always unshod. He had been present at the party and, in my opinion, was the one most in love with Socrates at that time. Not, however, that I have not asked Socrates too about some points that I had heard from Aristodemus; and Socrates agreed to just what Aristodemus narrated." "Why, then," Glaucon said, "don't you tell me? The way to town, in any case, is as suitable for speaking, while we walk, as for listening."

So as we walked, we talked together about these things; and so, just as I said at the start, I am not unprepared. If it must be told to you as well, that is what I must do. As for me, whenever I make any speeches on my own about philosophy or listen to others—apart from my belief that I am benefited—how I enjoy it! But whenever the speeches are of another sort, particularly the speeches of the rich and of moneymakers—your kind of talk— then just as I am distressed, so do I pity your comrades, because you believe you are doing something of importance, but in fact it's all pointless. And perhaps you, in turn, believe that I am a wretch; and I believe you truly believe it. I, on the other hand, do not believe it about you, I know it.

Comrade. You are always of a piece, Apollodorus, for you are always slandering yourself and others; and in my opinion you simply believe that—starting with yourself—everyone is miserable except Socrates. And how you ever got the nickname "Softy," I do not know, for you are always like this in your speeches, savage against yourself and others except Socrates.

Apollodorus. My dearest friend, so it is plain as it can be, is it, that in thinking this about myself as well as you I am a raving lunatic?

Comrade. It is not worthwhile, Apollodorus, to argue about this now; just do what we were begging you to do; tell what the speeches were.

Apollodorus. Well, they were somewhat as follows—but I shall just try to tell it to you from the beginning as Aristodemus told it.

He said that Socrates met him freshly bathed and wearing

fancy slippers, which was not Socrates' usual way, and he asked Socrates where he was going now that he had become so beautiful.[1]

And he said, "To dinner at Agathon's, for yesterday I stayed away from his victory celebration, in fear of the crowd, but I did agree to come today. It is just for this that I have got myself up so beautifully—that beautiful I may go to a beauty. But you," he said, "how do you feel about going uninvited to dinner? Would you be willing to do so?"

"And I said," he said, " 'I shall do whatever you say.' "

"Then follow," he said, "so that we may change and ruin the proverb, 'the good go to Agathon's feasts on their own.' Homer, after all, not only ruined it, it seems, but even committed an outrage [hybris] on this proverb; for though he made Agamemnon an exceptionally good man in martial matters, and Menelaus a 'soft spearman,' yet when Agamemnon was making a sacrifice and a feast, he made Menelaus come to the dinner uninvited, an inferior to his better's."

He said that when he heard this he said, "Perhaps I too shall run a risk, Socrates—perhaps it is not as you say, but as Homer says, a good-for-nothing going uninvited to a wise man's dinner. Consider the risk in bringing me. What will you say in your defense? For I shall not agree that I have come uninvited but shall say that it was at your invitation."

"With the two of us going on the way together,"[2] he said, "we shall deliberate on what we shall say. Well, let us go."

He said that once they had finished their conversation along these lines, they went on. And as they were making their way Socrates somehow turned his attention to himself and was left behind, and when Aristodemus waited for him, he asked him to go on ahead. When Aristodemus got to Agathon's house, he found the door open, and he said something ridiculous happened to him there. Straight off, a domestic servant met him and brought him to where the others were reclining, and he found them on the point of starting dinner. So Agathon, of course, saw him at once, and said, "Aristodemus, you have come at a fine

---

[1]The word beautiful (kalos), which is distinct from good (agathos), also means fair, fine, and noble; and everything outstanding in body, mind, or action can be so designated. What is lovable, either to sight or mind, is beautiful. It is the Greek term for what is moral, with the qualification that it designates what is beyond the sphere of obligation and duty, what one cannot expect everyone to do. It has a higher rank than the just.

[2]'Soft spearman' is from Iliad, 17.587; the uninvited Menelaus from 2.408; and "With the two of us going on the way together" from 10.224.

time to share a dinner. If you have come for something else, put it off for another time, as I was looking for you yesterday to invite you but could not find you. But how is it that you are not bringing our Socrates?"

"And I turn around," he said, "and do not see Socrates following anywhere. So I said that I myself came with Socrates, on his invitation to dinner here."

"It is a fine thing for you to do," Agathon said, "but where is he?"

"He was just coming in behind me. I am wondering myself where he might be."

"Go look, boy," Agathon said, "and bring Socrates in. And you, Aristodemus," he said, "lie down beside Eryximachus."

And he said the boy washed him so he could lie down; and another of the boys came back to report, "Your Socrates has retreated into a neighbor's porch and stands there, and when I called him, he was unwilling to come in."

"That is strange," Agathon said. "Call him and don't let him go."

And Aristodemus said that he said, "No, no, leave him alone. That is something of a habit with him. Sometimes he moves off and stands stock still wherever he happens to be. He will come at once, I suspect. So do not try to budge him, but leave him alone."

"Well, that is what we must do, if it is your opinion," he said Agathon said. "Well now, boys, feast the rest of us. Though you always serve in any case whatever you want to whenever someone is not standing right over you, still now, in the belief that I, your master, as much as the others, has been invited to dinner by you, serve in such a way that we may praise you."

After this, he said, they dined; but Socrates did not come in, and though Agathon often ordered that Socrates be sent for, Aristodemus did not permit it. Then Socrates did come in— he had lingered as long as was usual for him—when they were just about in the middle of dinner. Then he said that Agathon, who happened to be lying down at the far end alone, said, "Here, Socrates, lie down alongside me, so that by my touching you, I too may enjoy the piece of wisdom that just occurred to you while you were in the porch. It is plain that you found it and have it, for otherwise you would not have come away beforehand."

And Socrates sat down and said, "It would be a good thing,

Agathon, if wisdom were the sort of thing that flows from the fuller of us into the emptier, just by our touching one another, as the water in wine cups flows through a wool thread from the fuller to the emptier. For if wisdom too is like that, then I set a high price on my being placed alongside you, for I believe I shall be filled from you with much fair wisdom. My own may turn out to be a sorry sort of wisdom, or disputable like a dream; but your own is brilliant and capable of much development, since it has flashed out so intensely from you while you are young; and yesterday it became conspicuous among more than thirty thousand Greek witnesses."

"You are outrageous, Socrates," Agathon said. "A little later you and I will go to court about our wisdom, with Dionysus as judge, but now first attend to dinner."

After this, he said, when Socrates had reclined and dined with the rest, they made libations, sang a song to the god and did all the rest of the customary rites,[3] and then turned to drinking. Then Pausanias, he said, began to speak somewhat as follows. "All right, men," he said. "What will be the easiest way for us to drink? Now I tell you that I am really in a very bad way from yesterday's drinking, and I need a rest. I suspect many of you do too, for you were also here yesterday. So consider what would be the easiest way for us to drink."

Aristophanes then said, "That is a good suggestion, Pausanias, to arrange our drinking in some easier way, for I too am one of yesterday's soaks."

Eryximachus, he said, the son of Akoumenos, heard them out and then said, "What a fine thing you say. But I still have need to hear from one of you—from Agathon—how set he is on heavy drinking."

"Not at all," Agathon said, "nor do I have the strength."

"We seem to be in luck," Eryximachus said, "—myself, Aristodemus, Phaedrus, and those here—if you who have the greatest capacity for drink have now given up, for we are always incapable. And I leave Socrates out of account—as he can go either way, he will be content with whatever we do. Now, since in my opinion none of those present is eager to drink a lot of wine, perhaps I should be less disagreeable were I to speak the

---

[3]The customary rites at the end of a banquet are six in number: 1) a libation of unmixed wine to *agathos daimon* (the "good Genius"); 2) the clearing of the tables; 3) the washing of the hands; 4) the distribution of wreaths among the guests; 5) three libations, one each to Zeus Olympus and the Olympian gods, to the heroes, and to Zeus Soter; 6) the singing of a song to the god.

truth about what drunkenness is. For I believe this has become quite plain to me from the art of medicine. Drunkenness is a hard thing for human beings; and as far as it is in my power, I should neither be willing to go on drinking nor to advise another to do so, particularly if he still has a headache from yesterday's debauch.''

"Well, as for myself," he said Phaedrus the Myrrhinousian said, interrupting, "I am used to obeying you, particularly in whatever you say about medicine; and now the rest will do so too, if they take good counsel.''

When they heard this, all agreed not to make the present party a drinking bout, but for each to drink as he pleased.

"Since, then, it has been decreed,'' Eryximachus said, "that each is to drink as much as he wants to, and there is to be no compulsion about it, I next propose to dismiss the flute girl who just came in and to let her flute for herself, or, if she wants, for the women within, while we consort with each other today through speeches. And as to what sort of speeches, I am willing, if you want, to make a proposal.''

All then agreed that this was what they wanted and asked him to make his proposal. Eryximachus then said, "The beginning of my speech is in the manner of Euripides' *Melanippe*,[4] for the tale that I am about to tell is not my own, but Phaedrus' here. On several occasions Phaedrus has said to me in annoyance, 'Isn't it awful, Eryximachus, that hymns and paeans have been made by the poets for other gods, but for Eros, who is so great and important a god, not one of the many poets there have been has ever made even a eulogy? And if you want, consider, in their turn, the good Sophists, they write up in prose praises of Heracles and others, as the excellent Prodicus does. Though you need not wonder at this, for I have even come across a volume of a wise man in which salt got a marvelous puff for its usefulness, and you might find many other things of the kind with eulogies. So they employ much zeal in things like that, yet to this day not one human being has dared to hymn Eros in a worthy manner; but so great a god lies in neglect.' Now, Phaedrus, in my opinion, speaks well in this regard. So, as I desire to make a comradely loan to please him, it is, in my opinion, appropriate for those of

---

[4]The line from Euripides' (mostly lost) *Melanippe* is, ''The tale is not my own but from my mother''; and the fragment then goes on: ''how sky and earth were one shape; but when they were separated from one another, they gave birth to everything and sent them up into the light, trees, birds, wild beasts, those the salt sea nourishes, and the race of mortals.''

us who are now here to adorn the god. And if you share in my opinion, we should find enough of a pastime in speeches. For it is my opinion that each of us, starting on the left, should recite the fairest praise of Eros that he can, and Phaedrus should be the first to begin, inasmuch as he is lying on the head couch and is also the father of the argument.''

"No one,'' Socrates said, "will cast a vote against you, Eryximachus. For I would surely not beg off, as I claim to have expert knowledge of nothing but erotics; nor would Agathon and Pausanias beg off, to say nothing of Aristophanes, whose whole activity is devoted to Dionysus and Aphrodite. And none of the others I see here would refuse either. And yet it is not quite fair for those of us who lie on the last couches; but if those who come first speak in a fine and adequate way, we shall be content. Well, good luck to Phaedrus then. Let him make a start and eulogize Eros.''

All the others then approved and urged it as Socrates had done. Now, Aristodemus scarcely remembered all that each and every one of them said, and I in turn do not remember all that he said; but I shall tell you the noteworthy points of those speeches that, in my opinion, most particularly deserved remembering.

First of all, as I say, he said that Phaedrus began his speech at somewhat the following point: that Eros was a great and wondrous god among human beings as well as gods, and that this was so in many respects and not least in the matter of birth. "For the god to be ranked among the oldest is a mark of honor,'' he said, "and here is the proof: the parents of Eros neither exist nor are they spoken of by anyone, whether prose author or poet; but Hesiod says that Chaos came first—

> Then thereafter
> Broad-breasted Earth, always the safe seat of all,
> And Eros.[5]

After Chaos, he says, there came to be these two, Earth and Eros. And Parmenides says that Genesis,

> First of all gods, devised Eros.

---

[5]Hesiod, *Theogony*, lines 116, 117, 120. Our manuscripts of Hesiod read, after 117, "of all immortals, who hold the tops of snowy Olympus [118], and gloomy Tartarus in the recesses of the broad-wayed Earth [119].'' Line 118 is also not read by other sources; and the Hesiod scholium says that line 119 is athetized. After "Eros'' in line 120, Hesiod goes on: "who is the most beautiful among the immortal gods, the dissolver of care, who overpowers the mind and thoughtful counsel in the breast of all gods and human beings.''

Akousilaus agrees with Hesiod as well. So there is an agreement in many sources that Eros is among the oldest. And as he is the oldest, we have him as the cause of the greatest goods, for I can hardly point to a greater good for someone to have from youth onward than a good lover, and for a lover, a beloved. For that which should guide human beings who are going to live fairly throughout their lives can be implanted by neither blood ties, nor honors, nor wealth, nor anything else as beautifully as by love. Now what do I say this is? It is shame in the face of shameful things and honorable ambition in the face of beautiful things; for without them neither city nor private person can accomplish great and beautiful deeds. So I assert that in the case of any real man who loves, were it to come to light that he was either doing something shameful or putting up with it from another out of cowardice and without defending himself, he would not be as pained on being observed by either his father, his comrades, or anyone else as by his beloved. We observe that this same thing holds in the case of the beloved; he is exceptionally shamed before his lovers whenever he is seen to be involved in something shameful. So if there were any possibility that a city or an army could be composed of lovers and beloveds, then there could be no better way for them to manage their own city; for they would abstain from all that is shameful and be filled with love of honor before one another. And besides, were they to do battle alongside one another, then even a few of this sort would win over just about all human beings; for a real man in love would of course far less prefer to be seen by his beloved than by all the rest when it comes to deserting his post or throwing away his weapons; he would choose to be dead many times over before that happened. And, to say nothing of leaving behind one's beloved or not coming to his aid when he is in danger, there is no one so bad that, once the god Eros had entered him, he would not be directed toward virtue—to the point where he is like one who is best by nature: And simply, as Homer said, 'the strength that the god breathed'[6] into some of the heroes, Eros supplies from himself to lovers.

"And what is more, lovers are the only ones who are willing to die for the sake of another; and that is not only true of real men but of women as well. Alcestis, the daughter of Pelias, offers a sufficient testimony for Greeks on behalf of this argument. She alone was willing to die on behalf of her husband,

---

[6]At *Iliad*, 10.482, Athena breathes strength into Diomedes, and at 15.262 Apollo does the same for Hector.

though his father and mother were alive; but through her love she so much surpassed his parents in friendship that she showed them up as alien to their own son and only related to him in name. Her performance of this deed was thought to be so noble in the opinion not only of human beings but of the gods as well that, although there have been many who have accomplished many noble deeds, the gods have given to only a select number of them the guerdon of sending up their souls again from Hades, and hers they did send up in admiring delight at her deed. So gods, too, hold in particular esteem the zeal and virtue that pertain to love. Orpheus, the son of Oeagrus, they sent back from Hades unfulfilled; and though they showed him a phantom of his wife, for whom he had come, they did not give her very self to him, because it was thought he was soft, like the lyre player he was, and had not dared to die for love like Alcestis, but contrived to go into Hades alive. Consequently, they imposed a punishment on him, and made him die at the hands of women, and did not honor him as they had Achilles, the son of Thetis. For Achilles they sent away to the Isles of the Blest, because, though he had learned from his mother that he would be killed if he killed Hector, and that if he did not, he would return home and die in old age, still he dared to choose to come to the aid of his lover Patroclus; and with his vengeance accomplished, he dared not only to die on his behalf but to die after him who had died. On this account, the gods were particularly impressed and gave him outstanding honors, because he had made so much of his lover. Aeschylus talks nonsense in claiming that Achilles was in love with Patroclus (rather than the other way around), for Achilles was more beautiful than not only Patroclus but all the other heroes as well; and besides, he was unbearded, and thirdly, far younger than Patroclus, as Homer says.[7] Well, anyhow, though the gods really hold in very high esteem that virtue which concerns love, they wonder, admire, and confer benefits even more when the beloved has affection for the lover than when the lover has it for the beloved. A lover is a more divine thing than a beloved, for he has the god within him. This is the reason why they honored Achilles more than Alcestis and sent him to the Isles of the Blest.

"So this is how I assert that Eros is the oldest, most honorable, and most competent of the gods with regard to the acquisition of virtue and happiness by human beings both when living and dead."

---

[7] Homer, *Iliad*, 2.673; 11.786.

He said that Phaedrus made some such speech, and after Phaedrus there were some others that he scarcely could recall; he passed them over and told of Pausanias' speech. He said that Pausanias said, "Phaedrus, in my opinion it is not noble the way the argument has been proposed to us—commanding us to eulogize Eros in so unqualified a fashion. For were Eros one, it would be noble, but as it is, it is not noble, for he is not one; and as he is not one, it is more correct that it be declared beforehand which Eros is to be praised. So first I shall try to set the record straight, to point out the Eros who is to be praised, and then to praise him in a manner worthy of the god. We all know that there is no Aphrodite without Eros; and were she one, Eros would be one; but since there are two Aphrodites, it is necessary that there be two Erotes as well. Who would deny that there are two goddesses? One surely is the elder and has no mother, the daughter of Uranos, the one to whom we apply the name Uranian; the other is younger and the daughter of Zeus and Dione, the one we call Pandemus.[8] So it is necessary that the Eros who is a fellow worker with one correctly be called Pandemus, and the other one, Uranian. Now all gods must be praised, but one must still try to say what has been allotted to each god. Every action is of the following sort: When being done in terms of itself, it is neither noble nor base. For example, what we are now doing, either drinking, singing, or conversing, none of these things is in itself a noble thing, only in terms of how it is done in the doing of it does it turn out to be the sort of thing that it is. For if it is done nobly and correctly, it proves to be noble, and if incorrectly, base. So, too, in the case of loving and Eros, for Eros as a whole is not noble nor deserving of a eulogy, but only that Eros who provokes one to love in a noble way.

"Now the Eros who belongs to Aphrodite Pandemus is truly pandemian and acts in any sort of way. And here you have the one whom good-for-nothing human beings have as their love. Those who are of the same sort as this Eros are, first of all, no less in love with women than with boys; secondly, they are in love with their bodies rather than their souls; and thirdly, they are in love with the stupidest there can be, for they have an eye only to the act and are unconcerned with whether it is noble or not. That is how it happens that it turns out for them, however it turns out, with the same likelihood of its being good as the

---

[8]*Pandemus*, which is a cult title, literally means "common to all the people" and does not necessarily mean something vulgar and base. Pandemian has the same meaning.

opposite. For Eros Pandemus depends on the Aphrodite who is
far younger than the other goddess, and who partakes in her birth
of female as well as of male. But the other Eros is of Uranian
Aphrodite, who, first of all, does not partake of female but only
of male (and this is the love of boys); and secondly, is the elder
and has no part in outrage. That is how it comes about that those
inspired by this kind of love turn to the male, with an affection
for that which is naturally more vigorous and has more sense.
And one might recognize in pederasty itself those who have been
prompted purely by this kind of love; for they do not love boys
except when boys start having sense, and that is close to the time
when the beard first appears. For those who start loving a boy at
this point in time are in a position I believe to be with him and
live with him for their whole life and not—once they have
deceived and seized a young and foolish boy—to laugh at him
and then run away to another. There should have been a law as
well to prohibit the loving of boys, in order that a lot of zeal
would not have been wasted for an uncertain result; for it is not
clear where the perfection of boys has its end with regard to the
vice and virtue of both soul and body. Now, the good willingly
lay down this law upon themselves, but there should have been
applied the same sort of compulsory prohibition to those pandemian
lovers, just as we compel them as far as we can not to love
freeborn matrons. For here you have those who have made
pederasty a disgrace, so that some have the nerve to say that it is
shameful to gratify lovers. They say it is shameful with an eye to
those pandemian lovers, observing their impropriety and injustice, since surely any action whatsoever that is done in an orderly
and lawful way would not justly bring reproach.

"Now in general the law about love in other cities is easy to
understand, for it has been simply determined; but the law here
and in Sparta is complicated. In Elis and among the Boeotians,
and where they are not wise in speaking, the gratification of
lovers has been unqualifiedly legalized as noble, and no one,
whether young or old, would say that it is shameful. This is so, I
suspect, in order that they might have no trouble in trying to
persuade the young by speech, because they are incapable of
speaking. In Ionia, on the other hand, and in many other places
(wherever they live under barbarians), it has been customarily
held to be shameful. In the eyes of barbarians, on account of their
tyrannies, pederasty as well as philosophy and the love of gymnastics is shameful; for I suspect that it is not to the advantage of
the rulers that great and proud thoughts be engendered among

their subjects, any more than strong friendships and associations. It is precisely this that love, as well as all these other things, especially tends to implant. And the tyrants here [in Athens] actually learned this by deed; for the love of Aristogeiton and the friendship of Harmodius, once it became firm, dissolved the tyrants' rule.[9] So wherever it has been laid down as shameful to gratify lovers, it has been through the vice of those who have done so—the hankering after more on the part of the rulers, and the lack of manliness on the part of their subjects; and wherever the gratifying of lovers has been held to be a fine thing without qualification, it has been through the slothfulness of soul of those who have so ordained. But here [in Athens] there are much finer customs than elsewhere; yet just as I said, they are not easy to understand. Let one just reflect that it is said to be a finer thing to love openly than in secret; and particularly to love the noblest and best, even if they are uglier than others; and again, that everyone enthusiastically encourages the lover, and not as if he were doing anything shameful; and if a lover makes a successful capture, it is thought to be fine, and if he fails, shameful; and that, for making an attempt at seizure, the law grants the lover the opportunity to be praised for doing amazing deeds. If one dared to do any of these deeds in pursuing and wishing to accomplish anything else whatsoever except this, one would reap the greatest reproaches leveled against philosophy. For if, in wanting to take money from someone, or to take a governmental office, or any other position of power, one were willing to act just as lovers do toward their beloved—making all sorts of supplications and beseechings in their requests, swearing oaths, sleeping at the doors of their beloveds, and being willing to perform acts of slavishness that not one slave would—he would be checked from acting so by his enemies as much as by his friends, the former reproaching him for his flatteries and servilities, the latter admonishing him and feeling ashamed on his behalf. But if the lover does all of this, there is a grace upon him; and the law allows him to act without reproaching him, on the ground that he is attempting to carry through some exceedingly fine thing; and what is most dreadful, as the many say, is that, if he swears and then departs from his oath, for him alone there is pardon from the gods—for they deny that an oath in sex is an oath. Thus the gods and human beings have made every opportunity available to the lover, as the law here states. Now on

---

[9]Aristogeiton was the lover of Harmodius, with whom he slew Pisistratus' son Hipparchus in 514 B.C. It did not, however, end the tyranny but made it harsher.

these grounds one might suppose that it is customarily held to be a very fine thing in this city both to love and for lovers to have friends. But on the other hand, when fathers set attendants in charge of the beloveds and prohibit them from conversing with their lovers, and the attendant has this as a standing order, and the beloved's contemporaries and comrades blame him if they see anything like this going on; and the elders, in turn, do not stand in the way of those who cast reproaches or abuse them on the grounds that they are speaking incorrectly—then, if one glances in this direction, one would believe that such a thing is customarily held to be most shameful. This is to be explained, I believe, as follows. The matter is not simple; and, as was said at the start, it is neither noble nor base in itself, but if nobly done, noble, and if basely done, base. Now, it is base to gratify one who is no good and to do so in a bad way; while it is noble to gratify the good and to do so in a noble way. It is the pandemian lover who is no good, the one in love with the body rather than with the soul. He is not even, for example, a lasting lover, because he is in love with a thing that is not lasting either. As soon as the bloom of the body fades—which is what he was in love with—'he is off and takes wing,' having made a foul shame of many speeches and promises. But he who is in love with a good character remains throughout life, for he is welded to what is lasting. So our law, in good and noble fashion, really wants to test these and to have the beloved gratify one group of lovers and escape from the others. On account of this it exhorts lovers to pursue and beloveds to flee, setting up a contest so that there may be a test as to which group the lover belongs and to which the beloved. And because of this, first, to let oneself be caught too quickly is customarily held shameful, since it is precisely the passing of time that is thought to test many things nobly; and secondly, to be caught by money and political power is shameful, regardless of whether a hurt humbles the beloved and prevents him from resisting, or a benefit consisting of money or political favors prevents him from feeling contempt; for neither money nor political favors are thought to be stable or lasting, to say nothing of the fact that in the natural course of things no noble and generous friendship comes out of them. So there is only one way left according to our law, if a beloved is to gratify a lover in a fine way. For just as we have a law that in the case of lovers to be enslaved willingly in any slavery to the beloved is agreed not to be flattery nor a matter of reproach, so too there is only one other willing enslavement that is not a matter of reproach. This is the enslavement regarding virtue; for it is customarily held by us that if anyone is willing to devote his care to someone in the belief that he will be better because of him, either in regard to some kind of wisdom or any other part of virtue whatsoever, this willing enslavement is not disgraceful nor is it flattery. So these two laws (the law about pederasty and the law about philosophy and the rest of virtue) must contribute to the same end if it is going to turn out that a beloved's gratification of a lover is noble. For whenever lover and beloved come to the same point, each with a law, the one, in serving a beloved who has granted his favors, would justly serve in anything; and the other, in assisting him who is making him wise and good, would justly assist. And the one is able to contribute to prudence and the rest of virtue, while the other stands in need of them for the acquisition of education and the rest of wisdom. Then and only then—when these laws converge—does it result that a beloved's gratification of his lover is noble; but in any other circumstance it is not. Even to be deceived in this regard is no disgrace; but in all other cases, whether one is deceived or not, it does involve disgrace. If someone granted his favors to a lover for the sake of wealth because he thought him rich, and then were deceived and got no money when the lover was found to be poor, it is no less a disgrace; for a beloved of that sort is thought to display his very self as one who for the sake of money would serve anyone in anything, and this is not noble. So along the same line of argument, were someone to grant his favors because he thought that his lover was good and that he himself would be better through his friendship with this lover, then even if his lover is found to be bad and without virtue, the deception is noble all the same. For he too is thought to have made plain what holds in his own case—that strictly for the sake of virtue and of becoming better he would show his total zeal in everything, and this is the noblest thing of all. Thus, for the sake of virtue alone is it wholly noble to grant one's favors. This is the love of the Uranian goddess, and it is Uranian and very worthwhile for both city and private men, for it compels both the lover himself and the beloved—each in his own case—to exercise much concern for virtue. All the other loves are of the other goddess, the pandemian. Here, Phaedrus," he said, "you have my extemporary contribution to Eros."

With Pausanias' pausation—the wise teach me to talk in such balanced phrases—Aristodemus said that it was Aristophanes' turn to speak; however, he had just got the hiccups (from satiety or something else) and was unable to speak, but he did say—the doctor Eryximachus was lying on the couch next to him—"Eryximachus, it is only just that you either stop my hiccups or speak on my behalf until I do stop." And Eryximachus said, "Well, I shall do both. I shall talk in your turn, and you, when you stop hiccuping, in mine. And while I am speaking, see if by holding your breath for a long time, you make the hiccups stop; but if they do not, gargle with water. And if they prove very severe, take something with which you might irritate your nose, and sneeze; and if you do this once or twice, even if the hiccups are severe, they will stop." "Go ahead and speak," Aristophanes said. "I shall do the rest."

Then Eryximachus spoke. "Well, in my opinion, since Pausanias made a fine start to his speech but did not adequately complete it, it is necessary for me to try to put a complete end to the argument. Inasmuch as Eros is double, it is, in my opinion, a fine thing to divide him; but that he presides not only over the souls of human beings in regard to the beautiful but also in regard to many other things and in other cases—the bodies of all the animals as well as those things that grow in the earth, and just about all the things that are—that, in my opinion, I have come to see from medicine, our art. For how great and wondrous the god is in his comprehensive aims, both in terms of human things and in terms of divine things! I shall begin my speech with medicine, so that we may venerate that art as well. The nature of bodies has this double Eros, for the health and the sickness of the body are by agreement different and dissimilar; and the dissimilar desires and loves dissimilar things. Now, there is one love that presides over the healthy state, and another over the sickly. Just as Pausanias was saying, it is a fine thing to gratify those who are good among human beings and disgraceful to gratify the intemperate, so too, in the case of men's bodies taken by themselves is it a fine and needful thing to gratify the good and healthy things of each body (this is what has the name 'the medical'); but it is shameful to gratify the bad and sickly things, and one has to abstain from favoring them, if one is to be skilled. For the art of medicine is, to sum it up, the expert knowledge of the erotics of the body in regard to repletion and evacuation; and he who diagnostically discriminates in these things between the noble and base love is the one most skilled in medicine; while he who induces changes, so as to bring about the acquisition of one kind of love in place of the other, and

who, in whatever things where there is no love but there needs
must be, has the expert knowledge to instill it, or to remove it
from those things in which it is [but should not be], would be a
good craftsman. For he must, in point of fact, be able to make
the things that are most at enmity in the body into friends and to
make them love one another. The most opposite things are the
most at enmity: cold and hot, bitter and sweet, dry and moist,
and anything of the sort. Our ancestor Asklepios, who had the
expert knowledge to instill love and unanimity into these things—as
the poets here assert and as I am convinced is so—put together
our art. Not only medicine, as I say, is entirely captained by this
god, but likewise gymnastics and farming. And it is plain to
anyone who pays the slightest attention that music is also on the
same level as these—as perhaps Heracleitus too wants to say,
though as far as his actual words go, what he says is not fine.
For he says that the one 'alone in differing with itself agrees with
itself,' 'as is the harmony of lyre and bow.'[10] It is a lot of
nonsense to affirm that a harmony differs with itself or is composed of still differing things. But perhaps he wanted to say that,
from the prior differences between the high and the low, there
arises from their later agreement a harmony by means of the art
of music; for there surely would no longer be a harmony from
high and low notes while they were differing with each other; for
harmony is consonance, and consonance is a kind of agreement.
But it is impossible to derive agreement from differing things as
long as they are differing; and it is impossible, in turn, to fit
together the differing or nonagreeing—just as rhythm arises from
the fast and the slow, from their prior state of difference and
their subsequent agreement. Here, music inserts agreement in all
these things (just as, there, medicine does) as it instills mutual
love and unanimity; and music, in turn, is expert knowledge of
the erotics of harmony and rhythm. And in the simple constitu-
tion of harmony and rhythm it is not at all hard to diagnose the
erotics, for the double eros is not yet present there; but whenever
rhythm and harmony have to be employed in regard to human
beings, either by making rhythm and harmony (what they call
lyric poetry) or by using correctly the songs and meters that have
been made (what has been called education), it is difficult and a
good craftsman is needed. For the same argument returns here—

---

[10]The complete fragment (Diels-Kramz) runs: "They do not know how it [presumably
the one] in differing with itself agrees with itself: a counterturning fitting together
[harmony] as that of bow and lyre." "Counter-straining" is an old variant for "counterturning."

namely, that decent human beings must be gratified, as well as
those who are not as yet decent, so that they might become more
decent; and the love of the decent must be preserved. And this
love is the beautiful one, the Uranian, the Eros of the Uranian
Muse. But the pandemian one is Polyhymnia's, which must,
whenever it is applied, be applied cautiously, in order that it might
harvest its own pleasure but not instill any intemperance—just as
in our art it is a large order to employ in a fair way the desires
that cluster around the art of making delicacies so as to harvest
their pleasure without illness. And in general, in music, in
medicine, and in all other things—the human and the divine—
each Eros must be watched as far as practicable; for both of the
Erotes are present in these things. The composition of the seasons of the year, for example, is also full of both these Erotes;
and whenever the hot and the cold, and the dry and the moist,
which I mentioned before, obtain decent love for each other and
accept a moderate harmony and mixture, they come bearing
good seasonableness and health to human beings and to the rest
of the animals and plants and commit no injustice. But whenever
Eros with his hybris proves to be too strong with regard to the
seasons of the year, he corrupts and commits injustice against
many things. For plagues as well as many other diseases are
wont to arise for wild beasts and plants from things like that.
Frosts, for example, and hailstorms and blights arise from the
greediness and disorderliness of such erotic things in relation to
one another; and the science of these erotic things in regard to
the revolutions of stars and seasons of the years is called astronomy. Furthermore, all the sacrifices and things over which divination presides—these are concerned with the communing of
gods and human beings with one another—involve almost nothing else but the protection and healing of Eros. For impiety as a
whole is wont to arise if one does not gratify the decent Eros and
honor and venerate him in every deed, but instead gratifies and
honors the other one, in matters that concern parents, both living
and dead, and gods. And so it is, accordingly, that divination is
charged with the overseeing and healing of lovers; and divination, in turn, is the craftsman of friendship between gods and
human beings, since it has expert knowledge of human erotics,
as far as erotics has to do with sacred law and piety.

"This is the great and overwhelming power that Eros as a
whole has (and indeed it is rather close to total power); but the
Eros concerned with good things, consummately perfected with

moderation and justice, among us and among gods, this has the
greatest power and provides us with every kind of happiness,
making us able to associate with one another and to be friends
even with the gods who are stronger than we are. Now, perhaps
in praising Eros I too am omitting many things; but I have done
that unwillingly. For if I did omit anything, it is your job,
Aristophanes, to fill it in; or if you intend to make a different
eulogy of the god, proceed to do so, since you have stopped
hiccuping.''

He then said that Aristophanes accepted and said, "It has
stopped, to be sure; not, however, before sneezing had been
applied to it. So I wonder at the orderly decency of the body
desiring such noises and garglings as a sneeze is; for my hiccuping stopped right away as soon as I applied the sneeze to it.''

And Eryximachus said, "My good Aristophanes, look at
what you are doing. You have made [us] laugh just as you were
about to speak; and you compel me to be a guardian of your own
speech, lest you ever say anything laughable—though you did
have the chance to speak in peace.''

And Aristophanes laughed and said, "You have made a
good point, Eryximachus, and please let what has been said be
as if it were never spoken. But do not be my guardian, for in
what is about to be said I am not afraid to say laughable
things—for that would be a gain and native to our Muse—but
only things that are laughed at.''

"You believe you can hit and run, Aristophanes," he said,
"but pay attention and speak as though you are to render an
account; perhaps, however, if I so resolve, I shall let you go.''

"Well, Eryximachus," Aristophanes said, "I do intend to
speak in a somewhat different vein from that in which you and
Pausanias spoke. Human beings, in my opinion, have been
entirely unaware of the power of Eros, since if they were aware
of it, they would have provided the greatest sanctuaries and
altars for him, and would be making him the greatest sacrifices,
and not act as they do now when none of this happens to him,
though it most certainly should. For Eros is the most philan-
thropic of gods, a helper of human beings as well as a physician
dealing with an illness the healing of which would result in the
greatest happiness for the human race. So I shall try to initiate
you into his power; and you will be the teachers of everyone
else. But you must first understand human nature and its afflictions. Our nature in the past was not the same as now but of a

different sort. First of all, the races of human beings were three, not two as now, male and female; for there was also a third race that shared in both, a race whose name still remains, though it itself has vanished. For at that time one race was androgynous, and in looks and name it combined both, the male as well as the female; but now it does not exist except for the name that is reserved for reproach. Secondly, the looks of each human being were as a whole round, with back and sides in a circle. And each had four arms, and legs equal in number to his arms, and two faces alike in all respects on a cylindrical neck, but there was one head for both faces—they were set in opposite directions—and four ears, and two sets of genitals, and all the rest that one might conjecture from this. Each used to walk upright too, just as one does now, in whatever direction he wanted; and whenever he had the impulse to run fast, then just as tumblers with their legs straight out actually move around as they tumble in a circle, so did they, with their eight limbs as supports, quickly move in a circle. It is for this reason that the races were three and of this sort: because the male was in origin the offspring of the sun; the female, of the earth; and the race that shared in both, of the moon—since the moon also shares in both. And they themselves were globular, as was their manner of walking, because they were like their parents. Now, they were awesome in their strength and robustness, and they had great and proud thoughts, so they made an attempt on the gods. And what Homer says about Ephialtes and Otus,[11] is said about them—that they attempted to make an ascent into the sky with a view to assaulting the gods. Then Zeus and the other gods deliberated as to what they should do with them. And they were long perplexed, for the gods knew neither how they could kill them and (just as they had struck the giants with lightning) obliterate the race—for, in that case, their own honors and sacrifices from human beings would vanish—nor how they could allow them to continue to behave licentiously. Then Zeus thought hard and says, 'In my own opinion,' he said, 'I have a device whereby human beings would continue to exist and at the same time, having become weaker, would stop their licentiousness. I shall now cut each of them in two,' he said; 'and they will be both weaker and more useful to us through the increase in their numbers. And they will walk upright on two legs. But if they are thought to behave licentiously still, and are unwilling to keep quiet, then I shall cut them again

___
[11]Homer, *Odyssey*, 11.305–320; *Iliad*, 5.385–391.

in two,' he said, 'so that they will go hopping on one leg.' As
soon as he said this he began to cut human beings in two, just
like those who cut sorb-apples in preparation for pickling, or
those who cut eggs with hairs. And whenever he cut someone,
he had Apollo turn the face and half the neck around to face the
cut, so that in beholding his own cutting the human being might
be more orderly; and he had him heal all the rest. Apollo turned
the face around; and by drawing together the skin from everywhere toward what is now called the belly (just like drawstring
bags) he made one opening, which he tied off in the middle of
the belly, and that is what they call the navel. He shaped up the
chest and smoothed out many of the other wrinkles, with somewhat the same kind of tool as shoemakers use in smoothing the
wrinkles in leather on the last; but he left a few wrinkles, those
on the belly itself and the navel, to be a reminder of our ancient
affliction. When its nature was cut in two, each—desiring its
own half—came together; and throwing their arms around one
another and entangling themselves with one another in their
desire to grow together, they began to die off due to hunger and
the rest of their inactivity, because they were unwilling to do
anything apart from one another; and whenever one of the halves
did die and the other was left, the one that was left tried to seek
out another and entangle itself with that, whether it met the half
of the whole woman—and that is what we now call a woman—or
of a man; and so they continued to perish. But Zeus took pity on
them and supplies another device: He rearranges their genitals
toward the front—for up till then they had them on the outside,
and they generated and gave birth not in one another but in the
earth, like cicadas—and for this purpose, he changed this part of
them toward the front, and by this means made generation
possible in one another, by means of the male in the female; so
that in embracing, if a man meets with a woman, they might
generate and the race continue; and if male meets with male,
there might at least be satiety in their being together; and they
might pause and turn to work and attend to the rest of their
livelihood. So it is really from such early times that human
beings have had, inborn in themselves, Eros for one another—
Eros, the bringer-together of their ancient nature, who tries to
make one out of two and to heal their human nature. Each of us,
then, is a token of a human being, because we are sliced like
fillets of sole, two out of one; and so each is always in search of
his own token. Now all who are the men's slice from the
common genus, which was then called androgynous, are lovers

of women; and many adulterers have been of this genus; and, in turn, all who are women of this genus prove to be lovers of men and adulteresses. And all women who are sliced off from woman hardly pay attention to men but are rather turned toward women, and lesbians arise from this genus. But all who are male slices pursue the males; and while they are boys—because they are cutlets of the male—they are friendly to men and enjoy lying down together with and embracing men; and these are the best of boys and lads, because they are naturally the manliest. Some, to be sure, assert that such boys are shameless, but they lie. For it is not out of shamelessness that they do this but out of boldness, manliness, and masculinity, feeling affection for what is like to themselves. And there is a great proof of this, for once they have reached maturity, only men of this kind go off to political affairs. When they are fully grown men, they are pederasts and naturally pay no attention to marriage and procreation, but are compelled to do so by the law; whereas they would be content to live unmarried with one another. Now it is one of this sort who wholly becomes a pederast and passionate lover, always feeling affection for what is akin to himself. And when the pederast or anyone else meets with that very one who is his own half, then they are wondrously struck with friendship, attachment, and love, and are just about unwilling to be apart from one another even for a short time. And here you have those who continue through life with one another, though they could not even say what they want to get for themselves from one another. For no one would be of the opinion that it was sexual intercourse that was wanted, as though it were for this reason—of all things—that each so enjoys being with the other in great earnestness; but the soul of each plainly wants something else. What it is, it is incapable of saying, but it divines what it wants and speaks in riddles. If Hephaestus with his tools were to stand over them as they lay in the same place and were to ask, 'What is it that you want, human beings, to get for yourselves from one another?'— and if in their perplexity he were to ask them again, 'Is it this you desire, to be with one another in the very same place, as much as is possible, and not to leave one another night and day? For if you desire that, I am willing to fuse you and make you grow together into the same thing, so that—though two—you would be one; and as long as you lived, you would both live together just as though you were one; and when you died, there again in Hades you would be dead together as one instead of as

two. So see if you love this and would be content if you got it.'
We know that there would not be even one who, if he heard this,
would refuse, and it would be self-evident that he wants nothing
else than this; and he would quite simply believe he had heard
what he had been desiring all along: in conjunction and fusion
with the beloved, to become one from two. The cause of this is
that this was our ancient nature and we were wholes. So love is
the name for the desire and pursuit of the whole. And previously, as I say, we were one; but now through our injustice we
have been dispersed by the god, just as the Arcadians were dispersed
by the Spartans. There is the fear, then, that if we are not orderly
in our behavior to the gods, we shall be split again and go
around like those who are modeled in relief on stelae, sawed
through our nostrils, like dice. For this reason every real man
must be exhorted to be pious toward the gods in all his acts, so
that we may avoid the one result and get the other, as Eros is our
guide and general. Let no one act contrary to Eros—and he acts
contrary whoever incurs the enmity of the gods—for if we
become friends and reconciled to the gods, we shall find out and
meet with our own favorites, which few at the moment do. And
please don't let Eryximachus suppose, in making a comedy of
my speech, that I mean Pausanias and Agathon—perhaps they
have found their own and are both naturally born males. For
whatever the case may be with them, I am referring to all men and
women: our race would be happy if we were to bring our love to
a consummate end, and each of us were to get his own favorite
on his return to his ancient nature. And if this is the best, it must
necessarily be the case that, in present circumstances, that which
is closest to it is the best; and that is to get a favorite whose
nature is to one's taste. And were we to hymn the god who is the
cause of this we should justly hymn Eros, who at the present
time benefits us the most by leading us to what is our own; and
in the future he offers the greatest hopes, while we offer piety to
the gods, to restore us to our ancient nature and by his healing
make us blessed and happy.

"Here, Eryximachus," he said, "is my speech about Eros,
different from yours. So, just as I begged you, don't make a
comedy of it, in order that we may listen to what each of the
others—or rather, what each of the two—will say; for Agathon
and Socrates are left."

"Well, I shall obey you," he said Eryximachus said. "Your
speech was indeed a pleasure for me. And if I did not know that
both Socrates and Agathon were skilled in erotics, I should be

very much afraid of their being at a loss for words on account of the fullness and variety of what has been said; but as it is, I am confident.''

Socrates then said, ''That is because you yourself put up a fine show in the contest, Eryximachus; but if you were where I am now, or rather where I shall be when Agathon has spoken well, then you would really be afraid and as wholly baffled as I am now.''

''You want to bewitch me, Socrates,'' Agathon said. ''You would have me believe that the audience is full of expectation that I shall speak well, and in that way, I shall be in a turmoil.''

''I should surely be forgetful, Agathon,'' Socrates said, ''if I did that. I saw your courage and greatness of mind in mounting the platform with the actors and in facing so large an audience when you were about to display your own speeches, and I saw that you were in no way disturbed—should I now believe that you will be in a turmoil on account of us few human beings?''

''What's this, Socrates?'' Agathon said. ''You really do not believe that I am so wrapped up in the theater as not to know that to a man of sense a few who are sensible are more terrifying than many fools?''

''Well, I should surely be in disgrace, Agathon,'' he said, ''were I to presume any lack of urbanity in you; for I know very well that were you to meet any you believed wise, you would think more of them than of the many. But I suspect that we shall not prove to be of the wise, for we too were present there and were part of the many; but if you were to meet others who were indeed wise, then you might be ashamed before them—if you were perhaps to believe that you were doing something that is disgraceful. Is this what you mean?''

''What you say is true.''

''But you would not be ashamed before the many if you believed you were doing something disgraceful?''

Phaedrus then interrupted and said, ''Dear Agathon, if you answer Socrates, it will not make any difference to him what effect this might have on our present arrangements, provided only that he has someone to converse with, especially if he is beautiful. And I myself listen to Socrates' conversation with pleasure; but I am compelled to attend to the eulogy to Eros and to receive from each one of you your speech; so let each of you repay the god and then go on conversing as you were.''

''Well, what you say is fine, Phaedrus,'' Agathon said,

"and nothing keeps me from speaking; for it will be possible for me to converse with Socrates on many other occasions.

"I want first to say how I must speak, and then to speak. For in my own opinion all the previous speakers did not eulogize the god but blessed human beings for the goods of which the god is the cause; yet no one has said what sort is he who makes these gifts. There is one proper manner in every praise of anything: to tell in speech—whomever the speech is about—what sort he is and what sort of things he causes. This is the just way for us too to praise Eros—first what sort he is, and then his gifts. I declare that though all gods are happy, Eros (if sacred law allow it and it be without nemesis to say so) is the happiest of them, as he is the most beautiful and the best. As the most beautiful he is of the following sort: First, he is the youngest of gods, Phaedrus; and he by himself supplies a great proof for this assertion, for with headlong flight he avoids old age—swift though it plainly is, coming on us, at any rate, swifter than he should. It is precisely old age that Eros naturally detests; he does not even come within hailing distance of it. He is always with and of the young. For the old saying holds good, that like to like always draws near. Though I agree with Phaedrus in many other respects, I do not agree that Eros is more ancient than Kronos and Iapetos; but I affirm his being the youngest of gods and ever young. And the events of old about gods of which Hesiod and Parmenides speak belong to Necessity and not Eros, if what they say is true. Otherwise there would not have been castrations and bindings of each other, and many other acts of violence among the gods, had Eros been among them; but there would have been friendship and peace, just as there is now since Eros became king of the gods. So he is young, and besides being young, he is tender. But there is need of a poet as good as Homer was to show a god's tenderness. Homer says that Ate is a goddess and tender—her feet at any rate are tender—saying:

'Tender are her feet, for she does not on the threshold
    Draw near, but lo! she walks on the heads of men.'[12]

So in my opinion it is with a fine piece of evidence that he shows her softness, because she walks not on the hard but on the soft. And we too shall use the same piece of evidence about Eros to prove that he is soft; for not upon earth does he walk nor even

---

[12]Homer, *Iliad*, 19.92–3.

on skulls, which are hardly soft, but on the softest of beings he
walks and dwells. For he has set up his dwelling place in the
characters and souls of gods and human beings, and not in each
and every soul—for whichever soul he finds to have a hard
character, he goes away from, and whichever he finds to have a
soft one he dwells in. So, as he is always touching with his feet
and every other part the softest of the softest, it is necessary that
he be most tender. Now besides being youngest and tenderest, he
is supple in his looks. Otherwise he would not be able to fold
himself around everywhere, nor to be unobserved on first entering or on departing from every soul, if he were hard. The
harmony of his figure is a great piece of evidence for his
proportioned and supple appearance, and on all sides it is agreed
that Eros is exceptionally harmonious; for lack of harmony and
Eros are always at war with one another. The god's way of
living among blooming flowers means that his complexion is
beautiful; for Eros does not settle on what is fading and has
passed its bloom, whether it be body or soul or anything else,
but wherever a place is blooming and scented, there he settles and
remains.

    "Now this is enough about beauty as attributable to the
god, though many points are still omitted; but Eros' virtue must
next be spoken of. The greatest thing is that Eros neither commits injustice nor has injustice done to him, neither against a god
nor by a god, neither against a human being nor by a human
being. For it is not by violence that Eros is affected, if he is
affected at all—for violence does not touch him; nor does he act
with violence, for everyone of his own accord serves Eros in
everything. And whatever anyone of his own accord agrees upon
with another of his own accord, the 'royal laws of the city'
declare to be just. And besides the share he has in justice he has
his fullest share in moderation. For it is agreed that to be
moderate means to dominate over pleasures and desires; but no
pleasure is stronger than Eros; and if other pleasures are weaker,
they will be dominated by Eros; and since it is he who is
dominant, then in dominating pleasures and desires Eros must be
exceptionally moderate. And besides, in point of courage, 'not
even Ares resists' Eros; for Ares does not possess Eros (for
Aphrodite, as the story goes), but Eros Ares. And he who
possesses is stronger than he who is possessed; and in dominating the bravest of all the rest, he must be the bravest. Now that
the god's justice, moderation, and courage have been mentioned,
all that remains is wisdom; so, as far as I can, I must try to

supply the omission. And first—that I too might honor our art as Eryximachus did his—the god is a poet of such wisdom that he can make poets of others too; at any rate, everyone whom Eros touches proves to be a poet, 'though he be without the Muses before.' We can, accordingly, properly make use of this fact to infer that in every kind of musical making [i.e., poetry] Eros is a good poet [maker]; for what one does not have and does not know, one could neither give to another nor teach another. And who will oppose the fact that the making of all animals is nothing but Eros' wisdom, by which all the animals come to be and grow? And don't we know that, in the case of the arts, whomever this god teaches turns out to be renowned and conspicuous in craftsmanship, and that he whom Eros does not touch remains obscure? Archery, for example, medicine, and divination were invented by Apollo when desire and love were his guides; and thus he too must be a pupil of Eros, as are the Muses in music, Hephaestus in blacksmithing, Athena in weaving, and Zeus 'the captain of gods and human beings.' So it is plain that, when Eros came to be among them, the affairs of the gods were arranged out of love of beauty—for there is no eros present in ugliness. But before that, as I said at the start, many awesome events took place among the gods, as is said, through the monarchy of Necessity; whereas since the birth of this god, all good things have resulted for gods as well as for human beings from loving the beautiful things.

"Thus Eros, in my opinion, Phaedrus, stands first, because he is the fairest and the best, and, after this, he is the cause for everyone else of the same sort of fair and good things. It occurs to me to say something in meter too, that he is the one who makes

> Peace among human beings, on the open sea calm
> And cloudlessness, the resting of winds and sleeping of
> care.

He empties us of estrangement, he fills us with attachment; he arranges in all such gatherings as this our coming together with one another; in festivals, in dances, in sacrifices he proves himself a guide; furnishing gentleness, banishing wildness; loving giver of amity, no giver of enmity; gracious, good; spectacular to the wise, wonder-ful to the gods; enviable to the have-nots, desirable to the haves; father of luxury, splendor, glory, graces, yearning, and longing—caring for good ones, careless of bad ones; in toiling, in fearing, in longing, in speaking, the best governor, mariner, fellow warrior, and savior; the ornament of all gods and human beings, the fairest and best guide, whom every real man must follow hymning beautifully, and sharing the song Eros sings in charming the thought of all gods and human beings.

"Here, Phaedrus, you have the speech from me," he said. "Let it be dedicated to the god, sharing, as far as I am able, partly in playfulness, partly in measured earnestness."

Aristodemus said that when Agathon had finished speaking, all those present applauded vigorously, as the youth had spoken in a way as suited to himself as to the god. Socrates then said, with a glance at Eryximachus, "Son of Akoumenos," he said, "is it your opinion that my long-standing fear was groundless, and that I was not prophetic, when I said before that Agathon would speak in a marvelous way, and that I should be at a loss?"

"In my opinion," Eryximachus said, "your first point was indeed prophetic, that Agathon would speak well; but as to the other, that you would be at a loss, that I do not believe."

"You blessed innocent! How can you say that?" Socrates said. "Am I and anyone else whatsoever not to be at a loss after so fair and varied a speech has been made? Though the rest was not quite so marvelous, that bit at the end—who would not be thunderstruck on hearing the beauty of its words and phrases? I for my part, on reflecting that I myself should be unable to say anything nearly as beautiful, almost ran off and was gone in shame—if I had any place to go. For the speech reminded me of Gorgias; so I was simply affected as in the saying of Homer's. I was afraid that Agathon in his speech would at last send the head of the dread speaker Gorgias against my speeches and turn me to very stone in speechlessness.[13] And then I realized that, after all, I am to be laughed at for having agreed to eulogize Eros in turn with you, and for claiming that I was skilled in erotics; for as it has turned out, I know nothing of the matter, nor how one is to eulogize anything. For in my stupidity I believed the truth had to be told about anything that was given a eulogy, and that this was the underpinning, and that by selecting the most beautiful parts of the truth one was to arrange them in the seemliest manner possible. And I was quite filled with the proud thought that I should speak well, since I knew the truth about praising any-

---

[13]A pun on Gorgias and Gorgon, whose head Odysseus was afraid Persephone would send against him if he lingered in Hades (*Odyssey* 11.632). "Dread speaker" also means "skilled speaker."

thing. But it was not this after all, it seems, that was meant by the fair praising of anything, but the attribution to the matter at hand of the greatest and fairest things possible regardless of whether this was so or not. And if the praise were false, it was of no importance anyway; for the injunction was, it seems, that each of us should be thought to eulogize Eros, and not just eulogize him. It is for this reason, I suspect, that you leave no argument unturned and dedicate each and every argument to Eros. And you assert that he is of this sort and that sort and the cause of so many things, so that he may seem to be as beautiful and good as possible—plainly to those who do not know, for this surely is not the case for those who do know—and so the praise turns out to be beautiful and awesome. But after all I did not know that this was to be the manner of praise, and in ignorance I came to an agreement with you that I would take my turn in praising. 'So the tongue promised but the mind did not';[14] let me then call it quits. I am not a eulogist in this fashion: I am simply incapable of it. Not that I am unwilling—on the contrary I am willing—if you want, to tell the truth on my own terms, so long as my words are not to be compared with your speeches, lest I be laughed at. Decide, then, Phaedrus, if you have any need for such a speech too, for hearing the truth being said about Eros, even though the phrasing and arrangement of the sentences just fall as they come.''

He said that Phaedrus and the others urged Socrates to speak in whatever way he himself believed he had to speak.

''Allow me further, Phaedrus,'' he said, ''to ask Agathon about a few small points, in order that when I have got him to agree with me I can go ahead and speak.''

''Well, I allow it,'' Phaedrus said. ''Ask.'' After this he said that Socrates began from somewhat the following point.

''Well, dear Agathon, in my opinion you made a fine start to your speech, in saying that one had to show first what sort of being Eros himself is, and then his deeds. I very much admire this beginning. So come now, since you have explained fairly and magnificently all the rest about what sort he is, then tell me this as well about Eros: is Eros the sort that is love of something or of nothing? I am not asking whether he is of a mother or of a father (for the question whether Eros is love of mother or father would be laughable), but just as if I asked about this very word, *father*—is the father father of someone or not? You should

---

[14]Euripides, *Hippolytus*, 612: "The tongue swore, but the mind did not."

doubtless tell me, if you wanted to give a fair reply, that the father is father of a son or daughter. Isn't that so?''

"Of course," Agathon said.

"And the same is true of the mother?'' This too was agreed upon.

"Answer me just a little more," Socrates said, "so that you might come to understand better what I want. Suppose I asked, 'What about this point? Is a brother, just in terms of what he is, a brother of someone, or isn't he?' '' He answered that he is.

"And of a brother or a sister, right?'' He agreed.

"Do try, then,'' he said, "to tell about love as well. Is Eros love of nothing or something?''

"Of course he is of something.''

"Keep this fast in your memory, this something of which you claim he is,'' Socrates said, "but now say only this much: That Eros that is the love of something, does he desire this something or not?''

"Of course he does,'' he said.

"And is it when he has, or does not have, that which he desires and loves, that he desires and loves it?''

"It is at least likely that he does not have it,'' he said.

"Think,'' Socrates said, "is it not a necessity rather than a likelihood that the desirous thing desires what it is in need of, and does not desire unless it is in need? For in my opinion, Agathon, it is a marvelous necessity. What is your opinion?''

"It's my opinion too,'' he said.

"What you say is fair. Would anyone want to be tall if he were tall, or strong if he were strong?''

"From what has been agreed upon, that would be impossible.''

"For he surely would not be in need of those things that he already is.''

"What you say is true.''

"So that if he wanted to be strong being strong,'' Socrates said, "and swift being swift, and healthy being healthy—I say this so that we may not deceive ourselves, for one might perhaps suppose with regard to these and all cases of this sort that those who are of this sort and have these things desire those things that they have—but if you have these cases in mind, Agathon, then who would desire each of those things that of necessity he has at the moment when, whether he wants to or not, he has it? For whenever anyone says, 'I am healthy and want to be healthy or I am wealthy and want to be wealthy, and I desire those very things that I have,' we should tell him, 'You, human being, possessing wealth, health, and strength, want to possess them also in the future, since at the present moment at least, whether you want to or not, you have them. Consider then, whenever you say, ''I want the present things,'' if you mean anything else than, ''I want the things of the present moment to be present also in future time.'' Would he agree to that?'' Aristodemus said that Agathon consented.

Socrates then said, ''To want that those things be safe and present for him in future time, is to love that which is not yet at hand for him and which he does not have.''

''Of course,'' he said.

''So he and everyone else who desires what is not at hand desires what is not present; and what he does not have and what he himself is not and what he is in need of—it is things like that of which desire and love are, right?''

''Of course,'' he said.

''Come then,'' Socrates said. ''Let us draw up an agreement about what has been said. Eros is love, first of all, of some things, and secondly, of whatever things the need for which is present to him.''

''Yes,'' he said.

''Would you now think back then to what you asserted Eros to be of in your speech; but if you want, I shall remind you. I believe you spoke somewhat along these lines—that matters were arranged by the gods through love of beautiful things, for there would not be love of ugly things. Weren't you speaking somewhat along these lines?''

''I said so,'' Agathon said.

''And what you say is reasonable, comrade,'' Socrates said. ''And if this is so, Eros would be nothing else than love of beauty, but not of ugliness?'' He agreed.

''Hasn't it been agreed that that of which one is in need and does not have one loves?''

''Yes,'' he said.

''So Eros is in need of and does not have beauty.''

''Of necessity,'' he said.

''What about this? That which is in need of beauty and in no way possesses beauty, do you say that it is beautiful?''

''Certainly not.''

''Do you still agree then that Eros is beautiful, if this is so?''

And Agathon said, ''It's probable, Socrates, that I knew nothing of what I had said.''

"And yet spoke you beautifully, Agathon," he said. "But, still, tell me about a small point. Are the good things beautiful as well in your opinion?"

"Yes, in mine."

"So if Eros is in need of beautiful things, and the good things are fair, he would be in need of the good things as well."

"I, Socrates," he said, "would not be able to contradict you; so let it be as you say."

"Not at all, my dear Agathon. It is rather that you are unable to contradict the truth," he said, "since it is not at all hard to contradict Socrates.

"And I shall let you go for now, and turn to the speech about Eros that I once heard from a woman, Diotima of Mantineia. She was wise in these and many other things; when the Athenians once made a sacrifice before the plague, she caused the onset of the disease to be delayed ten years; and she is the very one who taught me erotics. The speech that she was wont to make, I shall now try to tell you all on the basis of what has been agreed on between Agathon and myself; and I shall try to do it on my own, as best I can. For just as you explained, Agathon, one must first tell who Eros himself is and what sort he is, and then tell his deeds. In my opinion, it is easiest to do this in just the same way that the stranger once did in quizzing me. For I came pretty near, in speaking to her, to saying the same sort of things that Agathon said to me now—that Eros was a great god, and was the love of beautiful things. She then went on to refute me with those same arguments with which I refuted him—that he is neither beautiful, according to my argument, nor good.

"And I said, 'How do you mean it, Diotima? Is Eros after all ugly and bad?'

"And she said, 'Hush! Or do you believe that whatever is not beautiful must necessarily be ugly?'

" 'Absolutely.'

" 'And whatever is not wise, without understanding? Or were you unaware that there is something in between wisdom and lack of understanding?'

" 'What is this?'

" 'Don't you know,' she said, 'that to opine correctly without being able to give an account [logos] is neither to know expertly (for how could expert knowledge be an unaccounted for [alogon] matter?) nor lack of understanding (for how could lack of understanding be that which has hit upon what is)? But surely correct opinion is like that, somewhere between intelligence and lack of understanding.'

" 'What you say is true,' I said.

" 'Then do not compel what is not beautiful to be ugly, or what is not good, to be bad. So too since you yourself agree that Eros is not good or beautiful, do not at all believe that he must be ugly and bad,' she said, 'but something between the two of them.'

" 'And yet,' I said, 'it is agreed on by all that he is a great god.'

" 'Do you mean by all who do not know,' she said, 'or by those who know?'

" 'No, by all together.'

"And she said with a laugh, 'And how, Socrates, could he be agreed to be a great god by those who deny even that he is a god?'

" 'Who are these?' I said.

" 'You are one,' she said, 'and I am one.'

"And I said, 'How can you say this?' I said.

"And she said, 'It's easy. Tell me, don't you assert that all gods are happy and beautiful? Or would you dare to deny that any one of the gods is beautiful and happy?'

" 'By Zeus, I would not,' I said.

" 'But don't you mean by the happy precisely those who possess the good things and the beautiful things?'

" 'Of course.'

" 'And do you hold to the agreement that Eros out of need for the good and beautiful things desires those very things of which he is in need?'

" 'Yes, I hold to it.'

" 'How then could he who is without a share in the beautiful and good things be a god?'

" 'In no way, it seems.'

" 'Do you see then,' she said, 'that you too hold that Eros is not a god?'

" 'What would Eros then be?' I said. 'A mortal?'

" 'Hardly that.'

" 'Well, what then?'

" 'Just as before,' she said, 'between mortal and immortal.'

" 'What is that, Diotima?'

" 'A great daemon, Socrates, for everything daemonic[15] is between god and mortal.'

---

[15]*Daemonic (daimonion)* is either a neuter diminutive of *daimon* or a neuter adjective, related to *daimon* as divine *(theion)* is to god *(theos)*. This neuter, in any case, is the theme of the dialogue up to Socrates' speech that concludes with "vulgar and low."

'' 'With what kind of power?' I said.

'' 'Interpreting and ferrying to gods things from human beings and to human beings things from gods: the requests and sacrifices of human beings, the orders and exchanges-for-sacrifices of gods; for it is in the middle of both and fills up the interval so that the whole itself has been bound together by it. Through this proceeds all divination and the art of the priests who deal with sacrifices, initiatory rituals, incantations, and every kind of soothsaying and magic. A god does not mingle with a human being; but through this occurs the whole intercourse and conversation of gods with human beings while they are awake and asleep. And he who is wise in things like this is a daemonic man; but he who is wise in anything else concerning either arts or handicrafts is vulgar and low. These daemons are many and of all kinds; and one of them is Eros.'

'' 'Who is his father?' I said, 'And who is his mother?'

'' 'It is rather long,' she said, 'to explain; but I shall tell you all the same. When Aphrodite was born, all the other gods as well as Poros [Resource] the son of Metis [Intelligence] were at a feast;[16] and when they had dined, Penia [Poverty] arrived to beg for something—as might be expected at a festivity—and she hung about near the door. Then Poros got drunk on nectar—for there was not yet wine—and, heavy of head, went into the garden of Zeus and slept. Then Penia, who because of her own lack of resources was plotting to have a child made out of Poros, reclined beside him and conceived Eros. It is for this reason that Eros has been the attendant and servant of Aphrodite, as he was conceived on her birthday; for he is by nature a lover in regard to the beautiful, and Aphrodite is beautiful. So because Eros is the son of Poros and Penia, his situation is in some such case as this. First of all, he is always poor; and he is far from being tender and beautiful, as the many believe, but is tough, squalid, shoeless, and homeless, always lying on the ground without a blanket or a bed, sleeping in doorways and along waysides in the open air; he has the nature of his mother, always dwelling with neediness. But in accordance with his father he plots to trap the beautiful and the good, and is courageous, stout, and keen, a skilled hunter, always weaving devices, desirous of practical wisdom

---

[16]Metis is the first goddess Zeus marries after the wars among the gods are over. He is warned in time not to allow her child Athena to be born, lest Athena's children overthrow him; he swallows Metis, and Athena is later born from the head of Zeus (see Hesiod, *Theogony*, 886–900).

and inventive, philosophizing through all his life, a skilled magician, druggist, sophist. And his nature is neither immortal nor mortal; but sometimes on the same day he flourishes and lives, whenever he has resources; and sometimes he dies, but gets to live again through the nature of his father. And as that which is supplied to him is always gradually flowing out, Eros is never either without resources nor wealthy, but is in between wisdom and lack of understanding. For here is the way it is: No one of the gods philosophizes and desires to become wise—for he *is* so—nor if there is anyone else who is wise, does he philosophize. Nor, in turn, do those who lack understanding philosophize and desire to become wise; for it is precisely this that makes the lack of understanding so difficult—that if a man is not beautiful and good, nor intelligent, he has the opinion that that is sufficient for him. Consequently, he who does not believe that he is in need does not desire that which he does not believe he needs.'

" 'Then who, Diotima, are the philosophizers,' I said, 'if they are neither the wise nor those who lack understanding?'

" 'By now it is perfectly plain even to a child,' she said, 'that they are those between them both, of whom Eros would be one. For wisdom is one of the most beautiful things, and Eros is love in regard to the beautiful; and so Eros is—necessarily—a philosopher; and as a philosopher he is between being wise and being without understanding. His manner of birth is responsible for this, for he is of a wise and resourceful father, and an unwise and resourceless mother. Now the nature of the daemon, dear Socrates, is this; but as for the one whom you believed to be Eros, it is not at all surprising that you had this impression. You believed, in my opinion, as I conjecture from what you say, that the beloved is Eros, and is not that which loves. It is for this reason, I believe, that Eros seemed to you to be wholly beautiful. For the beloved thing is truly beautiful, delicate, perfect, and most blessed; but that which loves has another kind of look, the sort that I just explained.'

"And I said, 'All right, stranger, what you say is fine. If Eros is of this sort, of what use is he for human beings?'

" 'It is this, Socrates,' she said, 'that I shall next try to teach you. Now, Eros is of that sort and was born in that way; and he is of the beautiful things, as you assert. But what if someone were to ask us, "What about those beautiful things of which Eros is, Socrates and Diotima?" It is more clearly ex-

pressed as follows: He who loves the beautiful things loves—
what does he love?'

"And I said, 'That they be his.'

" 'But the answer,' she said, 'still longs for the following
sort of question: What will he have who gets the beautiful
things?'

"I said that I was hardly capable of giving a ready answer
to this question.

" 'Well,' she said. 'What if someone changed his query
and used the good instead of the beautiful? Come, Socrates, the
lover of the good things loves: what does he love?'

" 'That they be his,' I said.

" 'And what will he who gets the good things have?'

" 'This,' I said, 'I can answer more adequately: he will be
happy.'

" 'That,' she said, 'is because the happy are happy by the
acquisition of good things; and there is no further need to ask,
"For what consequence does he who wants to be happy want to
be so?" But the answer is thought to be a complete one.'

" 'What you say is true,' I said.

" 'This wanting and this eros, do you suppose they are
common to all human beings, and all want the good things to be
theirs always, or how do you mean it?'

" 'That way,' I said. 'They are common to all.'

" 'Why is it, then, Socrates,' she said, 'that we deny that
everyone loves—given, that is, that everyone loves the same
things and always—but we say that some love and some do not?'

" 'I too,' I said, 'am amazed.'

" 'Well,' she said, 'don't persist in your amazement; for
we detach from eros a certain kind of eros and give it the name
eros, imposing upon it the name of the whole; while in the other
cases we employ several different names.'

" 'What are those?' I said.

" 'Like the following: You know that "making" has a
wide range; for, you see, every kind of making is responsible for
anything whatsoever that is on the way from what is not to what
is. And thus all the productions that are dependent on the arts are
makings, and all the craftsmen engaged in them are makers.'

" 'What you say is true.'

" 'But nevertheless,' she said, 'you know that not all craftsmen are called makers but have other names; and one part is
separated off from all of making—that which is concerned with
music and meters—and is addressed by the name of the whole.

For this alone is called poetry; and those who have this part of making are poets.'

" 'What you say is true,' I said.

" 'So too in the case of eros. In brief, eros is the whole desire of good things and of being happy, "the greatest and all-beguiling eros." But those who turn toward it in many other ways, in terms of either money-making, love of gymnastics, or philosophy, are neither said to love nor called lovers; whereas those who earnestly apply themselves to a certain single kind, get the name of the whole, love, and are said to love and called lovers.'

" 'What you say is probably true,' I said.

" 'And there is a certain account,' she said, 'according to which those who seek their own halves are lovers. But my speech denies that eros is of a half or of a whole—unless, comrade, that half or whole can be presumed to be really good; for human beings are willing to have their own feet and hands cut off, if their opinion is that their own are no good. For I suspect that each does not cleave to his own (unless one calls the good one's own and belonging to oneself, and the bad alien to oneself) since there is nothing that human beings love other than the good. Or is it your opinion that they do?'

" 'No, by Zeus,' I said, 'that is not my opinion.'

" 'Then,' she said, 'is it to be said unqualifiedly that human beings love the good?'

" 'Yes,' I said.

" 'What about this? Mustn't it be added,' she said, 'that they love the good to be theirs?'

" 'It must be added.'

" 'And not only that it be theirs,' she said, 'but always as well?'

" 'This too must be added.'

" 'So, in sum,' she said, 'eros is of the good's being one's own always.'

" 'What you say is most true,' I said.

" 'Since eros is always this,' she said, 'then in what manner and in what activity would the earnestness and intensity of those who pursue the good be called eros. What in fact are they doing when they act so? Can you tell?'

" 'If I could, Diotima, then I should not, you know, in admiration of your wisdom,' I said, 'resort to you to learn this very thing.'

" 'Well, I shall tell you,' she said. 'Their deed is bringing to birth in beauty both in terms of the body and in terms of the soul.'

" 'Whatever it is that you mean,' I said, 'is in need of divination, and I do not begin to understand.'

" 'Well, I shall speak more clearly,' she said. 'All human beings, Socrates,' she said, 'conceive both in terms of the body and in terms of the soul, and whenever they are at a certain age, their nature desires to give birth; but it is incapable of giving birth in ugliness, but only in beauty, for the being together of man and woman is a bringing to birth. This thing, pregnancy and bringing to birth, is divine, and it is immortal in the animal that is mortal. It is impossible for this to happen in the unfitting; and the ugly is unfitting with everything divine, but the beautiful is fitting. So Kallone [Beauty] is the Moira [Fate] and Eileithyia[17] for birth. It is for these reasons that whenever the pregnant draws near to beauty, it becomes glad and in its rejoicing dissolves and then gives birth and produces offspring; but whenever it draws near to ugliness, then, downcast and in pain, it contracts inwardly, turns away, shrinks up, and does not produce offspring, but checking the course of the pregnancy, has a hard time of it. So this is why someone who is pregnant, with breasts already swelling, flutters so much around the beautiful, because the one who has the beautiful releases him from great labor pains. For eros is not, Socrates,' she said, 'of the beautiful, as you believe.'

" 'Well, what then?'

" 'It is of engendering and bringing to birth in the beautiful.'

" 'All right,' I said.

" 'It is more than all right,' she said. 'And why is eros of engendering? Because engendering is born forever and is immortal as far as that can happen to a mortal being. From what has been agreed to, it is necessary to desire immortality with good, provided eros is of the good's always being one's own. So it is necessary from this argument that eros be of immortality too.'

"All of these things she used to teach me whenever she made her speeches about erotics. And once she also asked, 'What do you believe, Socrates, is the cause of this eros and desire? Or aren't you aware how uncanny is the disposition of all the beasts (the footed as well as the winged) whenever they desire to produce offspring? They are all ill and of an erotic disposition, first concerning actual intercourse with one another, then later concerning the nurture of what is generated. And they

---

[17]Fate and Eileithyia are goddesses who preside over birth, and Kallone is a cult name of Artemis-Hecate.

are ready to fight to the finish, the weakest against the strongest, for the sake of those they have generated, and to die on their behalf; and they are willingly racked by starvation and stop at nothing to nourish their offspring. One might suppose,' she said, 'that human beings do this from calculation; but as for the beasts, what is the cause of their erotic disposition's being of this sort? Can you say?'

"And I again said that I did not know; and she said, 'Do you really think you will ever become skilled in erotics, if you do not understand this?'

" 'But you see, Diotima, that is the reason—as I said just now—why I have come to you: I know I am in need of teachers. But do tell me the cause of these things as well as of the rest that concern erotics.'

" 'If you put your trust,' she said, 'in the statement that by nature eros is of that which we have often agreed to, don't persist in your amazement. For in the eros of the beasts, in terms of the same argument as that concerning men, the mortal nature seeks as far as possible to be forever and immortal. Mortal nature is capable of immortality only in this way, the way of generation, because it is always leaving behind another that is young to replace the old. For while each one of the animals is said to live and be the same (for example, one is spoken of as the same from the time one is a child until one is an old man; and though he never has the same things in himself, nevertheless, he is called the same), he is forever becoming young in some respects as he suffers losses in other respects: his hair, flesh, bones, blood, and his whole body. And this is so not only in terms of the body but also in terms of the soul; his ways, character, opinions, desires, pleasures, pains, fears, each of these things is never present as the same for each, but they are partly coming to be and partly perishing. And what is far stranger still is that in the case of our sciences too not only are some coming to be while others are perishing (and we are never the same in terms of the sciences either); but also each single one of the sciences is affected in the same way. For studying, as it is called, is done on the grounds that the science is passing out from us; for forgetfulness is the exiting of science; and studying, by instilling a fresh memory again to replace the departing one, preserves the science, so that it may be thought to be the same. For in this way every mortal thing is preserved; not by being absolutely the same forever, as the divine is, but by the fact that that which is departing and growing old leaves behind another

young thing that is as it was. By this device, Socrates,' she said,
'the mortal shares in immortality, both body and all the rest; but the
immortal has a different way. So do not be amazed if everything
honors by nature its own offshoot; for it is for the sake of
immortality that this zeal and eros attend everything.'

"And when I had heard her speech I was amazed and said,
'Really!' I said. 'Wisest Diotima, is it truly like this?'

"And she, like the perfect Sophists, said, 'Know it well,
Socrates,' she said, 'inasmuch as in the case of human beings, if
you were willing to glance at their love of honor, you would be
amazed at their irrationality unless you understand what I have
said and reflect how uncanny their disposition is made by their
love of renown, "and their setting up immortal fame for eternity";
and for the sake of fame even more than for their children, they
are ready to run all risks, to exhaust their money, to toil at every
sort of toil, and to die. For do you suppose,' she said, 'that
Alcestis would have died for Admetus' sake, or Achilles would have
died after Patroclus, or your own Codrus would have died
before his sons for the sake of their kingship, if they had not
believed that there would be an immortal remembering of their
virtue, which we now retain? Far from it,' she said, 'but I
believe that all do all things for the sake of immortal virtue and a
famous reputation of that sort; and the better they are, so much
the more is it thus; for they love the immortal. Now there are
those who are pregnant in terms of their bodies,' she said, 'and
they turn rather to women and are erotic in this way, furnishing
for themselves through the procreation of children immortality,
remembrance, and happiness (as they believe) for all future time.
But there are others who are pregnant in terms of the soul—for
these, in fact,' she said, 'are those who in their souls even more
than in their bodies conceive those things that it is appropriate
for soul to conceive and bear. And what is appropriate for soul?
Prudence and the rest of virtue; it is of these things that all the
poets and all the craftsmen who are said to be inventive are
procreators; and by far the greatest and most beautiful part of
prudence,' she said, 'is the arranging and ordering of the affairs
of cities and households. Its name is moderation and justice. So
whenever someone from youth onward is pregnant in his soul
with these virtues, if he is divine and of suitable age, then he
desires to give birth and produce offspring. And he goes round in
search, I believe, of the beautiful in which he might generate; for
he will never generate in the ugly. So it is beautiful bodies rather
than ugly ones to which he cleaves because he is pregnant; and if

he meets a beautiful, generous, and naturally gifted soul, he cleaves strongly to the two (body and soul) together. And to this human being he is at once fluent in speeches about virtue—of what sort the good man must be and what he must practice—and he tries to educate him. So in touching the one who is beautiful, I suspect, and in association with him, he engenders and gives birth to offspring with which he was long pregnant; and whether the [lover] is present or absent he holds the beautiful one in memory, and nurtures with him that which has been generated in common. Therefore, those of this sort maintain a greater association and firmer friendship with one another than do those who have children in common, because the children they share in common are more beautiful and more immortal. And everyone would choose to have for himself children like these rather than the human kind; and if one looks at Homer, Hesiod, and the other good poets, one envies them: what offspring of themselves they have left behind! For as these offspring are in their own right immortal, they supply the poets with immortal fame and memory. And if you want,' she said, 'think of the children that Lycurgus left behind in Sparta, the preservers of Sparta and, to exaggerate a little, of Greece. Solon too is honored among you through his engendering of the laws; and other men as well in many other regions, among Greeks and among barbarians, by their showing forth of many beautiful deeds, have engendered every kind of virtue. It is to these that many sanctuaries are now dedicated through children of this kind; while through the human sort there are no sanctuaries for anyone yet.

'' 'Now perhaps, Socrates, you too might be initiated into these erotics; but as for the perfect revelations—for which the others are means, if one were to proceed correctly on the way—I do not know if you would be able to be initiated into them. Now I shall speak,' she said. 'I shall not falter in my zeal; do try to follow, if you are able. He who is to move correctly in this matter must begin while young to go to beautiful bodies. And first of all, if the guide is guiding correctly, he must love one body and there generate beautiful speeches. Then he must realize that the beauty that is in any body whatsoever is related to that in another body; and if he must pursue the beauty of looks, it is great folly not to believe that the beauty of all bodies is one and the same. And with this realization he must be the lover of all beautiful bodies and in contempt slacken this [erotic] intensity for only one body, in the belief that it is petty. After this he must believe that the beauty in souls is more honorable than that in the body. So that even if someone who is decent in his soul has only a slight youthful charm, the lover must be content with it, and love and cherish him, and engender and seek such speeches as will make the young better; in order that [the lover], on his part, may be compelled to behold the beautiful in pursuits and laws, and to see that all this is akin to itself, so that he may come to believe that the beauty of the body is something trivial. And after these pursuits, he must lead [the beloved] on to the sciences, so that he [himself, the lover] may see the beauty of sciences, and in looking at the beautiful, which is now so vast, no longer be content like a lackey with the beauty in one, of a boy, of some human being, or of one practice, nor be a sorry sort of slave and petty calculator; but with a permanent turn to the vast open sea of the beautiful, behold it and give birth—in ungrudging philosophy— to many beautiful and magnificent speeches and thoughts; until, there strengthened and increased, he may discern a certain single philosophical science, which has as its object the following sort of beauty. Try to pay as close attention as you can,' she said. 'Whoever has been educated up to this point in erotics, behold- ing successively and correctly the beautiful things, in now going to the perfect end of erotics shall suddenly glimpse something wonderfully beautiful in its nature—that very thing, Socrates, for whose sake alone all the prior labors were undertaken—something that is, first of all, always being and neither coming to be nor perishing, nor increasing nor passing away; and secondly, not beautiful in one respect and ugly in another, nor at one time so, and at another time not—either with respect to the beautiful or the ugly—nor here beautiful and there ugly, as being beautiful to some and ugly to others; nor in turn will the beautiful be imagined by him as a kind of face or hands or anything else in which body shares, nor as any speech nor any science, and not as being somewhere in something else (for example, in an animal, or in earth, or in heaven, or in anything else), but as it is alone by itself and with itself, always being of a single form; while all other beautiful things that share in it do so in such a way that while it neither becomes anything more or less, nor is affected at all, the rest do come to be and perish. So whenever anyone begins to glimpse that beauty as he goes on up from these things through the correct practice of pederasty, he must come close to touching the perfect end. For this is what it is to proceed correctly, or to be led by another, to erotics—beginning from these beautiful things here, always to proceed on up for the sake of that beauty, using these beautiful things here as steps: from one to two, and from two to all beautiful bodies; and from beautiful bodies to beautiful pursuits; and from pursuits to beautiful lessons; and from lessons to end at that lesson, which is the lesson of nothing else than the beautiful itself; and at last to know what is beauty itself. It is at this place in life, in beholding the beautiful itself, my dear Socrates,' the Mantinean stranger said, 'that it is worth living, if—for a human being—it is [worth living] at any place. Should you ever see the beautiful itself, it will be your opinion that it is not to be compared to gold and garments and the beautiful boys and youths at whose sight you are now thunderstruck. And you and many others are prepared, in seeing the beloved and in always being with him, neither to eat nor drink, if it were somehow possible, but only to behold him and be with him. What then,' she said, 'do we believe happens to one, if he gets to see the beautiful itself, pure, clean, unmixed, and not infected with human flesh, colors, or a lot of other mortal foolishness, and can glimpse the divine beautiful itself as being of a single shape? Do you believe,' she said, 'that life would prove to be a sorry sort of thing, when a human being gazes in the direction of the beautiful and beholds it with the instrument with which he must and is together with it? Or don't you realize,' she said, 'that only here, in seeing in the way the beautiful is seeable, will he get to engender not phantom images of virtue—because he does not lay hold of a phantom—but true, because he lays hold of the true; and that once he has given birth to and cherished true virtue, it lies within him to become dear to god and, if it is possible for any human being, to become immortal as well?'

"Here, Phaedrus and you others, is what Diotima declared and what I am convinced of. And in this state of conviction, I try to persuade others that for this possession one could not easily get a better co-worker with human nature than Eros. Accordingly, I assert that every real man must honor Eros, as I myself honor erotics and train myself exceptionally in them; and I urge it on the rest, and now and always I eulogize the power and courage of Eros as far as I am able. Regard this speech, then, Phaedrus, if you want to, as spoken in eulogy of Eros; but if not, and your pleasure is to give it some other kind of name, so name it."

When Socrates had said this, some praised it; and Aristoph-

anes tried to say something, because Socrates in speaking had
mentioned him and referred to his speech. But suddenly a hammering on the courtyard door made a lot of noise—revelers they
thought—and they heard the sound of a flute girl. Then Agathon
said, "Boys, go look. And if it is any one of our close friends,
invite him in; but if not, say that we are not drinking but have
already stopped."

Not much later they heard the voice of Alcibiades in the
courtyard, very drunk and shouting loudly, asking where Agathon
was and commanding them to lead him to Agathon. Then the
flute girl who—together with some other of his attendants—
supported him and led him before them; and he stood at the door,
thickly crowned with ivy and violets, with many fillets on his
head. And he said, "Men, hail! Will you welcome a man who's
terribly drunk as a fellow drinker? Or shall we go away just as
soon as we have wreathed Agathon, for which single purpose we
have come? For I, you see," he said, "could not come yesterday, but now I have come with fillets on my head, so that from
my own head I might wreathe the head of the wisest and most
beautiful—well! And if I shall say that, what then? Will you
laugh at me because I am drunk? But all the same, even if you
do laugh, I know well that I am telling the truth. Well, tell me
on the spot, shall I enter on the said conditions or not? Will you
join me in drink or not?"

Then they all applauded loudly and asked him to enter and
lie down; and Agathon summoned him. And he came led by his
creatures; and as he was taking off the fillets to do the
crowning—he had had them before his eyes and so did not
observe Socrates—he sat down alongside Agathon, between him
and Socrates; for Socrates had made room for Alcibiades when
he saw him. On sitting down he embraced Agathon and bound
on the fillets.

Then Agathon said, "Take off Alcibiades' shoes, boys, so
that he may lie down in the third place."

"Certainly," Alcibiades said, "but who is here as our third
fellow drinker?" And at once he turned around and saw Socrates; and as soon as he saw him he leapt up and said, "Heracles!
What is the meaning of this? Socrates is here? Once again you
lie in ambush; and just as is your habit, you appear suddenly
wherever I believed you were least likely to be. And now, why
have you come? And why did you lie down here? For it is not
with Aristophanes, or with anyone else who is—or wants to

be—laughable that you lie; but you managed it so that you might lie down beside the most beautiful of those in this room."

And Socrates said, "Agathon, consider! Are you going to defend me? The love I have of this human being has proved quite bothersome. For since the time that I first loved him, it is no longer possible for me to look at or converse with even one beauty; or else in jealousy and envy of me he does amazing things, and abuses me and hardly keeps his hands off me. Take care lest he do something now, and do reconcile us; or if he tries to use force, defend me, since I really quake with fear at his madness and love of lovers."

"But," said Alcibiades, "reconciliation between you and me is impossible. Well, I shall take my vengeance on you for this at another time; but now, Agathon," he said, "spare us some of the fillets, so that I may wreathe this amazing head of his; and he need not reproach me because I wreathed you, and not him; for he conquers all human beings in speeches, and not just the day before yesterday as you did, but at all times." And at once he took some of the fillets, wreathed Socrates, and lay down.

And when he lay down, he said, "All right, men. In my opinion you're sober. This cannot be allowed; you must drink, for we have agreed to it. And I choose as leader of the drinking—until you have drunk enough—myself. But let someone do the fetching, Agathon, if there is any large beaker. But there is no need really; just bring that wine cooler there, boy," he said, as he saw that it had a capacity of more than eight pints. Once he saw that it got filled he was the first to drink it off; and then, as he asked that it be poured for Socrates, he said, "It is no sophistic stratagem of mine against Socrates, men; for as much as one asks him to, so much he drinks off without any risk of getting more drunk."

Then the boy poured and Socrates drank. And Eryximachus said, "What are we to do, Alcibiades? Is this to be our way, to say nothing at all over our cups, nor sing anything, but simply to drink like the thirsty?"

Then Alcibiades said, "Eryximachus, best son of the best and most moderate father, hail!"

"You too," Eryximachus said. "But what shall we do?"

"Whatever you order. For we must obey you—

'For a physician is worth the equivalent of many others.'[18]

---

[18]Homer, *Iliad*, 11.514.

Prescribe what you want.''

"Listen then," Eryximachus said. "It was our resolution before you entered that each of us in turn, beginning on the left, should make as fair a speech as he could about Eros, and eulogize him. Now all the rest of us have spoken; and since you have not spoken but have drunk up, it is just that you speak. And after your speech prescribe for Socrates whatever you want; and then let him prescribe for him on his right, and so on for the rest.''

"Well, Eryximachus," Alcibiades said, "what you say is fine, but I am afraid it is not quite fair for a drunkard to be matched against the speeches of the sober. And at the same time, you blessed innocent, has Socrates really convinced you of anything he just said? Don't you know that things are exactly the opposite of what he was saying? For if I praise anyone other than himself, whether god or human being, while he is present, he will not keep his hands off me.''

"Hush," Socrates said.

"No, by Poseidon," Alcibiades said. "Say nothing against this, since there is no one else I should praise while you were present.''

"Well, do so, if you want," Eryximachus said. "Praise Socrates.''

"What are you saying?" Alcibiades said. "Is it thought that I should, Eryximachus? Shall I assault the man and take vengeance on him in your presence?''

"You there," Socrates said. "What do you have in mind? To praise me for the sake of raising a laugh? Or what will you do?''

"I shall tell the truth. See if you allow it.''

"Well, if it is the truth," he said, "I both allow and order you to tell it.''

"Your word is my command," Alcibiades said. "Now you do as follows. If I say anything that is untrue, check me in the middle if you want to and say in what respect I am telling a lie; for as far as my will goes, I shall not lie. Now if in reminiscing I speak of one thing and then another, don't be surprised; for it is not at all easy for me in the condition I am in to enumerate fluently and consecutively your strangeness.

"I shall try in this way, men, to praise Socrates, through likenesses. Now he perhaps will suppose it is for raising a laugh; but the likeness will be for the sake of the truth, not for the sake of the laughable. I declare that he is most strictly like those silenuses[19] that sit in the shops of herm sculptors, the ones that craftsmen make holding reed pipes or flutes; and if they are split in two and opened up, they show that they have images of gods within. And I declare, in turn, that he bears a likeness to the satyr Marsyas. Now, that you are like them at least in looks, Socrates, surely not even you would dispute; and as for your likeness to them in other respects, just listen to what I have to say. You are hybristic, are you not? For if you do not agree, I shall get witnesses. Well, aren't you a flute player? You are far more marvelous, to be sure, than Marsyas. He used to charm human beings by means of instruments, with the power from his mouth, as anyone still does today who plays his flute songs. For I ascribe to Marsyas as what Olympus fluted since Marsyas had taught him; so that the songs of Olympus, whether a good flutist or a sorry sort of flute girl should play them, are the only ones—because they are divine—that cause possession and reveal those who are in need of the gods and initiatory rituals. And you differ from him only in that you do the same thing with bare words without instruments. We, at any rate, whenever we hear the speeches of anyone else—no matter how good a speaker he is—just about no one gets concerned. But whenever any one of us hears you or another speaking your speeches, even if the speaker is very poor, regardless of whether a woman, man, or lad hears them, we are thunderstruck and possessed. I, at any rate, men, were I not going to be thought utterly drunk, should tell you on oath exactly how his speeches have affected me, and still do to this very day. For whenever I listen, my heart jumps far more than the Corybants', and tears pour out under the power of his speeches; and I see that they affect many many others in the same way. When I heard Pericles and other good speakers, I thought they spoke well, but they could not affect me in any way like that, nor did my soul grow troubled and become distressed at my slavish condition. But I had so often been put in this state by this Marsyas you see before you that I came to the opinion that it was not worth living in the way I am. Now, Socrates, you will not say that this is not true. And even now I know within myself that were I willing to lend

---

[19]Silenus was a woodland god, depicted as an old man with the ears of a horse, often drunk, and riding an ass or wine jar. If caught, Silenus was supposed to reveal his wisdom; but nothing is known of his wisdom except that he said that it was better not to be born. He was associated since the sixth century with Dionysus. The *sileni* or silenuses were half-gods or spirits, with the same characteristics as Silenus, but often confused with the satyrs.

my ears, I should not be capable of holding out but should be affected in the same way. For he compels me to agree that, though I am still in need of much myself, I neglect myself and handle instead the affairs of the Athenians. So it was by main force that I stopped my ears and took off in flight, as if from the Sirens, in order that I might not sit here in idleness and grow old beside him. In regard to this human being alone have I been affected in a way that no one would suspect was in me—to feel shame before anyone at all. Only before him do I feel shame. For I know within myself that I am incapable of contradicting him or of saying that what he commands must not be done; and whenever I go away, I know within myself that I am doing so because I have succumbed to the honor I get from the many. So I have become a runaway and avoid him; and whenever I see him, I am ashamed of what has been agreed upon. And many is the time when I should see with pleasure that he is not among human beings; but again, if this should happen, I know well that I should be much more greatly distressed. I do not know what to do with this human being.

"And I and many others have been affected in such ways by the flute songs of this satyr here before us. But as to the rest, hear me tell how he is like those to whom I have likened him, and how amazing is the power he has. For know well that not one of you is acquainted with him; but I shall make it plain, inasmuch as I have started on it. You see that Socrates is erotically inclined to the beauties and is always around them, and that he is thunderstruck; and again that he is ignorant of everything and knows nothing. Now isn't this guise of his silenic? It certainly is. For he has wrapped this around himself on the outside, just as the carved silenus; but once he is opened up, do you suspect, fellow drinking men, how full he is of moderation? Know that he's not at all concerned if someone is beautiful—and he holds this in such great contempt that no one would believe it—any more than if someone is rich or has any other honor of those deemed blessed by the multitude. But he believes that all these possessions are worth nothing and that we are nothing, I tell you, and all his life he keeps on being ironical and playful to human beings. And when he is in earnest and opened up, I do not know if anyone has seen the images within; but I once saw them, and it was my opinion that they were so divine, golden, altogether beautiful, and amazing that one had to do just about whatever Socrates commanded. Believing him to be in earnest about my youthful beauty, I believed I had had a lucky find and an amazing piece of good luck: I had the chance—if I gratified Socrates—to hear everything that he knew; for I used to take an amazing amount of pride in my youthful beauty. So with this in mind, though I previously was not in the habit of being alone with him without an attendant, I then sent the attendant away and was alone with him. (For the whole truth must be told you, but pay attention, and if I lie, Socrates, try and refute me.) So I was alone with him alone, men; and I believed he would converse with me at once in just the way a lover would converse with his beloved in isolation, and I rejoiced. But exactly nothing of the sort happened; but just as he used to do, he would converse with me; and having spent the day with me he would take his leave. After this I challenged him to join me in stripping; and I stripped along with him. Here, I thought, I shall get my way. So he joined me in stripping and often wrestled with me when no one else was present. And what need is there to say more? I got no advantage from it at all. And when I made no headway in this manner, I resolved that the man must be set upon by force and not be released, since I was already committed to the attempt, and now I had to find out what was really the matter. I invited him then to join me at supper, simply as a lover plots against a beloved. And he did not quickly yield to me in this, but in time, at any rate, he was persuaded. And when he came for the first time, he wanted, once he had dined, to go away. And then out of shame I let him go; but I renewed my plottings once more. And this time when we had dined I kept on conversing far into the night; and when he wanted to go away, I pretended that it was too late and compelled him to remain. So he took his rest in the bed next to me on which he had dined; and no one else slept in the room but ourselves. Now, what I have said up to this point in my speech could properly be told to anyone at all. And you would not hear any more from me than this were it not that, first of all, as the saying goes, wine—with boys and without boys—is truthful, and in the second place, that it is patently unjust for me, once I have come to the point of praising Socrates, to keep hidden his magnificently overweening deed. Furthermore, the affliction of a victim of the viper's bite is also mine. For they say, as you know, that anyone who has been so afflicted is unwilling to speak of what sort of thing it is except to those who themselves have been bitten, since they alone will recognize it and pardon him if his pain brought him to the point of doing and saying anything. Take me, for instance. I was bitten by a more painful viper in the place that is most liable to pain—the heart or soul or whatever name it must have—bitten and struck by philo-sophical speeches, which grip in a more savage way than the viper, whenever they get a hold on a young soul that is not ill-favored by nature, and make it do and say anything whatsoever—and seeing in turn Phaedruses, Agathons, Eryximachuses, Pausaniases, Aristodemuses, as well as Aristophaneses . . . and what need is there to speak of Socrates and all the others? You all have shared in the philosophic madness and bacchic frenzy—so accordingly you all will hear; for you will pardon the things then done and now said. But you house servants—and if there is anyone else who is profane and rustic—put large gates over your ears.

"So, men, when the lamp was extinguished and the boys were outside, I resolved that I should in no way complicate the issue before him, but freely speak what were my opinions. And I nudged him and said, 'Socrates, are you asleep?' 'Certainly not,' he said. 'Do you know then what I have resolved?' 'What in particular?' he said. 'You, in my opinion,' I said, 'have proved to be the only deserving lover of mine; and it seems to me that you hesitate to mention it to me. Now I am in this state: I believe it is very foolish not to gratify you in this or anything else of mine—my wealth or my friends—that you need; for nothing is more important to me than that I become the best possible; and I believe that, as far as I am concerned, there is no one more competent than you to be a fellow helper to me in this. So I should be far more ashamed before men of good sense for not gratifying a man like you than I should be before the many and senseless for gratifying you.'

"And when he heard this, he said very ironically, and exactly as he is, and in his usual fashion, 'Really, my dear Alcibiades, you're no sucker if what you say about me is really true and there is some power in me through which you could become better. You must see, you know, an impossible beauty in me, a beauty very different from the fairness of form in yourself. So if, in observing my beauty, you are trying to get a share in it and to exchange beauty for beauty, you are intending to get far the better deal. For you are trying to acquire the truth of beautiful things in exchange for the seeming and opinion of beautiful things; and you really have in mind to exchange "gold for bronze."[20] But, blessed one, do consider better: without your being aware of it—I may be nothing. Thought, you know, begins to have keen eyesight when the sight of the eyes starts to decline from its peak; and you are still far from that.'

[20]Homer, *Iliad*, 6.236.

"And I heard this, and said, 'This is the way matters stand on my side—not one of my words has been said in a way different from what I think; but you yourself take whatever counsel you believe to be best for yourself and me.'

" 'Well,' he said, 'what you say is good; for in the future, after deliberating, we shall do whatever looks best to us two concerning these things and the rest.'

"So I, when I had heard and said these things, and had shot my darts as it were, thought he had been wounded. And I got up, and did not allow him to speak any more, but wrapped my mantle around him—for it was winter—and lay down under his blanket; and I threw my arms around this truly daemonic and amazing being, and lay down beside him the whole night. And not even in this, Socrates, will you say that I lie. But when I had done this, he so far prevailed over me and despised and laughed at my youthful beauty and committed an outrage against it (and in that regard I believed I was something special, men of the jury—for you are the judges of Socrates' arrogance) . . . for know well, by the gods, by the goddesses, that though I slept the night through with Socrates I got up without anything more untoward having happened than would have been the case if I had slept with my father or elder brother.

"So after this, what notion do you suppose I had? I believed I had been dishonored, and yet I still admired his nature, moderation, and courage; I had met a human being whose prudence and endurance were such as I believed I should never encounter. Consequently, I did not know how I could be angry at him and be deprived of his association; nor did I have any resources whereby I could attract him. I knew well that—on all sides—he was far more invulnerable to money than Ajax was to iron; and even at that one point where I believed he could be taken, he had escaped me. So I was in a quandary; and enslaved by this human being as no one has been by anyone else, I wandered about in distraction. Now, all this had happened to me earlier; and after this we went together on the expedition to Potidaea, and we shared our mess there. Now first of all he faced trials not only better than I did but better than all others. Whenever we were cut off somewhere and compelled to go without food, as happens in campaigns, the others were nothing compared to him in self-control. And again at festivities he alone was able to take pleasure in other things, and in drinking as well; for even though he wasn't willing to drink, whenever he was compelled to do so, he outdid everybody; and what is the most amazing thing of all, no human being has ever seen Socrates drunk. Now it is my opinion that there will soon be a test of this. And again, in regard to resistance against the winter—for winters are terrible there—all the rest that he did was amazing. And once when the frost was the most terrible imaginable, and no one went outdoors (or if any did go out, they wrapped themselves in an amazing number of garments and put on shoes and tied up their feet in felt and sheepskins), he went out among them with the same sort of mantle as he wore at any time, and without shoes he marched through the ice more easily than the others did shod; and the soldiers looked askance at him as if he were despising them. And that is the way things were.

" 'What sort of thing the strong man did and dared'[21] there on campaign once, is worth hearing. Once, he had gotten a thought, and he stood on the same spot from dawn on, considering it; and when he made no progress, he did not let up but stood searching. And it was already noon, and the men became aware of it; and in amazement one said to another that Socrates had stood there in reflection since dawn. And finally some Ionians, when it was evening and they had dined—for it was then summer— brought out their pallets and slept in the cold and watched to see if he would also stand during the night. And he stood until it was dawn and the sun came up; and then having made a prayer to the sun he went away. And in combat, if you want to hear about it—for it is just to credit him with this—once when there was a battle for which the generals gave me the prize of excellence, no other human being saved me but he; for he was not willing to leave me wounded, but saved both myself and my weapons. And I even then, Socrates, asked the generals to offer you the prize of excellence. And in this too you will not blame me and say that I lie; but as a matter of fact, when the generals looked to my rank and wanted to offer me the prize of excellence, you proved more eager than the generals that I take it rather than yourself. Furthermore, men, it was worthwhile to behold Socrates when the army retreated in flight from Delium; for I happened to be there on horseback and he was a hoplite. The soldiers were then in rout, and while he and Laches were retreating together, I came upon them by chance. And as soon as I saw them, I at once urged the two of them to take heart, and I said I would not leave them behind. I had an even finer opportunity to observe Socrates there than I had had at Potidaea, for I was less in fear because I was on

---

[21]Homer, *Odyssey*, 4.242, 271.

horseback. First of all, how much more sensible he was than Laches; and secondly, it was my opinion, Aristophanes (and this point is yours); that walking there just as he does here in Athens, 'stalking like a pelican, his eyes darting from side to side,'[22] quietly on the lookout for friends and foes, he made it plain to everyone even at a great distance that if one touches this real man, he will defend himself vigorously. Consequently, he went away safely, both he and his comrade; for when you behave in war as he did, then they just about do not even touch you; instead they pursue those who turn in headlong flight.

"Now, one could praise Socrates for many other amazing things; but whereas for the rest of his pursuits—one might perhaps say the like about someone else as well—what deserves all wonder is that respect in which he is like no human being, neither the ancients nor those of the present day. For one might liken Brasidas and others to such a one as Achilles was; and, in turn, liken the sort that Pericles was to both Nestor and Antenor (and there are others as well); and of the rest one might make likenesses in the same way. But the sort that this human being in his strangeness proved to be, both in himself and in his speeches, one could not even come close to finding, whether one looked among the men of today or among the ancients; unless, after all, one were to liken him in himself and in his speeches to those I say—to no human being but to silenuses and satyrs.

"And what is more, I omitted to say at the beginning that his speeches too are most like the silenuses when opened up. For were one willing to hear Socrates' speeches, they would at first look altogether laughable. The words and phrases that they wrap around themselves on the outside are like that, the very hide of a hybristic satyr.[23] For he talks of pack-asses, blacksmiths, shoe-makers, and tanners, and it looks as if he is always saying the same things through the same things; and hence every inexperi-enced and foolish human being would laugh at his speeches. But if one sees them opened up and gets oneself inside them, one will find, first, that they alone of speeches have sense inside; and, second, that they are most divine and have the largest number of images of virtue in them; and that they apply to the largest area, indeed to the whole area that it is proper to examine for one who is going to be beautiful and good.

"Here, men, is what I praise Socrates for; and I mixed in with it what, in turn, I blame him for, when I told you how he

---

[22]Aristophanes, *Clouds*, 362.
[23]An allusion to the flaying of Marsyas by Apollo.

committed an outrage against me. And what is more, he not only did this to me, but to Charmides the son of Glaucon, Euthydemus the son of Diocles, and many many others—for while deceiving them into thinking of him as the lover, he brings it about that he is the beloved rather than the lover. It is this that I am telling you, Agathon. Do not be deceived by him; but with the knowledge of our afflictions be on your guard, and do not, as in the proverb, like a fool realize it after you have suffered.''

When Alcibiades said this, there was laughter at his outspokenness because it was thought that he was still erotically inclined toward Socrates. Then Socrates said, ''You are sober, in my opinion, Alcibiades, for otherwise you would never have so elegantly cast a screen about yourself and tried to conceal why you said all this; for you spoke of it as if it were a side-issue by inserting it at the end, as though you had not said everything for its sake—to set Agathon and me at odds, believing that I must love you and no one else, and that Agathon must be loved by you and by no one else. But you did not get away with it; this satyr and silenic drama of yours was quite obvious. Well, my dear Agathon, see that he does not get the advantage—and prepare yourself against anyone setting you and me at odds.''

Then Agathon said, ''Why, Socrates, I am afraid that what you say is true. My evidence is the fact that he lay down between you and me so that he may hold us apart. Well, he will not get the advantage, but I shall come and lie down beside you.''

''Yes,'' Socrates said, ''do come lie down in the place beside me.''

''Zeus!'' Alcibiades said. ''What the fellow does to me! He believes he must surpass me everywhere. Well, if nothing else, you wondrous being, let Agathon lie down between us.''

''But that is impossible,'' Socrates said. ''For you praised me, and I in turn must praise the one on the right; surely if Agathon lies down next to you, he will not praise me again, will he, before he has been praised by me? But leave it as it is, daemonic being, and do not begrudge the lad's being eulogized by me, for I want very much to sing his praises.''

''Now I get it, Alcibiades,'' Agathon said. ''It is impossible for me to remain here; and I shall not fail to change my place so that I may be praised by Socrates.''

''This is the usual thing,'' Alcibiades said. ''When Socrates is present it is impossible for someone else to get hold of the beauties, just as now you see how resourcefully he has found a persuasive argument to get Agathon to lie down beside him.''

Now Agathon got up to lie down beside Socrates; but suddenly a large crowd of revelers came to the door; and finding it open—someone had gone out—they walked straight in among the guests and lay down. And everything was full of commotion, and everybody was compelled—but no longer with any order—to drink a great deal of wine. Now Aristodemus said that Eryximachus, Phaedrus, and some others went away, but he himself was overtaken by sleep. And he slept very deeply, because the night was far gone and the cocks were already singing when he woke toward daybreak. And on awakening he saw that the rest were sleeping or had gone away; but Agathon, Aristophanes, and Socrates were the only ones who were still awake, and they were drinking from a large cup, passing it from left to right. Socrates was conversing with them. And Aristodemus said, he did not remember the other points of the speeches—for he was not only absent at the start, but was dozing—however, the chief point, he said, was that Socrates was compelling them to agree that the same man should know how to make comedy and tragedy; and that he who is by art a tragic poet is also a comic poet. They were compelled to admit this, though they were not following too well and were nodding. Aristophanes went to sleep first, and then, when it was already day, Agathon. Then Socrates, having put them to bed, got up and went away, and he (Aristodemus) followed, just as he was accustomed to; and Socrates went to the Lyceum, washed up, and spent the rest of his day just as he did at any other time. And once he had passed the time in this way, toward evening he took his rest at home.

GORGIAS
Part III

Translated by W. C. Hembold

Editor's note: Gorgias is a dialogue in three distinct parts. The first is a discussion between Socrates and the rhetorician Gorgias of the professed and real aims of Gorgias' art. The second is a discussion between Socrates and Polus, a follower of Gorgias, on the ethics of power. In the third section, which follows, Socrates discusses with the cynical character Callicles the themes of rhetoric and power. Socrates opens by responding to Callicles' demand for a clarification of his statement that rhetoric is nothing but a tool of persuasion for those intent to deceive and that the virtuous man needs only the power of the truth.

Socrates. Callicles, if human beings did not have certain feelings in common (though they may vary a bit from man to man), if each of us had merely his own private sensations unshared by the rest, it would not be easy to demonstrate to another what one feels. I say this with reference to the fact that at the moment you and I are both experiencing somewhat the same emotion and each of us has two objects of his love: I Alcibiades, the son of Clinias, and philosophy; you the Athenian Demos and the son of Pyrilampes. Now I have noticed that in each instance, whatever your favorite says, however his opinions may go, for all your cleverness you are unable to contradict him, but constantly shift back and forth at his whim. If you are making a speech in the Assembly and the Athenian Demos disagrees, you change and say what it desires; and in the presence of this beautiful young son of Pyrilampes your experience is precisely similar. You are unable to resist the plans or the assertions of your favorite; and the result of this is that if anyone were to express surprise at what you say on various occasions under the influence of your loves, you would tell him, if you wanted to speak true, that unless your favorites can be prevented from speaking as they do, neither can you. Imagine, then, that you are hearing just the same kind of excuse from me. Don't be surprised at my remarks, but rather prevent my love, Philosophy, from making them. It is she, my dear friend, who continues to say what you are hearing from me now; she is, in fact, far less capricious than any other love. For my Alcibiades says now one thing, now another; but Philosophy speaks always the same and, though you are now surprised at her words, you were present at the whole discourse. So either refute her on the point I just made and prove that wrongdoing, together with impunity from punishment, is not the very worst of all evils; or, if you are going to leave this unrefuted, Callicles, by the Dog, god of the Egyptians, Callicles will not agree with you and will be at variance with you your whole life long. And yet, for my part, dear friend, I do believe that it would be better for me that my lyre or a chorus I directed should be out of tune and loud with discord, and that multitudes of men should disagree with me rather than that my single self should be out of harmony with myself and contradict me.

Callicles. Socrates, you seem to me to be going mad with eloquence, like a true politician! And now you are prattling this way because Polus has fallen victim to the very treatment which he accused Gorgias of having received at your hands. For he said, I believe, that when Gorgias was questioned by you as to whether, when anyone came to him desiring to learn rhetoric but without a knowledge of justice, Gorgias grew ashamed and said he would teach him, complying with conventional morality, because people might grow indignant if he said he wouldn't; and it was through this very admission that he was forced to contradict himself, which is exactly what you are so fond of. On this occasion Polus was laughing at you, and rightly, too, as I think: but now, in his turn, he has suffered this same fate. From my point of view, what I cannot approve of in Polus' performance is precisely this: he conceded to you that doing wrong is uglier than suffering it, and it was from this concession that he got completely tangled up in the argument and, being ashamed to say what he really thought, had his mouth gagged. Now, Socrates, you know you really do divert the argument into such cheap and vulgar paths, saying that you're pursuing the truth, but really getting us into what is beautiful, not by nature but by convention. Yet these two are for the most part opposed to each other, nature and convention; so that if a man is timid and doesn't have the courage to speak his mind, he must necessarily contradict himself. So this is the clever trick you have devised to cheat in your arguments: if a man makes his assertions according to convention, in your questions you slyly substitute ''according to nature,'' and if he speaks according to nature, you reply according to convention. So in the present instance, when doing and suffering wrong were being examined, Polus spoke of what was uglier according to convention, but you followed it up as though it were a natural principle. By nature, in fact, everything that is worse is uglier, just as suffering wrong is; but to do wrong is uglier merely by convention. For to suffer wrong is not the part of a man at all, but that of a slave for whom it is better to be dead than alive, as it is for anyone who is unable to come either to his own assistance when he is wronged or mistreated or to that of anyone he cares about. I can quite imagine that the manufacturers of laws and conventions are the weak, the majority, in fact. It is for themselves and their own advantage that they make their laws and distribute their praises and their censures. It is to frighten men who are stronger than they and able to enforce superiority that they keep declaring, to prevent aggrandizement, that this is ugly and unjust, that injustice consists in seeking to get the better of one's neighbor. They are quite content, I suppose, to be on equal terms with others since they are themselves inferior.

This, then, is the reason why convention declares that it is unjust and ugly to seek to get the better of the majority. But my opinion is that nature herself reveals it to be only just and proper that the better man should lord it over his inferior: it will be the stronger over the weaker. Nature, further, makes it quite clear in a great many instances that this is the true state of affairs, not only in the other animals, but also in whole states and communities. This is, in fact, how justice is determined: the stronger shall rule and have the advantage over his inferior. By what principle of justice, then, did Xerxes invade Greece or his father Scythia? One could, of course, cite innumerable examples of the same sort of thing. To my mind men are acting in accordance with natural justice when they perform such acts, and, by heaven, it is in accordance with law, too, the law of nature—though, no doubt, it hardly coincides with the one we frame when we mold the natures of the best and strongest among us, raising them from infancy by the incantations of a charmed voice, as men do lion cubs; we enslave them by repeating again and again that equality is morality and only this is beautiful and just. Yet I fancy that if a man appears of capacity sufficient to shake off and break through and escape from all these conventions, he will trample under foot our ordinances and charms and spells, all this mass of unnatural legislation; our slave will stand forth revealed as our master and the light of natural justice will shine forth!

It seems to me that Pindar, too, illustrates my point of view in the ode in which he declares that

> Convention is the Lord of all
> Mortals and immortals;

and it, he continues,

> Justifies the utmost violence
> With sovereign hand. My witness is
> The deeds of Heracles, for without payment—

I am only quoting approximately, for I don't know the whole poem by heart. But he does say that Heracles didn't pay for the cattle nor did Geryon give them to him when he drove them off, as though it were by right of nature that the better and stronger should possess the herds and all the rest of the property of his inferiors, those weaker than himself.

Here, then, you have the truth of the matter. You will become convinced of it if you only let philosophy alone and pass on to more important considerations. Of course, Socrates, philosophy does have a certain charm if one engages with it in one's youth and in moderation; but if one dallies overlong, it's the ruin of a fellow. If a man, however well endowed, goes on philosophizing throughout his life, he will never come to taste the experiences which a man must have if he's going to be a gentleman and have the world look up to him. You know perfectly well that philosophers know nothing about state laws and regulations. They are equally ignorant of the conversational standards that we have to adopt in dealing with our fellow men at home and abroad. Why, they are inexperienced even in human pleasures and desires! In a word, they are totally innocent of all human character. So, when they come to take part in either a private or a public affair, they make themselves ridiculous—just as ridiculous, I dare say, as men of affairs may be when they get involved in your quibbles, your "debates." Euripides put his finger on it when he wrote:

> Each shines in that which can attract him most,
> The task on which he spends the livelong day,
> The work in which he can surpass himself . . .

whereas a man shuns and vilifies whatever he can't do well, but praises his other work out of regard for himself, with the notion that this is the way to praise himself.

But the best course, no doubt, is to be a participant in both. It's an excellent thing to grasp as much philosophy as one needs for an education, and it's no disgrace to play the philosopher while you're young; but if one grows up and becomes a man and still continues in the subject, why, the whole thing becomes ridiculous, Socrates. My own feeling toward its practitioners is very much the same as the way I feel toward men who lisp and prattle like a child. When I see a child, who ought to be talking that way, lisping and prattling, I'm pleased, it strikes me as a pleasant sign of good breeding and suitable to the child's age; and when I hear a little lad speaking distinctly, it seems to me disagreeable and offends my ears as a mark of servile origin. So, too, when I hear a grown man prattling and lisping, it seems ridiculous and unmanly; one would like to strike him hard! And this is exactly the feeling I have about students of philosophy. When I perceive philosophical activity in a young lad, I am pleased; it suits him, I think, and shows that he has good breeding. A boy who doesn't play with philosophy I regard as illiberal, a chap who will never raise himself to any fine or noble action. Whereas when I see an older man still at his philosophy and showing no sign of giving it up, that one seems to me, Socrates, to be asking for some hard knocks! For, as I said just now, such a man, even if he's well endowed by nature, must necessarily become unmanly by avoiding the center of the city and the assemblies where, as the Poet[1] says, "men win distinction." Such a fellow must spend the rest of his life skulking in corners, whispering with two or three little lads, never pronouncing any large, liberal, or meaningful utterance.

Now, Socrates, since I have only the most friendly feelings toward you, my experience seems to be that of Zethus toward Amphion in Euripides' play (which I just mentioned). It occurs to me, in fact, to say to you much the sort of thing he says to his brother: "You're neglecting, Socrates, the things you ought to care for; in a childish guise you're warping the noble soul that

---

[1] The Poet is Homer (*Iliad*, 9. 441).

Nature gave you. Never will you be able to counsel aright or persuade others with plausibility. Never will you devise a gallant plan for the service of a friend.'' And yet, dear Socrates—don't be angry with me, for I'm speaking as your friend! Don't you think it's disgraceful for you to be in the state I think not only you are in, but all those who go faring deeper and deeper into the abysses of philosophy? For as the situation is now, if anyone were to arrest you or any of your kind and drag you off to prison, declaring that you'd broken the law though you hadn't done a thing, you know perfectly well that you wouldn't be able to help yourself. You'd stand there, reeling and gaping and not have a thing to say. If the fellow hales you into court, though his accusations are never so unproven and false, you'll die the death if he chooses to claim the death penalty. How can this be wisdom, Socrates, this art that takes a good man and makes him worse, unable to help himself or save himself from the gravest dangers, save neither himself nor anyone else, this art that lets him be stripped by his enemies of all his possessions and suffers him to live in his own country with absolutely no legal status? Such a man, if I may use a vulgar phrase, is one you can slap in the face with impunity! Now, my dear friend, take my advice: stop your refutations, take up the Fine Art of Business, and cultivate something that will give you a reputation for good sense. Leave all these oversubtleties to someone else. Should one call them frivolities or just plain nonsense? They'll only land you in a house where you'll be the only visitor! You must emulate, not those whose very refutations are paltry, but men of substance and high repute and everything else that is good.

Socrates. If my soul happened to be golden, Callicles, don't you think I should be overjoyed to find a stone to test the metal, the best stone possible, which, when I applied it, if it agreed that my soul had been well cared for, then I would know that I was in a satisfactory state and never needed another touchstone?

Callicles. What is the motive behind this question, Socrates?

Socrates. I shall tell you. I think, now that I've met you, I've met just such a lucky stone.

Callicles. How so?

Socrates. Because I am convinced that whenever you agree with me about any opinion my soul proposes, then it must be the whole truth. It is my belief that a man who is going to test a soul on the correctness (or the reverse) of its life must have three qualities: knowledge, good will, and candor. You have them all. I run into many people unable to test me because they are not wise, as you are; others have wisdom, but won't tell me the truth because they don't care for me, as you do; and your two guests here, Gorgias and Polus, are both wise men and friends of mine, but they are somewhat deficient in candor and more modest than they should be. This must be so; for both of them have gone to such an extreme of modesty as to venture to contradict themselves before a large audience, and this on matters of the gravest importance. But you have all these qualifications which the others do not possess. Your education is a good one, as many an Athenian can testify, and you are well-disposed toward me. How may I prove this? I shall tell you. I am aware that there are four of you who have gone into partnership in the pursuit of wisdom: you, Callicles, Tisander of Aphidnae, Andron the son of Androtion, and Nausicydes of Cholarges. Once upon a time I overheard you deliberating about how far one should cultivate wisdom. I remember that some such opinion as this prevailed: philosophy ought not to be pursued to the point of pedantic minutiae. Rather than that, you exhorted each other to make certain you did not become overwise and be ruined before you knew it. Now when I hear you giving me the same advice you gave your most intimate friends, it is a satisfactory proof that you are really well-disposed toward me. Finally, that you are frank of speech and not bashful, you yourself assert and the speech you made a little while ago confirms it. This, then, is clearly the present state of the question: if there is any point on which we both agree, we may regard it as sufficiently tested by both of us, and we shall never again have to submit it to further proof. You could not have conceded it either through a failure in wisdom or by excess of modesty; nor again through a wish to deceive me, for you are my friend, as you yourself declare. Any agreement of us both must in very fact bear the stamp of a final truth. And, Callicles, the investigation for which you rebuked me is the noblest of all possible inquiries: what a man's character ought to be, what he should study and up to what point, whether he is old or young. As for me, be sure of this: if there is any error in my own way of life, it is not an intentional one, but comes solely from my ignorance. Please, therefore, do not stop the lessons you have begun to give me, but show me clearly what it is that I ought to pursue, and how I may come to possess it; and if ever you catch me agreeing with you now on any subject, and later neglecting to act on it, then consider me a complete dunce and don't waste time teaching me any more lessons, for I won't be worth it. Now please begin at the beginning and tell me again what it is that you and Pindar declare natural justice to be. Is it that the stronger should plunder the property of the weaker, that the better should rule the worse, and that the superior man should have the advantage over the inferior? Does my memory fail me, or is this what you said justice was?

Callicles. This is what I said it was, and I say so now again.

Socrates. Do you also say that "better" and "stronger" are one and the same? For, to tell the truth, I wasn't able on your first statement to grasp what you meant. Is it the more powerful whom you call "stronger" and is it the feebler who must pay attention to the more powerful? This is what you seem to have been demonstrating by the statement that large states proceed against small ones in virtue of natural justice because they are stronger and more powerful. It appears to assume that "stronger" and "more powerful" and "better" and "stronger" are the same. Please define this precisely for me. Are "stronger" and "better" and "more powerful" the same or are they different?

Callicles. I shall be glad to tell you precisely: they are the same.

Socrates. Then are not the many naturally stronger than the one, inasmuch as they make the laws to regulate the individual, as you yourself said just now?

Callicles. Of course.

Socrates. The ordinances of the many are therefore those of the stronger.

Callicles. Quite so.

Socrates. And they are therefore those of the better? For the stronger are much the better in your account.

Callicles. Yes.

Socrates. Then their ordinances are beautiful by nature since, to be sure, they are those of the stronger.

Callicles. I agree.

Socrates. Is, then, the opinion of the multitude that, as you just stated, justice consists in sharing equally and that it is uglier to do wrong than to suffer it? Is this so or is it not? And see to it that you, in your turn, don't get involved in false modesty. Does the multitude, or does it not, believe that justice consists in having a share that is equal, and no more? That to do wrong is uglier than to suffer it? Please don't begrudge me your answer, Callicles, so that if you agree with me, I shall have confirmation from you, obviously a man well able to discern the truth.

Callicles. Well, yes. That is the multitude's opinion.

Socrates. So, then, it is not solely by convention that to do wrong is uglier than to be wronged and that justice is sharing equally. It is thus by nature also. It looks, then, as though you were not correct in your former statements, nor right in criticizing me by affirming that convention and nature are opposed and that I knew it and so took an unfair advantage in argument by diverting to "convention" what was meant by "nature" and to "nature" what was meant by "convention."

Callicles. Here's a fellow who'll never be done with trifling! Tell me, Socrates, aren't you ashamed to be playing with words at your age? If a chap makes a slip in a term, you pounce on it as though it were a treasure trove! Do you really think I meant anything by the "stronger" except the "better"? Didn't I inform you long ago that to me the better and the stronger are the same? Or do you seriously believe that if a pack of slaves and ne'er-do-wells, who have nothing "strong" about them except perhaps their bodies, get together and make pronouncements, I mean that these are ordinances?

Socrates. So, wisest of Callicles', that's what you say, is it?

Callicles. It certainly is.

Socrates. Well, dear friend, I too have had for some little time now a suspicion that your definition of "stronger" was something like this; so I now repeat my question in real anxiety to know precisely what you do mean. For of course you don't think that two are better than one, or that your slaves are better than you because their combined strength is stronger than you are. Please start again at the beginning and tell me what on earth you mean by "better," since it can't be "more vigorous." And please, my gifted friend, try to teach me my primer in a milder tone, so that I won't run away from your school.

Callicles. What a piece of sarcasm, Socrates!

Socrates. No, Callicles; that I swear by Zethus, he whose name you took in vain just now to indulge in a good deal of sarcasm against me. But come and tell me who it is you mean by "the better."

Callicles. I mean the worthier.

Socrates. But can't you see for yourself that it is you who are uttering words with no meaning? Please tell me whether you mean that the better and stronger are the more intelligent or whatever they may be.

Callicles. Aha! Yes, good heavens, it is just exactly this and that most emphatically!

Socrates. By your account, then, one intelligent man is many times stronger than ten thousand fools: he should rule, and they be ruled, and the ruler should have the advantage over the ruled. This seems to me to be what you are implying—and I'm not playing with words—if it is true that one is stronger than ten thousand.

Callicles. Yes, that is just what I mean. This, in fact, I conceive to be justice according to nature: he who is better and more intelligent should rule and have the advantage over baser men.

Socrates. Stop there a moment. What do you say to this? Suppose there are a great number of us in the same spot, as on the present occasion, and we have in the common stock ample provisions to eat and drink. Suppose further that we are men of all sorts, some strong, some weak, but that one of us is more intelligent than the rest about such matters, being a physician. Though he is in all probability stronger than some and weaker than others, will he not still be better and stronger to care for the provisions, since he is more intelligent than the rest of us?

Callicles. Quite so.

Socrates. Then should he, because he is better, receive more of the provisions than the rest of us? Or ought he, in virtue of his authority, have control over everything, yet in the consumption of food and its use for his own person should he refrain from taking advantage of us on pain of punishment? Should he merely have more than some, but less than others? And if, Callicles, he happens to be the weakest of all, should he, the best of all, have the least? Is that the way of it, my friend?

Callicles. You keep talking about food and drink and doctors and all such nonsense! But that's not what I mean at all.

Socrates. Well then, by "better" do you mean the more intelligent? Say yes or no.

Callicles. I do.

Socrates. But shouldn't the "better" have more?

Callicles. But not necessarily of food and drink.

Socrates. I see. You mean, perhaps, more clothes? Should the most skillful weaver have the biggest coat and go about dressed in the most and the finest garments?

Callicles. What's this about clothes?

Socrates. Well, shoes then. The man who is best and most intelligent about shoes should have the advantage. The shoemaker should, no doubt, have the biggest shoes and walk about shod in the largest possible number.

Callicles. What's this about shoes? You do insist on talking nonsense!

Socrates. Well, if that's not what you mean, perhaps this is it: a farmer who is intelligent and genteel about cultivating the soil should no doubt have a larger share of seed and use the greatest possible amount of it on his own property.

Callicles. Socrates, you always keep saying the same thing over and over again!

Socrates. Not only that, Callicles, but on the same subjects, too.

Callicles. I swear you absolutely never stop talking about shoemakers and cleaners and cooks and doctors! As though our conversation were about them!

Socrates. Well then, will you tell us what things there are in which the stronger and more intelligent have the right to a larger share? Since you won't accept my suggestions, won't you tell us yourself?

Callicles. But I have been telling you for ages. In the first place, the stronger men I'm talking about are not shoemakers or cooks, but those who use their brains for directing politics in the way it should go; they are, in fact, not merely intelligent, but also courageous and capable of converting their designs into fact; they are not the sort to shrink back through any feebleness of spirit.

Socrates. Now, best of Callicles', don't you see how different our complaints about each other are? You declare that I am always repeating myself and you censure me for it. I, on the contrary, maintain that on the same subject you never say the same thing twice. First, you defined "the better and stronger" as "the more vigorous," then as "the more intelligent," and now you come along with still another solution: "the better and stronger" are to be described as "more courageous." Come, friend, tell us finally once and for all who you say are the "better and stronger" and with reference to what.

Callicles. But I have already told you that they are the intelligent and courageous in politics. These are the men who should rule the state, and justice consists in this: they should have more than the rest, since the rulers should have more than the ruled.

Socrates. How's that again? More than themselves, my friend? What's this about rulers and ruled?

Callicles. What do you mean?

Socrates. That every man is his own ruler. Do you think it unimportant for a man to rule not himself, but only others?

Callicles. How do you mean, "his own ruler"?

Socrates. Nothing subtle, merely the general definition: temperate and self-controlled, having mastery over his own pleasures and desires.

Callicles. How simple-minded you are! You mean those fools, the "temperate"!

Socrates. What! Anyone can see what my meaning is.

Callicles. Of course he can, Socrates! How can a man be happy if he's a slave to anything? No, my friend; what is beautiful and just by nature I shall now explain to you without reserve. A man who is going to live a full life must allow his desires to become as mighty as may be and never repress them. When his passions have come to full maturity, he must be able to serve them through his courage and intelligence and gratify every fleeting desire as it comes into his heart. This, I fancy, is impossible for the mob. That is why they censure the rest of us, because they are ashamed of themselves and want to conceal their own incapacity. And, of course, they maintain that licentiousness is disgraceful, as I said before, since they are trying to enslave men of a better nature. Because they can't accomplish the fulfillment of their own desires, they sing the praises of temperance and justice out of the depths of their own cowardice. But take men who have come of princely stock, men whose nature can attain some commanding position, a tyranny, absolute power; what could be lower and baser than temperance and justice for such men who, when they might enjoy the good things of life without hindrance, of their own accord drag in a master to subdue them: the law, the language, and the censure of the vulgar? How could such men fail to be wretched under the sway of your "beauty of justice and temperance" when they can award nothing more to their friends than to their enemies? And that, too, when they are the rulers of the state! The truth, which you claim to pursue, Socrates, is really this: luxury, license, and liberty, when they have the upper hand, are really virtue, and happiness as well; everything else is a set of fine terms, man-made conventions, warped against nature, a pack of stuff and nonsense!

Socrates. With what fine nobility, Callicles, your lack of reserve enables you to tackle the argument. The fact is that you are now putting into words what other men think, but don't care to state aloud. And so I beg you to keep right on so that we shall really discover how to live. Now tell me this: you say that we should not repress our desires if we're going to live the way we ought to; we should let them grow as great as possible and procure their satisfaction from any source we can; and that this, in fact, is virtue?

Callicles. That's what I say.

Socrates. In that case it is wrong to say that those who want nothing are happy.

Callicles. Of course; otherwise stones and corpses would be happiest of all.

Socrates. But life would be terrible as you put the matter, too. I shouldn't, you know, be at all surprised if Euripides were right to say

> Who knows if all this life of ours is death,
> And death is life?

And perhaps we are really dead. At any rate I once heard a wise man declare that we are, in fact, dead here and now: the body is really our tomb, and the part of the soul in which the desires are located is such that it easily yields to persuasion and shifts back and forth. So a clever fellow, doubtless from Sicily or Italy, put this into a fable and, playing on the word because of its susceptible character, he gave it the name of "wine-jar" and the foolish he called the uninitiated.

In the uninitiated, that part of the soul where the desires are located, the unprincipled part, the very opposite of watertight, he compared to a leaky jar, because it could never be filled. So now he, in contradiction to you, Callicles, points out that of the inhabitants of Hades (he means, of course, the world invisible) —these, the uninitiated, will be the most wretched since they have to carry water to their leaky vessel in a similarly perforated sieve. Now by the sieve, as my informant expressly told me, he meant the soul and he compared the souls of the foolish to a sieve because it is leaky: by their lack of conviction and their forgetfulness they cannot retain anything. All this, to be sure, is rather strange stuff; yet it does point out what I want to demonstrate, if there is any way I can, in order to make you change your mind and choose a life that is ordered and content with what it has in place of one of insatiable self-indulgence. Well, now, am I succeeding at all in persuading you to come around to the view that the ordered life is happier than the unrestrained? Or could any amount of such fables have any effect in changing your mind?

Callicles. The very opposite would be more correct, Socrates.

Socrates. Come now, let me give you another metaphor from the same crop as the former. See if you don't say that, in a fashion, it expresses the difference between the two lives, the self-controlled and the unrestrained. There are two men, both of whom have many jars; those of the first are sound and full, one of wine, another of honey, a third of milk, and many others have a multitude of various commodities, yet the source of supply is meager and hard to obtain and only procurable with a good deal of exertion. Now the first man, when he has filled his jars, troubles no more about procuring supplies, but, so far as they are concerned, rests content; but the other man, though his source of supply is difficult also, yet still possible, and his vessels are perforated and rotten, is forced to keep on trying to fill them both night and day on pain of suffering the utmost agony. If such, then, is the nature of these two lives, do you still assert that the self-indulgent is happier than the orderly one? Am I, or am I not, succeeding in persuading you by such arguments that the orderly life is better than the unrestrained?

Callicles. No, you are not, Socrates. For the man who is full has no longer the slightest taste for pleasure; his life, as I said just now, is the life of a stone. Once he's sated, he no longer feels pleasure or pain. But in the other life is the true pleasure of living, with the greatest possible intake.

Socrates. So then, if there's much intake, there must also be much outlet; there will have to be large perforations for the excess to flow away.

Callicles. Why, of course.

Socrates. Now it's a pelican's life you are describing, not that of a corpse or a stone. But tell me: is the life of pleasure you mean more or less the sort in which one feels hunger and consequently eats?

Callicles. That's it.

Socrates. And feels thirst and consequently drinks?

Callicles. Yes, that is what I mean; and one should have all the other desires and be able to fulfill them and enjoy them and so live in happiness.

Socrates. Splendid, my dear fellow! Please go on just as you've begun and try not to feel the slightest shyness, which I too, it seems, must endeavor to avoid. Now first tell me whether a man who itches and scratches, and has abundant opportunity for scratching, can live his life happily by continually scratching.

Callicles. What a strange creature you are, Socrates, just a plain old pettifogger at heart!

Socrates. Yes, Callicles, that is how I came to startle Polus and Gorgias and brought out their shyness; you, however, must not be startled or shy, for you are a courageous fellow. Just answer the question, please.

Callicles. Well, I'll admit that one can lead a pleasant life scratching.

Socrates. And if pleasant, then happy also?

Callicles. Of course.

Socrates. And is it only my head that I scratch—or shall I extend the range of my questions? Just consider, Callicles, what you are going to answer if I ask you one after another all the questions which logically follow, the climax of which would be the life of a catamite. Is not such a life dreadful and ugly and wretched? Or will you dare to assert that men of this sort are happy if only they have an abundant supply of what they want?

Callicles. Aren't you ashamed, Socrates, to take the argument in this direction?

Socrates. Is it I who take this direction, my moral friend, or is it the man who declares with such abandon that all who have pleasure, no matter how, are happy; the man who refuses to distinguish between good and bad pleasures? But come now, tell me once more whether you assert that the pleasant and the good are the same thing or whether there is any pleasure which is not good.

Callicles. If I say they're different, I'll be contradicting myself; so I say they're the same.

Socrates. Callicles, you are going back on our original agreement. It will be impossible to continue our search for truth together if you are going to make statements you don't really believe.

Callicles. That's what you do, too, Socrates.

Socrates. If that's really what I do I'm quite wrong in doing it, and so are you. My dear fellow, please consider whether pleasure from any source whatever is not the good. But if it is so, then not only the many shameful consequences I have hinted at just now will obviously follow, but many others as well.

Callicles. That's what you think, Socrates.

Socrates. So you really hold to this opinion?

Callicles. I do.

Socrates. Then shall we take you to be serious and attack the question?

Callicles. By all means.

Socrates. Well, if you do think so, please clear up one point. May I suppose that there is such a thing as knowledge?

Callicles. There is.

Socrates. And didn't you say just now that, besides knowledge, there was something else you called courage?

Callicles. That also.

Socrates. And you meant, didn't you, to speak of them as two things, since courage is different from knowledge?

Callicles. Quite.

Socrates. What follows then? Do you call pleasure and knowledge different or the same?

Callicles. Different, of course, you universal genius.

Socrates. Then courage, again, is distinct from pleasure?

Callicles. To be sure.

Socrates. Now, now, this we must not forget: Callicles of Acharnae has declared that pleasure and good are the same thing, but that knowledge and courage are different both from each other and from the good.

Callicles. And we can't get Socrates from Alopece to agree to it! Or does he agree?

Socrates. He does not; nor do I believe Callicles will either, when he takes the true view of himself. Now tell me this: don't you think that good and evil fortune are opposite conditions?

Callicles. I do.

Socrates. Then, since these are mutually opposed, the relation between them must be the same as that between sickness and health; for obviously a man is not going to be sick and well at the same time or be simultaneously free of both health and disease.

Callicles. How's that?

Socrates. Take as an illustration any part of the body you like. I suppose a man may have a disease of the eyes called ophthalmia?

Callicles. Of course.

Socrates. And while his eyes are sick they can't be well at the same time?

Callicles. No, they can't; not at all.

Socrates. But suppose he gets rid of his ophthalmia; does he then get rid of his eyes' health and finish up by losing both simultaneously?

Callicles. Certainly not.

Socrates. Such a result would, in fact, be astonishing and irrational, would it not?

Callicles. Extremely so.

Socrates. Whereas, I imagine, a man gains and loses sickness and health alternately.

Callicles. I agree.

Socrates. And is it the same with strength and weakness?

Callicles. Yes.

Socrates. And speed and slowness?

Callicles. Quite.

Socrates. And is it so with the other good things and happiness, and with their opposites, evil things and wretchedness; does one alternately gain and lose each one of them?

Callicles. Yes, certainly.

Socrates. Consequently, if we hit upon anything that a man may lose and possess simultaneously, it is obvious that this cannot be what is either good or bad. Are we agreed on this point? Think it over carefully before you answer.

Callicles. But I do agree beyond any question whatever.

Socrates. Then let us return to our former admissions. Did you say that hunger was pleasant or painful? By hunger, I mean the state itself.

Callicles. Painful; it is, however, pleasant to eat when one is hungry.

Socrates. I understand. Yet hunger itself is painful, is it not?

Callicles. I agree.

Socrates. And thirst also?

Callicles. Very.

Socrates. Then must I go further with my questions or do you admit that every sort of want and desire is painful?

Callicles. I admit it without further questions.

Socrates. Good. But you do admit, don't you, that drinking when one is thirsty is pleasant?

Callicles. I do.

Socrates. And this phrase of yours "when one is thirsty" implies pain?

Callicles. Yes.

Socrates. But drinking is the satisfaction of a want and is a pleasure?

Callicles. Yes.

Socrates. So you affirm that pleasure is felt in the act of drinking?

Callicles. Certainly.

Socrates. "When one is thirsty," at least?

Callicles. I agree.

Socrates. While one feels pain?

Callicles. Yes.

Socrates. Then do you see the consequence of this? You are declaring that pleasure and pain are felt at the same time when you say that a man drinks when he is thirsty. Or does this not occur at the same time or place, whether in the soul or the body, as you prefer? I fancy there is here no difference. Is this so or is it not?

Callicles. It is.

Socrates. Yet you state that it is impossible for a man to fare well and ill at the same time.

Callicles. Yes, and I say so again.

Socrates. But you have admitted that it is possible to feel pleasure while in pain.

Callicles. It looks that way.

Socrates. Then to feel pleasure is not to fare well, nor is to feel pain to fare badly. And the result of this is that what is pleasant is different from what is good.

Callicles. I have no notion what you're quibbling about, Socrates.

Socrates. I rather think you do, Callicles; you're only pretending. But let us continue on our forward march, so that you may acquire some notion of what a clever fellow you are to take me to task. Isn't it true that in all of us both the thirst and the pleasure derived from drinking ceases simultaneously?

Callicles. I have no notion what you mean, I tell you.

Gorgias. Don't say that, Callicles. Answer him for our sake, also, so we may properly come to the end of the argument.

Callicles. But Socrates is always like this, Gorgias. He keeps on asking piffling little questions until he's got you!

Gorgias. What's that to you? Your reputation is not at stake. Just let Socrates refute you in any way he likes.

Callicles. Well then, go on asking your finicky little questions, since Gorgias wants it that way.

Socrates. You are a lucky man, Callicles, to be initiated into the Greater Mysteries before the Lesser. I didn't think they allowed it. So let us begin again where we left off. Is it true that everyone ceases from his thirst and his pleasure at the same time?

Callicles. I agree.

Socrates. And is it the same with hunger? Does one cease from all the other desires and pleasures simultaneously?

Callicles. That is true.

Socrates. Then pains and pleasures cease together?

Callicles. Yes.

Socrates. But on the other hand, as you once admitted, good and evil do not cease together. Do you still admit that now?

Callicles. I do. What of it?

Socrates. The consequence, my friend, is that good is not the same as pleasure, or bad the same as pain. One pair of them ceases simultaneously, the other does not, for its members are different. How then could pleasure be the same as good, or pain as bad? If you like, look at it this way, though this, too, may fail to satisfy you. Yet consider: those that you call good, don't you call them good because of the presence of goodness in them, just as you call beautiful those in whom beauty is present?

Callicles. I do.

Socrates. Well then, do you call fools and cowards good men? At any rate you didn't just now when you were talking about brave and wise men. Is it not these that you call good?

Callicles. Of course it is.

Socrates. Well now, have you ever seen a foolish child pleased?

Callicles. I have.

Socrates. And have you never seen a foolish man enjoying himself?

Callicles. I believe I have. But what of it?

Socrates. Nothing; merely answer.

Callicles. Yes, I have.

Socrates. Have you seen a sensible man in sorrow or pleasure?

Callicles. I have.

Socrates. Which one receives the greater pleasure and pain, the sensible or the foolish?

Callicles. I don't believe there's very much difference.

Socrates. Even that will do. In war-time have you ever observed a coward?

Callicles. How could I avoid it?

Socrates. Well then, when the enemy withdrew, which did you think received greater pleasure, a coward or a brave man?

Callicles. Both had pleasure, about equally, I think.

Socrates. Never mind the difference. The point is that cowards also feel pleasure.

Callicles. Yes, tremendously.

Socrates. Fools also, it appears.

Callicles. Yes.

Socrates. When the enemy is coming at you, do only cowards feel pain, or do brave men also?

Callicles. Both.

Socrates. To the same degree?

Callicles. Cowards more, perhaps.

Socrates. And at the moment of retreat, don't they feel more pleasure?

Callicles. Perhaps.

Socrates. Then fools and wise men, cowards and brave men, all feel pleasure and pain to a similar degree according to your statement; but cowards feel them more than brave men?

Callicles. That is correct.

Socrates. But are wise and brave men good, while cowards and fools are bad?

Callicles. Yes.

Socrates. Then both good and bad feel pleasure and pain to a similar degree?

Callicles. They do.

Socrates. Are good and bad men, then, good and bad to a similar degree? Or are the bad even more so than the good?

Callicles. I swear I haven't the faintest notion what you're talking about.

Socrates. Don't you realize that you are maintaining that the good are good because of the presence of good in them, and the bad are bad in the same way; and good things are pleasant and bad things painful?

Callicles. Yes, I do.

Socrates. Then when men feel pleasure, good is present— that is, pleasure, since they are pleased?

Callicles. Of course.

Socrates. Then those who feel pleasure are good because of the presence of good?

Callicles. Yes.

Socrates. And with those who feel pain, it is because evil is present, that is, pain?

Callicles. Yes, evil is there, all right.

Socrates. So it is because of the presence of evil that you term bad men bad. Do you still maintain this position?

Callicles. I do.

Socrates. So the good are those who feel pleasure, and the bad those who feel pain?

Callicles. Quite so.

Socrates. And are they more so if they feel more, and less so if they feel less, and about the same if they feel the same?

Callicles. Yes.

Socrates. And do you maintain, then, that wise men and fools, cowards and brave men, feel pleasure and pain in a similar way, and that cowards experience them even more than the others?

Callicles. I do.

Socrates. Then reckon up with me the results of our points of agreement, for whatever is excellent material for conversation and inquiry is still excellent when used twice over and again. We maintain that the wise and brave man is good, do we not?

Callicles. Yes.

Socrates. And the fool and coward bad?

Callicles. Quite so.

Socrates. And, yet again, a man who feels pleasure is good?

Callicles. Yes.

Socrates. And one who feels pain is bad?

Callicles. Necessarily.

Socrates. But good and bad feel pain and pleasure equally, and perhaps the bad man feels them more?

Callicles. Yes.

Socrates. Then the consequence will be that the bad man is equally bad and equally good with the good man—or even better! Aren't those and our former conclusions the result of maintaining that pleasure and good are the same? Aren't they a necessary result, Callicles?

Callicles. It's quite a time now, Socrates, that I've been listening to you while I spoke my agreeable answers, perfectly well aware that if for a joke anyone gives you an inch, you'll seize upon it with childish glee! As if you really believed that I or anyone else in the world didn't realize that some pleasures are better and some worse!

Socrates. Ah, ah, Callicles! What a rascal you are to treat me like a child! Sometimes you say one thing, then you say another, just to deceive me. Little did I think when I started out that you were going to mislead me on purpose; I thought you were my friend. But as things are, I see that I was mistaken. It looks as though I'd have to obey the old proverb and make the best of it and take whatever you're willing to offer me. Well, now it seems that you maintain that some pleasures are good, some bad. Right?

Callicles. Yes.

Socrates. Are beneficial ones good, and harmful ones bad?

Callicles. Quite so.

Socrates. Those are beneficial which do some good, and bad those which effect some evil?

Callicles. I agree.

Socrates. Would these be the sort you mean, if we took, for example, the physical pleasures we just mentioned, those of eating and drinking: are the ones good which create health or strength or any other physical capacity, and bad those which have the opposite effect?

Callicles. Certainly.

Socrates. So, in the same way, some pains are useful, and some are bad?

Callicles. Of course.

Socrates. Then is it the useful pleasures and pains that we must choose and set in operation?

Callicles. Certainly.

Socrates. Not the bad ones?

Callicles. Quite obviously not.

Socrates. In fact, if you remember, Polus and I agreed that all our actions should be performed for the sake of good results. Is it also your opinion that the aim of absolutely all our actions is the good and that for its sake all other things are to be done, not the good for the sake of the rest? Will you add your vote to ours and make a third?

Callicles. I will.

Socrates. Then what is pleasant is like everything else: it is performed for the sake of the good, not the good for pleasure's sake?

Callicles. Certainly.

Socrates. Is it, then, in every man's power to choose from among pleasures those which are good and those which are bad, or is there in each case a need for professional knowledge?

Callicles. Professional knowledge is required.

Socrates. Let us, then, recall my remarks to Polus and Gorgias. If you remember, I said that some activities were concerned solely with pleasure, procured this only, and paid no attention to what might be better or worse; and there were others which recognized good and evil. Among those concerned solely with pleasure I put cookery as a knack, not an art; and among those concerned with the good I set medicine as an art. And now by the love of friendship, Callicles, please don't think that you

ought to play with me or that your answers should be at random
or contrary to your true opinion; on the other hand, don't take
what I say as a joke, either. You do see, surely, that our
conversation is on the subject which should engage the most
serious attention of anyone who has a particle of intelligence: in
what way should one live one's life? Should it be the one to
which you urge me as being the activity which best befits a
man—speaking in public, practicing rhetoric, engaging in politics in the current fashion? Or should it be this present life of
mine immersed in philosophy? And what is the difference between the two of them? Perhaps the best way to discover this is
to begin with the distinction I attempted to make a little while
ago: when we have made it and agreed upon the fact that these
two lives are actually distinct, we must inquire what the difference is and which one of them we should choose to live. It is
possible that you do not yet catch my meaning.

Callicles. I certainly don't.

Socrates. I'll try to make it clearer. Since we have both
agreed that there is such a thing as a good thing and a pleasant
thing, and that the pleasant differs from the good, and that there
is a practical way of attaining each of them, a search for the
good and a search for pleasure, will you tell me first whether or
not you still agree with this position? Do you?

Callicles. I do.

Socrates. Then to proceed: in regard to what I was saying to
our friends here, please reassure me that my remarks seemed to
you to be accurate. I was maintaining, in effect, that cookery
didn't appear to be an art, but a knack; yet medicine was an art.
My meaning was that the medical art has made an inquiry into
the nature of what it treats and the reasons for the treatment and
can give an account of each of them. The other, however, directs
absolutely all of its unprofessional efforts toward producing the
pleasure which is its only end and aim; yet it has not studied the
nature of pleasure nor its causes. It proceeds with complete
irrationality, so to speak, and no hint of calculation; only by
mere routine and a sort of knack does it preserve any memory of
the usual results, by which, of course, it may procure its pleasures. This, then, you must first consider and see whether it has
been adequately stated. Consider also whether there are certain
other activities that involve the soul, some of them artistic, so
that they take some thought for the soul's best interests; whereas
others ignore this and are, as in the case of cookery, concerned
solely with the soul's pleasure, making no study of how it comes

about or which pleasures are better or worse, caring for nothing but the gratification they bring, be it worse, be it better. To me, Callicles, it appears that there are such activities which I maintain to be a flattery whether of body or soul or anything else, whenever they are employed to minister to pleasure without consideration of better or worse. Now tell me: do you share our views on these matters or do you disagree?

Callicles. Oh, all right, I agree—to help you finish up your argument and out of "gratification" to Gorgias here.

Socrates. And does this hold for one soul only and not for two or more?

Callicles. Oh no; it holds for two and for many more.

Socrates. Then is it possible to "gratify" a large crowd, all together at the same time, without taking into consideration what is best?

Callicles. Yes, I imagine so.

Socrates. Can you tell me, then, what activities there are that indulge this practice? Or rather, if you please, when I ask you, if you think one of them belongs to this class, say so; if not, say no. First, let us think of flute-playing. Does it not seem to you, Callicles, that it seeks our pleasure only and has no other object?

Callicles. Yes, I think so.

Socrates. And is it so with all similar activities, such as playing the harp?

Callicles. Yes.

Socrates. And the singing of tragic choruses and dithyrambic poetry? Does it seem to be of this sort to you? Do you imagine that Cinesias, son of Meles, cares at all whether his utterances will make the audience better? Or is he preoccupied merely with gratifying the crowd of spectators?

Callicles. The latter is obviously the case, Socrates, at least with Cinesias.

Socrates. Well then, what about his father, Meles? When he played his harp, do you think he kept his gaze upon the highest good? And perhaps he didn't even aim at great pleasure, for his music used to annoy the audience. Now think: don't you believe that all harp-music and all dithyrambic poetry have been invented solely for pleasure's sake?

Callicles. I do.

Socrates. And what about the effort of that stately marvel, tragic poetry? Is all her aim and concern merely to gratify the audience? Or does she also strive not to make any pronouncement which, though it may be pleasant and delightful, is also bad? Does she boldly sing out what is useful, though unpleasant, whether the audience likes it or not? Which attitude do you believe to be displayed by tragic poetry?

Callicles. Why, it seems quite obvious, Socrates, that the effort is rather toward pleasure and the gratification of the spectator.

Socrates. Did we not assert just now, Callicles, that such an attitude was flattery?

Callicles. Quite.

Socrates. Suppose we examine any sort of poetry: if one were to strip away the music and the rhythm and the meter, would there be anything left but bare prose?

Callicles. Nothing, of course.

Socrates. Is this bare prose to be directed at great crowds of people?

Callicles. It is.

Socrates. Then poetry is a kind of public address.

Callicles. So it seems.

Socrates. It should, consequently, be a rhetorical kind of public address; for you do think, do you not, that poets make use of rhetoric in their plays?

Callicles. I do.

Socrates. Then we have now hit upon a kind of rhetoric addressed to a crowd of people made up of men and women and children alike, of slaves as well as free men. We are not able to admire it very much because we maintain that it is a form of flattery.

Callicles. Quite.

Socrates. Good. What, then, is the nature of the rhetoric addressed to the people of Athens and of the other cities of free men? Does it seem to you that orators always speak with an eye on what is best and aim at this: that their fellow citizens may receive the maximum improvement through their words? Or do they, like the poets, strive to gratify their fellows and, in seeking their own private interest, do they neglect the common good, dealing with public assemblies as though the constituents were children, trying only to gratify them, and caring not at all whether this procedure makes them better or makes them worse?

Callicles. This question you are asking is no longer a simple one. There are, in fact, some orators who say what they say with deep concern for their fellow citizens; but there are also others such as you describe.

Socrates. That's good enough. For if this matter is really

two-fold, part of it will doubtless be a form of flattery and a
shameless method of addressing the public; the other may well
be beautiful, a genuine attempt to make the souls of one's
fellows as excellent as may be, a striving always to say what is
best, whatever the degree of pleasure or pain it may afford the
audience. But a rhetoric such as this you have never encountered. Or, if you are able to mention such an orator, why have
you not already told me his name?

Callicles. Well. . . . I swear I can't name a single one, at
least among the orators of today.

Socrates. Are you then able to mention any of the older
statesmen through the influence of whose public career the
Athenians became better than they were before? For my part, I
haven't a notion who such a man might be.

Callicles. What! Have you never heard what a good man
Themistocles was? And Cimon and Miltiades and our Pericles,
who died only recently and you yourself heard him speak?

Socrates. Yes, Callicles, if the definition you once gave of
virtue is really true: to fulfill desires, both one's own and those
of others. But if it is not true, if we must substitute what we
were compelled to accept in the subsequent discussion, that we
should fulfill only those desires which make a man better, not
those which make him worse, and suppose this to be an art—I
am unable to name such a man from the group you proposed.

Callicles. If you only looked hard enough, you could.

Socrates. Then let us examine the question impartially to
see if this is so. Consider: will a good man, whose speeches are
for the maximum improvement of his fellows, say anything at
random? Will he not always have some definite end in view?
Just as all other craftsmen keep their eye on the task in hand and
select and apply nothing at random, but only such things as may
bring about the special form he is bent upon effecting. Consider,
if you like, painters and architects and shipwrights and any other
craftsman you please; each one of them disposes every element
of his task in a fixed order and adjusts the parts in a suitable and
harmonious scheme until the whole has been constituted as a
regularized and well-ordered object. And so it is also, of course,
with the rest of the craftsmen, including those we just mentioned, who occupy themselves with the human body, trainers
and physicians; they too, I presume, direct their efforts toward
regularizing and harmonizing the body. Shall we accept this
view or shall we not?

Callicles. Good enough.

Socrates. Then a house which has order and harmony is a good house, and one in disorder is bad?

Callicles. I agree.

Socrates. And the same is true of a sailing vessel?

Callicles. Yes.

Socrates. And may we further apply the principle to our own bodies?

Callicles. Quite.

Socrates. Now what about the soul? If it is in disorder, can it be excellent? Or must it have some sort of order and harmony?

Callicles. We shall have to grant this, too, to agree with our former conclusions.

Socrates. What name, then, may we apply to the results of order and harmony in the body?

Callicles. I suppose you mean health and strength.

Socrates. I do. Next, what name do we give to the results of order and harmony in the soul? Please try to think of the word and tell me as you did before.

Callicles. Why don't you tell us yourself, Socrates?

Socrates. Well, if you like that better, I shall. And if you think I'm right, say so; if not, refute me, please, and don't let it pass. I think that "healthy" is the right word for order in the body; from it health and the other physical excellencies arise. Is this so or is it not?

Callicles. It is so.

Socrates. And the word for harmony and order in the soul is "lawful" and "law," by which men become law-abiding and orderly. These qualities, then, are justice and self-control. Do you agree or do you not?

Callicles. Let it stand.

Socrates. Then it is these qualities which the moral artist, the true orator, will have in view in applying to men's souls whatever speech he may use; to these he will apply absolutely every one of his actions. Whether he bestows a benefit or takes one away, he will always fix his mind upon this aim: the engendering of justice in the souls of his fellow citizens and the eradication of injustice, the planting of self-control and the uprooting of uncontrol, the entrance of virtue and the exit of vice. Do you agree or not?

Callicles. I agree.

Socrates. One must, I think; for what would be the use in offering to a sick, wretched body abundant food, no matter how delicious, or wine or anything else, when, properly considered, these may sometimes do no more good than their very opposites, or rather do it even less good? Is this true?

Callicles. Let it stand.

Socrates. There is no advantage, then, I take it, for a man with a wretched body to live at all; for his way of life also must be wretched. Isn't this true?

Callicles. Yes.

Socrates. It is, in general, only when a man is healthy that the doctors let him fulfill his desires, such as eating as much as he wants when he is hungry, and drinking all he likes when thirsty; but if he is sick, they practically never allow him to satisfy his appetites. Do you also agree to this?

Callicles. I do.

Socrates. And, my dear friend, will not the same hold true for the soul? As long as it is in a bad way, it will be witless and uncontrolled, unjust and impious, and we must keep it from its desires and allow it no action except what will improve it. Do you agree or do you not?

Callicles. I do.

Socrates. Because this is presumably better for the soul itself?

Callicles. Quite.

Socrates. Then to keep it from its desires is to punish it?

Callicles. Yes.

Socrates. So punishment is better for the soul than the lack of control which you recently advocated?

Callicles. I haven't a notion what you're getting at, Socrates. Suppose you try your questions on someone else!

[*Socrates.* Here's a man who can't endure benefaction. He can't stand what we're talking about: punishment.][2]

Callicles. I don't give a damn for a single word you say! I only answered your questions to please Gorgias.

Socrates. Well, well. What shall we do now? Break off the argument in the middle?

Callicles. You're the judge.

Socrates. They say, you know, that it's contrary to good morals to break off even a story in the middle; it needs a head, so it won't have to go running around without one. Why not complete your answers, so our argument can get ahead?

Callicles. What a slave-driver you are, Socrates! If you'll

---

[2]The bracketed speech is probably an interpolation; at the very least it gives an odd turn to the methods of Socrates.

take my advice, you'll let this argument alone, or else do your talking to someone else.

Socrates. Yet who else is willing? Let's not have our conversation go by the board.

Callicles. Why can't you finish it yourself? Talk to yourself and give yourself answers!

Socrates. So that the words of Epicharmus may be fulfilled:

Where two men spoke before

I alone am to be equal to the task, though single handed! But it looks very much as though that's just what I shall have to be. Yet, if this is what we must do, I think that all of us should vie with each other in the struggle to learn what is true in the matters under discussion, and what is false; for it is to the common good of everyone of us that this should be made clear. So, then, I shall continue the discussion as seems best to me; but if anyone of you thinks that any statement of mine is contrary to the truth, he should take issue with me and refute it. For it is by no means from any real knowledge that I make my statements: it is, rather, a search in common with the rest of you, so that if my opponent's objection has any force, I shall be the first to admit it. This, however, is merely stated on the supposition that you wish to complete the argument; if not, let's say good-bye and go home.

Gorgias. As far as I'm concerned, Socrates, I think you should not go yet. You must complete your argument and this, I believe, is the opinion of all the others, too. Personally, I have a strong wish to hear you continue the remaining portion by yourself.

Socrates. Well, Gorgias, I too should have been pleased to go on conversing with Callicles here until I had paid him back Amphion's speech in exchange for Zethus'. But since you, Callicles, are unwilling to help me finish the argument, at any rate please listen and take issue with me whenever I seem to be going wrong. And if you will be kind enough to refute me, I'll not be annoyed with you, as you have been with me; on the contrary, you'll be nominated my greatest benefactor.

Callicles. Go on and finish it up by yourself, friend.

Socrates. Then listen while I recapitulate the argument from the beginning:

Are pleasure and good the same?

—They are not the same; on this Callicles and I are agreed.

Is pleasure to be pursued for the sake of the good, or good for the sake of pleasure?

—Pleasure for the sake of the good.
Is that pleasant which, by its presence, gives us pleasure; and that good which, by its presence, makes us good?
—Quite.
But further: are we good, both we ourselves and everything else that is good, by reason of some excellence present in us?
—To me, Callicles, this seems a necessary consequence.
And again: the excellence of each thing, whether of utensil or of body or (to extend the definition) of soul or of any living thing—this excellence surely cannot be best acquired by mere chance, but by correct arrangement and by an art which is peculiar to each class individually. Is this true?
—I heartily agree.
Then is the excellence of each thing produced by order and arrangement?
—I should say so.
Then a certain order present in each existent thing and peculiar to it renders it good?
—That is my opinion.
So then a soul which has its own order is better than one which has none?
—This must follow.
And a soul which possesses order is an "ordered" soul?
—How could it fail to be?
And an "ordered" soul has self-control?
—Quite necessarily.
Then the self-controlled soul is good.
My dear Callicles, I have no desire to change any of these statements. But if you do, please tell me.
Callicles. Keep on talking, friend.
Socrates. I go on, then, to state that if the self-controlled soul is good, that which has the opposite disposition is bad; and this, of course, is the soul devoid of sense and discipline.
—Quite so.
Further, the self-controlled man will do what is right in regard both to gods and to men; for surely he would have no control if he did not?
—This is a necessary consequence.
And in his conduct toward men, when he does what is fitting, he will be doing what is just; in his conduct toward the gods, he will be doing what is holy. So a man whose conduct is just and holy must be a just and holy man.
—True.

Then, too, he must be courageous as well; for it is not the act of a self-controlled man either to pursue or to avoid what one ought not, but, on the contrary, to avoid and pursue what one ought, both actions and men, both pleasures and pains; he must stand his ground and resist when it is his duty. So that the self-controlled man, Callicles, as we have defined him, just and brave and holy, must of necessity be completely good; and that the good man must do well and fairly whatever he does; and that, since he does his work well, he must be happy and blessed by the gods; and that, on the contrary, the wicked evil-doer must be wretched. Such a man will be one whose make-up is precisely opposite to that of the self-controlled man; in a word, the profligate whom you praised.

My position, then, is this and these are the things which I hold to be true. And if they are true, it appears that a man who wants to be happy must both pursue and practice self-control, and also flee from profligacy, each one of us as fast as his legs can take him. We must strive so far as possible never to stand in need of punishment; but if we or any one of our associates, either an individual or a government, needs chastisement, then they and we must submit to justice and be punished, if we are going to be happy. To me, at least, this seems to be the end and aim which a man must keep in mind throughout his life. He must turn all his own efforts and those of his country to bring it about that justice and self-control shall effect a happy life. He must not allow his desires to run riot nor, by striving to fulfill the endless torment of satisfying them, live the life of a brigand. Such a man could not be on friendly terms with any other man, nor with God, for he would be incapable of sharing; and where there is no sharing, there can be no friendship. Wise men say, Callicles, that heaven and earth, gods and men, are held together by the principles of sharing, by friendship and order, by self-control and justice; that, my friend, is the reason they call the universe "cosmos,"[3] and not disorder or licentiousness. Clever though you are, you seem not to have paid enough attention to these matters; it has, in fact, escaped you what a mighty power is exercised, both among men and gods, by geometrical equality. And it is your neglect of geometry which brings about your opinion that one should strive for a share larger than that which other men possess.

Well, then, either we must refute the present argument and

---

[3]That is, "order."

prove that it is not the possession of justice and self-control which makes men happy, and the domination of evil which makes them wretched; or, if the argument is true, we must examine the consequences. There will be, Callicles, all those consequences that preceded your question as to whether I was in earnest when I maintained that if a wrong is done, one will have to accuse oneself or one's son or friend, and it is for this purpose that we must use rhetoric; also the point that you thought Polus conceded to me through shame is, after all, quite true: namely, that to do injustice is worse than suffering it in proportion as it is an uglier act; and, finally, the fact that one who is going to be a true rhetorician must first be a just man himself and conversant with the principles of justice, which again was a point which Polus said that Gorgias had conceded through shame of denying it.

On the basis of these facts, then, let us try to examine the reproaches that you lodge against me and see whether or not they hold good. You say that I am unable to help either myself or any friend or intimate, not even to save them from the gravest dangers; that like an outlaw who is everyone's target I am at the mercy of anyone who wants to slap my face (to use your own spirited phrase), or to steal my money, or to banish me or, if it comes to the worst, to kill me. And to be in such a situation, according to your argument, is the most disgraceful fate of all. Yet what my account of it is, though it has often been stated already, may well be presented again. I deny, Callicles, that to be struck in the face unjustly is the most disgraceful of fates, nor is the mere fact of having my body or my purse slit. No! It is the act of striking and slitting me or my possessions wrongfully that is worse and more disgraceful; it is robbery and kidnapping and housebreaking and, in a word, doing me or my possessions any wrong that is worse and more disgraceful to the doer than it is to me who suffers it. These points, as I am stating them now, have already been set forth in our previous discussion and there fastened down and chained (if I may put it rather bluntly) by arguments of adamant and steel—or so it would appear. If you or someone yet more vigorous are not able to break through them, then it will be impossible for anyone to speak correctly on such a subject in any way other than the way I am speaking now. Remember that my position has always been the same: though I have no real knowledge of the truth of these matters, yet just as on the present occasion, I have never encountered anyone who was able to maintain a different position in such a discussion and

not come off covered with ridicule. Accordingly, I must assume
that matters stand as stated; if they really do so and if injustice is
the greatest of evils to the malefactor and if it is a still greater
evil than this (if such were possible) for the wrongdoer not to be
brought to justice, what sort of help should a man be able to
bring to his aid which, if he fail to do so, will render him truly
ridiculous? It will be, of course, the one which may avert from
us the greatest harm. Yet surely this must be the sort of aid that
it is shameful not to be able to give to oneself and one's friends
and intimates; and second in importance to it comes the inability
to ward off evil of the next importance; and third, evil of the
third importance, and so on. In proportion to the magnitude of
each evil is the glory of being able to ward it off and the shame
of not being able to do so. Is this true, Callicles, or is it
otherwise?

Callicles. Not otherwise.

Socrates. So given two evils, the doing of injustice and the
suffering of it, we must state that to do injustice is a greater evil,
and to suffer it a lesser one. With what, then, shall a man
provide himself to secure this double advantage: insurance from
doing wrong and from suffering it? Is it power that he needs, or
will-power? What I mean is this: can a man escape from being
wronged merely by willing to escape it, or may he escape it by
acquiring power to prevent it?

Callicles. Well, this at least is obvious: by acquiring power.

Socrates. And what about insurance from wrongdoing? Is it
sufficient if he merely wills to do no wrong? Will he then not do
it? Or, to prevent his going astray, must he have acquired a
certain power and art? And if he does not learn them and practice
them, he may do wrong? Will you be kind enough to answer at
least this question, Callicles: is it your opinion that Polus and I
were right in our earlier argument when we were forced to admit
that no one does wrong of his own free will and that it is against
his will that everyone who does wrong commits such an action?

Callicles. Let it stand as you have it, Socrates, so that
you may finish the argument.

[*Socrates.* For this end, accordingly, that we may escape
doing wrong, we must acquire a certain power and art.

Callicles. Quite.][4]

Socrates. What, then, may be the art which renders us
immune from suffering unjustly, or suffering to the least possible

---

[4]The bracketed speeches appear to be a later insertion or amplification.

degree? See if you agree with me on its identity, which I take to be as follows: one must either be a ruler in one's own country, or even a tyrant, or at least a friend of the existing government.

Callicles. Now see, Socrates, how eager I am to praise you when you put things nicely! This definition of yours, it seems to me, has been stated very well indeed.

Socrates. Well then, see if you think this too is well stated: it appears to me that the strongest bond between friends is, as the wise men of old say, "Like to like." Don't you agree?

Callicles. I do.

Socrates. So, then, when a savage and ignorant tyrant is the governing power, any man in the state who is far better than the tyrant will, of course, be feared by him and could never wholeheartedly become a friend of his.

Callicles. That's right.

Socrates. Nor could a man who was much worse; for the tyrant would despise him and would not be likely to take his friendship seriously.

Callicles. That, too, is correct.

Socrates. There remains worth mentioning, then, only one possibility of friendship for such a man: a person of like character who blames and praises the same things and at the same time is willing to be ruled and remain subordinate to his ruler. This man will have great power in that state and no one will wrong him with impunity. Isn't this true?

Callicles. Yes.

Socrates. If, then, a young man under such a government should happen to reflect, "How can I acquire great power so that no one will wrong me?"—this, it seems likely, will be his method: from his youth he will accustom himself to share the same likes and dislikes as his master and make himself over into as exact a duplication of the tyrant as he may. Isn't that true?

Callicles. Yes.

Socrates. So then the young man will bring it about, according to our account, that he gets great power and that no one wrongs him.

Callicles. Quite so.

Socrates. But what about doing no wrong himself? Will he have gained immunity from that? Isn't this most unlikely, if he is going to resemble the tyrant who is unjust, and with whom he will have great power? The very opposite, I think, will occur: he will acquire the means of doing all the wrong he can and at the same time remain exempt from the penalty of his misdeeds. Right?

Callicles. So it seems.

Socrates. So, then, the greatest of evils will befall him: his soul will become vicious and deformed by the imitation of his master and his master's power.

Callicles. I don't know how it is, Socrates, that you always manage to twist the argument around until it's upside down! Surely you know that the man who imitates a tyrant can kill, if he likes, anyone who doesn't imitate his master. He can seize all his property.

Socrates. Yes, I know it, friend Callicles, if, at least, I haven't grown deaf, for I've heard it many, many times already, from you and from Polus and from practically everybody else in town. But you may also hear from me that if he likes he can kill his victim, all right; but it will be a ruffian killing a good man.

Callicles. Well, isn't that the very thing that arouses indignation?

Socrates. Not in a sensible man, as the argument will tell you. Do you really think that this is the object of our lives: to live as long as possible, to lavish all our care upon the cultivation of those arts which may save us from danger—just as you keep urging me to cultivate the rhetoric that may keep me safe in the law courts?

Callicles. Yes, and I swear it's good advice I'm giving you.

Socrates. Well, well, friend. And do you also have a high opinion of the art of swimming?

Callicles. Of course I don't.

Socrates. And yet it too saves men from death when they chance to be immersed in something that makes such an art necessary. But if you think this too trivial, I'll mention a more important art, that of navigation, which not only saves men's lives, but their very bodies and all their property from the gravest dangers—just like rhetoric. And, moreover, this art is orderly and modest and does not put on airs or strike attitudes as if it were performing some terrific feat; yet it performs the same feat as forensic eloquence and brings you here safely from Aegina for the price of two obols; and if it be from the Black Sea or Egypt or some far place, in return for this great service, for having saved a man and his children and property and wife and disembarked them at the harbor here, it charges a couple of drachmae. And the master of the ship, the possessor of the art and the performer of this feat, comes ashore and walks along the quay by his ship with an unassuming demeanor. He is reflecting, I imagine, upon the uncertainty of whether he has benefited any of his passengers by not letting them drown, whether he has not actually injured some of them, aware as he is that he has put them ashore no better in either body or soul than when they embarked. He reflects, therefore, that anyone who has escaped drowning, yet is afflicted in his body with grave and incurable ailments, continues to be wretched because he is not dead and has not been benefited at all by the navigator; and, similarly, anyone who has in his more valuable part, the soul, many incurable ailments, will receive no benefit from continued life, whether he be saved from the sea or the law courts or anything else. He knows, this navigator, that it is not better for a wicked man to live; for his life must of necessity be an evil one.

Now this is why it is not customary for the navigator to put on airs, even though he saves our lives—nor indeed, my worthy friend, does the engineer preen himself, though from time to time his capacity for saving lives is not a bit less than that of the general or anyone else you please, to say nothing of the navigator. Sometimes, indeed, the engineer is able to preserve whole cities. Do you think that this is in the power of the legal pleader? And yet, Callicles, if he wanted to talk as the rest of you do and glorify his business, he could tunnel you under with his arguments, exhorting you to the duty of becoming engineers since nothing else is of any importance. Believe me, he has plenty to say. You, however, despise both him and his art and, as though it were a reproach, you call him a mere "engineer." You would never consent to marry your daughter to his son, or yourself marry his daughter. Yet after the praises you bestow on your own pursuits, what right have you to despise either the engineer or the others I just mentioned? You may say, obviously, that you are the better man and better born. But if "better" does not mean what I say it means and if virtue is merely this: to save oneself and one's property irrespective of one's character, then your disparagement of the engineer and the physician and of all the arts which have been devised for the preservation of life becomes ridiculous. Yet consider, my dear friend, whether what is noble and good may not be something rather different from the mere saving of human life; whether existence, over however many years, is not something which a human being, who is at the same time a rational man, must disregard. He must not cling to life, but surrender such considerations to God and have faith in the old wives' proverb that "None can escape his Destiny." Thereafter he must reflect upon how he may best employ his allotted span of years, whether, for instance, he should adapt himself to the form of the government under which he happens to be living. That is, in the present case, whether you should make yourself as similar as possible to the Athenian people since you intend to be congenial to it and acquire great power in the state. Consider closely, my dear friend, whether such a proceeding would really be beneficial to you and to me. We do not want to meet the fate they say overtakes Thessalian witches when they charm the moon down from the sky; and upon the choice of such power in the state our dearest interests may well be staked. If you believe that there is any man on earth who can teach you an art that will at once make you powerful in the state and at the same time unlike it in temper (whether for better or for worse), in my opinion, Callicles, you're quite wrong. It is not merely an imitator that you will be, it is your very nature that will conform to the mob if you are going to enter into a real bond of friendship with the Athenian people and, I swear, with the son of Pyrilampes as well. Whoever, then, may render you most like them will also make you the politician and orator you desire to be. Everyone, of course, is pleased with speeches that accord with his own way of looking at things and annoyed with a foreign point of view. Or do you have any objection, my dear fellow? Shall we reply to this, Callicles?

Callicles. I don't know how it is that your words attract me, Socrates. Yet I feel as most people do: You can't quite convince me.

Socrates. It is because the love of Demos dwells in your soul, Callicles, and resists me. Yet if we go back to these same questions again and again and examine them more thoroughly, perhaps you will be convinced. Just remember that we decided that there were two ways of cultivating anything, whether it was of the body or the soul: one procedure is to aim at its pleasure, the other at its best good. The latter uses no soothing methods, it combats them. Was not this the distinction we made before?

Callicles. Quite so.

Socrates. So the one method, that of pleasure, is worthy of no honor and amounts to nothing but flattery. Right?

Callicles. Have it so if you like.

Socrates. But the aim of the other is to make the object of one's care as good as possible, be it body, be it soul?

Callicles. Quite so.

Socrates. So then, when we take under our care the state

and its citizens, must we not try to make them as good as possible? For without this endeavor, as we discussed sometime ago, there will be no use in any other benefaction we may attempt to provide; but first, in the case of those who are going to receive great wealth or authority over others or any other power whatever, their hearts must be made honest and good. Shall this be our statement?

Callicles. All right, if it suits you.

Socrates. Suppose then, Callicles, that we were going to engage in public affairs and were urging each other on to architectural feats, the building of important edifices, walls or docks or temples: ought we first to examine ourselves and discover if we do or do not understand the art of building and elicit, too, the identity of our teacher? Should we or should we not do this?

Callicles. Of course we should.

Socrates. Then, in the second place, we should consider this point: whether we have ever had occasion to construct a private building for ourselves or for any of our friends, and whether this building was beautiful or ugly. And if, after consideration, we found that we had sound and famous teachers and that, in collaboration with them, we had built many beautiful buildings, and even after graduating from their tuition we had continued to erect numerous works on our own initiative—under these conditions we might sensibly proceed to public structures. On the other hand, if we were unable to point out our instructor, or if we could point out either no building at all or only a number of worthless edifices, then it would surely be folly to attempt public works or to urge each other on to their perpetration. Shall we or shall we not accept these conclusions?

Callicles. Of course we shall.

Socrates. And is this not true of all other cases? Suppose you and I were seeking the office of state physician and were encouraging each other to apply, on the supposition that we were competent for the job. We should, of course, look into each other's records: "Tell me, now, how is Socrates' personal health? Has anyone, slave or free man, ever been cured by him?" And I should conduct the same inquiry about you. If we did discover that no one, foreigner or citizen, man or woman, had ever been cured by us, I swear to God, Callicles, would it not be really ridiculous that any human being should come to such a pitch of folly as to attempt public service as a physician or to encourage others to such a task before there had been even any private practice, often with indifferent results, yet with a number of

successful cures and a proper training in the art? It would be like
the proverb: try to learn pottery by starting on a wine jar! Don't
you think such conduct would be folly?

Callicles. I do.

Socrates. But as the case is now, my dearest friend, since
you yourself are just beginning to enter on public affairs, and are
encouraging me to do the same and censuring me for not doing
so, should we not first look into each other's records: "Tell me
now, has Callicles ever improved any of his fellow citizens? Is
there anyone, foreigner or citizen, slave or free, who was previously bad, unjust or licentious or stupid, and has become
through Callicles' efforts a good and decent man?" Tell me,
Callicles, if anyone examined you so, what would you reply?
Who can you say has become better through association with
you? Can you hesitate to reply if you are really able to point to
any of your own handiwork done in private practice, before you
attempt public service?

Callicles. You are trying to pick a quarrel with me, Socrates.

Socrates. Believe me, it is not from quarrelsomeness that I
ask this question, but because I really wish to know how you
think politics should be conducted among us. When you have
entered upon the business of the city, will your chief care be the
maximum improvement of us, your fellow citizens? We have
repeatedly acknowledged that this is the chief obligation of the
politician, have we not? Have we or have we not? Please answer. Well, I shall answer for you: we have acknowledged it.
Now if this is what an upright man ought to provide for his own
city, cast your mind back to what you said a little while ago
about the prominent figures of the past and tell me whether you
still believe them to have been good citizens: Pericles and Cimon, Miltiades and Themistocles.

Callicles. Yes, I do.

Socrates. Then if they were good, it is obvious that everyone of them tried to improve the citizens. Did he try or didn't
he?

Callicles. He did.

Socrates. So at the moment when Pericles began to make
his harangues before the people the Athenians were worse than
on the occasions when he delivered his final speeches?

Callicles. Perhaps.

Socrates. My dear man, there is no "perhaps" to it at all.
This is a necessary consequence of our admissions if, indeed, it is
true that he was a good citizen.

Callicles. All right. What then?

Socrates. Nothing at all. Just tell me this, too: is it commonly reported that the Athenians became better under Pericles' influence, or the exact opposite, that they were corrupted by him? This is the way I hear it: Pericles made the Athenians idle and cowardly and loquacious and greedy by instituting the system of public fees.

Callicles. That's the sort of thing, Socrates, you hear from the boys with the battered ears.[5]

Socrates. But here is something else I do not have merely on hearsay, but you know it as well as I do: at first Pericles had a splendid reputation and the Athenians never involved him in any sentence which carried disgrace, so long as they were "worse"; but when they had been made "good and honest" by him, at the end of his life, they found him guilty of embezzlement and all but sentenced him to death, clearly under the impression that he was a scoundrel.

Callicles. All right. Does that make Pericles a bad man?

Socrates. Yet if he were the keeper of asses or horses or cattle, he would be thought a bad one if the animals, when he received them into his care, did not kick or butt or bite him, but became wild enough to do all these things before he was through with them. Doesn't any keeper of any sort of animal seem to you a bad one if he takes over comparatively tame animals and makes them wilder than when he got them? Do you think so or don't you?

Callicles. All right, all right, anything to please you.

Socrates. Then please me further by answering this question: is man also an animal or is he not?

Callicles. Of course he is.

Socrates. And did Pericles have men in his care?

Callicles. Yes.

Socrates. Well then, as we just now agreed, should they not have become more just under his care, instead of less, if it is indeed true that he was a good politician?

Callicles. Quite so.

Socrates. Then, further, the just are gentle, as Homer says. Do you agree? Is it so?

Callicles. Yes.

Socrates. And yet he left them wilder than he found them, and that too against himself, which he could hardly have desired.

---

[5]Excessively given to boxing in imitation of Spartan discipline: hence unpatriotic.

Callicles. Do you want me to agree with you?

Socrates. If I seem to you to be speaking the truth.

Callicles. Let it stand, then.

Socrates. If, then, he made them wilder, did he make them also more unjust and worse?

Callicles. Let it stand.

Socrates. From this argument, then, Pericles was not a good politician.

Callicles. You're the one who says he wasn't.

Socrates. And you too, in view of your admissions. But now tell me about Cimon. Didn't the very men he tried to serve ostracize him so that they could have ten years' respite from hearing his voice? And didn't they behave in precisely the same way toward Themistocles and, in addition, punish him with exile? And Miltiades, the victor at Marathon, didn't they vote to throw him into the Public Pit and, if it hadn't been for the president of the Assembly, in he would have gone? And yet these persons, if they had been good men in the way that you say they were, would never have suffered such a fate. At least it is certainly true that good charioteers are not those who keep their footing in their chariots at the beginning; then, when they have trained their horses and have themselves become more proficient in the art of driving, fall out. Such a state of affairs is impossible either in charioteering or in any other occupation. Or don't you think so?

Callicles. Yes, I do.

Socrates. Then what we said before, it seems, is correct: we are unaware of the existence of a single good politician in our state. You admitted that there was none now, but mentioned some former examples and selected these we have just reviewed. They, however, have been shown to be on a par with present-day specimens. So, even if they were orators, they did not make use of the true art of rhetoric (otherwise they would not have been discarded) or even of the sort that merely flatters.

Callicles. Yet surely, Socrates, not one of the present breed has come within miles of accomplishing such feats as did any one at all of the elder statesmen.

Socrates. Nor am I, my dear friend, censuring them, at least as servants of the state; they seem to me, in fact, to have been more serviceable than the present generation, and more capable of giving the state what it wanted. But as for transforming its desires instead of toadying to them, as for persuading and coercing fellow citizens to the point of self-improvement, there is not, in a word, a whit of difference between generations. Yet this and this alone is the task of a truly good citizen. I freely acknowledge that the former age was cleverer at providing ships and walls and docks and the rest of it than are our contemporaries.

In our argument, therefore, you and I are doing something quite ridiculous: during the entire extent of our conversation we have been continuously circling round to the same point—and each in complete ignorance of what the other was trying to say. I, for instance, thought that on many an occasion you had grasped and acknowledged the fact that our method of treating the problem was a double one, concerned as it is with both body and soul, and that one of them was subservient to the other. It is by that treatment that we are able to provide food if our bodies are hungry, drink if thirsty, clothes if cold, and bedding and shoes and anything else we may physically desire. (I purposely repeat the same examples to make it easier for you to grasp the point.) Now the provider of these things may do so either wholesale or retail or be a manufacturer of them himself, a baker or a cook, a weaver or a cobbler or a tanner; so that there is nothing surprising in the fact that he regards himself as mainly concerned with the care of the body and is so regarded by others—at least, that is, by any others who do not realize that there exists an art which transcends all these, the combination of medicine and gymnastic. This art it is which is really concerned with the body's care and to it rightfully belongs the governance of the other crafts and the utilization of their products, for it alone understands what food and drink is good or bad for the perfection of the body, while all the other crafts ignore this cardinal principle. This is the reason, then, that they are servile, subservient, and illiberal in the treatment of the body, while the art of medicine and gymnastic is by right their master.

Now sometimes you seemed to comprehend that the very same facts and principles hold good for the soul as well, and then you agreed with my statements as though you understood what they meant; but a little later you came along with the opinion that there have been good and honest citizens in our state. When I ventured to ask you who they may be—look at the politicians you brought up! Do you know what seems to me to have the closest resemblance to them? It's just as though I should question you about physical culture and asked what men have been, or are, good trainers of the body and you were to answer in all seriousness, "Thearion the baker, and Mithaecus who wrote the treatise on Sicilian cookery, and Sarambus the shopkeeper: these have been wonderful physical trainers, since the first makes marvelous bread, the second cooks well, and the third provides excellent wine." And perhaps you would be offended if I were to say to you, "Man alive, you have no comprehension of true physical culture! You're merely listing servile fellows who cater to the appetites and have no understanding of the fine points. They, it may be, fill and fatten men's bodies and so win their praise, yet finally bring about the destruction of the flesh they had to start with. Yet people will be too ignorant to hold the fellows who indulge them with banquets responsible for their maladies and their loss of weight; but much later in life, when their former surfeit, indulged without regard to health, comes home accompanied by disease, then they will blame those who happen to be in the vicinity and venture to offer advice; they will revile these innocent bystanders and will even do them harm if they are able; but their predecessors, those really responsible for their misfortunes, they will praise to the skies. And what you are now doing, Callicles, is something extremely similar: you praise men who wined and dined our fellow citizens and crammed them full of what they desired. Men say that they made our city great, not perceiving that it is swollen and ulcerous because of its ancient counselors. With no regard for self-control or justice they stuffed our state with harbors and docks and walls and tribute-money and all such nonsense; so when this presumed attack of illness finally comes, they will blame the advisers who happen to be about at the time, while praising to the skies Themistocles and Cimon and Pericles, though they were the true authors of the trouble. On you too they may perhaps lay their hands if you don't watch out, and on my friend Alcibiades. This they may do when they are losing all their empire, both the recent additions and the ancient possessions, though you are not responsible for their troubles—yet perhaps partially responsible.

Be that as it may, there is one quite irrational thing that I perceive happening every time a discussion of the elder statesmen comes up. When the state lays hands on its politicians as offenders, one hears them complaining and crying out against their harsh treatment; they have done, they say, many splendid services to the state and yet are unjustly brought to destruction by it. This is nothing but a pack of lies; no leader of the state, not one, could be unjustly ruined by the very city he controls. And it is likely that the case of the self-styled politician is the same as that of those who call themselves sophists. Sophists, in fact, with all their cleverness, commit this extraordinary blunder: they pretend to teach virtue, yet time and time again they accuse their pupils of misdeeds, either of defrauding them of wages or of showing no gratitude for the benefits they have received. Now what could be more illogical than such a case? The pupils have become good and just; all injustice has been purged by their master; they have a firm hold on justice; how should they do wrong through a quality which is no longer theirs? Don't you think this is a strange blunder, my friend?—Callicles, you have actually forced me into public speaking by your constant refusal to reply!

Callicles. So you're the one who couldn't talk if there was no one to answer you?

Socrates. It looks as though I could. This time, at any rate, I've had to go to great lengths because you simply wouldn't answer. But now, dear friend, please tell me in the name of friendship, don't you think it is illogical for one who asserts that he has made another man good to blame him for being bad, though *ex hypothesi* he has been made and guaranteed good by the very man who blames him?

Callicles. Yes, I think so.

Socrates. And do you hear such statements from those who profess to educate others in the path of virtue?

Callicles. I do; but why mention such worthless fellows?

Socrates. And why do you, then, mention those who profess to be masters of the state and devoted to its maximum improvement, yet who turn around and accuse it, when occasion serves, of the vilest wickedness? Do you think there is much difference between these classes of men? A sophist and an orator are identical, dear man, or at any rate they closely approximate one another, as I tried to tell Polus. It is your ignorance which makes you admire the one art, rhetoric, and despise the other. [Yet the truth is that sophistic is finer than rhetoric to the same degree that legislation is superior to judicial procedure and gymnastic to medicine.][6] For my own part, I should have thought that public speakers and sophists were the only ones who had no right to blame, for causing mischief to themselves, the very thing they teach—if, that is, they are not going to accuse themselves, in one and the same breath, of doing no good to those whom they claim to benefit! Isn't that true?

Callicles. Quite.

---

[6]The bracketed words are probably an interpolation.

Socrates. And, it seems, they should also be the only ones who could afford to make their services available to the public without a fee—if only what they said were true. Where some other kind of service is concerned, for example, when one is taught by a trainer to run fast, the defrauding of a reward is perhaps more comprehensible, in that the service may be thought to be gratuitous or there was no stipulation that the fee should be paid at exactly the moment the speed was imparted; for it is not, one would think, through lack of swiftness that men do wrong, but through injustice. Is this the case?

Callicles. Yes.

Socrates. Then whoever removes precisely this, injustice, need never again fear to be treated unjustly; and he is the only one for whom it is quite safe to impart this benefit without stipulation, if, that is, anyone can really make others good. Is it not so?

Callicles. I agree.

Socrates. Then this, it seems, is the reason why there is nothing disgraceful about taking money for advice on other matters, such as architecture or any of the arts.

Callicles. Yes, so it seems.

Socrates. Yet only about this matter, how one may become as good as possible and govern one's house or one's country in the best way, it has come to be considered disgraceful to decline to impart one's advice until one receives money for it. Isn't that the case?

Callicles. It is.

Socrates. The obvious reason is that this is the only benefit capable of making its recipient eager to requite it, and it has this result: it is thought to be a valid proof that the benefit has actually been conferred if it is requited; if not, not. Isn't this how matters stand?

Callicles. It is.

Socrates. Then to which sort of treatment of our city do you urge me? Please define it for me. Is it to combat the Athenians until they become as virtuous as possible, prescribing for them like a physician; or is it to be their servant and cater to their pleasure? Tell me the truth, Callicles. It is only fair that, since at the beginning you were quite candid with me, you should continue in the same vein. So now speak out frankly and freely.

Callicles. Well, then I say: be their servant!

Socrates. So, frankest of friends, you urge me to flatter them.

Callicles. Call yourself the lowest of the low, Socrates, if it gives you any satisfaction. But if you won't do as I say—

Socrates. Please don't repeat what you've already said a hundred times, that anyone who wants to can kill me, so that I don't have to say again, "It will be a ruffian killing a decent man!" Don't say that anyone can strip me of whatever goods I may possess, so that I won't have to repeat, "But if he takes them, he won't know how to use them; since he took them unjustly, he will use them unjustly; and if unjustly, disgracefully; and if disgracefully, then to his harm."

Callicles. How confident you seem to be, Socrates, that nothing like this could ever happen to you, that you dwell out of harm's way, that you could never be dragged into court, quite possibly by some utterly vicious and debased creature.

Socrates. Then, Callicles, I must really be a fool if I believe that in this city of ours anyone at all is exempt from the risk of any possible form of calamity. Of this, however, I am perfectly certain: if I ever am dragged into court and exposed to any of these risks, it will be, as you say, some vicious fellow that brings me there (for no honest man could ever so deal with the innocent); and, indeed, it would not be surprising if I were put to death. Do you want me to tell you why I expect such an outcome?

Callicles. I certainly do.

Socrates. In my opinion I am one of the few Athenians (not to say the only one) who has attempted the true art of politics, and the only one alive to put it into practice. For this reason, then, I never carry on my habitual discussions with a view to gratification, but with my eyes fixed on the highest good, not on that which is merely pleasant. Being unwilling to follow your advice as to the employment of rhetorical tricks, I shall have nothing to say in the court room. The same situation that I described to Polus will apply to me: I shall be like a physician tried before a jury of children on the accusation of a cook. Just consider what defense such a man could make if he were caught in the toils of such a circumstance! His accuser will say, "Children, the defendant here has committed many offenses against all of you. The youngest of you he continues to maim by amputation and cautery; he drives you to despair by his starving and stifling; he forces you to hunger and thirst, then the drink that he gives you is bitter. How unlike he is to me, who have always regaled you with choice dainties of a tempting variety!" What do you think the physician caught in such a predicament could say?

If he admitted the truth and declared, "Yes, children, I did every one of these things—for your good health!" How much of an outcry do you think a jury like that would make? It would be loud, wouldn't it?

Callicles. Perhaps; one would naturally think so.

Socrates. And the physician would be at a complete loss what reply to make?

Callicles. Quite.

Socrates. Such, however, is the experience I expect to have if I'm ever brought into court. There will be no pleasures provided by me that I can tell them about, pleasures which they count as benefactions and services (yet I am far from feeling envy for either the purveyors or those for whom they are provided). And if anyone accuses me of corrupting the younger men by perplexing them with doubts, or says that I criticize their elders with bitter words both in private and public, I shall be able neither to tell the truth ("Yes, and it is right for me to say all this and in doing so I am serving your interests, gentlemen of the jury") nor to utter anything else at all; so that, in all probability, there is no telling what may happen.

Callicles. Then, Socrates, do you think a man in such a situation and yet unable to defend himself is safe in this city?

Socrates. Yes, Callicles, if he has this one advantage which time and time again you have agreed to acknowledge: if he were his own defense through never having said or done anything unjust to man or God. This line of self-defense we have repeatedly acknowledged to be the best one. If, therefore, anyone were to convict me of inability to provide this sort of aid either for myself or for anyone else, I should be utterly ashamed, whether my conviction took place before many or before only a few, or even man to man; and if it were this inability that brought me to my death, I should be very sorry indeed. If, on the other hand, it is merely through lack of the art of flattery that I meet my end, I am perfectly certain that you will see me face death with composure. Of death itself surely no one who is not an absolute fool or coward can be afraid; it is to do injustice that men fear. And if the soul arrives in Hades burdened with a load of iniquities, that is the worst and last of all evils. And now, if you are agreeable, I should like to tell you a story to show that this is true.

Callicles. Well, since you've got through all the rest, you may as well finish this, too.

Socrates. Then listen, as they say, to a very fine tale, which you may consider a myth, but I regard as a true story; for I want you to take everything I shall say as strict truth.

When, as Homer says, Zeus and Poseidon and Pluto took over the rule of the universe from their father, they divided it among themselves. Now in the time of Cronus there was a law concerning mankind, which holds to this very day among the gods, that any man who had passed his life in a just and holy fashion should at his death proceed to the Islands of the Blessed and dwell there in complete happiness out of the reach of evil; while the doer of evil and impious deeds should be sent to a prisonhouse of retribution and judgment; and this they call Tartarus. Now in the time of Cronus and in the earlier portion of Zeus' reign the judges were living men who judged their fellows while they too were still alive, since the arraignment of a man was held on that day when he was about to die; and for this reason the judgment was conducted badly. So both Pluto and the overseers of the Islands of the Blessed came to Zeus and reported that improper persons were being sent to both places. Then Zeus said: "I shall put a stop to this proceeding. It is quite true that the judgments are now conducted badly, for the defendants are brought to trial clothed and judgment is passed while they are still alive. There are many," he said, "who have wicked souls, but are clad in beautiful bodies and pride of race and wealth and, when judgment comes, many witnesses advance to their aid, testifying to the justice of their lives. The judges are overawed by these; furthermore, they themselves are clothed, with the veil of eyes and ears and indeed the whole body interposed before their souls as they sit in judgment. All this becomes an obstacle for them, both their own clothing and that of those they judge. Now first," said he, "we must terminate men's foreknowledge of death, which they now possess. I have already given orders to Prometheus to put an end to it. Next, they must all be judged in nakedness, for judgment must not be passed till they are dead. The judge also must be naked and dead in order that the judgment shall be just, his very soul contemplating the naked soul of each man who has died without warning, bereft of all his kin, and all his trappings left behind him upon earth. Accordingly, since I recognized this state of affairs even before the rest of you, I have appointed my own sons to be judges, two of them from Asia, Minos and Rhadamanthys, and one from Europe, Aeacus. So these, when they are dead, shall give judgment in the Meadow at the Crossroads from which the Two Roads lead, one to the Islands of the Blessed, the other to Tartarus. And

Rhadamanthys shall judge those from Asia and Aeacus those from Europe; but to Minos I shall give the prerogative of passing sentence on appeal when the other two have any doubts. And so the judgment as to a man's last journey shall be rendered with the utmost justice."

This, Callicles, is what I have heard and I believe it to be true; and from the narrative I draw some such inference as this: Death, as I think, turns out to be merely a divorce of two things, the soul and the body; and when they have been separated one from the other, each of them still retains much the same condition as it had while the man was alive. The body retains its natural contours with the marks of its upbringing and its experiences quite manifest. For example, if a man's body was quite large while he was alive, either naturally, or as a result of diet, or both, when he dies his corpse will be large; if he was fat, the corpse will be fat; and so on. If, again, he used to wear his hair long, the corpse will have long hair. Or if he used to be beaten and had the marks and scars of lashes or blows or other wounds on his body while he was alive, these may all be seen on the body when he is dead. Or if he had any limbs broken or distorted during life, in death the same are plainly visible. In a word, whatever characteristics a man's body presented in life, these remain visible in death, either all of them, or most of them for some little time.

Now this same state of affairs appears to me to hold true for the soul also, Callicles. When it has been stripped of the body, everything in it becomes visible, all its natural traits as well as those acquired from every habit and each pursuit. When, therefore, the dead appear before the judge, those from Asia before Rhadamanthys, he causes them to halt before him and examines each soul with no knowledge of its identity; often indeed, he has laid hold on the King of Persia or some other monarch or despot and discerned nothing sound in the soul; for it is deeply scarred by the whip and full of festering wounds brought on by perjury and crime, the imprint on the soul of its every act. He sees all of it twisted by lies and impostures, crooked because it has received no nourishment from truth; he sees it compact of distortion and hideousness by reason of the irresponsibility and licentiousness, the insolence and intemperance of its acts. And when he has seen such a soul, he sends it, in all dishonor, straight off to the prison where it is destined to enter and undergo the sufferings that are its due.

Everyone who is punished, and rightly punished, ought

either to be benefited and become better, or serve as an example to others that they may behold these sufferings and through fear become better. Those who are benefited by their punishment at the hands of men and gods are they that have committed only curable sins; none the less their improvement must come through the pangs of suffering both here and in Hades. Only in this way can they be rid of their wrongdoing. But those who have committed the extreme of injustice, and have thus become incurable, serve as an example to others; they themselves benefit not at all, since they are incurable, yet others may do so when they observe these malefactors suffering in the greatest, the most painful, and the most fearful torments because of their sins, strung up forever in that prisonhouse of Hades, an example, a portent, and a warning to the unjust as they arrive below.

And one of these I say Archelaus will be, if what Polus tells about him is true, and any other tyrant who resembles him. One may believe, in fact, that most of these dread examples are drawn from tyrants and kings, despots and politicians, for it is they who, through irresponsible power, commit the most fearful and incurable crimes. Homer also is a witness to this, for he has represented kings and despots, Tantalus, Sisyphus, Tityus, as the ones who suffer eternal punishment in Hades; but no one has represented Thersites and other wicked persons of private status as suffering great torments on the ground that they are incurable. [A private person has not the power for great sin, and in this he is more fortunate than those who have.][7] It is, Callicles, from the ranks of the powerful that the supremely wicked are drawn. Yet there is nothing to prevent good men from being found in this class also; and they, when they occur, are entirely admirable, for it is both difficult and most praiseworthy, Callicles, to live a just life when one has great opportunities to do wrong. Few, therefore, have survived this test, yet here and elsewhere they have sprung up in the past and there will, I don't doubt, be further examples in the future, honorable men endowed with the virtue of administering justly whatever one places in their charge. One most praiseworthy example, famed throughout Greece, was Aristides the son of Lysimachus; on the other hand, my dear friend, most powerful men become evil.

And so, as I was saying, the mighty Rhadamanthys receives such a man, knowing nothing else about him, neither name nor lineage, but only that he is bad; and on perceiving this he packs

---

[7]The bracketed words are probably an interpolation.

him off to Tartarus, putting a mark upon him to indicate whether
he seems curable or not; and the criminal proceeds to prison and
suffers whatever is his due. On occasion the judge may perceive
a soul that has lived in holiness and truth, the soul of some
private person or another; but most often, Callicles, as I should
say, it will be the soul of a philosopher who has kept to his own
business and has not meddled with others' affairs during his
lifetime. Whereupon the judge is struck with admiration and
sends him on to the Islands of the Blessed. Aeacus' role is just
the same, [each of them sits in judgment with a staff in his
hand][8] while Minos, as overseer, sits apart; he alone has a
golden scepter, just as Homer's Odysseus says he saw him,

Holding a scepter of gold and judging among the dead.[9]

So, Callicles, I have been convinced by these accounts; it has
become my concern how I may present to the judge my soul in
its healthiest condition. I relinquish, therefore, the honors that
most men pursue and shall endeavor, by cultivating the truth, to
be as good as I may during my life and, when I come to die, in
my dying. And insofar as I am able I urge all other men (and you
in particular I summon, thus countering your former summons to
me) to such a life and such a contest as this, which I affirm to be
worth all the contests here on earth put together. And I retort to
your reproaches that it is you who will be unable to help yourself
when that trial and that judgment which I have just described
comes upon you. You will have to appear before the judge,
Aegina's son; when he lays hands upon you and drags you before
him, it is you who will stand there with gaping mouth and
reeling head no less than I here; and it will be you, perhaps, whom
they will shamefully slap in the face and mistreat with every
indignity.

It is quite possible that all this may seem to you only a
myth, an old wives' tale, and you will despise it; nor would your
contempt be surprising if with all our searching we could find
anything better or truer than this account. But as it is, you will
observe that the three of you, the wisest of all the Greeks alive at
this moment, you and Polus and Gorgias, are unable to demonstrate
the necessity of living any other life than this, which clearly
brings advantage after death as well. Yes, in all our long discussion the other arguments have been refuted and this alone stands

---

[8]The bracketed words are probably an interpolation.
[9]Homer, *Odyssey*, 11.569.

immovable: doing wrong must be avoided more sedulously than suffering it. Above all else, a man must study, not how to seem good, but to be so, both in public and in private life. And if he grows bad in any way, he must be punished; for this is the good which is to be rated second after being just: to become so through making amends by punishment. Flattery of every kind, whether of oneself or of others, whether of the few or of the many, is to be avoided; and so rhetoric, like every other practice, is always to be used to serve the ends of justice, and for that alone.

Then join with me and be my companion on the journey to the place where, as the argument shows, you will be happy both in life and in death. And let others, if they like, despise you for a fool and insult you; even, God help us, confidently endure from them that ignominious slap on the cheek. There will be nothing terrible in this experience if you are a truly honorable man in the pursuit of virtue. Then at length, when we have really practiced virtue together as we should, we may, if it seems appropriate, apply ourselves to politics or deliberate about whatever else may attract us; for then we shall be better fitted for such deliberation than we are now. It would be disgraceful for men in what appears to be our present condition to put on airs as though we amounted to something, we who never hold twice the same opinion about the same subjects, and that, too, though they are of the greatest importance. Such are the depths to which our lack of true education has brought us. For our guidance, then, let us make use of the argument which has now revealed itself, declaring that this is the best way to spend one's days: to live and die in the pursuit of justice and the other virtues. Let us follow it, then, and urge on everyone else to do the same and to abandon that way in which you put your confidence and your exhortations; for your way, Callicles, has no value whatever.

SELECTED BIBLIOGRAPHY
(English-language works)

Barker, E. *The Political Thought of Plato and Aristotle*. 1906. Reprint. New York and London: Dover Publications, 1959.

Crombie, I.M. *An Examination of Plato's Doctrines*. 2 vols. London: Humanities Press, 1962–1963.

Dover, K.J. *Greek Popular Morality in the Time of Plato and Aristotle*. Oxford: Oxford University Press, 1974.

Friedlander, P. *Plato*. 3 vols. New York: Pantheon Books, 1958–1969.

Gould, J. *The Development of Plato's Ethics*. Cambridge: Cambridge University Press, 1955.

Grube, G.M.A. *Plato's Thought*. London: Methuen, 1935.

Guthrie, W.K.C. *A History of Greek Philosophy*. Vols. 3, 4, and 5. Cambridge: Cambridge University Press, 1962–1978.

Hare, R.M. *Plato*. Oxford: Oxford University Press, 1982.

Havelock, E.A. *Preface to Plato*. Oxford: Basil Blackwell, 1963.

Keaney, J.J. "Plato," in *Ancient Writers: Greece and Rome*, ed. T. James Luce. New York: Scribners, 1982.

Kerferd, G.B. *The Sophistic Movement*. Cambridge: Cambridge University Press, 1981.

Kirk, G.S., and J.E. Raven. *The Presocratic Philosophers*. Cambridge: Cambridge University Press, 1963.

Raven, J.E. *Plato's Thought in the Making*. Cambridge: Cambridge University Press, 1965.

Robinson, R. *Plato's Earlier Dialectic*. Oxford: Oxford University Press, 1953.

Ross, W.D. *Plato's Theory of Ideas*. Oxford: Oxford University Press, 1951.

Shorey, P. *What Plato Said*. Chicago: University of Chicago Press, 1978.

Taylor, A.E. *Plato: The Man and His Work*. New York: Meridian Books, 1957.

Vlastos, G., ed. *Plato: A Collection of Critical Essays*. 2 vols. New York: Doubleday, 1970–1971.

———, ed. *The Philosophy of Socrates*. New York: Doubleday, 1971.

———. *Platonic Studies*. Princeton: Princeton University Press, 1973.

There are various articles on Platonism as well as its influence throughout the ages all through the five-volume *Dictionary of the History of Ideas* (ed. Philip P. Wiener. New York: Charles Scribner's Sons, 1968–1974).

(N.B.: Dates are not necessarily those of original publication—only of convenient, latest editions.)